Revolutionary Camden

ALSO BY DEREK SMITH
AND FROM MCFARLAND

Bloody Savannah: The City's Most Violent Era as Seen by a Crime Reporter (Exposit, 2023)

South Carolinians in the Battle of Gettysburg (2021)

Revolutionary Camden
South Carolina's Bloody Epicenter in the War of Independence

DEREK SMITH

McFarland & Company, Inc., Publishers
Jefferson, North Carolina

LIBRARY OF CONGRESS CATALOGING-IN-PUBLICATION DATA

Names: Smith, Derek, 1956 November 3– author.
Title: Revolutionary Camden : South Carolina's bloody epicenter in the War of Independence / Derek Smith.
Other titles: South Carolina's bloody epicenter in the War of Independence
Description: Jefferson, North Carolina : McFarland & Company, Inc., Publishers, 2024 | Includes bibliographical references and index.
Identifiers: LCCN 2024038827 | ISBN 9781476696164 (paperback : acid free paper) ∞
 ISBN 9781476653792 (ebook)
Subjects: LCSH: Camden (S.C.)—History—Revolution, 1775-1783. | Camden (S.C.)—History, Military—18th century. | South Carolina—History—Revolution, 1775-1783.
Classification: LCC F279.C2 S65 2024 | DDC 975.7/87—dc23/eng/20240822
LC record available at https://lccn.loc.gov/2024038827

BRITISH LIBRARY CATALOGUING DATA ARE AVAILABLE

ISBN (print) 978-1-4766-9616-4
ISBN (ebook) 978-1-4766-5379-2

© 2024 Derek Smith. All rights reserved

No part of this book may be reproduced or transmitted in any form or by any means, electronic or mechanical, including photocopying or recording, or by any information storage and retrieval system, without permission in writing from the publisher.

Front cover images: *Battle of Camden—Death of DeKalb* (Emmet Collection of Manuscripts Etc. Relating to American History, The New York Public Library); *background* plan of the battle fought near Camden, August 16, 1780 (Library of Congress).

Printed in the United States of America

McFarland & Company, Inc., Publishers
 Box 611, Jefferson, North Carolina 28640
  www.mcfarlandpub.com

Table of Contents

Preface	1
Notable Events and Dates in Camden's Revolutionary War Timeline	5
Introduction	7
1. Camden's Beginnings	11
2. "To win over the wavering" and the Gathering Storm	17
3. A Scarlet Hurricane Roars Ashore: 1780	32
4. "I have cut 170 Off'rs and Men to pieces"	37
5. "The Carolinas have been conquered"	48
6. "Our Army is like a dead whale upon the Sea Shore"	62
7. "I resolved … to attack the rebel army"	77
8. "The most tremendous firing I ever heard"	93
9. "A perfect scene of horror and confusion"	105
10. "The firmest troops in the field"	113
11. "A prisoner of war … with one of my legs quite broke by a musket ball"	119
12. "We made our retreat like lost sheep"	133
13. Dance of the Devils	145
14. "The late affair has almost broke my heart": 1781	156
15. "To the plains of Zama"	166

16. "In the flush of victory and pursuit": Hobkirk Hill — 176

17. "Camden" Has "an evil genius about it" — 190

18. "He conquers by magic" — 200

19. The Leaders in the Postwar Period — 213

20. "Loud and long were the cheers of the multitude" — 224

21. Women "Reapers" of the Camden Region: 1780 — 231

22. African Americans at Camden and Beyond — 233

23. DeKalb's First Grave: "in the 'custom of knighthood'" — 236

24. DeKalb, Major Benjamin Nones and the "Hebrew Legion" — 239

Appendix: Beyond the Battles: Camden Military Lore — 243
Chapter Notes — 249
Bibliography — 273
Index — 283

Preface

"Camden seems to have an evil genius about it. Whatever is attempted near that place is unfortunate."
—American Major General Nathanael Greene,
May 4, 1781, days after his defeat at Hobkirk Hill

The metal detector hummed loudly and I dropped to my knees to dig into the grayish sandy soil. It was a flamingly humid South Carolina afternoon in the 1970s, and sweat stung my eyes as the shovel cut into the ground where the Revolutionary War battle of Camden was fought on August 16, 1780.

Shooing away the devilish gnats, I heard—and felt—the shovel clink against something possibly metallic in the dirt, brushing away the soil to uncover the treasure. It was a pancaked musket ball that no one had seen or touched since that terrible, bloody morning when it was likely fired in anger during the combat.

I thought about some of the global events that had occurred since that deadly messenger was triggered on its errand, left forgotten and unfound before that day: America's independence, the Civil War, Wright brothers, Einstein, penicillin, the world wars, first man on the moon…

I also tried to gauge who fired the shot, most likely in a volley, and at whom. We'll revisit that little mystery sometime later, so you'll have to read on.

I grew up in Bishopville, S.C., some 20 miles from Camden, but always had strong ties there. My mother's side of our family included several relatives in Camden, primarily Harvey and Mildred Hall, who owned a TV and stereo equipment store for many years. We went to Camden—a bigger town than Bishopville—to shop, visit the dentist, and eat some of the best hot dogs on the planet at the Little Midget (when it was only a small red and white structure). Even earlier, my kindergarten class boarded the train in Camden and rode the rails about fifteen miles to Bethune, S.C., for a picnic lunch! Does it get any better for a five-year-old in 1961 or so?

Before I-20 was built (I can't believe I just typed that), my family traveled down Highway 34 to U.S. 1 through Camden for outings to Columbia, passing the big watch plant at Elgin and Blaney Drag Strip, among other sites. A few years later my friends and I would hit some of Camden's night spots, play tennis in the parks or catch a flick at the Little Theater, all this while my love of American history was ever blossoming, especially the Civil War, the Revolutionary War a close second. Then there were some intriguing billboards near Camden, beckoning motorists to "Come see where Cornwallis spent a tough winter," or words to that effect.

My brother Mark and I bonded with our dad as we all discovered the fun of metal detecting, a very unique hobby in the late 1960s and early 1970s. We found coins, rings, and a whole lot of chewing gum wrappers and can pop tops at various places. But the best day was when we unearthed a fat Mason jar of mostly Mercury dimes, part of a cache buried years earlier by a bootlegger.

This was all great fun with everlasting memories, but my interest was more toward finding military artifacts—and thus we return to the sun-roasted afternoon and my musket ball. Based on the spot where I found it, the bullet likely was fired by a Loyalist soldier in the Volunteers of Ireland toward troops of the Delaware Continentals in the American army. Its flattened condition meant that it had hit *something* that disfigured it. There were no large rocks on the field, but it could have struck a tree; hunters dug lead balls out of tree trunks for years after the battle to remold and reuse to shoot game, but this one was in the ground. Still, nature and geology could have buried this bullet over time. My teenaged mind then—and even now, still teenaged, some might say—tells me it likely smashed into some military equipment—like a gun stock, bridle, belt buckle or canteen—or shattered the bone of a living creature—be it an unfortunate soldier or horse. Your guess is just as good as mine.

Over several trips—at least one in a torrential summer thunderstorm—I uncovered several other musket balls and part of a light-weight horseshoe, possibly belonging to a cavalryman and mount of Armand's Legion, leading the American advance that fateful morning in 1780.

The most amazing thing I discovered, however, was the overlooked but crucial role that Camden played in the Revolutionary War. Two major battles were fought there, as well as more than a dozen lesser clashes in the general vicinity and the most infamous—and still controversial—"massacre" of scores of American soldiers at the Waxhaws settlement. Camden itself was central to the British army's plan to quell the rebellion in the South and gradually smother it completely. After Charleston's capture in May 1780, the British established a chain of outposts across South Carolina, Camden being the critical link as a stronghold, inland base of operations and supply depot. "During the last year and a half of the war, the history of the State—we might say, of the United States—was making in that small district of which Camden was the capital," stated a 1905 account.[1]

My artifacts came from the wilderness battlefield of 1780, but there is so much more to the rich—and true—story of Camden during the conflict. Even today it's not hard to imagine the rival armies roaming the fields and pine thickets amid the violent clatter of combat or to see village residents often sharply choosing sides against each other.

Our very real cast includes the Kershaws' turbulent and tragic family, and Earl Cornwallis, Andrew Jackson, Francis Rawdon, Horatio Gates, Nathanael Greene, "Bloody Ban" Tarleton, Sarah McCalla, Mary Gill, Guinea Cato and other slaves and freemen whose names are lost in time, the mysterious Agnes of Glasgow, Waterees, Catawbas, Loyalists, Americans, Continentals, Redcoats and backwoods militiamen shouldering their slim but deadly accurate rifles for either side.

Join me on this high adventure.

Notable Events and Dates in Camden's Revolutionary War Timeline

November 5, 1774—Judge William Henry Drayton and members of the Camden District grand jury issue what is considered the first American declaration of independence.

April 19, 1775—Battles of Lexington and Concord spark the conflict.

June 15, 1775—Continental Congress appoints George Washington commander-in-chief of the new Continental army.

June 28, 1776—Repulse of the British naval and land assault on Charleston, S.C.

June 1776—Lafayette, DeKalb and other French officers land near Georgetown, S.C., intent on joining the American cause.

March 29, 1780—British forces under Clinton open siege of Charleston.

April 16, 1780—DeKalb leads Continental troops south from Morristown, N.J., to try to reinforce and relieve Charleston.

May 12, 1780—General Benjamin Lincoln surrenders Charleston and the American army defending it to the British.

May 29, 1780—Battle of the Waxhaws. Buford's command of Continentals destroyed by Tarleton.

June 1, 1780—Cornwallis's British troops enter and occupy Camden.

July 25, 1780—General Horatio Gates assumes command of Southern army, taking over from DeKalb.

August 8, 1780—Joseph and Ely Kershaw sail from Charleston, exiled to Bermuda due to their anti–British activities.

August 16, 1780—Battle of Camden. Cornwallis routs Gates, DeKalb mortally wounded and captured.

August 18, 1780—Battle of Fishing Creek; Tarleton surprises and overwhelms Sumter's force.

August 19, 1780—DeKalb dies in Camden.

October 7, 1780—Battle of Kings Mountain—American victory.

October 29, 1780—Cornwallis retreats from North Carolina, establishing headquarters at Winnsboro, S.C.; Rawdon sent back to Camden in early November to command the outpost, strengthening defenses over the coming months.

November 10-11, 1780—Ely Kershaw dies from lingering illness aboard ship off the Bermuda coast.

December 3, 1781—Major General Nathanael Greene relieves Gates as commander of the Continental Southern army.

January 17, 1781—Battle of Cowpens—American victory.

March 15, 1781—Battle of Guilford Court House—British victory.

April 25, 1781—Battle of Hobkirk Hill—Rawdon defeats Greene.

May 9-10, 1781—Camden evacuated and burned by the British; Americans entering the village on the second day.

September 8, 1781—Battle of Eutaw Springs—British victory.

October 3, 1781—Joseph Kershaw returns to Camden from exile in Bermuda.

October 19, 1781—Cornwallis surrenders at Yorktown, but war continues.

December 14, 1781—British abandon Charleston.

September 3, 1783—Treaty of Paris ends the war and recognizes the U.S. as an independent nation.

November 1785—William Kershaw dies in Charleston.

Introduction

Spring in South Carolina is usually an Eden of stunning natural radiance, yellow jessamine (jasmine) cheering the woods, swamps and foothills. Bees buzzing in the warm, sweet air accent the perfume of azalea, wisteria, honeysuckle, crepe myrtle, and dogwood blossoms, while birds sing, swirl and nest in the glorious greenery.

In spring 1780, however, South Carolina—and very soon Camden itself—was at the epicenter of the American Revolutionary War. Like a scarlet tidal wave, a British army under Lt. Gen. Sir Henry Clinton landed near Charleston in February, aided by a formidable naval force. During the coming weeks, the Redcoats slowly wrapped their martial coils around the provincial capital and seaport.

Even as the British entrenched outside Charleston, the Revolution already had been raging for five years as Great Britain's 13 North American provinces—or colonies—sought to break away and gain their independence from the mother empire.

The rebellion had simmered over time before becoming open warfare at Lexington and Concord, Massachusetts, on April 19, 1775. In June, a tall, dignified Virginian named George Washington was appointed commander-in-chief of the Continental Army, the burgeoning force being raised and funded by the Second Continental Congress, the first governing body of what the insurgent colonists hoped would be a new nation. Congress also set about establishing a navy in October.

Still, this flagrant and violent challenge to the iron rule of the proud and formidable British realm would not be tolerated by King George III. Reinforcements of British troops, warships, artillery and all the other accoutrements of war were soon under sail across the vast Atlantic to suppress this uprising by the "rebels." Washington, meanwhile, worked feverishly to recruit, organize, train and supply the Continental Army, augmented by separate units of militiamen from the various colonies. Something would have to give.

Another aspect of this period would prove to be one of the most bloody, terrible and divisive—a most uncivil civil war among the colonists themselves. Loyalists—also known as Royalists and Tories—remained supporters of the Crown, aiding and fighting alongside the British forces. Their foes were fellow colonists—often relatives, neighbors and friends—who backed the rebellion and were called Americans, Patriots, rebels, Whigs, all describing men and women who wanted independence and freedom from British rule. As is discussed later, clashes between these rival forces would be among the most savage, almost medieval in nature, especially in South Carolina where there were instances of brutality on both sides.

The years 1775 to 1778 were studded with immortal battles—Bunker Hill, Montreal (Quebec), the British evacuation of Boston, Harlem Heights, Trenton, Oriskany, Brandywine, Saratoga and Monmouth, all in the northern colonies or Canada.

A British land and sea attack against Charleston in June 1776 was repelled (more on this later), but other than the Redcoats' almost bloodless capture of Savannah, Georgia, in December 1778 and scattered fighting between Loyalists and Patriots in South Carolina, this period was relatively quiet in the South. The most important development of 1778 was France's entry into the war on the side of the Americans.

The year 1779 brought more action to South Carolina and Georgia as fighting in the north continued, but at a lessening pace as the Crown shifted its military emphasis to the South. A British thrust at Port Royal Island, S.C., was blunted in February while Georgia was bloodied by battles at Kettle Creek—an American victory 11 days after Port Royal—and a Redcoats triumph at Brier Creek on March 3. A British strike from Savannah toward Charleston climaxed in a brief but savage clash at Stono Ferry on June 20.

A major military action occurred with the siege of British-held Savannah by a combined American-French force lasting about four weeks over September and October 1779. The operation's zenith was a massive infantry assault targeting the Redcoats' defenses at the Spring Hill Redoubt, just west of the city. The British repulsed the attack after desperate, heavy fighting.

Thus, we turn to early April 1780, cannon and musketry blasts echoing across the salt marshes and palmetto groves as Clinton opened his siege of Charleston. The British trenches and the fortifications of the defending American army led by Major General Benjamin Lincoln scarred the coastal landscape as the fighting stretched into weeks. Spring's soft beauties and aromas were maimed by the stench of dead horses and mules, burnt gunpowder and soldiers' corpses baking in shallow graves. The British gripped Charleston in a stranglehold by May's second week, leaving its beleaguered defenders with little or no hope of reinforcements or escape.

Introduction

On May 10, Major General Lincoln received several petitions signed by hundreds of his troops, urging him to surrender. Among the signatures on at least two of the documents were members of the Camden District Militia Regiment. They included Zach Cantey, Willis Whitaker, James Cantey, Samuel Wyly, Samuel Mathis, John Whitaker, John Chesnut, Isaac DuBose, David Weatherspoon, John Witherspoon and Samuel Glasgow. Overwhelmed, surrounded and with food and other supplies dwindling, Lincoln finally surrendered on May 12, his bedraggled army of about 5,200 laying down its arms after 42 days under siege. Within a week or so, the British looked to capitalize on their triumph and momentum by destroying an American force retreating from the Charleston area and then establishing an inland base to solidify their foothold in South Carolina, eventually North Carolina and possibly beyond. That outpost would be Camden. The frontier village suddenly became the centerpiece of the Crown's effort to reconquer its Southern provinces and quell the rebellion with Brown Bess and sabers.

1

Camden's Beginnings

In their 1540 quest for gold, power and territory, Spanish explorer Hernando De Soto and his conquistadores ventured into the wilds of what are now the Carolinas, traversing the region where the roots of colonial Camden would be seeded more than two centuries later.

The Catawbas—or "people of the river"—who hunted, fished and farmed along the Catawba River were known for their fierceness in battle and likely encountered De Soto's party on its westward trek. At that time the proud and powerful Catawba nation is estimated to have numbered over 8,000, in the eastern territories, where they and their ancestors had reigned and flourished for thousands of years.[1]

Twenty-eight various tribes of Native Americans inhabited the wilderness of what is now South Carolina when the first English immigrants began arriving in the 1650s. Along the future border with North Carolina, Cherokees ruled the western hills and lands, while the Catawbas were the monarchs of the east. The region was also home to lesser tribes, including the Congarees, Santees, Stonos, Waterees, Waxhaws and others. Pestilence, war, time and the overwhelming—and often shameful—expansion of colonial powers extinguished many of these peoples, whose names live on today in the names of rivers, creeks and communities across the state.[2]

The coastal settlement of Charles Town was established in 1670 on the west bank of the Ashley River and was named in honor of British King Charles II. The English settlers relocated to the present-day site of Charleston ten years later. (The town would be called Charles Town until 1783 when it was renamed "Charleston.") Early immigrants to South Carolina also included the Spanish and French, but their presence was soon overshadowed by the English. The colony's agricultural roots brought in other, less-fortunate, "immigrants" and by 1708 African slaves composed the majority of the population. By 1730, the colonization of the "New World,"—what is now North America—was a continuing and ever-tense struggle of European powers intent on expanding their global sovereignties. That year, King George ordered Robert Johnson, the royal governor of the South Carolina colony—also referred to as a province—to establish townships there. In turn, Johnson issued directives for the survey of 11 townships, including Fredericksburg on the Wateree River. The survey led to a scattering of Welsh and Scottish immigrants establishing the tiny settlement of Fredericksburg in early 1734, despite protests from the Catawba and Wateree tribes. In a few years the crossroads evolved into Pine Tree, or Pine Tree Hill, a remote, frontier village along the east side of the Wateree about 100 miles inland from Charleston. The rustic community was so named because Indians used a pine log to cross a nearby stream, later called Pine Tree Creek.[3]

A group of Irish Quakers settled in the area about 1750, led by Samuel Wyly (sometimes spelled "Wiley" "Wyllie" or "Wylly" in various sources) and Robert Millhouse, described as "two very sensible and respectable men." In early 1748, a young man named Joseph Kershaw emigrated from Great Britain to the colonies, landing in Charleston shortly after his 21st birthday. He had left his home in Sowerby, Yorkshire, England, at age 13 to find "menial" work in London, staying there several years before sailing for the colonies. He and two brothers who would later join him, settled in South Carolina, "bringing with them considerable funds or property." By April 1756, Joseph was operating a grocery in Charleston, based on an advertisement in the *South Carolina Gazette* newspaper. At least one other source varies slightly, stating that Joseph was a clerk in the store of James Laurens & Co. in the provincial capital. Both may have been accurate. About 1758, Kershaw was an agent of the commercial firm of Ancrum, Lance and Loocock and relocated to Pine Tree Hill to establish "a country branch of the firm."[4]

Kershaw set up a "trading establishment" there and "soon became one of the most extensive and influential proprietors in that section." Duncan McRae (or "McRa"), John Chesnut and Zach Cantey, all of whom would soon be among the settlement's "wealthy and influential" first families were employed in Kershaw's mercantile endeavors. Chesnut in particular showed promise, first as an apprentice, clerk and later as a partner "in this extensive country store" which flourished with branches at Granby (near present-day Columbia) and "the Cheraws" or "Cheraw Hill" where Cheraw, S.C. now stands on the Pee Dee River. Chesnut's family had been in the Camden region since at least spring 1762. We will meet them shortly. Joseph also dabbled in other business ventures, primarily in wheat cultivation, flour milling and a brickyard. Still, he appears to have been proud of Chesnut, McRae and Cantey, supposedly stating "that he was raising up chickens to pick out his own eyes" meaning they would possibly take over his business or start some on their own. Kershaw "engaged in commerce upon an enlarged and liberal scale," a Camden newspaper noted in 1855, "and enjoyed in the highest degree, the confidence of the people of that part of the country."[5]

Samuel Wyly, meanwhile, was surveying land and trading with the Catawbas, possibly operating an inn and/or store in the region in the early 1750s. From about 1752 to 1755 he obtained some 600 acres in the area, already owning land along Swift Creek. In 1759 his home near Pine Tree Hill was called "Mount Pleasant." Wyly also served as a justice of the peace and soon was operating a gristmill and a saw mill.[6]

The Catawbas had primarily friendly interactions with the Pine Tree settlers, both benefiting from the election, about 1754, of King Hagler (Nopkehee) to leadership of the tribe. His decade-long tenure was a period of expansion for the Catawbas as well as goodwill for the pioneers, so much so that he is widely referred to as the "patron saint of Camden." King Hagler's reign was one of coexistence with the newcomers while the Catawbas flourished with their fine pottery making and as traders, especially in furs. However, smallpox savaged the tribe in 1759, almost half of the Catawbas succumbing to the scourge, but Hagler and the survivors endured. Tragically, King Hagler, the dynamic leader who meant so much to the Catawbas and to Camden's growth, was killed by members of a rival tribe—possibly Shawnee raiders—in August 1763.[7]

The Pine Tree Hill community grew slowly between 1758 and 1768, but Kershaw continued to prosper in his many business endeavors. One often overlooked aspect of his success was his expertise in flour milling, which he had learned in England years earlier. By 1760, Ancrum, Lance and Loocock were advertising "Fine Carolina Flour" likely produced by Kershaw's mills on Pine Tree Creek. During this time only about a dozen families lived within a mile radius of what is now modern-day Camden. About 1763, Kershaw married Sarah Mathis, a young Quaker, whose parents, Daniel and Sophia, were among the early Quaker settlers. Two of his brothers, Ely and William Kershaw, arrived in the colony from England during this period. Ely, who was about 20, joined Joseph as an apprentice in the store and was soon appointed as a tax collector. At age 16, William was the youngest of the three, but began thriving in Charleston's mercantile realm. William did spend time in the Camden area, however, and was a property owner there, based on various records.

Meanwhile, Joseph Kershaw used his clout to persuade the settlers to lay out streets and lots in the community and to change the name from Pine Tree Hill to Camden, honoring the British statesman Lord Camden who was a champion of colonial rights. The town was laid out in 1760 and chartered two years later. Surprising to some, the original village was situated about a half mile south of today's Camden and along both sides of what is now Broad Street. That north-south route originated as the

Catawbas' trading path, linking them to the coast as well as the mountains and further north. As more settlers arrived, the road was improved and known as the Great Wagon Road, a key component in Camden's evolution.

Local historians Thomas J. Kirkland and Robert M. Kennedy noted that possibly the first mention of the name Camden was found in the Act of Assembly dated April 12, 1768, calling for a court to be established in Camden, "lately called Pine Tree Hill." That same year, Joseph Kershaw acquired a tract of 250 acres two to three miles north of the village. He called the tract "Log Town"; it and a low, wooded ridge a bit further north destined to figure prominently in Camden's war history. The town also lost one of its so-called "founding fathers," Samuel Wyly passing away in February and buried in the Quaker cemetery. The year also saw the establishment of the Camden District, which would encompass portions of what would later be at least nine South Carolina counties. Within the district, Camden was located in St. Mark's Parish.[8]

Returning to the story of Joseph Kershaw's business associate John Chesnut, we find an ironic and fateful twist for one family in Camden's history. Chesnut's mother and stepfather, Mary Chesnut Sutton and Jasper Sutton, along with Mary's other two children, settled on a 100-acre tract on Gum Swamp Creek, a branch of Sanders Creek about seven miles north of Pine Tree Hill on the Catawba Path. Mary had married Jasper after the death of her first husband, James Chesnut, in Virginia in 1749. With the French and Indian War raging in some of the northern provinces, the Suttons worried the conflict could spread into Virginia where they lived. They moved south about 1755, eventually coming to South Carolina. By May 1762, Sutton had gradually acquired about 1,500 acres in the Gum Swamp area, where he farmed and built a popular local tavern. Years later, another war would bring bloodshed and violence to their very doorstep.[9]

By the late 1760s, Camden also had become a backcountry trade center, bringing in quantities of items including tobacco, indigo and animal skins. Cargoes were sent to Charleston via the Wateree or by land, the river deep enough to accommodate boats large enough to carry 50 or 60 hogsheads of tobacco. The enterprising Kershaw also was dispatching some 40 wagons per day to Charleston during this period. Meanwhile, after thriving in Camden as a businessman and property owner, Ely Kershaw established his own store and company in Cheraw. He continued to be a vital cog in Cheraw's development, so much so that he is considered one—if not the most important—of the town's founders. Among his accomplishments was overseeing construction of the Old St. David's Church. In 1769 he married Mary Cantey, from one of Camden's first families.[10]

On a March day in 1767, a pregnant widow and her two young sons stood over a fresh grave in a country churchyard, some 40 miles north

1. Camden's Beginnings

of Camden, mourning the loss of a husband and father. Elizabeth Jackson—better known as Betty—and her husband, Andrew Jackson the elder, had come to South Carolina two years earlier. After landing at Charleston, the Jacksons and their sons, Hugh and Robert, trekked about 160 miles inland to the Waxhaws, a settlement of Scotch and Irish immigrants that was named after the Waxhaw tribe, who once inhabited the area. Waxhaw Creek meandered through the region which was on the boundary between South and North Carolina. The Jacksons were poor, but already had relatives in the settlement and were eager to carve out a new life on the colonial frontier. They built a log cabin along Twelve Mile Creek and started raising farm crops before fate dealt them a cruel hand. Andrew had sickened and died, Betty giving birth to their third son, Andrew, on March 15, 1767, a few days after the funeral. Since then, the widow and her boys continued the grueling existence of pioneer life, even as relations between the colonists and the mother country deteriorated. Infant Andrew's life would be forged by his experiences as a teenaged prisoner of war in Camden after being attacked by a British soldier. Fate and destiny later rode with him to the U.S. presidency.[11]

Another future giant in the Camden story was barely visible on the horizon by then. In 1768, a tall, 47-year-old French army officer in civilian garb was traveling across the northern provinces, secretly gauging the level of interest the colonists had in revolting against Great Britain, France's perpetual enemy on the world stage of warring powers. John Kalb did not reach South Carolina on his mission; but 12 years later he would be revered forever in Camden—and across the United States—as Baron Johann DeKalb.[12]

In late 1771, an English immigrant named John Bartlam and his family settled in Camden a few years after landing in Charleston. Bartlam was a master potter and established South Carolina's first pottery works about 1765 on the Wando River a few miles from the capital. When this business closed, the Bartlams relocated to Camden where residents were already familiar with the Catawbas' fine creations. There were a few lean years ahead for the Bartlams before some prosperity, which the war brought to a halt, as will be seen.[13]

A court house was built at Camden in 1771–1772, establishing the village as the seat of the Camden District. This development, along with the Quaker meetinghouse, an early Presbyterian presence, and the stores of Kershaw and Wyly, began to attract more settlers to the burgeoning inland town on the Wateree. A two-story brick jail—or gaol, the spelling of the day—was also completed during that time, across the street from the court house. Both structures stood at the intersection of present-day King and Broad streets. A contract for construction of both buildings was let to Kershaw, John Chesnut, William Ancrum and Aaron Loocock in 1770. Chesnut's work ethic and business sense had resulted in his being promoted to "a member of the firm." A female admirer described Chesnut as "one of the handsomest men of his day" and in 1770 he married Sarah Cantey, "born in the Wateree." Despite the construction, Camden remained but a tiny flicker of civilization in the vast South Carolina wilderness, the scant houses of worship a major public issue since they were so few and far between. The first grand jury presentment in the initial court session at Camden in November 1772 contained a grievance regarding that complaint:

"The Parish of St. Mark, in our District, being so extensive that the numerous inhabitants are deprived of the comfort of the Preaching of the Gospel and divine service, some of the Inhabitants being one hundred and Forty miles distant, and consequently subject to many evils too notorious to be overlooked in a Christian part of the world." The "evils" apparently included "many villainies and Roberies [sp] committed." The myriad hazards of living in an untamed land predominated in another grand jury grievance submitted during the April 1773 Camden court term: "The want of Law to encourage the killing and destroying of Beasts of Prey, such as Wolves, Tygers [sp], Bears &c., which, it is found, grow very numerous and of course detrimental to the inhabitants." The complaint also mentioned "idle and disorderly vagrants constantly hunting in the woods and destroying Deer for their skins, especially when they do it in the night by fire light, whereby great numbers of cattle are destroyed, and the lives of the people endangered."[14]

The master potter John Bartlam and his family, meanwhile, were struggling to survive in the village. Bartlam traded at Joseph Kershaw's store in 1772, but by October he was jailed for "bad debts." Accounts are sketchy as to how Bartlam resolved his financial woes and raised money to build another business—Kershaw may have had a hand in this salvation—but by spring 1774 a "pottworks" was thriving in the Camden area. Soon, he was selling and shipping his "queens ware, cream ware and earthen ware" in Charleston. Bartlam's creations were "equal in quality and appearance and can be afforded as cheap, as any imported from England," said the *South Carolina Gazette*. Bartlam, however, would soon be wielding a musket, possibly for both sides at different times, it will be seen.[15]

2

"To win over the wavering" and the Gathering Storm

1774

A convention was convened at Charleston on July 6, 1774, to express South Carolina's outrage and opposition to the closing of the port at Boston in retaliation for the famous Boston Tea Party the previous December. At this meeting, delegates were elected to participate in the First Continental Congress, held in Philadelphia in September. Additionally, a committee of 99 members was appointed from all over the colony "to correspond with similar committees from the other colonies." The Camden District was represented at the convention and on the committee, but any records listing these officials have not been found. A most notable incident occurred in the town on November 5 when Judge William Henry Drayton, a fervent patriot who was temporarily presiding over the circuit court in Camden, "delivered the first of those stirring charges to grand juries that were so effective in arousing the people of upper Carolina to a sense and assertion of their rights," said one account. Impassioned by Drayton, the Camden District grand jury responded with what has been described as a "veritable little Declaration of Independence."[1]

Here is an extract of the most important segments from the third clause of that presentment:

> We present, as a grievance of the most dangerous and alarming nature, the Power exercised by the Parliament to tax, and to make Laws to bind the American Colonies in all cases whatsoever. We conceive such a Power destructive of our Birthrights as Freemen, descended from English Ancestors, seeing such freemen cannot be constitutionally taxed or bound by any law without their consent, expressed by themselves or implied by the representatives of their own election—a consent which the good people of this colony never have signified, to be taxed or bound by Laws of the British Parliament in which they never have had any constitutional representation.

And whereas we rather choose to die Freemen than to live Slaves, bound by Laws in the formation of which we have no participation,

So now that the Body of this District are [sic] legally assembled, as one step towards the defense of our constitutional Rights, which are dearer to us than our Lives and Fortunes, we think it is our indispensable Duty, to the people of this District, to ourselves the Grand Jurors for the Body of the People, and to our Posterity, thus clearly to express the sense of this large and populous District, touching our Constitutional Rights and the very imminent Danger to which they are exposed from the usurped power of the British Parliament, taxing and by Law binding the Americans in all cases whatsoever, being

Resolved to maintain our Constitutional Rights at the Hazard of our Lives and Fortunes, we do most earnestly recommend that this Presentment, in particular, be laid before our Constitutional Representatives in General Assembly, who, we doubt not, will do all in their power to support us in our just Rights.

Included in the presentment were the names of the jurors: Matthew Singleton, foreman; Joshua English, Sylvester Dunn, Jasper Sutton, John Payn, Isham Moore, John Cantey, John Witherspoon, John Gamble, Robert Carter, Henry Hunter, David Neilson, Thomas Casity, John Perkins, Sen.; Henry Cassels, Samuel Bradley, James Conyers, David Wilson, Aaron Frierson, Moses Gordon, Samuel Cantey, and Edward Dickey. Drayton's oratory later inspired similar presentments at Georgetown and Cheraw where he also presided as circuit judge. The year also saw the construction of a Presbyterian meetinghouse near the Quaker cemetery, on land donated by Joseph Kershaw. The widening of the town's streets, based on the work of John Heard, a deputy surveyor, was another positive development.[2]

By summer 1774, Kershaw's Camden firm under his partnership with Ancrum, Lance and Loocock of Charleston was thriving as a multi-tiered enterprise composed of "storehouses, store of goods, mills, wagons, horses," and about 100 "valuable" African Americans—"coopers, millers, bakers, wagoners [sp], jobbing carpenters, boatmen, and field slaves employed in carrying on the business," claimed a *South Carolina Gazette* advertisement. "Many thousand acres" of land on the Wateree River were also for sale in "convenient lots of from one hundred to hundred acres to suit purchasers of all ranks."[3]

After his Charleston partners retired in December, Kershaw's agreement with them was dissolved. His business acumen, however, was unaffected. He established Kershaw and Company located near the Exchange Building in Charleston, selling a variety of produce from the Camden area and beyond. He also dealt with the firm of George Ancrum, Jun., and Company, which was the successor to his former partnership in the city. Additionally, Kershaw was a partner in other stores in Camden—Kershaw and Wyly, Kershaw and Hoyle and John Wylly and Company. "Thus a successful venture in back-country trade had raised an obscure country trader to the rank of a great Charleston merchant," stated one account.[4]

1775

Despite the banshees of coming war screeching ever louder over the provinces, Camden's growth was ongoing, the village continuing to be the economic and political mecca of inland South Carolina. By spring 1775 about 30 families lived in or near the town, grist mills for grinding wheat brought in by local farmers contributing to the prosperity. The most prominent, obviously, was that of Joseph and Sarah Kershaw and their six children, James, John, Joseph, Mary, George and infant Sarah, born this year. Some of these families were likely among area Baptists who gathered to hear the Rev. Richard Furman conduct the first Baptist service held in Camden. Camden's location on the Great Wagon Road was increasingly important, the route essentially a segment of interstate for travelers and commerce at the time. Roads to Cheraw, Augusta, and Cross Creek (present-day Fayetteville, N.C.) also intersected there, adding more significance to Camden as a transportation hub. This distinction would soon be magnified as troop and supply movements began.[5]

Weeks earlier, the Congress of the Province of South Carolina had gathered in Charleston on January 11, 1775, the *South Carolina Gazette* describing the assembly as "the most complete representation of all the good people throughout this colony that ever was and perhaps ever will be." Delegates from the Camden area (east of the Wateree) of St. Mark's Parish were Robert Carter, Aaron Loocock, Joseph and Ely Kershaw, Robert Patton, Col. Richard Richardson, William Richardson, Matthew Singleton, Thomas Sumter and William Wilson. All of these members, along with John Marshall and Isaac Ross from the outlying Camden region, were appointed to a provincial committee charged with implementing guidelines from the Continental Association regarding law processes and other legal matters. John Chesnut was a delegate at large and also on this committee.[6]

An Irish immigrant who would become one of the leading Loyalists in Camden District was James Miller, who settled there in February 1775. He had bought 200 acres in the area of Jackson's Creek for two pounds an acre. That spring Miller was among Loyalists who refused to sign one of the documents circulating in the province proclaiming opposition to the Crown. This eventually made him a target of the local Patriots and he was later imprisoned for some 19 weeks in spring 1776. After his release, Miller appears to have enlisted in a Loyalist unit led by Captain James Phillips.

Little is known of his activity over the next three years, but his "steadfast loyalty" was rewarded in August 1780 when he was appointed as captain in the Jackson's Creek Loyalist militia. At some point during the war, Miller and at least some portion of this detachment served under British Lieutenant Colonel George Turnbull of the New York Volunteers, but Miller's combat record is unknown.[7]

Joseph Kershaw, meanwhile, had raised a local militia regiment of about 200 Patriots by March 1775. Among these men was John Bartlam, the master potter who had thrived in Camden, apparently beholding to Kershaw for helping him out of financial problems enroute to his success. Bartlam continued to remain an enigmatic figure in the Camden story throughout the coming conflict.[8]

The clashes at Lexington and Concord in April intensified the urgency of decisions and conviction in all of the colonies. "South Carolina, on hearing of the outbreak on the plains of Lexington, was ablaze with excitement...," said one account, the Provincial Congress again convening at Charleston on June 1. A "Declaration of Association" was written and was to be circulated among all the men of the province, "the signers pledging themselves to be ready to sacrifice life and fortune to secure the freedom and safety of South Carolina...." The document went further, stating that the Congress would be "holding all persons inimical [hostile] to the liberties of the colonies who should refuse to subscribe to the Association."[9]

The Carolina politicians also voted to raise two infantry regiments—also called "regiments of foot," as the British referred to them—and a regiment of rangers, or mounted infantry, 500 men in each unit. William "Danger" Thomson of Orangeburg was chosen as lieutenant colonel of the rangers, whose other officers included notable Camden men—Ely Kershaw elected one of the captains; Francis Boykin, a first lieutenant; and Dr. Thomas Charlton, a second lieutenant. Isaac DuBose, who later lived in Camden, was named a second lieutenant in one of the regiments of foot.

In other matters, Joseph Kershaw and John Chesnut were appointed to the Committee of Continental Association to represent St. Mark's Parish, which included Camden. Samuel Boykin of Saxe Gotha Parish was named to the same committee. The most momentous decision reached by the Provincial Congress, however, was the formation of a Council of Safety, which was empowered by the Carolinians for the governance of the colony in defiance of the Crown. The Council was composed of 13 prominent Charleston Patriots with Henry Laurens as president. The Provincial Congress adjourned on June 22. It was not a coincidence in timing that Lord William Campbell, the newly appointed royal governor of South Carolina, had arrived in Charleston on June 18. He stepped ashore in a

2. "To win over the wavering" and the Gathering Storm

provincial capital that was seething with a rebellious atmosphere. Trying to maintain order, Campbell soon dissolved the Crown-sanctioned colonial assembly, a majority of members who had also served in the Provincial Congress. Unsure of the severity of the crisis he faced, Campbell then sought refuge aboard a British vessel in the harbor.[10]

At the time, the province was also divided into 12 military districts. One of these was Camden, consisting of "the country between Lynch's Creek and the Congaree" River, making up the present counties of Kershaw, Richland, Sumter, Fairfield and Chester. The other districts were: Charleston, Berkeley County, Granville County (the present counties of Beaufort and Hampton), Craven County, Colleton County, Orangeburg, Cheraw in present-day Chesterfield County, Ninety Six, The Forks of Saluda, Upper Saluda and the "New District" or "New Acquisition" consisting of present-day York County. Militia leaders in the Camden District were the Kershaws, Colonel Richard Richardson, Lt. Colonel James McGirth and Major Samuel Cantey. The province also was in the process of raising a body of regular troops, or professional soldiers. Possibly overlooked in some histories are the Taylor brothers—Thomas and John, the latter sometimes referred to as James—who also were organizing troops in the Camden area after the conflict flamed. Originally from Virginia, the Taylors were among the first settlers in the region east of the Congaree River and soon became the most influential. The brothers fought as partisans under Thomas Sumter and in other capacities. We will see them again later.[11]

The Camden colonists, including Joseph Kershaw, also were negotiating with members of the Catawba tribe, encouraging their allegiance to the American cause. Renowned for being staunch fighters, Catawbas under King Hagler's rule had fought in the French and Indian War under George Washington, on the side of the British. Ironically, Washington, and the Catawbas were still on the same side, but opposed to the Crown in the Revolution. On July 22, 1775, Col. Thomson wrote to the provincial Council of Safety that "King Prow, with about 50 of the Catawbas, are now in Camden on a friendly visit." Three days later, patriot Governor John Rutledge wrote to Kershaw regarding the Catawbas. "Your assurances that those people are hearty in our interest, and your hopes that forty or fifty of them will cheerfully enter into the service of the colony affords the Council [of Safety] additional satisfaction...." Rutledge noted. The result was that a militia company of Catawba warriors would be assigned to the rangers, the company led by Captain Samuel Boykin of Camden.[12]

Still, even as the Catawbas and other colonists were being organized into military units that summer, the province was much divided by the question of whether to oppose or support a possible break from

King George III. Much of the opposition or indifference came from people who lived in the South Carolina upcountry—or "backcountry." Particularly in the settlements between the Saluda and Broad rivers, support for the Crown remained generally strong. These settlers lived a more isolated existence, and had not been as greatly affected as the Carolinians who lived in the central or coastal sections of the province.

In Camden, however, there was also division, especially when the rebellion seeds were first sown. Among those embracing the American cause during this tempestuous time in addition to Joseph and Ely Kershaw were John Chesnut; Thomas Charlton; Duncan McRae; Isaac DuBose; James and Zach Cantey; John and Willis Whitaker; and Samuel, John and Francis Boykin, to name a few.

Daniel McGirtt, Henry Rugeley, his brother Rowland, along with James and Nathaniel Cary were the most prominent Loyalists in the area as tensions heightened. McGirtt, who lived just south of town, would eventually flee to British Florida, where he became a partisan fighter against the Americans. Before the war, Henry Rugeley had operated a mercantile business in Charleston with branches in the Carolina interior. One of these was at his country estate near the fork of Grannys Quarter and Flat Rock Creeks, where he also operated a mill. James Cary's family had immigrated to Virginia from Ireland, also living in North Carolina before relocating to the South Carolina low country in 1764. He and his family settled west of the Wateree six years later, eventually buying a plantation there. Camden's Quakers were as split as anyone else. Based on their religious beliefs, some chose to remain neutral. Others, like Robert and Joshua English, Jonathan Belton and John Adamson, sided with the Loyalists. The Wylys—John and Samuel—along with Samuel Mathis were among those standing with the Americans.[13]

In late July, the Council of Safety decided to dispatch a delegation "to explain to the people the nature of the present unhappy public disputes between Great Britain and the American Colonies." The delegation—Joseph Kershaw, Col. Richard Richardson "of the Camden regiment" Judge William Henry Drayton, the Baptist Rev. Oliver Hart, and the Presbyterian Rev. William Tennent of Charleston—set out from Charleston on August 2, 1775, to raise funds and enthusiasm for the independence cause. The trip was described as "a tour through the upper country [of South Carolina], to strengthen the friends of resistance and to win over the wavering." Tennent in particular was a daring firebrand. After his sermons in various rural churches and meeting-houses he "harangued the people on the state of the country [and] gave them a 'touch of the times.'" Drayton and Tennent as well encountered some Loyalist leaders and "many of their followers" on the tour, but other than some tension and perhaps harsh words, no violence was done. Tennent and possibly the other delegates, also kept a keen eye on and encouraged military preparations among their supporters, the Presbyterian checking on cannon platforms along the Savannah River, and even raising a company of mounted rangers amid his journey. On the whole, however, this campaign of persuasion was a failure.[14]

Meanwhile, weeks had passed and Captain Samuel Boykin had yet to organize his company of Catawba warriors. He wrote to the Council of Safety on October 16, 1775, that the Catawbas were not yet ready to muster due to widespread illness. Three men died "and several more [were] very sick," the Captain related, adding that he also "was taken extremely ill with the feaver [sp] but had recovered." Boykin had been to "Catawba Town" a few days before penning the letter "and the Indians has [sp] got much better, and are willing to come down at any time you may think proper, as the sickly season of the year is now over." He also stated that he had paid 25 Catawba fighters ten pounds each and requested reimbursement from the Council.

Despite some of their men joining Boykin, the Catawbas near Camden were puzzled by the military activities and sent two "runners" to Charleston to determine what was happening. They met with members of the Council of Safety and were told that "our brothers on the other side of the water wanted to take our property from us without our consent, and that we would not let them, and that we expected their warriors to join ours" said one account. The Catawbas were asked to relay this message to the Cherokees in the northern part of the province. By this point, Lord Campbell, the royal governor, was ashore and rallying Loyalists in the upstate under leaders including Patrick and Robert Cunningham, Moses Kirkland, Daniel Browne, Jacob Bowman, Joseph Robinson and Thomas Fletchall. These men were organizing Loyalist militia to quell the rebellion while British agents were inciting the Cherokee against the Americans. In mid- to late October the Council of Safety decided to try to appease the Cherokees—and possibly avoid an uprising by them—with a gift of 1,000 pounds of gunpowder and lead to use in hunting. Bearing this cargo, a small wagon train, escorted by Camden's Lt. Thomas Charlton and a party of rangers, was bound for Keowee, the Cherokees' main village, when they were surprised by a large group of mounted Loyalists led by Patrick Cunningham and Bowman. Overwhelmed and outnumbered, Charlton surrendered, the Loyalists making off with the lead and powder.[15]

Patriot Major Andrew Williamson and about 500 men made an attempt to recover the munitions but were surrounded by a larger force of Loyalists and besieged for three days and nights near the South Carolina village of Ninety Six, a critical hub where 12 roads and paths intersected.

Despite being little more than a skirmish over November 19–21, this action is considered by some to be the first battle of the war fought south of New England. The "siege" ended in a stalemate and truce, but Williamson did not retake the lead and powder. Even before this action occurred, however, the Council of Safety in Charleston had decided on a stronger military response. On November 8, the members voted to send Colonels Richard Richardson—who some accounts claim commanded the Camden militia—and William Thomson to organize and lead a sizeable force on a strike into the heart of the Loyalists' enclaves in the "backcountry." By late November, Richardson had gathered about 3,000 militiamen who swept through the region arresting or driving out many of the prominent Loyalists there. Some of these fugitives fled to the mountains of western North Carolina; others relocated to Crown havens in eastern Florida. The latter included Daniel McGirtt, one of the Camden area's leading Loyalists, mentioned earlier. The operation was called the Snow Campaign, since heavy snow began falling on December 23. A substantial amount of gunpowder and weapons was seized in the operation, including some 200 muskets that were sent to the Patriots in Camden.[16]

On December 21, 1775, the British government passed an act of Parliament, which effectively cut the last strands of the cord still binding South Carolina and her sister colonies to the mother country. The act called for the confiscation of property belonging to rebellious Americans, denied them any further protections, and authorized the seizure of all American ships. It would take weeks for news of the act to reach the provinces but it struck like a hammer blow when received.[17]

Before this legislation, the Carolinians and others had lobbied for liberty from unjust and unreasonable laws, intolerable taxes and other unequal treatment from the Crown, even as they prepared to defend themselves. Cries for liberty had gone unheard across the vast Atlantic. Now the shouts were louder and different. From Camden to Charleston and up the colonial coast it rose: *Independence!*

1776

In Charleston, a legislative committee of the Provincial Congress had been working to draft a framework constitution establishing a new government for South Carolina. The Provincial Congress on March 6 had approved a constitution submitted by the committee, but the arrival of a copy of the act of Parliament on March 21 from Savannah caused the Carolinians to backtrack, based on the stern and even shocking measures they read in the British document. On May 26, a revised constitution was adopted, a momentous decision, making South Carolina the first of the 13 provinces to declare itself a free state. Joseph Kershaw was a member of the first Legislative Council, a body that later evolved into the state Senate. John Rutledge was elected as president, Henry Laurens as vice president, and William Henry Drayton as the chief justice of the fledgling state. Early on, the legislators passed an act providing for the punishment of rebellion and treason against the state. Drayton supervised the reopening of the courts, which had been closed during the turmoil of the past 12 months. Other measures followed with the intent of "putting the new constitution into active operation." In other words: "South Carolina was the first to set up a formal government in opposition to the King's, and to provide for it a constitution."[18]

The other provinces were engaged in similar activities which would also make them independent of British rule. At the same time, all of them knew that hell was on the way. The proud British Empire was the mightiest power on earth, with a formidable navy and army enforcing the Crown's prestige and influence to the globe's far reaches. But even the storied lion of Europe couldn't wave the Union Jack over its vast holdings without being stretched thin somewhere over thousands of miles. Amid this uncertainty, foreboding and excitement, the South Carolinians began bolstering Charleston for an expected British attack by sea.

In early February, Samuel Boykin of Camden and his company of Catawba warriors had taken the field "as lately ordered" and were encamped "within a few miles of Charleston, the captain reported to the Council of Safety." In the coming weeks these fighters conducted scouting patrols in the parishes of St. George, Dorchester, and St. Paul's. Boykin had orders to cooperate with local patriot leaders in these locales "or to perform other public services in the line of their [the Catawbas] duty, from time to time" until about March 10 when the company was discharged and paid. Boykin was instructed to "inform said Indians that, when their further services are required, the public will expect them to obey the call."[19]

Boykin's Catawbas were recalled to duty when a British fleet indeed menaced Charleston in late June 1776, launching a land and sea attack. The men were part of a 750-man force under Colonel William Thomson which successfully defended Sullivan's Island against British troops trying to reach the island across a narrow channel from Long Island—modern-day Isle of Palms—on June 28, 1776. That same day, the enemy fleet was repulsed by the defenders of Fort Sullivan—an incomplete sand and palmetto log bastion guarding the harbor entrance. Despite being heavily outgunned by the British navy, the Carolinians held their own, the ships' cannonballs sinking harmlessly into the spongy texture of the palmettos.

The overall assault failed and the enemy vessels withdrew. The victory was one of the most historic events in South Carolina history, the palmetto tree later joining the familiar crescent moon on the state flag.[20]

The names of the Catawbas who fought and shared in this American triumph are largely lost to history, but one of them apparently was Abram Kelley of the later-named Kershaw District who was 85 when he died in 1832. His obituary stated that he was in Francis Boykin's Rangers—more specifically Samuel Boykin's Catawbas—during the Revolution and that he also served with the "Swamp Fox" Francis Marion in several engagements. In the Sullivan's Island combat, Kelley was said to have gathered "broken bombs" fired by the British, the projectiles reused by the Carolina defenders when their artillery was almost exhausted.[21]

Within days of the British repulse, violence flared in northern South Carolina with an uprising by the Cherokees on or about July 1. The action appears to have been instigated by British agents Alexander Cameron and John Stuart. Colonists fled south as far as Orangeburg to escape the havoc and "the people around Camden were also terror stricken." A number of militiamen from the Camden area who were posted near Charleston were rightly concerned about loved ones at home. "Several of the officers and privates have rec'd letters from their Friends in the Back Country on account of the Indians breaking out, which gives them a great deal of uneasiness in regard to their families," William Thomson wrote to Governor Rutledge on July 11 from his camp on Sullivan's Island.

Among the worried was Lt. Thomas Charlton, posted on the island with the rest of Capt. Ely Kershaw's company. Charlton, a Camden merchant and family man before the war, had been an officer in Thomson's Rangers since 1775. On the morning of the 11th, he had received a letter from Camden regarding the uprising and had immediately made "application for leave to go there to secure his Family from a presumed insurrection of the" Cherokees. When Thomson refused his request, Charlton resigned his commission. After much carnage, the Cherokees were defeated by colonels Williamson and LeRoy Hammond near the Keowee River and a severe vengeance was wreaked on them.[22]

Yet underscoring the perplexing but perpetual schism of ideals in Camden and beyond in this monumental year is the resume of James Cary, the Irish immigrant who had lived with his family along the Wateree since 1770. The Provincial Congress appointed him as a justice of the peace for the Camden District in 1776, Still, Cary was a well-known supporter of the Crown and had received a major's commission with authorization to raise a Loyalist regiment in the region.[23]

Indeed, the blades of war were already bloodied, but Camden's sanguine reckoning was still to come.

1777–1778

Camden continued to flourish as an inland crossroads and commercial center, primarily due to Joseph Kershaw's enterprises. Its role in military importance also heightened with the state ordering construction of a powder magazine there, the project to be under Kershaw's direction. The site would be well outside the village—a safety measure due to the danger of explosion—and on a slight hill about a quarter mile southwest of where Kershaw's mansion was then being built. Some 36 slaves—including carpenters and laborers—from surrounding plantations worked for some 114 days to complete the magazine under foreman James Brown, an engineer and master carpenter. Most, if not all, of the slaves belonged to Kershaw, John Wylly and Joseph Habbersham (or Habersham). Of the slaves only one worked the entire time, others varying from two to 74 days. Locally dug clay was hauled to the site and baked into bricks, the latter for the structure's four-feet-thick walls supporting a vaulted roof. The cost was about 9,000 English pounds and consisted of some 225,140 bricks. By this time, Kershaw's landholdings were such that he owned most of the town as well as the surrounding acreage.[24]

Possibly the most crucial victory of the war occurred not on any battlefield but at the negotiating table on February 6, 1778, when France and the U.S. agreed to two treaties in which France became directly involved in the conflict. The treaties meant the French would send troops, ships, armaments and financial aid, along with military advisers, to fight side-by-side with the Americans.

France had secretly been shipping much needed gunpowder and other supplies to the Americans since spring 1776. American war fortunes flagged later that year, but Washington's triumphs at Trenton in December and Princeton in January 1777, reenergized the Patriot cause prompting the French to increase covert military shipments to the colonists. The witty, crafty and suave Benjamin Franklin was the key negotiator for the Americans, having spent some time in Paris charming his way through diplomatic and social circles. The treaties' momentum also was sustained by the Patriots' stunning victory at Saratoga in October 1777. Many decades of war and bad blood between the French and British also contributed to France entering the fray. The French still seethed over their defeat by the British in the Seven Years' War, of which the French and Indian War from 1754 to 1763 in North America was a part. That debacle resulted in France losing most of its territory on the continent, including all of Canada. The international power and pride of empires was soon to hang in the balance again as a result of the Franco-American agreements.

By fall 1778 the British high command was becoming increasingly convinced that the war in the northern provinces was stalemated, and that military operations in the South might prove more advantageous. Near "the close of the year 1778, the scene of action was transferred to the South ... and from this time on to the end of the war no State was so harried and fought over as" South Carolina, said one account. At Camden, about half of 100 or so Loyalists moving through the region and attempting to escape to British East Florida were confined in the town jail after the entire number were captured by American militia.[25]

With Savannah being threatened by the British in December, an American force under Brigadier General William Moultrie moved from Charleston to the village of Purrysburg (also known as Purrysburg Landing or Purrysburgh) on the 27th. The village was situated on the Carolina side of the Savannah River and just north of Savannah. From there the Americans could guard against an enemy strike across the river and toward Charleston. Brigadier General Richard Richardson's state militia were a part of this force, the Camden District militia regiment of Colonel Joseph Kershaw included in Richardson's ranks. Kershaw's senior captain was John Marshall, who would lead the regiment in Kershaw's absence. Marshall—or Marshel—was a local landowner and member of the 1775 Provincial Congress. Kershaw's other company captains were Luke Petty, George Summerville, Middleton McDonald, Robert Crawford, George Dunlap, Robert Montgomery, Josiah Evans and Edward Kennington. Kershaw's other militiamen, however, were hardly fit for service. "This militia was in a wretchedly undisciplined state," stated one account, "the men going off when they chose, and refusing to move without being told why and where they were going." With minimal resistance from its garrison, Savannah was captured by the Redcoats on December 29, but there was no immediate thrust by the British to cross the river.[26]

However, trouble was boiling over at Purrysburg, and Kershaw's rowdies were stirring a pot of insubordination, mutiny and possible cold-blooded murder if tempers got any hotter.

1779

In the early days of January 1779, Pvt. John Cayle in the Camden militia was on guard duty at Purrysburg when he abandoned his post for several hours. Caught and reprimanded by his company commander, Capt. Petty, Cayle "became abusive and was ordered under arrest." At this the soldier threatened to "put a bullet through the captain's brain" but another soldier "threw up his gun in the nick of time." The private underwent a court-martial on a charge of insubordination with General Richardson

2. "To win over the wavering" and the Gathering Storm 29

serving as president of the court and the other judges also being militiamen. The question soon arose: should the man be judged based on the "Continental rules of war" or were these not applicable since he was in the militia?

By this time, Major General Benjamin Lincoln had replaced Brigadier General Robert Howe as Southern commander. Lincoln contended that the militiamen were being paid and provisioned by the Continental army and thus were subject to army discipline. Otherwise, he would discontinue their provisions and they could return home.[27]

The discipline was the sticking point, since punishment for insubordination under Continental army guidelines was death, while under militia rules was merely a small fine. The situation was widely debated, Lincoln criticized for his opinion. In frustration and as a way out of this matter, Lincoln turned over command of the state militia to General Moultrie. The South Carolina general assembly eventually decided the issue, calling for stricter rules for the militia, but maintaining the latter were not bound by Continental regulations.[28]

During this period, a regally uniformed foreign officer at the head of his cavalry force trotted through the streets of Camden. Brigadier General Casimir Pulaski and his Legion were passing through the village on their way to the coast and actually stayed in the area for several days resting and recuperating. The Polish-born count, who turned 34 in March, was among a number of European soldiers, enamored by the Patriot cause, who had come to America to fight, Pulaski raising an independent corps in Maryland in 1778. Likely unknown to anyone at the time of his Camden sojourn, some of his troopers were infected with smallpox, which would start to spread through area farms, plantations and tentacle out even further in the coming summer weeks.[29]

On April 20, Lincoln led a force of about 2,000 troops, primarily Continentals augmented by some of his better organized militia regiments, in a strike toward Augusta. At Purrysburg, he left behind Kershaw's militiamen and a force of North Carolina militia led by Brigadier General Griffith Rutherford. Learning of Lincoln's operation, Major General Augustine Prevost, the British commander at Savannah, launched a blow against Charleston, the city's defenses weakened by Lincoln's departure. Prevost and the bulk of his army of about 4,000 troops crossed into South Carolina on April 28, causing Moultrie and his scattered militia units— including some of Kershaw's men under newly promoted Major John Marshall—to fall back toward the capital.

Apparently the remaining three quarters of Kershaw's regiment were sent home for a brief period of reorganization between Lincoln's move against Augusta and the time the alarm was raised about Prevost's incursion. These Camden soldiers and the contingent of Catawba braves led by Samuel Boykin, drew supplies from the Kershaw & Wyly company on May 12 preparing to return to the coast. This Camden force was ordered to Dorchester, about 24 miles northwest of Charleston, the village being a marshaling point during Moultrie's retreat in the previous few days. At Camden, Kershaw left behind a company under Capt. John Chesnut—his young business associate—to guard the magazine.[30]

As Kershaw and Boykin prepared to leave Camden, much had already happened: Moultrie and a patchwork of militias had reached Charleston on May 9, Prevost's Redcoats nearing the city the next day. Pulaski and his Legion had departed Camden and were active around the city by the 8th. There had been a series of negotiations about the possible surrender of Charleston stretching into May 12, but with little result. Meanwhile, Lincoln, ever cautious as was his nature, was slowly marching to Charleston's relief. Prevost was aware of this, but unaware of Lincoln's whereabouts. Early on the morning of the 13th, American lookouts in Charleston were surprised to see the enemy lines across the way empty of Redcoats. With the possible threat of Lincoln closing in on him from behind, Prevost retreated toward Savannah. The British did leave behind a strong rear-guard force at Stono Ferry on John's Island, south of Charleston. This was a key position since it linked the island to the mainland, leaving open the possibility of a future British offensive against Charleston along the Carolina coastal islands.

Kershaw's militia, now a part of Brigadier General Andrew Williamson's brigade, were posted near Charleston about the first week of June, but the brigade was plagued by desertions, leaving it weakened and in disarray. On June 8, Kershaw's soldiers outdid the rest of the command, an entire company of 30 men—a captain, "one subaltern" and 27 privates deserting. Twelve days later, on June 20, the remainder of Williamson's troops, including Kershaw's men, joined in an American attack on Stono Ferry where it appears that the "rest of the regiment [the Catawbas, Marshall's and Petty's companies] bore its part becomingly" in the "severe little battle." On a different note, a much more joyous occasion that year was celebrated by the Kershaws, Joseph and Sarah, welcoming baby daughter Rebecca—their seventh child—into a tumultuous world.[31]

From hundreds of miles away, even stiffer winds of war were soon to shift not only toward Camden, but the rest of South Carolina as well, beginning on December 26, 1779. On that day a formidable British fleet under Admiral Marriot Arbuthnot, composed of warships and transports, set sail from New York. The vessels contained some 8,500 of the Crown's troops, many of whom were battle hardened and considered among the finest in the world, as well as an array of the most modern arms and other

2. "To win over the wavering" and the Gathering Storm

equipage. When augmented by reinforcements from Savannah and local Loyalists, the force would eventually swell to about 12,000. The army was commanded by Major General Sir Henry Clinton, and among the officers aboard the ships were men named Cornwallis, Tarleton and Rawdon, all of whom would play major roles in Camden's war history. At this point, however, the British had another objective in mind. Once again, their target was Charleston.[32]

3

A Scarlet Hurricane Roars Ashore: 1780

As winter squalls ravaged the southbound enemy armada, Camden bustled as a key inland supply post and crossroads for American forces moving to reinforce Charleston or to other points.

After several brutal weeks at sea, most of the British fleet arrived off the Georgia coast at Tybee Island near Savannah in early February and inched north toward Charleston, troops being landed at several locations. Much equipment and most of Clinton's horses—artillery and cavalry—were lost during the turbulent voyage, but the British slowly regrouped, troops edging into defensive positions on the neck of the Charleston peninsula, north of the city, by March 20. Heavy guns were posted and Arbuthnot's vessels soon blockaded the port.

In Charleston, General Lincoln and his few thousand American defenders helplessly watched the foe's buildup, the stranglehold slowly tightening in the coming days. Lincoln had few options for relief. Savannah was held by the King's men. There were a few American ships in Charleston harbor, but they were too weak to puncture this British sea wall and no help was foreseen from the infant American navy from outside the enemy perimeter. Essentially, Lincoln's only hope was to receive supplies and reinforcements by land—and any major effort of this kind would likely go through Camden and its roads network.[1]

In his role as a militia colonel, Joseph Kershaw superintended the Camden powder magazine, located about a quarter mile from his home, and oversaw the distribution of its always meager munitions to the passing soldiers. News of the British army's landing and not knowing the enemy's intent prompted the Americans to abandon the magazine in February. Seventeen wagons transported the gunpowder and other stores to Charlotte for safekeeping. After determining the Redcoats were not an immediate threat, the munitions were returned to Camden about ten days later. Still, with the war edging closer in March and April, the Patriots constructed earthwork fortifications in an effort to protect the magazine from possible surprise attack by Loyalists. "We have thrown up some works about our Magazine to prevent any surprise from the disaffected," Kershaw informed Governor John Rutledge.[2]

In an April 25 letter from Camden, Kershaw wrote to Rutledge about various other matters. Corn was scarce there, although some was available for about $20 a bushel, a hefty price. Other supplies also were scant due to wartime shortages that had only worsened since the British besieged Charleston. Many, if not all, of the villagers relied on Kershaw's longtime generosity to help feed their families. He told Rutledge,

> [I]t is unfortunate for the Publick that stores of Provisions were not laid in 4 or 5 months ago when it might have been done for much less than half the Price. The Publick Credit here is at a very low ebb. I shall be obliged to make all Purchases on my own Account. I am Pretty Largely in advance for the Publick for Supplys [sp] as Long ago as Christmas 1778. [H]owever I doubt not the Publick's doing me Justice as whatever I have done for them ... has been without fee or Reward.
>
> I inform you that a Colo. Beaufort [sp] is just arrived with about 300 Continental Troops. Our commissary is out of Money or Credit. No Rum or Sperits [sp] of any kind which they hanker after much.

Kershaw was referring to a force of Virginia Continentals led by Col. Abraham Buford on its way to reinforce Charleston. A few days before Buford's appearance, four wagons from Brigadier General Andrew Williamson's command trundled in with a request for ammunition from the magazine. Kershaw noted that Williamson "was supplyd [sp] as far as we could. We had only about 1,000 lb. of Lead of which [we] sent him half tho' his Request was 2000 lb." After this order was filled, the magazine's inventory consisted of an undisclosed quantity of powder, some 30 boxes of cartridges "each containing abt 110 dozen. and not a flint."[3]

It was on or about this same time that Kershaw also wrote to Rutledge:

> I am sorry to say I have lost all influence & command amongst the People here, but shall do everything in my power towards furnishing the Troops to be assembled at Wright's Bluff with corn flour, in which shall be assisted by my brother Ely Kershaw, but with respect to Beef it is not to be had in this quarter, the severity of the winter has carried off a great number of Cattell, and those which have survived are so miserable poor as scarcely to be able to get out of a Bog.

A few days earlier, Brigadier General Richard Caswell and about 500 North Carolina militia passed through Camden en route to Charleston. Caswell had requested and received a supply of ammunition from the Camden magazine, Kershaw informed Rutledge. Also in Camden were six brass fieldpieces and a "quantity of Baggage wagons" belonging to Brigadier General William Woodford's brigade of Continentals who had already marched on to Charleston. "You may depend upon my utmost exertions for the carrying [of] every desire of your excellency into Execution." As Woodford's column left Camden, his entourage likely included Captain Robert Porterfield, a Virginian and aide-de-camp. In the months ahead, Porterfield's brother would become one of the most tragic figures in Camden's war story.[4]

Within days of these communications, two of the three Kershaw brothers in South Carolina returned to Charleston—whether they traveled together or separately is unclear, but the city remained under siege. Ely had already seen more than his share of battle, participating in the Snow Campaign, Sullivan's Island and Kettle Creek fighting, all of which had taken their toll on him, mentally and physically. He arrived in Charleston not only to check on his business interests, but to try to regain his overall health. Joseph apparently went there to lead elements of the South Carolina militia in defending the city.

The third brother, William, also was in Charleston where he continued his career as a merchant, but also apparently serving in the city's defenses. William also was a "Brigade Major" of "South Carolina troops" starting in 1776, based on one source, and complained to a relative about "marching, counter marching, camping, & doing garrison duty for some years and much against my inclination at some periods...." while in the Americans' service. William's complaint was rooted in his conflicting loyalties. He was more inclined toward remaining under Crown rule—or at least considering it—which caused friction, especially with brother Joseph.[5]

Lincoln and his slowly starving, ragged soldiers held on into early May, despite dwindling provisions and the British siege lines drawing the noose around Charleston ever tighter. However, a heavy and prolonged two-day bombardment by Clinton's artillery was too much to withstand. With no hope of relief or supplies, and wanting to curtail further needless bloodshed, Lincoln and his approximately 6,600 troops surrendered on May 12. Among the prisoners were Joseph and Ely Kershaw. William Kershaw also was captured, as part of the Fort Moultrie garrison. One observer wrote of seeing William "going to Camden on Foot" after the city's fall. We will learn more about him a bit later. The separate American forces under General Caswell and Colonel Buford that had left Camden for Charleston did not reach the city before its fell. One unit would later earn battle glory near the inland village; the other would be essentially destroyed in one of the worst, and still controversial, slaughters of the Revolution.[6]

3. A Scarlet Hurricane Roars Ashore: 1780

After Charleston's capture, Clinton set about implementing plans to control the South Carolina interior with the further goal of subduing the rebellion in North Carolina as soon as possible. Clinton also was preparing to return to New York with a portion of his army, but his three-pronged South Carolina operation would come first, all originating from Charleston. One thrust would be made northwest along the Savannah River—the border of Georgia and South Carolina—toward the vicinity of Augusta, Georgia. Another would pass the Saluda River further inland and target the critical crossroads village of Ninety Six, mentioned earlier.[7]

The third point of the spear was the most important and involved Camden: Clinton's second-in-command, Lt. General Charles Lord Cornwallis, was to lead a force of about 2,500 troops and five cannon across the Santee River proceed up the north bank and try to intercept an American column led by Colonel Abraham Buford. This force—the Third Virginia Detachment—was composed of about 350 Virginia Continentals from the Eleventh Virginia "and detachments of regiments." two six-pounder cannon and a number of supply wagons, was on the march to reinforce Charleston, but did not reach the city before the British closed a mailed fist around it. Unsure of how to proceed, Buford camped at Lenud's Ferry on the Santee on May 6 and sent an "express"—a mounted messenger—to Brigadier General Isaac Huger of South Carolina, the highest-ranking officer he could reach—for orders. This brief lull allowed his exhausted troops and horses some respite from their weeks-long march from Petersburg, Va., and across the Carolinas as the southern spring simmered toward summer.[8]

Huger soon replied with instructions for Buford to retreat to Hillsborough, North Carolina, via Camden, where Buford was to "remove the ammunition and military stores deposited there" and bring along on his retreat 30 or 40 previously captured British prisoners being held in the town. Buford began his retreat from the Santee on May 12, within hours of Lincoln's capitulation. It would be a laboriously slow march—much as it had been from Petersburg to the Charleston area. Now, however, the Virginians' supply wagons were pulled by increasingly fatigued horses even after a few days of rest at Lenud's. The column was soon joined by South Carolina's patriot Governor Rutledge and his small entourage who had managed to escape Charleston, as well as about 40 Virginia Light Dragoons who also had evaded the British net. The Dragoons raised Buford's force to about 400 troops.

Within days, Buford also linked with Caswell and his 600 or so North Carolina militia, both commands retreating to Camden and further north. Reaching Camden on May 26, Buford "executed the order [from General Huger] with precision," supplies that could not be brought off "thrown into a neighbouring creek" possibly Pine Tree Creek. Now, however, his wagons would be heavier and overburdened with the additional stores and ordnance to be removed. Buford's troops encamped in and around the town, as did Caswell's men, teamsters, played-out horses, dragoons, and Governor Rutledge with two Council members. It was a scene of despair, frustration and bone-tired endurance that was destined to only deepen in the coming days.[9]

Buford at some point, probably that night, composed a letter to the Virginia Assembly from "Camp Camden," as he worded it. "Everything here is in the greatest confusion," he wrote of the South Carolina situation.

> The enemy has [captured] Georgetown.... How far they proceed to the northward will I believe entirely depend on the opposition they meet with.... I wish any stay/delay[?] may not occasion the loss of many military stores and baggage ... which we are now much incumbered [sp] with.... Gen. Caswell has begun his retreat ... with about 600 militia which are all the troops here in service except my Battalion, the Gov. of this State having discharged his militia to prevent them from being taken in arms. I am sorry to inform you that the people of this state are now about to make terms for themselves with the British army. My regt. [regiment] with the stores move[s] tomorrow. My march is by way of Salisbury.... I am apprehensive of the loss of stores and baggage as the enemy are now ahead of us.... Our horses are worn down by constant marching, which makes our retreat the more dangerous. Nothing but large reinforcements can occasion a thought of stopping the enemy....

It is unclear what happened to the Redcoat prisoners Huger mentioned, or even if there were any. There is no word about them from Buford or Tarleton. Perhaps Huger was misinformed, or the men had been sent elsewhere.[10]

Caswell's and Buford's troops both left Camden sometime on May 27—times are unknown—but it proved to be a major turning point in the events soon to follow. "At Camden these two corps unfortunately separated," recalled Robert Brownfield, a surgeon's mate in the Second South Carolina Continentals who was with Buford's command. Both forces were bound for North Carolina, but with different destinations, Caswell moving toward Cross Creek and Buford, still accompanied by Rutledge, on the march toward Salisbury on the Great Waxhaw Road, also known as the Great Wagon Road. Buford was unaware that his command would soon be in catastrophic peril from a fast-riding enemy thundering ever closer. Brownfield added what could have been an epitaph for Buford's men: "This measure was accounted for by the want of correct intelligence of Tarleton's prompt and rapid movements...."[11]

4

"I have cut 170 Off'rs and Men to pieces"

Cornwallis did not begin his pursuit of Buford until May 18, moving towards Camden along the same route taken by his intended prey. The British crossed the Santee at Lenud's Ferry and continued their march "some days," but Cornwallis, "finding him [Buford] too far advanced to be overtaken by the main body" had to choose another option. He dispatched Lt. Col. Banastre Tarleton to take a mounted detachment and, by forced marches, bring Buford to bay. Tarleton commanded the British Legion, a contingent of cavalry and infantry—the latter sometimes mounted—composed of northern Loyalists known for their green uniform jackets and burgeoning battle tenacity. Tarleton and his men, most of whom were recent Scottish immigrants to the provinces, had only just returned to the army after a foray to Georgetown. Now, leading his strike force out of Cornwallis's bivouac at Nelson's Ferry on May 27, Tarleton's command consisted of 230 of his Legion troopers, 40 horsemen from the 17th Light Dragoons regiment, and a three-pounder cannon.[1]

Over the next few days Tarleton would become not only a major figure in Camden's war history, but ride to infamy as one of the most aggressive, feared and bloodthirsty commanders of the Revolution, especially in South Carolina.

His life's road to Camden began on August 21, 1754, when he was born in Liverpool, England, the third of seven children in the family of John and Jane Parker Tarleton. His father had made a comfortable living primarily in the slave trade and shipping, owning plantations in the West Indies, Jamaica and Curacao. When Banastre was ten, his father was elected mayor of Liverpool. There is sparse information about the boy's early schooling, but he was described as solidly built, although small for his age during this time. Even as a youngster, he excelled more as an aggressive and savvy athlete than as a student. Cricket, especially was his game and he shone as a batsman. Headed to college at Oxford in fall, 1771, Tarleton's storyline was much the same: an average and unmotivated teenager gifted with natural physical talents in cricket, boxing and riding. His parents had hoped to steer him toward a legal career, but this ended—about the same time as his withdrawal from Oxford—with his father's death. Tarleton found himself with about 5,000 pounds—a small fortune left to him—and moved to London. His lifestyle quickly devolved from any law studies to drinking, gambling and womanizing, his vices soon devouring much of his inheritance.[2]

With no direction and little money, Tarleton turned to the army, purchasing a commission as a cornet in the First Regiment of the King's Dragoon Guards on April 20, 1775, the day after the battles at Lexington and Concord. Over the coming weeks and months, the British military readied its forces to be sent to America. Among these troops were elements of an infantry division commanded by Lord Cornwallis. Eager for action and with his unit still awaiting orders, Tarleton volunteered and was granted permission to sail to the colonies in December with Cornwallis's force. Tarleton participated in Clinton's failed campaign to take Charleston in June 1776 and also saw action at the battle of White Plains, New York, in October. He also was present for the British seizure of Forts Washington and Lee in November. Tarleton's grandest act in the conflict to this point occurred on December 13, 1776, when he led a patrol that captured the infamous General Charles Lee, a British officer who had resigned from the army the previous year to join the Patriots' cause. During brief lulls in action Tarleton, yearning for more battle thrills and accolades, refocused his energies on drinking and the carnal pleasures offered by colonial lasses. He also was becoming known for his hair-trigger temper and for mercilessness toward the enemy. Tarleton was with Cornwallis's forces who fought George Washington in the January 1777 battles near Princeton and Trenton. He was in combat at Brandywine in September, the operations resulting in the British capture of Philadelphia that same month, and also was engaged in the October battle of Germantown. Tarleton had risen steadily in the ranks and on August 1, 1778, was given command of the British Legion with the temporary rank of lieutenant colonel.[3]

As the epic chase of Buford unfolded on its second day—May 28— some of Tarleton's horsemen ransacked and torched the summer home of Thomas Sumter, a noted patriot and former soldier, whose plantation was near the present-day village of Stateburg, S.C., in the High Hills of Santee, an area of rolling wooded hills about 20 miles south of Camden. Sumter escaped after being warned that a Legion cavalry detachment led by Captain Charles Campbell was approaching. In the coming months, he would exact a measure of revenge for this incident by bedeviling the British as a highly effective partisan commander, but this day was all about Tarleton trying to close the gap on his distant foe—Buford. He related that his men "followed the Americans without anything material happening on the route, except the loss of a number of horses, in consequence of the rapidity of the march, and the heat of the climate."[4]

"By pressing [or seizing] horses on the road," Tarleton and at least some of his troops were nearing Camden about 10 a.m. on May 28, when they were met by Joseph Kershaw—recently returned after being paroled at Charleston—and a small group of others representing the town. They had left Camden about four hours earlier, riding south with a petition from the residents asking the British for protection. Kershaw recalled that after learning of their intent, Tarleton "assured us it was his Order & Earl Cornwallis ['s] particular desire that Our Property Should remain untouched" other than needed military supplies "and that their intention was only to put the Country into a State of Peace & tranquility."[5]

Tarleton reached Camden about 1 p.m. There he learned that Buford had left Rugeley's Mill, about 12 miles to the north, a day or so earlier and "was marching with great diligence" to join a North Carolina militia unit moving southwest from Salisbury toward Charlotte. "This information strongly manifested that no time was to be lost, and that a vigorous effort was the only resource to prevent the junction of the two American corps," Tarleton related.

The weary British rested for a few hours at Camden before the relentless Tarleton again ordered them into the saddle about 2 a.m. on the 29th, "being tolerably refreshed" to continue the pursuit. The Redcoats reached Rugeley's about daylight, finding that Buford's column was some 20 miles ahead. They narrowly missed capturing Governor Rutledge, who had spent the night there, moving north separately and on a different route from Buford's force. An oddity in this phase of the chase is that Rutledge stayed at Clermont, home of the mill's operator Henry Rugeley, a supposedly staunch Loyalist and colonel of Loyalists troops. At least one account, however, claims that Rugeley, "courting both the British and rebels," awoke the governor and his aides, who were soon in the saddle galloping north toward safety.[6]

Tarleton claimed that at this juncture he faced a decision on how to proceed, based on the discretion Cornwallis had given him. He "might have contented himself with following them [Buford's troops] at his leisure" to the boundary line of the Carolinas and then "returned upon his footsteps to join the main army, satisfied with pursuing the troops of Congress out of the province" but "animated by the alacrity … both in officers and men, to undergo all hardships … put his detachment in motion…" to engage Buford. Tarleton also decided to adopt a "stratagem to delay the march of the enemy" and sent Capt. David Kinlock of his command to ride ahead and deliver a surrender demand to Buford. By this ploy and by "magnifying the number of the British," he "might intimidate him [Buford] into submission, or at least delay him whilst he deliberated on an answer."[7]

Kinlock reached the American column about 1 p.m., near the Waxhaws settlement, and Tarleton's message was delivered to Buford. What thoughts must have raced through the Virginian's mind as he read these words:

> Sir,
>
> Resistance being vain, to prevent the effusion of human blood, I make offers which can never be repeated:—You are now almost encompassed by a corps of seven hundred light troops on horseback; half of that number are infantry with cannon, the rest cavalry: Earl Cornwallis is likewise within a short march with nine British battalions.
> I warn you of the temerity of farther inimical proceedings, and I hold out the following conditions, which are nearly the same as were accepted by Charles town [sp]. But if any persons attempt to fly after this flag is received, rest assured, that their rank shall not protect them, if taken, from rigorous treatment.[8]

The dispatch then laid out five articles of capitulation. Briefly, they were: (1) All officers to be prisoners of war, but paroled and allowed to return home until exchanged. (2) All Continental soldiers to go to Lamprie's Point near Charleston or any other British outpost in that area, remaining there until exchanged. Also, to "receive the same provisions as British soldiers." (3) All militiamen to be prisoners upon parole at their homes. (4) "All arms, artillery, ammunition, stores, provisions, wagons, horses, &c. to be faithfully delivered." (5) Officers "to be allowed their private baggage and horses, and to have their side arms returned."

Tarleton's ominous message closed with an even more ominous demand: "I expect an answer to these propositions as soon as possible; if they are accepted, you will order every person under your command to pile his arms in one hour after you receive the flag: If you are rash enough to reject them, the blood be upon your head."[9]

As Kinlock awaited an answer from Buford, Tarleton was racing to catch up to him as well as the enemy column, but his ranks had dwindled somewhat due to the almost non-stop and merciless pace of the pursuit. "By this time many of the … cavalry and mounted infantry were totally worn out, and dropped successively into the rear," he wrote, "the horses of the three pounder were likewise unable to proceed." Buford, meanwhile, was mulling the enemy demand and did not halt his column, in direct defiance of Tarleton's threat of "rigorous treatment." He did, however, immediately call a council of his officers to discuss the summons and offered "three distinct propositions"—or courses of action: "Shall we comply with

Tarleton's summons? Shall we abandon the baggage, and, by a rapid movement, save ourselves, or shall we fortify ourselves by the waggons [sp], and wait his approach?"[10]

The officers unanimously rejected the first two options, "declaring it to be incompatible with their honor as soldiers, or the duty they owed their country, either to surrender or abandon the baggage on the bare statement of Tarleton," Brownfield related. "They had no certainty of the truth of his assertion, and that it might be only a *ruse de guerre* to alarm their fears and obtain a bloodless victory." The third option—making a stand with the wagons—also was opposed, the officers making the case that even if they held their ground against Tarleton "no succor was near, and as Tarleton could, in a short time, obtain reinforcements from Cornwallis," they would eventually be overwhelmed by superior numbers.

At least one part of Tarleton's "ruse" had worked, since Cornwallis was advancing, but still was within two or three days march of even reaching Camden, much less the Waxhaws. Buford's council resolved to continue the march, "maintaining the best possible order" for repelling the Redcoats. Thus, "after detaining the flag [Kinlock's] for some time," Buford "returned a defiance," informing Tarleton in no uncertain terms:

> SIR,
> I REJECT your proposals, and shall defend myself to the last extremity.
> ABR. BUFORD, Colonel.[11]

Tarleton was quick to react, even though he was outnumbered. He "determined as soon as possible to attack, there being no other expedient to stop their [Buford's troops] progress, and prevent their being reinforced the next morning" by the North Carolina militia en route to Charlotte. At 3 p.m., the British "advanced guard" galloped toward the end of the American column capturing a sergeant and four light dragoons. These soldiers were apparently part of a rear guard or stragglers, since they were behind the infantry still in column on the road.

Tarleton made no mention of bloodshed in this initial clash, but Brownfield presented a vastly different, more grotesque, version of what occurred:

> In a short time Tarleton's bugle was heard, and a furious attack was made on the rear guard, commanded by Lieut. [Thomas] Pearson. Not a man escaped. Poor Pearson was inhumanely mangled on the face as he lay on his back. His nose and lip were bisected obliquely; several of his teeth were broken out in the upper jaw, and the under completely divided on each side. These wounds were inflicted after he had fallen, with several others on his head, shoulders and arms. This attack [on the rear guard] gave Buford the first confirmation of Tarleton's declaration by his flag [demanding surrender].[12]

"The event happening under the eyes of the two commanders," Tarleton related, "they respectively prepared their troops for action." Buford deployed his soldiers first. "He chose his post in an open wood, to the right of the road," Tarleton wrote, "he formed his infantry in one line, with a small reserve; he placed his colours in the center; and he ordered his cannon, baggage, and wagons, to continue their march." "Unfortunately," said Brownfield, "he [Buford] was … compelled to prepare for action, on ground which presented no impediment to the full action of cavalry." The American line actually stretched across the road, facing south, although the bulk of the Virginians were to the right—or east of the route.[13]

Tarleton posted his force based on how the Americans were positioned in front of him. On this May afternoon, he was the master of the field, opposed to a numerically superior foe but playing a deadly chess game with an overmatched king across the field. The British right wing consisted of 60 dragoons and about the same number of mounted infantry, all led by Major Charles Cochrane, Tarleton's second in command. Cochrane was to dismount his infantry "to gall the enemy's flank" as Captain Kinlock, with a portion of the Legion cavalry, and Captain William Talbot's detachment of the 17th Dragoons assailed the American center. On the British left, Tarleton with 30 "chosen horsemen and some infantry" coiled to assault Buford's right flank and reserve.[14]

The Virginian's delay in replying to the summons played directly into Tarleton's gauntlets, allowing time for more Redcoats to reach the field. Many of the British stragglers and their lone cannon "as they could come up with their tired horses, were ordered to form something like a reserve, opposite the enemy's center, upon a small eminence that commanded the road…." Tarleton noted. "This disposition afforded the British … troops an object to rally to, in case of a repulse…." He added that the one solid advantage enjoyed by his force was "the known inferiority of the continental cavalry, who could not harass their [the British] retreat to…. Cornwallis's army, in case they were repulsed by [Buford's] infantry." The Redcoats completed their deployment within about 300 yards of the line of Continentals, who held their fire. It was about 3:30 p.m.[15]

Bugles blared from the British positions as Tarleton ordered the main attack, the Redcoats surging across the fields "with the horrid yells of infuriated demons." In a matter of seconds, the Brit cavalrymen closed within some 50 paces of the blue line, the Continentals raising their muskets to their shoulders. But there was no volley of scything lead, the British hearing American officers shouting to their men to hold fire until the enemy riders were even closer. Finally, with the British about ten yards from them, the Continentals' muskets blazed in a storm of noise and smoke. Several horses were hit and tumbled, as did a handful of wounded or killed

Redcoats, but the charge was unbroken, the Americans unable to trigger even a ragged second volley before being overrun. "Some officers, men, and horses suffered by this fire"; Tarleton noted of the volley, "but the [American] battalion was totally broken...." Cochrane's infantrymen swept over Buford's soldiers in that sector, wielding their bayonets to deadly purpose without firing a shot, although some of the Continentals on the Americans' left flank rallied and reformed about 50 yards to the rear.[16]

Perhaps the most incredible incident of the fighting involved Capt. John Stokes, a Virginian who encountered a dragoon in one-on-one combat early in the battle. The cavalryman "aimed many deadly blows" at the captain's head, but Stokes "easily parried" them "by the dexterous use of the small sword" he carried. Another Brit trooper, however, coming at him from a different direction, landed a saber stroke that tore off Stokes's right hand. Both soldiers continued to assail Stokes, who "attempted to defend his head with his left arm until the forefinger was cut off, and the arm hacked in eight or ten places from the wrist to the shoulder. His head was then laid open" from the crown to his eyebrows by another sword strike. By then Stokes had fallen, suffering "several cuts on the face and shoulders" as he lay on the ground.[17]

Leading his dragoons in the attack, Tarleton's horse was killed by at least one ball in the volley and fell, momentarily pinning the Legion commander's leg under its weight. Before he could remount "slaughter was commenced," Tarleton recalled, adding that "a report amongst the cavalry, that they had lost their commanding officer ... stimulated the soldiers to a vindictive asperity not easily restrained." In other words, when Tarleton and his mount tumbled, word quickly spread among his troopers that he was killed, inflaming them to avenge him.[18]

The violent miasma of how the battle evolved—or devolved, depending on viewpoints—over the next fifteen minutes or so will likely forever be lost in the confused fog of war. Conflicting accounts, some written decades after the Revolution, are still debated by modern-day historians. What is known is that Buford, seeing that the brief battle was getting out of hand, decided to surrender and sent a mounted officer with a truce flag toward the British. The identity of the officer—Buford's adjutant, Henry Bowyer claimed to be the messenger, while other accounts state the rider was Ensign John Cruit—and the minutiae of his encounter with the Redcoats remains unclear, the surrender request was either ignored, refused or never seen in the chaotic span of when Tarleton fell under his horse.[19]

"Buford now perceiving that further resistance was hopeless, ordered a [truce] flag ... and the arms to be grounded, expecting the usual treatment sanctioned by civilized warfare," Brownfield noted, adding that Cruit was "instantly cut down" while advancing with the truce flag. It is unclear how many—if not all—of the Americans put down their weapons, or even had a chance to do so amid the havoc of a few violent minutes. Brownfield added: "Viewing this [Cruit's fall] as an earnest of what they [the Americans] could expect, a resumption of their arms was attempted, to sell their lives as dearly as possible…." By then, however, it was too late, Brownfield continuing that before the Continentals could rearm,

> Tarleton with his cruel myrmidons was in the midst of them, when commenced a scene of indiscriminate carnage never surpassed by the ruthless atrocities of the most barbarous savages.
>
> The demand for quarters, seldom refused to a vanquished foe, was at once found to be in vain;—not a man was spared—and it was the concurrent testimony of all the survivors, that for fifteen minutes after[,] every man was prostrate. The [British] went over the ground plunging their bayonets into every one that exhibited any signs of life, and in some instances, where several had fallen one over the other, these monsters were seen to throw off on the point of the bayonet the uppermost, to come at those beneath.[20]

The only British troops present and equipped with muskets fitted for bayonets were the infantry of Tarleton's Legion. Thus, unless some of his other soldiers picked up muskets from the Continentals, any bayonet mayhem would have to be primarily from these men. "The Americans remained steady until the British were within ten yards and then fired a volley, which produced little effect," wrote 19th-century British military historian Richard Cannon, "and before the smoke cleared away, their ranks were broken, and the British were cutting them down with a terrible carnage. In a few minutes the conflict had ceased; one hundred Americans lay dead on the spot…."[21]

His hand hacked off and also bleeding heavily from numerous other wounds, Capt. John Stokes lay helpless as the nightmare flurried around him. An enemy soldier "passing on in the work of death" paused and asked if he expected quarters, meaning mercy. Stokes replied, "I have not, nor do I mean to ask quarters, finish me as soon as possible." The soldier bayonetted him twice before moving on. Stokes was still alive when another Redcoat approached him. The earlier scenario was repeated with basically the same brief conversation before Stokes was again speared twice in the body with the bayonet. Amazingly, Stokes was still alive, his eyes locked on a wounded British officer sitting a short distance away when a Redcoat sergeant came up, "addressed him [Stokes] with apparent humanity, and offered him protection from further injury at the risk of his life." Stokes told him that all he wanted was to be "laid by that officer that I may die in his presence." It is unclear why this was so important to Stokes, but the sergeant complied, carrying him toward the injured officer. Twice the soldier had to lay the Virginian back on the ground and "stand over him to defend him against the fury of his comrades." Whether this "fury" was ignited by blood lust, Tarleton's perceived death, or a combination of both is unknown.[22]

Laid next to the Brit officer, Stokes saw that the man's wounds were being dressed by a "Doct. Stapleton, Tarleton's surgeon, whose name ought to be held up to eternal obloquy [contempt]...." Stokes, who "lay bleeding at every pore," asked the surgeon for aid, but was "scornfully and inhumanely refused." This was until the doctor was "peremptorily ordered by the more humane [Redcoat] officer" to assist Stokes "and even then [he] only filled the wounds with rough tow, the particles of which could not be separated from the brain for several days." Stokes suffered 23 wounds at Waxhaws, but survived not only the battle but the war. At least one account states that Tarleton "immediately wrote Cornwallis: 'My Lord, I am extremely fatigued with overtaking the Enemy & beating them—I summoned the Corps—they refused my terms—I have cut 170 Off'rs and Men to pieces.'"[23]

"The loss of officers and men was great on the part of the Americans, owing to the dragoons so effectually breaking the infantry.... Upwards of one hundred officers and men were killed on the spot...." Tarleton stated after the war. "The execution done in this action was severe," added Major Charles Stedman, a Loyalist officer, who was not at the battle. "The king's troops were entitled to great commendation for their activity and ardour on this occasion, but the virtue of humanity was totally forgot."[24]

"The wounded of both parties were collected with all possible dispatch, and treated with equal humanity," Tarleton wrote. That being said, the more seriously injured Continentals apparently were left on the field until the next day. "The American officers and soldiers who were unable to travel, were paroled the next morning [May 30], and placed at the neighbouring [sp] plantations and in a meeting house, not far distant" from the battlefield, Tarleton related. "Surgeons were sent for from Camden and Charlotte ... to assist them, and every possible convenience was provided by the British." The meeting house was the log sanctuary of the Waxhaws Presbyterians where the wounded were treated by members of the congregation and others from the settlement. Many of these civilians had been drawn by the combat cacophony and began separating the slain from the wounded, using their wagons to carry the latter to the meeting house, but the task was overwhelming.[25]

Among the merciful angels was an Irish immigrant widow, Elizabeth Hutchinson Jackson, aided by her sons—Robert and 13-year-old Andrew, who would later become a president of the United States. A third son, Hugh, fought with American forces at the battle of Stono Ferry in June 1779, but died of heat and fatigue shortly after the action. "Mrs.

Jackson was one of the kind women who ministered to the wounded soldiers in the church, and under that roof her boys first saw what war was," a 19th-century Jackson biographer wrote. "For many days Andrew and his brother assisted their mother in waiting upon the ... men; Andrew, more in rage than pity, though pitiful by nature, burning to avenge their wounds and his brother's death." The teen "first saw the demon of war in its most horrid form, and all that misery and British power and oppression, were ever afterward associated in his mind," said another account. Young Andrew played an interesting role in Camden's Revolutionary history, a role to be discussed much more later.[26]

Tarleton and his force were still at the Waxhaws on the 30th when he again wrote to Cornwallis about his triumph. He had every reason to be highly proud of his achievements and the performance of the soldiers who followed his banner. To cover 105 miles in 54 hours, and to engage and annihilate an enemy force of superior number which enjoyed a ten-day lead over rough roads in the steamy Carolina wilderness was an epic military accomplishment in that age, or even now.

Tarleton wrote:

> My Lord,
>
> I have the honour to inform you that, yesterday ... the rebel force were [sp] brought to action.
>
> After the summons, in which terms similar to those accepted by Charlestown were offered, and positively rejected, the action commenced in a wood: the attacks were pointed at both flanks, the front and reserve by 270 cavalry and infantry blended, and at the same time all were equally victorious, few of the enemy escaping, except the commanding officer, by a precipitate flight on horseback.
>
> It is above my ability to say anything in commendation of the bravery and execution of officers and men. I leave their merit to your Lordship's consideration.[27]

The British also had received word that the American force that Buford was trying to link with near Charlotte "had fallen back upon the report of the late affair." That evening—the 30th, Tarleton "commenced his march towards Earl Cornwallis" It would necessarily be a slow but certainly a grandly triumphal parade for the Green Dragoon, an "express" messenger—apparently the second rider dispatched after the first one on the 29th—already galloping ahead through the deepening darkness to find and inform Cornwallis of the victory. In addition to his own soldiers, Tarleton's column included fifty-three prisoners, a haul of three colors, two brass cannon, two royals, two ammunition wagons, an artillery forge cart, fifty-five barrels of gunpowder, and 26 wagons "loaded with new cloathing [sp], arms, musquet [sp] cartridges, new cartridge boxes, flints, and camp equipage." Meanwhile the local residents were burying some eighty or more dead Continentals in a mass grave on the battlefield where a pitted, old monument later stood sentinel for decades bearing the Loyalist Stedman's haunting words: "the virtue of humanity was totally forgot." Other Americans, too severely mangled to live, died in the coming days and were interred in the graveyard next to the meeting house, where Andrew Jackson's father, Andrew Sr., also rests.[28]

Tarleton gave this assessment of the battle in his postwar memoir:

> The complete success of this attack, may, in great measure, be ascribed to the mistakes committed by the American commander: If he had halted the wagons as soon as he found the British troops pressing his rear, and formed them into a kind of redoubt, for the protection of his cannon and infantry against the assault of the cavalry, in all probability he either would not have been attacked, or by such a disposition he might have foiled the attempt: The British troops in both cases, would have been obliged to abandon the pursuit, as the country in the neighborhood could not have immediately supplied them with forage or provisions; and the [C]ontinentals might have decamped in the night, to join their reinforcement. Colonel Buford also, committed a material error, in ordering the infantry to retain their fire till the British dragoons were quite close; which when given, had little effect either upon the minds or bodies of the assailants, in comparison with the execution that might be expected from a successive fire of platoons or divisions, commenced at the distance of three or four hundred paces.[29]

Tarleton's aggressive nature makes at least the first part of this assessment hard to believe since he and his force had ridden so hard and fast to reach and bring Buford's column to bay. Tarleton was, by far the superior commander on the field, Buford appearing inept in basically every decision that May afternoon. At least one account states that some of the British were riding double on their horses. This has some possible accuracy in the middle or latter stages of the pursuit as animals were lost due to the rapidity, length, dehydration, heat and general exhaustion of the chase, coupled with Tarleton's drive to bring as many soldiers as possible to a confrontation with Buford.

5

"The Carolinas have been conquered"

As Tarleton continued his march south from the Waxhaws on May 31, Cornwallis was nearing Camden, moving through the "High Hills of Santee," a region of heavily forested, rolling hills in the central part of the province. Suddenly several gunshots rang out from the woods. In short order "two boys" identified as Kit Gales and Sam Dinkins were seized and accused of shooting at the soldiers. No injuries were recorded, but Gales was hanged from a tree and Dinkins was manacled, joining the column as a prisoner bound for confinement or worse in Camden. Cornwallis's Redcoats had not suffered for rations on the expedition, "supported from the country through which they passed," related the Pennsylvanian Major Stedman, Cornwallis's commissary officer. "A number of negroes, mounted on horses, were employed under proper conductors in driving in cattle for ... the army, and, though they were in general very small, the army was plentifully supplied," Stedman wrote. "The cattle were delivered alive to the regiments, who found their own butchers."[1]

Cornwallis was destined to be not only the British general most associated with Camden in the Revolution but also in South Carolina, and a place called Yorktown, Virginia, as well.

A portly aristocrat, politician and combat-seasoned professional soldier thus far in his life, Cornwallis turned 41 during the fleet's voyage south. His family traced its origins to four centuries earlier in Cornwall and Suffolk, having the prestige of English nobility, but not the wealth that often accompanied it. Young Charles was educated at Eton, where he suffered an injury that influenced his life forever. During a field hockey match, he was hit in the face by an opponent's stick, resulting in permanent damage to one of his eyes. Thereafter, he was self-conscious about his appearance, which likely contributed to his reserved nature. At length Cornwallis, still a teenager, chose a career in the army, his family purchasing a commission for him in the First Grenadier Guards, a common practice in the Empire at that time. Before becoming a Guardsman, Cornwallis traveled and enrolled in an Italian military academy in Turin in 1757, eventually joining the Guards several months later. Ever yearning for action, he proved to be a natural soldier and leader, serving with zeal and distinction in the Seven Years' War and rising to the rank of lieutenant colonel by 1761. A year later, the death of his father—the first Lord Cornwallis—required him to return to England and replace his father as a representative in Parliament's House of Lords. Cornwallis married Jemima Tulleken Jones in July 1768, the couple settling into his family's estate in Suffolk. Their first of two children, Mary, was born in June 1769.[2]

In Parliament, Cornwallis, quite surprisingly, was a supporter of the colonies and opposed to key legislation that contributed to the causes of the coming conflict. He voted against the Stamp Act in 1765 and the next year resisted passage of the Declaratory Act, in which Parliament claimed the right to legislate for the colonies in all matters. The war clouds were darkening almost daily by the time Lady Cornwallis birthed their son, Charles, on October 19, 1774. When the conflict flamed, Cornwallis was ordered to assume command of an army division and "notwithstanding his opinions of the injustice of that war, he considered that as a military man, he could not decline" the position, related Charles Ross, an officer and friend who served with the earl. As with most soldiers, Cornwallis was obviously reluctant to leave his family, but he sailed for America in February 1776, as a lieutenant general. Rumors abounded at the time that Lady Cornwallis so adamantly opposed his decision that she appealed to Cornwallis's uncle, the Archbishop of Canterbury, to request the King to allow the Earl to "relinquish his appointment." The effort failed. Cornwallis had his first brush with an American general named Nathanael Greene later that year. The British were focused on taking Fort Lee, a stronghold about ten miles north of what is now New York City, and Cornwallis led the surprise attack. The garrison commander Greene, however, was warned of the strike by a deserter and managed to slip away with about 4,000 troops, evacuating the fort and an immense quantity of supplies.[3]

In the days after George Washington's famous crossing of the Delaware and Christmas morning assault on the British post at Trenton, Cornwallis's and Washington's forces confronted each other over ten days in late December and early January 1777, in the snowy New Jersey countryside between Trenton and Princeton. The earl turned 38 on January 1, but this went likely unnoticed as Cornwallis maneuvered to destroy Washington's force which quite possibly could have ended the Revolution, some historians contend. It was not to be. Washington tricked the British commander, using soldiers to tend campfires while sending his main body around Cornwallis's flank to successfully attack Princeton. General

Clinton strongly criticized Cornwallis's performance, stating that it was "the most consummate ignorance I ever heard of in any officer above a corporal."[4]

Cornwallis returned to England on leave in January 1778, but again embarked for the colonies in April, Jemima and the children accompanying him to Portsmouth to see him off. Traveling on the same vessel, Lord Carlisle wrote in a letter to a friend: "Poor Lord Cornwallis is going to experience perhaps something like what I have felt, for he has brought with him his wife and children, and we em-bark [sp] tomorrow, if the wind serves. My heart bleeds for them." Lady Cornwallis sullenly returned to the family's home at Culford "where she resumed the solitary life she had led since his first departure." Her grief was so great that it gradually eroded her health, Ross noted, bringing "on a kind of jaundice" that would eventually kill her. Learning of Jemima's serious condition, Cornwallis left the army and tried to reach her side as quickly as possible, arriving a few weeks before her death on February 14, 1779. "Lady Cornwallis always declared to her confidential attendant that she was dying of a broken heart" and requested that a "thorn-tree" be planted above her burial vault "as nearly as possible over her heart—significant of the sorrow which destroyed her life." She also directed that no stone "should be engraved to her memory." Both wishes were granted.[5]

Poised to occupy Camden on June 1, Cornwallis dispatched Major Stedman to enter the village ahead of the troops, post some sentinels and "take charge of such stores as might be found in the town." When Cornwallis himself rode toward the village, the "citizens met him outside the limits with a flag of truce and besought his protection; they were treated as prisoners on parole." In conversation with Dr. Thomas Charlton, a local physician, and Charles Ogilvie, an area landowner and merchant, among possibly others in the delegation, Cornwallis promised protection for the town's civilians in return for provisions. To that end, Joseph Kershaw ordered three officers who had served under him in the militia to round up cattle along Lynches Creek. He also asked Camden area residents to bring corn and other food or edible crops to his store so that any "plundering" by the British soldiers could possibly be avoided.[6]

With its central location near the Wateree River and its roads hub, Camden was to be the keystone outpost for the British army. It would also serve as a staging point or main inland base of operations for Cornwallis's expected strike into North Carolina. "Other small posts were [soon to be] established in the front and on the left of Camden...." Cornwallis wrote to Lord George Germain, Secretary of State for the Colonies, "and the main body of the corps was posted at Camden, which, for this country, is reckoned a tolerably healthy place, and where the troops could most conveniently subsist, and receive the necessary supplies of various kinds" from Charleston.[7]

Fanning out through the village and the immediate area, the Redcoats first seized a mill "belonging to ... colonel Kershaw" which contained some flour and wheat. In the store owned by Joseph and Ely Kershaw, Stedman and his soldiers discovered a trove of assorted "merchandize" including "21 rice tierces, 3 hogsheads and a half of indigo, some tea, sugar, coffee, and linen, which were sent to the general hospital" in Charleston. Also confiscated were salt, "20 barrels of flour, 18 ditto Indian corn meal," a hogshead of rum, and a quantity of "bacon, hams, butter, brimstone, axes and wedges, sent to the engineer department," Stedman noted. Some "rhubarb in root" used for medical purposes also was shipped to the general hospital, despite being damaged. "A number of hats, and some green cloth [were] distributed to the troops." Some 90 hogsheads of tobacco were uncovered in a barn near the Wateree; some of which were destroyed by the troops and the rest Cornwallis ordered sent to Charleston. About 100 head of cattle and some sheep were also seized in and around the town. The Redcoats also discovered quantities of "silver plate" and other supplies "sent from the low country" by those vainly hoping to keep them from just such a confiscation. Joseph Kershaw's deeds and reputation as a patriot rabble-rouser and soldier made him a conspicuous target of the British. "Lord Cornwallis ordered the commissaries to give no receipt to colonel Kershaw for the property taken from him, as he was deemed a very violent man, and who was said to have persecuted the loyalists," Stedman explained. "A return was made every night to…. Cornwallis of all species of property taken in the course of the day, of its distribution, and of the amount in hand."[8]

It is unclear when Tarleton's "first express" arrived with news of the Waxhaws victory, or even if there was a second messenger. Tarleton wrote: The main army had not moved more than 40 miles from "Nelson's [F]erry" when Cornwallis was informed "of the advantage obtained by the light troops." Whatever the time frame, the British were either approaching Camden or settling in there on June 1 when Cornwallis issued the following: "Orders. Lord Cornwallis desires that Lieut. Colonel Tarleton, Major Cochrane, and the officers and soldiers of the Legion and detachment serving with them, will accept ... his warmest acknowledgements for the splendid services they have rendered their country by the gallant action of the 29th of May." Tarleton's column reached Camden a "few days afterwards" with the "addition of the American cannon, royals, and wagons, which were delivered to the artillery and quarter-master-general's departments."[9]

Other than surveying possible defensive positions at Camden what most attracted the eyes of the British was Joseph Kershaw's beautiful, two-and-a-half-story residence crowning Magazine Hill, certainly the finest house, by far, in the vicinity. Facing west, the Georgian-style mansion—modeled after the William Washington house in Charleston—stood at the south end of what is now Lyttleton Street. Also known as the "Great White House," due to its painted exterior, Cornwallis chose it for his headquarters despite construction of the house still incomplete, railings still to be installed on the hall stairways and the ballroom unfinished. Cornwallis allowed Kershaw's wife and young children to stay in their home temporarily, although restricted to an upper floor room. An "old store" owned by the Kershaws was used as a barracks by the Redcoats, and possibly as a hospital later in the occupation. Initially, the kitchen building behind the Kershaw House was used as a hospital. The Kershaws had more serious and immediate troubles. Ely was still declining physically, possibly due to smallpox contracted in Charleston, ironically where he had gone to restore his health. Cornwallis had decided to banish both brothers from the colony immediately, but Joseph had pleaded for more time to allow Ely to recuperate. The general relented—at least temporarily.[10]

Meanwhile Camden's transformation into a military installation was ongoing. Tarleton noted that "huts, of proper materials to resist the hot weather, were constructed" for the troops at least in the early stages of the occupation. Nathaniel Cary, a local Loyalist, later claimed that 23 houses—and "gardens"—he owned in and around Camden were used to quarter British troops. Most of the Redcoats were billeted in and about the village. The six-year-old Presbyterian meetinghouse was dismantled, the wood and nails used to build huts or other crude barracks for the soldiers. Other structures were likely torn down as well. Lieutenant Henry Haldane of the Royal Engineers—who oversaw the housing project—was plagued throughout by supply shortages and delays. The British soon organized a Loyalist militia regiment led by James Cary, by then a militia major. Later promoted to colonel, it was on the grounds of his estate, "Cary's Place," that a redoubt called "Carey's Fort" was eventually erected to guard Wateree Ferry on the river about a mile west of Camden.[11]

The British's strengthening and expansion of the magazine near the Kershaw House was underway as well. The magazine's existing defenses were incorporated into a star-shaped redoubt to guard the brick armory. The "Star," as it became known, measured some 150 feet across from point to point. Related Tarleton:

> Rum, salt, and other stores, that were wanted by the regiments, by the artillery, by the quarter-master-general's, and by the commissariat departments, were ordered to be conveyed from Charleston to Camden. The magazine was formed at that place on account of water carriage by the river from Nelson's [F]erry, and because it [Camden] was the most eligible position to support the

communication between the army and Charleston, when the King's troops moved forward to North Carolina.

The British would make further—and more significant—efforts to bolster Camden's fortifications, but these were yet to come.[12]

As expected, Camden's road system quickly became a vital link for the British to send supplies and reinforcements from Charleston to Loyalist units further west along the Broad and Saluda rivers. Equally important, these routes were critically essential to British communications within the province and beyond. Essentially, the British lifeline began in Charleston, supplies sent by water to Monck's Corner and transported by wagon to a landing near Nelson's Ferry where they were boated to Camden via the Wateree. Amid all this activity, the Loyalist officer and Camden landowner Zacharias Gibbs had been released in April 1780 after serving some 15 months as a war prisoner at Ninety Six and returned to Camden. He remained there until Charleston fell to the British in May and then resumed his soldierly activity in July, promoted to major and later colonel of his Loyalist regiment. During this period, Gibbs, 39, also bought his second large parcel of land in the Camden area from his friends Drury Bishop and John Brown, a further indication that Gibbs had complete faith and confidence that South Carolina would remain a province of the King. During imprisonment at Ninety Six, the captain and 22 other Loyalists being held were sentenced to death. Eighteen of them were reprieved, but five others, including Gibbs's brother-in-law, were executed.[13]

Cornwallis was still busily engaged in transforming Camden into a military post when he wrote to Clinton on June 2, regarding plans to reestablish the Crown's control of North Carolina:

> I have sent emissaries to our friends in North Carolina, to state my situation to them, and to submit to them whether it would not be prudent for them to remain quiet, until I can give them effectual support, which could only be done by a force remaining in the country. At the same time, I assured them that, if they thought themselves a match for their enemies without any regular force, and were determined to rise at all events, I would give them every assistance in my power, by incursions of light troops, furnishing ammunition, &c. Although in this sanguine moment, I may appear slow and cautious to some who overflow with zeal, I must trust you will find my conduct in this business both active and vigorous.[14]

In other words, the British had decided to temporarily postpone their thrust into North Carolina. "The heat of the summer, the want of stores and provisions, and the unsettled state of Charleston and the country, impeded the immediate invasion of North Carolina," Tarleton stated. The Loyalists there were encouraged to "attend to the harvest" and "prepare provisions" for the army before Cornwallis struck north in late August or early September. Cornwallis had the "charge of prosecuting the war in North Carolina as soon as the season of the year, and other circumstances, would permit," related Charles Stedman. Beyond the sweltering fact of the Carolinas summer, the other "circumstances" included "the impossibility of subsisting an army in that province [North Carolina] until the harvest was over" and the necessity of "forming magazines, with a chain of communications properly secured before the expedition was begun...." Still, with matters so well in hand, Clinton issued a June 3 proclamation "requiring the inhabitants of the Province of South Carolina, including prisoners on parole, to return to their allegiance, or be treated as rebels to the government of the king." "Almost the whole of South Carolina was now restored to its legal government"; a British sergeant wrote, "but the calm was only temporary; the submission was only nominal...."[15]

Over time that summer, the British presence attracted an untold number of Loyalists from the immediate region and beyond to Camden. Some sought safety within the outpost to escape violence and/or other retribution from those on the American side. Others set up businesses, drawn by the "presence of such a substantial military establishment" and the fact that most of the village's stores were closed down due to the flight or arrests of their Patriot owners. Thomas Hopper, or Hooper, came to Camden from his home in Charleston to supply horses for the British army. He soon partnered with a local resident, Thomas Charlton, to operate a store within the outpost, "selling mostly goods of British origin." Charlton—whom we met earlier—appears to have been a man of divided loyalties to say the least. As will be seen, he was later accused of spying by both sides and also served as a physician, aiding the wounded no matter the uniform they wore. He had ridden to Waxhaws to treat the battle casualties there, but found that the British had confiscated some of his medical supplies after he returned to Camden. There will be more about this shadowy figure later on.[16]

Charleston merchant Michael Egan, along with fellow Loyalists Robert and Joseph English, ran a dry goods store in Camden. They built a storehouse and dealt in wagons, horses, cattle, sugar and rum. A "Major Downes," a former Camden merchant, returned to town after the Redcoats took over. He operated a blacksmithery and a turner's shop. These Loyalist-run businesses would survive only as long as the British controlled Camden and the surrounding countryside. While Camden was now a safe haven for Loyalists, residents who had been disloyal were now pariahs—like the Kershaw brothers—jailed, exiled or forced to flee, abandoning homes and property. Much of the confiscated land was redistributed to local Loyalists. John Phillips, meanwhile, had been a hard-shell Loyalist since war broke out and had been imprisoned—including four months in the Camden jail—for refusing to "take the oath to the state." He and his large family had come to South Carolina from Ireland in 1770. When Cornwallis occupied Camden, Phillips organized his like-minded neighbors on Jackson's Creek, near Winnsboro and offered their service to the British. The Jackson's Creek Regiment became one of the best and most active Loyalist militia units in the province.[17]

The "great common" in front of the Kershaw House became a parade ground, assembly area and bivouac for the British. Even today, it's not hard to imagine Cornwallis or [Lieutenant Colonel Francis Lord] Rawdon standing at rigid attention there while the ranks of Redcoats passed in review amid the shrill swirl of fifes and the rumble of drums. Officers may have used trees in the front yard as points from which to direct the movement of troop formations. "The very hawthorn trees by which Lord Rawdon and Colonel [Nisbet] Balfour ranged their scarlet lines of war are yet among us," an 1830 article in the *Camden Journal* stated. From the outset of the occupation and for weeks afterward, the British at Camden were "wholly supported by supplies from the neighboring districts," Stedman recalled. "The [Loyalist] militia were employed in collecting Indian corn to be ground into meal, which, issued when new, made a good substitute for wheat. They were also employed in collecting cattle and sheep" and were paid four shillings and eight-pence per head of cattle, and two shillings and 11-pence sterling per head for sheep (for driving only). "The owners had either a receipt, or a certificate, given them (unless avowedly hostile)."[18]

Amid intermittent rain, some sullen survivors of Buford's destroyed command reached the Moravian community of Salem, N.C.—present-day Winston-Salem—on June 7–8. Others, including wounded soldiers "moaning piteously" were at nearby Abbotts Creek before apparently continuing toward Virginia, the Moravians learned. On foot, three of the men with what must have been minor wounds wandered into the village, where a man identified only as "Br. Bonn" found they had neither food nor money. He "bandaged them and gave them half a loaf of bread, and they left again," a Bishop Graff noted in the Moravians' Salem diary. He added: The Collect under the Doctrinal Text today was: "Lord, teach us both faithful and useful to prove, / That friend and foe may believe in our love."

The Americans "gave us some details concerning the bloody action" at Waxhaws, Graff related. "Before they [Buford's troops] were aware of it they had been surrounded by the English, and laid down their arms, but as the English commander [apparently Tarleton] rode up one man seized a gun and shot at him, and then the massacre began. Between three and four hundred were killed or taken prisoner, and those who could ran away." (Graff wrote the battle was at Hanging Rock, but editor Fries in a footnote stated that location was erroneous, the bishop referring to the Waxhaws instead.)[19]

Across the Atlantic, news of Tarleton's overwhelming victory contributed greatly to the already healthy morale of the British populace, the positive developments adding to the momentum of an expected suppression of the colonial rebellion. It also greatly added to Tarleton's reputation. Certainly, he had fought well in the northern campaigns, but Waxhaws was his triumph alone, and he flourished as a result. Suddenly—by 18th-century standards—he was a war hero, young, dashing and full of soulful fire to scorch the traitorous rebels. "Colonel Tarleton knew, that having taken a command of the King's troops, the duty he owed to his country directed him to fight and conquer," noted the *London Chronicle*.[20]

With a welcome lull in action after Charleston and the Waxhaws, Major Charles Cochrane of Tarleton's command requested leave to return home to England, since he had been abroad for almost seven years. Certainly, he wanted to reunite with his family, but there were other personal matters to take care of as well. His father died during Cochrane's time away and his father-in-law, Major John Pitcairn of the British marines, was mortally wounded at Bunker Hill. Cornwallis was in Camden on June 10 and promptly granted Cochrane's request, adding: "Dear Sir,—I cannot let you go from hence without expressing the very sincere regret I feel at your leaving my corps, and assuring you that on any future occasion I shall be happy in serving with so able and spirited an officer. I heartily wish you a prosperous voyage, and a happy meeting with your family...."[21]

Shortly after Camden's occupation, Lt. Col. Rawdon and his Volunteers of Ireland, accompanied by some of Tarleton's horse, "made a short expedition" into the Waxhaws settlement to gauge the degree of Loyalists support, primarily among Scotch-Irish immigrants in the area. Rawdon and his troops met with a rude welcome. "The sentiments of the inhabitants did not correspond with his lordship's expectations," Tarleton related. "He there learned what experience confirmed, that the Irish were the most adverse of all other settlers to the British government in America." Still, many of the settlers "gave their paroles" vowing not to fight against the Crown, but it was "an obligation they readily violated, when called to arms" by the Americans. Rawdon wrote to Cornwallis: "I had the fullest proof that the people who daily visited my camp not only held constant correspondence with the rebel militia, but used every artifice to debauch the minds of my soldiers and persuade them to desert from their colors." With the sights, sounds and stench of Buford's defeat by Tarleton still raw, it was no wonder that the British received such a harsh reception. The recently filled mass grave for many of Buford's soldiers on the battleground also didn't help the Crown's cause.[22]

After pocketing a signature victory with Charleston's fall, the surrender of Lincoln's army, the capture of a vast array of military hardware, supplies and even ships, Clinton was justly proud of his achievements as he prepared to return to New York in early June. He already had the "agreeable intelligence of the Americans at Wacsaw [sp]," Tarleton related, "a circumstance that evinced the total extirpation of the [C]ontinental troops" in Georgia and South Carolina. The submission of the American post at Ninety Six and the dispersal of some patriot militia in the province's northwest region "put a temporary period to all resistance in South Carolina." In addition to Charleston's occupation, Redcoats marched through Savannah's streets, still a strongly-held British provincial capital and seaport after the ferocious siege and climatic attack by American and French forces was thwarted the previous October.[23]

In Charleston, Clinton was a military peacock, glorying in the seeming subjugation of his fiefdom. "I am clear in opinion that the Carolinas have been conquered in Charleston," he wrote to a friend about this time. The British also set about a vigorous recruitment of Loyalists for several provincial corps, composed of men who would undergo substantial military training, and establishing a militia which could be called up as needed. This served a dual purpose in that it was meant to further discourage the already downtrodden Americans and encourage the general populace to renew its allegiance to the Crown. What both sides soon learned, however, was that there was a solid core of supporters for each cause and that there were also many Carolinians who were swayed by results on the battlefields. On June 5, Clinton boarded the *Romulus* at Charleston harbor for the voyage to New York, along with several thousand British troops on other vessels. Cornwallis was left in command of the Crown's army in South Carolina, statistics varying on how many soldiers he had. Stedman states about 4,000 troops remained after Clinton's departure. Tarleton stated there were about 5,400 troops in South Carolina and a total of some 1,100 British, Hessians and Loyalists in Georgia, primarily posted in Savannah and Augusta.[24]

Despite his compliance in gathering cattle and foodstuffs for the Redcoats, Joseph Kershaw's life was about to take a harsh turn due to his earlier record as a "violent" rebel. When Charleston fell, General Clinton had offered parole to the captured American militia, allowing them to go home if they swore loyalty to the Crown. The situation changed, however, when Clinton returned to New York, leaving Cornwallis in command. Cornwallis believed in sterner measures against militiamen—like Kershaw—who had fought against the King, and others who had held office in the rebellious provinces. These men deserved to be punished by losing their protections and being paroled—essentially exiled—to South Carolina's coastal islands. Joseph and Ely Kershaw were paroled on June 10 and prepared to depart Camden, Ely's grace period for recovery having run out. Joseph's arrangements included taking care of his family left behind and trying to ensure that Ely, whose health remained fragile, had the best possible chances to survive exile.

His greatest concern for Sarah and the children was the very real threat of smallpox. The pestilence had already savaged the colony like a rogue poltergeist twice in the 18th century and was on the brink of doing so again that summer, tearing through Charleston and the Redcoat entrenchments during the siege. Joseph received permission to have his family moved out into the country where they would be less likely to become sick. Joseph also asked that he and Ely be confined at Port Royal, Bermuda, which Cornwallis allowed. It is unclear why this request was made, but possibly could be that Joseph believed the climate there would be healthier for Ely.[25]

With the North Carolina offensive delayed, Cornwallis set about establishing a belt of outposts across the province, with Camden being the keystone. The troops would be concentrated in these "cantonments as to cover the frontiers both of South Carolina and Georgia, and secure their internal quiet." The Camden force consisted of the 23rd and 33rd regiments of foot (infantry), the Volunteers of Ireland, Tarleton's Legion infantry, Daniel Browne's Loyalist force and Lieutenant Colonel John Hamilton's First Royal North Carolina Regiment of provincials, and an artillery unit, all under Rawdon's command. Also, Camden would be the site for the "principal magazine for the intended (North Carolina) expedition." Camden was linked with the district and village of Ninety Six—the most populous in the province—by a post at Rocky Mount on the Wateree River garrisoned by Lieutenant Colonel George Turnbull's New York Volunteers and some Loyalist militia. At Ninety Six, three provincial battalions and a force of light infantry held a fort commanded initially by Lieutenant Colonel Nisbet Balfour and later by Lieutenant Colonel John H. Cruger.

Major Archibald McArthur of the 71st Highlanders and two of his battalions were posted at Cheraw on the Pee Dee, assigned to cover the region between Camden and Georgetown, the latter on the coast north of Charleston. McArthur also was to "correspond with the highland settlement" at Cross Creek in North Carolina. A Loyalist detachment of Queen's Rangers led by Captain John Saunders held Georgetown, while Lieutenant Colonel Thomas Brown and his South Carolina Loyalists, augmented by units from other regiments, were stationed at Augusta, "the frontier town of Georgia." Brown had earlier been tarred, feathered and otherwise tortured by Whigs, but exacted some revenge during the Savannah siege. There, he and his men held the Spring Hill redoubt, a key point in the city's defenses, and had helped repel the massive assault, resulting in a British victory. The remaining Crown troops were at Charleston,

Savannah and Beaufort, the latter on the South Carolina coast between the other two posts. Additionally, a mobile force headed by Major Patrick Ferguson patrolled the region between the Saluda and Wateree rivers, and "sometimes approached the borders of North Carolina."[26]

Tarleton's troopers, meanwhile, were to endure excruciating and exhausting duty amid this arrangement and establishment of outposts. The 17th Light Dragoons, which had been assigned to the Legion and fought so well against Buford at the Waxhaws, were gone, transferred to New York. Thus it fell to Tarleton's dragoons to "keep the communications open between the principal posts of this extended cantonment." Tarleton continued: "This service injured them infinitely more than all the preceding moves and actions of the campaign, and though hitherto successful against their enemies in the field, they were nearly destroyed in detail by the patroles [sp] and detachments required of them during the intense heat of the season."[27]

With "everything wearing the face of tranquility and submission," Cornwallis rode out of Camden on June 21, returning to Charleston and his many duties there. At Camden he left Lord Rawdon in command of the Crown's troops on the South Carolina frontier. Rawdon, after Brigadier General James Paterson, the commandant at Charleston, was the next officer of rank in the province. "Upon earl Cornwallis ... devolved also the care of adjusting the internal affairs, and establishing such regulations, whether civil or commercial, as might be necessary for its (South Carolina's) future prosperity," Stedman noted, adding that it was an "arduous task." There was at least one troubling aspect to deal with, however. In the weeks after their early-June foray into the Waxhaws settlement, desertions wracked Rawdon's Volunteers of Ireland. The problem was so serious by July 1, that Rawdon issued orders for anyone harboring these deserters to be punished with "invariable severity." He also made this offer in the grim vein of apparently unintended gallows humor: "I will give the inhabitants ten guineas for the head of any deserter belonging to the Volunteers of Ireland and five guineas only if they bring him in alive. They shall likewise be rewarded, though not to that amount, for such deserters ... belonging to any other Regiment." All that being said, British recruitment efforts in the province were initially successful, mustering some 2,500 soldiers in a varying number of regiments within two months after the fall of Charleston. The King's forces had the momentum during this time; whether it could be sustained would be another story.[28]

Rawdon

"In person he was tall and dark," a British soldier from another generation wrote of 25-year-old Lt. Col. Francis, Lord Rawdon. "He was said to be 'the ugliest man in England,' but his bearing was stately and dignified. His manner was genial, and it was said of him that 'No man possessed in a higher degree the happy but rare faculty of attracting to him all who came within the sphere of his command.'"[29]

Rawdon was born in December 1754 and was the eldest son of John, Lord Rawdon by his third wife, Lady Elizabeth Hastings. Young Francis was known by the courtesy title of Lord Rawdon beginning in 1761. He received his early education at Harrow. In August 1771 he was "gazetted" as an ensign in an infantry regiment (the 15th Regiment of Foot), but apparently never joined it, enrolling in October at University College Oxford, where he "did not take a degree," a British account noted. Within two years he was serving in the Fifth Regiment of Foot and at age 19 was promoted to lieutenant in October 1773. With tensions worsening in the provinces, the Fifth was among British units sent to America, landing at Boston in July 1774. The Fifth's grenadier company was engaged in the historic clash at Lexington on April 19, 1775, and Rawdon was soon assigned to the grenadiers, replacing an officer wounded there. It was at the battle of Bunker Hill outside Boston on June 17, however, that Rawdon emerged as a tough, unflappable soldier and promising centurion for the Crown's arms. "It was here that he first made his mark," said one report. When the grenadiers' captain fell wounded, Rawdon took over, leading the company through the rest of the fighting. He barely escaped death or serious injury when two bullets pierced his hat. "Lord Rawdon has this day stamped his fame for life," wrote British General John Burgoyne.[30]

Within weeks Rawdon was promoted to captain and assigned to the 63rd Foot, as the British abbreviated their infantry regiments. Eventually he was posted as aide-de-camp to General Clinton and was at the 1776 New York battles of Brooklyn and White Plains, as well as the capture of Fort Washington, New York, and Fort Lee, New Jersey, later that year. Rawdon also accompanied Cornwallis on his march through New Jersey to the Delaware River in December 1776. He accompanied Clinton home to Britain soon afterward and in early spring 1777 met a Frenchman named Lafayette—who would figure so mightily in America's war fortunes—at a ball in London.

Returning to America with Clinton, Rawdon saw service in Pennsylvania, and raised the Volunteers of Ireland, a Loyalist regiment composed almost "entirely of Irish deserters from the American Army" in Philadelphia and New York in 1778–1779. Rawdon was promoted to major in 1778, Clinton replacing William Howe as commander of British forces in America. In short order, likely due to his friendship with Clinton, Rawdon rose to lieutenant colonel and adjutant-general of the army in the provinces, three days before the Redcoats abandoned Philadelphia in June 1778. The

Volunteers of Ireland, meanwhile, were bloodied at the battle of Monmouth, New Jersey, on June 28, during the evacuation operations. The British concentrated the bulk of their forces in New York after Philadelphia was lost.[31]

When Clinton decided to shift British military efforts to the Southern provinces in December 1779, sending a fleet and some 7,600 troops to take Charleston, Rawdon remained in New York, attending to his duties there. With Charleston besieged in spring 1780, however, he was soon back in a combat zone. Clinton had sent for reinforcements from New York, and Rawdon arrived on April 18, with about 2,500 men. He wasted little time before getting into action, leading an assault that overwhelmed an American strongpoint at Haddrell's Point, just north of the Cooper River and opposite Charleston.[32]

Soon after the Carolina capital was surrendered in mid–May, Rawdon found himself riding deeper into this unfamiliar province with the force led by Cornwallis. Somewhere in the many miles ahead, through the plush vegetation and tormenting heat, was the frontier village of Camden, where the destiny of his life would be changed forever.

6

"Our Army is like a dead whale upon the Sea Shore"

About a month earlier, on April 16, 1780, about 1,400 Maryland and Delaware Continental troops left their encampment at Morristown, N.J., on the first leg of their trek south, hopefully to relieve Charleston. Led by Major General the Baron Johan DeKalb, the army marched through a portion of New Jersey and Pennsylvania before boarding ships to land at Petersburg, Virginia. From there they were to proceed south across country into South Carolina. With the approval of Congress, General George Washington, the American commander in chief, had authorized this movement. He fully realized it would likely be too late to save Lincoln and Charleston, but DeKalb's troops could possibly "assist to arrest the progress of the enemy and save the Carolinas."

Time would have been of the essence under any circumstances, but the expedition was beset with delays, including getting the Maryland soldiers paid, routing and logistics issues and DeKalb being held up in Philadelphia for about three weeks in making preparations. The general reached his army at Petersburg on or about May 22, his newly assigned regiment of Virginia artillery—12 guns—already on the march south with an infantry escort. A shortage of wagons and supplies, however, forced more time lost into the first week of June, some of the troops moving out on the 1st and more on the 6th. On that latter day, DeKalb received the "unwelcome news" that Charleston had fallen on May 12, Lincoln surrendering his army en masse.[1]

Some six-feet-tall and with an athletic frame, the 58-year-old DeKalb "seemed formed for the hardships of war, and for encountering the toils of our then rude and toilsome campaigns," stated a 19th-century account. DeKalb also had "a talent and a knowledge of greater use to the soldier: the talent of reading men and the knowledge of human nature." He was a Spartan warrior of old, drinking only water and subsisting on the sparest of diets, "often living on beef-soup and bread, at other times contented with a short allowance of cold meat."[2]

6. "Our Army is like a dead whale upon the Sea Shore"

John Kalb was born into a peasant family on June 29, 1721, at the village of Huettendorf, a village in the principality of Brandenburg-Bayreuth, a German territory. His parents, John Leonard Kalb and Margaret Putz Kalb, had three sons, of whom young John—or Johan—was the middle child. There is scant information about his boyhood, other than that his early schooling was at Kriegenbroun and that in his youth he worked as a waiter, before going abroad when he was barely 16. His biographer, Kapp, wrote: "At this point his trace is lost for years" but there is "but little doubt that he soon found his way to France" where John appears to have joined the army in late 1743, identifying himself as Hans Kalb and later as Jean DeKalb, a lieutenant in a French infantry regiment. With no blue blood in his veins, Kalb apparently on his own assumed the false title of baron and the prefix "de" in the hope that such importance would advance his army career. "The title of nobility was simply the password which unlocked the world to him," Kapp related, "the indispensable starting point for all further operations. One more scruple on his part, and the world would probably have gained a sturdy yeoman, but lost a hero!"[3]

In late 1767, the French initiated a plan to determine the depth of unrest among the English colonists in North America with their mother country, Great Britain, France's seemingly perpetual enemy at the time. DeKalb was chosen for the "secret mission" and also was to try to examine the colonists' "resources in troops, fortified places, and forts, and will seek to discover their plan of revolt, and the leaders who are expected to direct and control it," as well as other military information. "Great reliance is placed in the intelligence and address of M. DeKalb in the pursuit of a mission requiring an uncommon degree of tact and shrewdness, and he is expected to report progress as often as possible." DeKalb arrived in Philadelphia in January 1768, also spending time in Boston, New York, and Halifax. In all, he gathered intelligence over about six months, also surviving a shipwreck off New York before returning to France. In 1777, DeKalb embarked from France for America with the Marquis de Lafayette, intent on joining the rebellion. Lafayette and DeKalb landed at North Island, on the South Carolina coast near Georgetown, both soon earning renown and generalships in Washington's army.[4]

With his objectives now clouded and uncertain due to Charleston's fall, DeKalb requested further orders and readied the rest of his army to proceed from Petersburg and regroup with the advanced elements—already halted, per his instructions—in North Carolina. He also was awaiting the promised arrival of Virginia and North Carolina militia forces to strengthen his numbers. DeKalb also took into account that any British troops he encountered in South Carolina would likely outnumber him greatly. Still, the decision was made for DeKalb's army to continue into South Carolina, the presence of a sizeable body of Continentals there hopefully bolstering pro-patriot spirits after the Charleston disaster and slowing the British momentum, as Washington wanted. Again, however, the lack of supplies, haunted the increasingly desperate Americans, the march slowed to a snail's crawl that barely reached the village of Goshen, some 15 miles inside the North Carolina border, by June 20. "Here I am at last, considerably south, suffering from intolerable heat, the worst of quarters, and the most voracious of insects of every hue and form," DeKalb wrote his wife the next day, the epitome of a European soldier campaigning in the maw of a southern summer.

> The most disagreeable of the latter is ... called the tick, a kind of strong black flea, which makes its way under the skin, and by its bite produces the most painful irritation and inflammation.... My whole body is covered with these stings. I do not yet know whether the strength and the movements of the enemy, and the difficulty of feeding my little army, will permit me to advance two hundred miles further to the borders [of the two Carolinas]. Of the violence of thunderstorms in this part of the world Europeans cannot form any idea.[5]

Learning of Lincoln's Charleston catastrophe, Congress in June appointed Major General Horatio Gates—the hero of Saratoga—to head the Southern Department. It was a title and not much else since Lincoln and his army had been swallowed up and Buford was destroyed at Waxhaws, the Britons also in firm control of Savannah and the rest of the Georgia coast. Amazingly, the politicians had chosen Gates without consulting George Washington. The commander-in-chief would have preferred Major General Nathanael Greene for the post, Greene being his most dependable and trusted lieutenant from his performance in the northern campaigns. Gates, meanwhile, prepared to ride south and take command of the hodge-podge army DeKalb was leading.[6]

DeKalb's listless column reached Hillsborough on June 22, but there, the Baron "was compelled to lie idle a number of days [until June 30], to give his exhausted soldiers an opportunity to rest and refresh themselves as far as possible." By this point rations were almost non-existent, foraging parties returning with little if anything to feed the men. "We marched ... without an ounce of provision being laid in at any one point, often fasting for several days together," noted an unidentified "correspondent"—possibly a soldier—with the army. The gaunt ranks were "subsisting frequently upon green apples and peaches; sometimes by detaching parties [foragers] we thought ourselves feasted, when by violence they seized a little fresh beef, and cut, threshed out, and ground a little wheat; yet under all these difficulties, we had to press forward." The troops trudged on, reaching Buffalo Ford on the Deep River on July 19, some 87 miles from Hillsborough.

"At this time, we were very much distressed for want of provisions," noted Sergeant-Major William Seymour of the Delaware Continentals, "insomuch that we were obliged to send out parties through the country to thrash out grain for our sustenance; and this availed not much, for what was procured after this manner could scarce keep the troops from starving, which occasioned a vast number of men to desert...."[7]

At Deep River, DeKalb first learned of Gates's appointment and apparently had no outward reaction since he was a professional soldier cut from the stoic cloth of European military tradition. It was also about this time that the army was joined by Armand's Legion, a small force of about 60 cavalry and an equal number of infantry. Known as the First Partisan Corps, in its early organization, the Legion was led by Colonel Charles Armand, and composed mainly of foreign volunteers. Armand, 30, was yet another French officer in the Continental Army. His Legion had seen combat under Washington before being sent south and in February 1780 had absorbed the remnants of the Pulaski Legion, whose Count Pulaski was mortally wounded in the Savannah siege the previous year. For many of the disgruntled around the campfires, however, these new arrivals and their horses were just more mouths to feed.[8]

En route to reach his army, Gates already was well aware of the serious supply issues he was inheriting. At Hillsborough on July 19, he wrote to North Carolina Governor Abner Nash regarding the "deplorable" conditions of his army's commissary and quartermaster departments as well as a lack of powder magazines. Gates asked Nash to correct these problems and also to provide the troops with provisions, forage and other supplies.

> Without these Things done, our Army is like a dead whale upon the Sea Shore—a monstrous Carcass without Life or Motion... [he penned]. With proper Exertions, I have no doubt that the Enemy might be confined to Charles Town [Charleston] and finally expelled from it; but on the contrary should Inactivity or Neglect continue, their Baleful Influence must be fatal to the Army, and ruinous to the Southern States....

On the 21st, DeKalb received a message from Thomas Sumter, the partisan chief apprising the former of conditions in South Carolina and offering his opinion on possible strategies. "Having been well informed that you are marching to the relief of this country, I think it my duty to give you the earliest intelligence of the situation and force of the enemy, with such other things as appear the most interesting from the best accounts," the Gamecock noted in this July 17 letter. Sumter informed DeKalb of the locations of the British posts and troop strengths at each, estimating a total of 3,482 men. He also wrote that it would take Cornwallis about two weeks to marshal them, plus 10,000 Loyalist militia, at Camden and that such a concentration could be prevented by seizing Nelson's and another ferry on the Santee. Knowing that Gates was coming to take over from him, DeKalb simply wrote, "I will lay the letter before General Gates at his arrival," but did not reply to Sumter.[9]

To artillery salutes amid a martial ceremony, Gates arrived on July 25 to assume command from DeKalb. "The success of (Gates) in the northern campaigns of 1776 and 1777, induced many to believe that his presence as commander of the southern army, would re-animate the friends of independence," said one 19th-century account.

Ironically, the man selected to spearhead the effort to halt Cornwallis's tear through South Carolina and beyond was the British-born, 52-year-old Gates, who had spent years of service in the King's army. He has been described variously as a "man of total self-assurance," who had a "youthful appearance" and whose "manner was reserved and his appearance intellectual." Beginning in 1745, Gates was posted in Europe, the West Indies, Ireland and North America, the latter where he served in General Edward Braddock's ill-fated force in 1755 during the French and Indian War and was wounded. As major in the Forty-fifth Regiment of Foot, he returned to England after that conflict, but sold his army commission and returned to North America in 1769. Aided by George Washington—the two having fought together in the French and Indian hostilities—Gates purchased land for a plantation, "Traveller's Rest," in Berkeley County, Virginia, and settled there with his wife, Elizabeth Phillips Gates, and teenaged son Robert about 1772. He also became a slave owner, acquiring an untold number to work his lands.[10]

Gates's military reputation as a disciplinarian resulted in Congress appointing him adjutant-general of the Continental army—with the rank of brigadier general—when that service was organized in June 1775. Washington was chosen as commander-in-chief the same day. Gates having "become warmly attached to his adopted country, he felt bound to offer his services in the time of danger." Under Washington, Gates performed efficiently enough to warrant promotion to major general in the army's Northern Department in May 1776 serving as commandant of Fort Ticonderoga. He saw action in New Jersey that fall and held several inconsequential positions in the first part of 1777. This changed in August 1777 when Congress chose him to command the Northern Department, replacing Major General Philip Schuyler, who was perceived as being weak in blunting a British strike from Canada. Gates's greatest hour came at Saratoga—actually two battles fought on September 19 and October 7, 1777. His defensive strategy, coupled with the hard-hitting combat tactics of Major General Benedict Arnold, resulted in Lt. Gen. John Burgoyne's defeat—the first surrender of a British army in world history.[11]

Congress appointed Gates president of its Board of War in late

November, making him responsible for retooling the inner workings and management of the army. At the same time, Washington was facing criticism for his lackluster performance in 1777, including the British capture of Philadelphia in September. There was talk of Gates supplanting Washington as commander-in-chief, some historians contending that Gates tried to undermine Washington's credibility for his own gain. In short, the effort to replace Washington never amounted to much in the war's grand scheme. Over the next two and a half years, Gates's "military services were of little account," stated one report, and included commands of the Highlands Department and Eastern Department.

Possibly one of the most prophetic lines of all time is attributed to Gates's close friend, General Charles Lee, another Briton and army veteran who had migrated to Virginia, also later taking up the patriot cause. As Gates prepared to head south and assume command from DeKalb, Lee told him "Take care that you do not exchange Northern laurels for Southern willows." In other words, Lee was warning Gates not to let his Saratoga glory be sullied by defeat in the Carolinas. Despite his record as a seasoned professional soldier, DeKalb was not even considered for army command since he was a foreigner and possessed little, if any, influence with Congress. In contrast, Gates had allies among the politicos in addition to his Saratoga accolades.[12]

The exchange of power at Deep River was cordial. DeKalb agreed to lead the Maryland division, consisting of the Maryland and Delaware Continentals, and thus he became second-in-command under Gates, not much of a demotion since the rest of the army was then composed of Armand's Legion and a small artillery detachment from Virginia. The biggest surprise was that Gates ordered the troops to "hold themselves in readiness to march at a moment's warning" which was greeted as "a matter of great astonishment to those who knew the real situation of the troops." Major Thomas Pinckney, a new aide to Gates, however, had a much different take on the situation. He recalled that when Gates joined DeKalb, "the American Army had been in that neighborhood three weeks & exhausted all the provisions within their reach. I therefore admired Genl Gates ['s] prompt decision, when on being informed of the condition of the Army in this respect, then we may as well march on & starve, as starve lying here."[13]

Before Gates's arrival, DeKalb had been advised during a war council to divert his route off the main road to Camden toward "the well cultivated settlements in the vicinity of the Waxhaws," which would provide more farm crops and other rations for the men and animals of the army. Gates, however, did not heed this advice, deciding to take the shorter road toward Camden. This would be one of the significant decisions of the campaign. The shorter route led through barren countryside, basically devoid of farmlands and populated by remote homesteads. The troops had suffered from scarce rations throughout their journey, but as they marched into the hardships of that July-August their hunger was even more aggravated, as were their spirits for the cause. There were grumblings of mutiny and profane complaints in the ranks, but "the officers who shared every calamity in common with the privates" tried to soothe the stomach gnawing frustration with "a patient sufferance of their (own) hard lot."[14]

Still, encouraging words went only so far. Clouds of whining gnats swirled and stung, as did other winged tormentors. The merciless sun baked all, even a small passing cloud offering a few seconds of relief to the toiling soldiers in their heavy uniforms and laden with equipment. Col. Otho H. Williams, Gates's deputy adjutant general, noted that

> the supplies of grain were scarcely sufficient, even for the present subsistence of the troops and the only meat ration that could be procured, was lean beef, daily driven out of the woods and the cane-breaks [sp], where the cattle had wintered themselves. Inaction, bad fare, and the difficulty of preserving discipline, when there is no apprehension of danger, have often proved fatal to troops and ruined whole armies. But here, the activity of the officers, and the persevering patience of the privates, preserved order, harmony, and even a passion for the service.[15]

As the army neared the Pee Dee River about August 1, two Continental cavalry officers rode into camp. Colonels William Washington and Anthony White had been active in the clashes around Charleston, but their horsemen were roundly defeated by Tarleton at Monck's Corner and Lenud's Ferry and had taken refuge in North Carolina. Washington, 28, was a distant relative of George Washington. Expecting to join forces with Gates, the officers were surprised when the General rejected their services, feeling that cavalry would be ineffective on the southern terrain. Gates had not had to rely on cavalry at Saratoga. Indeed, the hilly land there was not conducive to mounted operations. But the topography of central South Carolina was very different—much of it flatlands with open pine woods ideal for mounted troops who could use the swamps for concealment or defensive barriers.

At the Waxhaws slaughter, Tarleton himself had already demonstrated how horse soldiers could be used with speed, skill and deadly efficiency, an early form of blitzkrieg from a future age. Gates had only the 60 or so troopers of Armand's Legion and reportedly also refused offers from Washington and White to recruit a mounted force from his ranks. A lack of cavalry, employed as scouts or a "shock arm" as historian Henry Lumpkin put it, would factor into Gates's legacy in the coming weeks. A dearth of horses, however, may have been the most critical reason for Gates's decision about a mounted force; DeKalb had been forced to leave ten of the army's 18 field guns in North Carolina because there weren't enough animals to pull them.[16]

On or about August 4, Gates was joined by about 100 Virginian State troops led by Lieutenant Colonel Charles Porterfield, just south of the Pee Dee. Porterfield had retreated after Charleston fell and "had found means of subsisting his men in the Carolinas" until joining Gates's army. Porterfield was "a most excellent officer, on whose abilities General Gates particularly depended," said one account. Porterfield was combat-tough, and as a captain of Virginia Continentals had made his mark at the battle of Brandywine.[17]

Meanwhile, the army's severe shortage of rations worsened with every passing hour. Col. Williams related:

> The distresses of the soldiery daily increased, they were told that the banks of the Pee Dee ... were extremely fertile—and so indeed they were; but, the preceding crop of corn (the principal article of produce) was exhausted, and the new grain ... was unfit for use. Many of the soldiery, urged by necessity, plucked the green ears and boiled them with the lean beef, which was collected in the woods, made for themselves a repast, not unpalatable to be sure, but which was attended with painful effects.

The men also picked unripe peaches, substituted for bread, with "similar consequences," Williams continued:

> Some of the officers, aware of the risk of eating such vegetables, and in such a state, with poor fresh beef, and without salt, restrained themselves from taking anything but the beef itself, boiled or roasted. It occurred to some that the hair powder, which remained in their bags, would thicken soup, and it was actually applied.

The Delaware soldier, William Seymour, added:

> We were so much distressed for want of provisions, that we were fourteen days and drew but one-half pound of flour. Sometimes we drew half a pound of beef per man, and that so miserably poor that scarcely any mortal could make use of it—living chiefly on green apples and peaches, which rendered our situation truly miserable, being in a weak and sickly condition, and surrounded on all sides by our enemies....[18]

At this point, Cornwallis was aware of enemy movements in the general region—as early as June 21 or so—but there were no imminent or immediate threats to his realm. His intelligence told him that DeKalb was at or near Hillsborough, N.C., with about 2,000 Maryland and Delaware Continentals; some 300 Virginia infantry members, led by "General Porterfield," were somewhere along the Carolinas border; there were militia mustered at Salisbury and Charlotte, and a larger body—about 1,000—at Cross Creek under General Caswell, a former provincial governor of North

Carolina. "As all these corps were at a great distance from us, and as I knew it to be impossible to march any considerable body of men across.... North Carolina before the harvest, I did not expect that our posts on the frontier would be much disturbed for two months...." Cornwallis wrote to Lord George Germain.[19]

During this period—late June or early July—a force of about 800 North Carolina Loyalists, led by Colonel Samuel Bryan, made its way into South Carolina and found safe haven in the British post at Cheraw, moving eventually to Camden. Bryan's men claimed that they had intended to wait for Cornwallis's movement into their province, but that the Loyalists' persecution, harassment and suffering at the hands of the Americans there had caused them to come south. "Never was a finer body of men collected," recalled the British officer Charles Stedman, "strong, healthy, and accustomed to the severity of the climate...." Bryan's troops marched into Camden where "they presented to our view the horrors of a civil war." Stedman continued:

> Many of them had not seen their families for months, having lived in the woods to avoid the persecution of the Americans. Numbers of them were in rags, most of them men of property. There were men in Bryan's corps who possessed some hundred acres of land, farms highly cultivated.... These, with families and friends, they abandoned to manifest their attachments to the British government.

By July's end, the North Carolinians had been assimilated into Rawdon's force. If Bryan's men were "strong" and "healthy" as Stedman noted, the Camden post, in general, was not. Rawdon related on August 1 that he had sent some of his soldiers outside the village to try to avoid illness, and that he himself had suffered a "severe attack of the ague," or acute fever with chills.[20]

Thomas Sumter's raiders, meanwhile, assailed the British camp at Rocky Mount, near modern-day Great Falls, S.C., on July 30. Lt. Col. George Turnbull commanded about 150 Redcoats there, opposing the Gamecock's 600 men. This was a planned and simultaneous attack with Maj. William R. Davie and a small force of partisans launching a diversionary assault against another enemy post at Hanging Rock, about 15 miles to the east. After an eight-hour struggle, Sumter was repulsed. Davie also was repelled, but had a bit more success. With only about 100 mounted infantry and cavalry, he was too weak to attempt a large-scale strike against Major John Carden and his 500 Loyalists there. But the camp of three companies of Bryan's only recently arrived Loyalists, located at a farmhouse away from the main bivouac, was an inviting target. Davie split his troops and surprised Bryan's men, who were caught in a blistering crossfire—the fact that both sides wore civilian garb instead of uniforms contributing to Davie's success. Before Carden could counterattack from the main camp, the Americans fled with some prisoners, supplies and without a casualty. Bryan's Carolinians were utterly routed.[21]

Gates's army was reinforced significantly on August 6 with the arrival of some 2,000 North Carolina militiamen led by Brigadier General Richard Caswell. These men were expected sooner, but Caswell had balked when ordered to join DeKalb, before Gates took command. Caswell's hesitancy was likely due to his last foray south when he and a lesser force of his militia narrowly escaped the sanguine fate of Buford at Waxhaws, taking a different route from Camden when their troops separated there on May 27.[22]

Sumter, meanwhile, rested his men for several days after Rocky Mount and then joined Davie to coordinate an August 6 strike against Carden at Hanging Rock, about 25 miles north of Camden. Combined, their troops totaled between 700 and 800, outnumbering the Redcoats. The attack came near dawn, but confusion roiled the Americans, most of whom assaulted the left of the British line. This pressure overwhelmed the Loyalists there, who broke and fell back as the Patriots roared after them, an officer exhorting them: "Give it to them my boys! Give it to them hotter and hotter!" The Americans overran one of the Loyalist camps, but the assault sputtered there, the soldiers stopping to plunder and uncovering a supply of liquor which many of them could not resist. Sumter rode among them, vainly chiding them to return to the action. Seeing this chaos, some Loyalist cavalry charged, but were repulsed by Davie's horsemen as the bloodshed ended. Carden's loss was about 200 killed and wounded while American casualties were 12 dead and 41 wounded.[23]

In Davie's ranks were young Andrew Jackson and his brother Robert from the Waxhaws settlement. The boys may have served as messengers, based on some accounts, but this likely would have been their only participation in the battle. Both Jacksons admired Davie not only for his bravery and combat savvy, but also because their brother Hugh was in Davie's command at Stono Ferry, where Hugh died. Davie "was a man after Andrew's own heart," related Jackson biographer James Parton, "swift, but wary; bold in planning enterprises, but most cautious in execution; sleeplessly vigilant; untiringly active; one of those cool, quick men who apply mother-wit to the art of war; who are good soldiers because they are earnest and clear-sighted *men*." After helping aid American wounded after Tarleton's lopsided victory at the Waxhaws in May, the Jacksons were becoming ever-more hardened to the war, but their toughest personal trials were yet to come.[24]

Learning of Sumter's attack, Rawdon at Camden ordered the British 23rd Regiment, led by Maj. Thomas Mecan, to Hanging Rock, where the latter was to "put the post in security." Mecan's arrival also allowed

Bryan to "collect his people, who were scattered over the face of the countryside," Tarleton noted, adding that the North Carolinians were "greatly dispersed, but did not suffer considerably by the fire of the enemy." The wounded were taken to Camden, where a number of other British officers and men had also been sent for medical care due to "the climate."[25]

Also in Camden, more than 160 local men, "many of them gentlemen of the highest character and standing," were languishing in the "small common jail" after defying the Crown. In early August after learning of Gates's approach, the British called on "all the male inhabitants in and around the town, to take up arms" with the Redcoats in opposing the possible American threat. Those who refused were arrested, some manacled to the floor. Among the notables incarcerated was a Mr. Strother, described as a "decided and independent patriot" who died in custody; Colonel Few, "Mr. Kershaw"—in all probability Joseph Kershaw, John Boykin, Colonel Alexander, Mr. Irvin, Colonel [Richard] Winn, Colonel Hunter, John Chesnut and James Bradley, with others whose names are lost to history. The British had earlier seized a supply of indigo, valued at $5,000, from Chesnut, who had been among the Camden soldiers captured and paroled when Charleston fell. He was arrested after one of his slaves claimed Chesnut was corresponding with the rebels, thus violating his parole.[26]

Joseph and Ely Kershaw would not be allowed to remain in Camden very much longer. About the first week of August, Cornwallis had them sent to Charleston, destined to be banished from the province. The brothers, Ely still ailing, were put aboard the schooner *Savannah*, which sailed from Charleston on August 8 bound for Nassau on New Providence Island in the Bahamas. This was the first leg of their journey, their ultimate destination being Port Royal, Bermuda, where they were to be confined. Their brother William Kershaw had also returned to Charleston during this period, but already strongly leaning toward support for the Crown, continued his life as a merchant there. Meanwhile, hundreds of miles north of Camden, there was a major development in the overall war effort about this time. On July 10, 1780, Lt. Gen. the Comte de Rochambeau and about 5,500 French troops arrived by naval transports at Newport, Rhode Island. King Louis XVI of France had dispatched this force to aid the Americans with a promise of some 6,000 more men to follow. French aid would prove crucial to the war's outcome.[27]

Rawdon, meanwhile, had exacted another imposition on the Kershaw family soon after assuming command at Camden. Mrs. Kershaw and the children were ordered to leave the main house and stay in an outbuilding on the grounds that had earlier sheltered smallpox victims. Other families were ordered out as well, the Redcoats—throughout their occupation—still needing adequate quarters for their troops and other buildings for various military functions. At some point the Kershaws were allowed to move to Burndale, a small farm outside of town. "Here they suffered many indignities, and, tradition says, were saved from starvation only by the exertions of faithful slaves, notably one, Guinea Cato, who hid cattle and other provisions for them out in the swamps." Despite the family's presence, the house was frequently used by young Redcoat officers for "Bacchanalian festivities" or dances and "doubtless riotous carousals" said one account.

The Kershaws were roused about midnight on one occasion as the British searched for patriot officer Wade Hampton, whom Mrs. Kershaw "was suspected of harboring." Hettie Cummings, a young Loyalist woman living with the Kershaws at the time, was angered by the soldiers' suggestion that a man, possibly Hampton, might be hiding in her room. Despite her objections and known allegiance, the soldiers searched the room, jabbing their bayonets into her mattress, but finding no one. On another occasion, Hampton *had* sought refuge at the home, narrowly escaping through a back door as enemy troopers—possibly Tarleton himself, according to some accounts—dashed into the front yard, trying to capture him. Fortunately for the family, Mrs. Kershaw's brother, Samuel Mathis, was on hand during this period offering at least some protection. Mathis was a Camden militiaman captured and paroled when Charleston fell. He was allowed to "come up often into the Town on business, but had always to go to Head Quarters for a pass to go out."[28]

On August 9, two expresses arrived in Charleston informing Cornwallis that Gates was moving south from North Carolina. With him was an American army of about 6,000 men advancing toward Lynch's Creek about 20 miles northeast of Camden. As if this development was not foreboding enough, Sumter and his 1,000 or so partisans were likely still in that area after their clashes at Rocky Mount and Hanging Rock days earlier. If Sumter or other patriot militia joined Gates, the manpower pendulum would swing even more against the British, with few, if any, reinforcements in sight.

Rawdon was keeping an eye on the enemy's movements, and would not back away from a confrontation, if necessary, to delay Gates's march at Lynches Creek. At the same time, he also was withdrawing his outposts in readiness to marshal his forces in Camden. Still, he had enough troops on hand to bloody Gates if the Americans were brash enough to attack him frontally. To this end, Rawdon posted his men—consisting of elements from most of the units in his Camden garrison—and four guns, in a "commanding position" on the south bank of Little Lynches Creek, by the overnight hours of August 9–10. "The hospital, the baggage, the provisions, the ammunition, and the stores, remained under a weak guard at Camden," some 14 miles to the south, Tarleton noted.[29]

Gates broke camp about 4 a.m. on August 10, the Continentals of Brigadier General William Smallwood's First Maryland Brigade leading the main column. Nearing the creek, the Americans learned the British were arrayed in force on the opposite side. Unwilling to make a contested crossing, Gates bivouacked that night, his soldiers receiving a rum ration but also put on the alert for any enemy assault. Early on the 11th, the army marched "by the right flank" up the north bank, bypassing Rawdon's potential trap, the latter withdrawing toward Camden. Tarleton had an interesting take on the situation which may have cast the campaign in a much different light: Gates "declined an attack; but he had not sufficient penetration to conceive, that by a forced march up the creek, he could have passed Lord Rawdon's flank, and reached Camden; which would have been an easy conquest, and a fatal blow to the British."[30]

From the Charleston area, Tarleton himself, recently recovered from a "fever," joined Rawdon at the creek position sometime on the 10th, after gathering more of his Legion troopers, including convalescents, and also mounted militia from various posts over several days. Assisted by Major George Hanger, his new second-in-command replacing Major Cochrane, about 70 cavalrymen were assembled by August 6 when Tarleton crossed the Santee—and then embarked on a brief raid beyond the Black River. This strike was primarily to eliminate any rebel ambitions to hit British supply convoys moving inland, Kingstree being a particular hotbed of insurrection. "The vicinity of the rivers Santee and Wateree, and of all the [Charleston] communications with the royal army, rendered it highly proper to strike terror into the inhabitants of that district," Tarleton said. Reaching Camden with a few prisoners before joining Rawdon, Tarleton appears to have been startled by the condition of his horsemen there. He saw "evident proof" that the legion cavalry were nearly destroyed by the constant duties of detachment and patrole [sp], adding that he "collected all the dragoons at that post, and in the neighbourhood" to reinforce Rawdon.[31]

Rawdon and Tarleton would become a dynamic duo for the Crown in the operations in and around Camden. One reason may have been that they were almost the same age—both 25—when the British occupied the town. Tarleton was the older by about four months. Both were educated at Oxford although it is unknown and unlikely that they knew each other before joining the military. Rawdon was serving in the provinces and already distinguished by his gallantry at Bunker Hill well before Tarleton arrived in 1776. Both saw action at Monmouth and in the Charleston siege. Cornwallis, meanwhile was still engaged in establishing a provincial government in Charleston, planning his fall campaign into North Carolina and directing his troops from his headquarters at Drayton Hall plantation. Rawdon sent regular dispatches keeping Cornwallis informed of enemy movements as well as those of "the King's troops, on the frontier," related Tarleton.[32]

It appears that Rawdon sent two express riders south as early as August 8 via Camden to reach Cornwallis in Charleston sometime on the 9th. Cornwallis wrote to Clinton on the 10th, stating that "Gates, with Caswall [sp] and Rutherford, was advancing and making every appearance of attacking Lord Rawdon" at Little Lynches Creek. "Our troops are in general sickly, the 71st [Highlanders] so much so, that the two battalions have not 274 men under arms." Cornwallis went on to inform Clinton of the battle at Hanging Rock and the "considerable" British casualties there. "These accounts [of troop losses due to sickness and combat], adding to the infidelity of our militia, are not pleasing." Cornwallis added: "I am just going to join the army, and hope to get there before anything of consequence happens...."

"The appearance of a formidable army in the province prevented a methodical completion of the system of government, and called the attention of Earl Cornwallis to objects of more immediate importance," Tarleton recalled.[33]

Cornwallis left Charleston on the evening of the 10th with an escort of light dragoons bound for Camden. What thoughts must have occupied him as he rode through the sticky Carolina night? Somewhere in the distant blackness Gates was coming, the victor of Saratoga who had conquered "Gentleman Johnny" Burgoyne in a shocking triumph amid the New York hill country. Gates outnumbered him, based on limited intelligence reports, but Cornwallis also realized that his British troops—illnesses be damned—were among the finest combat soldiers of the Empire and thus the world. The immediate issue, though, was not having enough regulars and his forced dependence on Loyalist militia, some of whom were fine soldiers, but others who were unreliable or chose sides based on which benefited them the most. Still, he was developing great trust and dependability in Rawdon and Tarleton, both young, ambitious officers who exhibited an inner flame, coolness in battle and natural, savvy leadership.

Certainly, there also would have been time to reminisce about his beloved, lost Jemima and their two children. Cornwallis also knew that monumental decisions, awaiting him at Camden, could influence not only his military career but the fate of the King's army in South Carolina and the other Southern provinces as well.

Withdrawing from Little Lynches Creek, Rawdon commenced a slow pullback toward Camden. "The situation of the British hospital and magazine, and the present distance of the army, pointed out to ... Rawdon the propriety of ... concentrating his force near Camden," Tarleton recalled. The British reached the Camden vicinity on or about the 12th, "without any molestation from the enemy." Expecting a possible American attack, Rawdon decided that his troops should encamp at Log Town, a few miles north of the village. Although overlooked by a ridge named Hobkirk Hill, Rawdon apparently believed Log Town offered the best defensive terrain available to repel an assault on the vital British inland base, Tarleton noting that Camden "did not afford any naturally-advantageous position for defensive operations."[34]

Gates on the 11th derived significant intelligence about Camden's defenses and its garrison from a British soldier who had either deserted or been captured, records being unclear. The man certainly could have been a spy as well, but whatever his status, artillery Sergeant Elias Langham had been in Camden long enough to give the Americans detailed information. He listed the specific regiments at the outpost, including their numbers—amounting to 2,365 total troops. Of these about 1,000 were British regulars, the rest Loyalist units and militia. The intelligence report noted:

> The Fortifications of the Enemy are on this Side of Town & not extensive, containing six six-pounders; the flanks of the works are open, no morasses or other impediments obstructing the passage of troops into the Town. There are no boats at the ferry more than three common scows; the troops are sickly, numbers suppos'd about six hundred.

The report added that no supplies—military or otherwise—were removed "previous to his [Langham] leaving that place. 'Twas reported that Lord Corn Wallace [sp] was near with a reinforcement of Hessians, said to be at the Congaree [River]."[35]

An August 12 reconnaissance dispatch from Thomas Sumter, a portion of which focused on Camden, only bolstered Gates's optimism. Sumter was not the most articulate general, but his points were reasonably clear:

> Camden altogether Defenseless, without the Troops have Retreat to it, Which I judge is Not the Case. They are busy in preparing Works at the Saw mill ... but if they think to Make a Stand there, it will prove an excellent Trap for them, as the General Cant [sp] fail of having a proper Description of the Country about Camden. I am Cleare they mean to Make no great oppossisseon [sp] at that place; these preperations [sp] are meare [sp] amusements by which they expect to gain time to Remove their Sick & Wounded, Which are Very Numerous. They have also Considerable Stores; three Large Boats has Just Come up in Which are a quantity of Salt, Rum & Sugar, Cloathing, &c.[36]

7

"I resolved ... to attack the rebel army"

Crossing Wateree Ferry, Cornwallis rode into Camden about 4 a.m. on August 14, "after a most expeditious and painful journey." The general's presence was reassuring and "to the great joy of Lord Rawdon and the whole Army," noted Royal Governor Josiah Martin of North Carolina, who was in the village then. Rawdon had already reassembled his troops there from the Log Town position. Additionally, four companies of light infantry, led by Captain Charles Campbell and "in a very weak state" had marched in from Ninety Six during the day of the 13th. "The arrival of the noble earl and of the light infantry were fortunate events," Tarleton noted.

Cornwallis almost immediately began preparing for battle. "The following day he spent in examining the condition of his own force," related Major Stedman, adding that almost "eight hundred British troops were sick at Camden." The number of troops "really effective" was about 2,000, including officers, "of whom about fifteen hundred were regulars, or belonged to established provincial corps, and the rest, militia and refugees from North Carolina." Another, equally reliable account stated that on the morning of August 15, Cornwallis had 2,239 officers and men "present and fit for duty."[1]

Cornwallis also "adopted the most likely measures to obtain intelligence of" Gates's manpower and position, Tarleton wrote. The earl "likewise directed his attention to strengthen the British regiments and provincial corps, by mustering the ablest convalescents; and he was not unmindful of his cavalry." Cornwallis "ordered all the horses of the army, belonging both to regiments and departments, to be assembled. The best were selected ... for the cavalry, and ... they were delivered up to the British Legion. These active preparations diffused animation and vigour [sp] throughout the army," Tarleton added. Still, a formidable task awaited Cornwallis. "He found on his arrival no small difficulties to encounter," stated a British account of that period. "Gates was advancing, and at hand, with a very decided superiority of force ... whilst the name and character of the commander [Gates] increased the idea of its force." His troops decimated by "sickness and casualties," the earl had an even larger problem: "The position of Camden, however advantageous or convenient in other respects, was a bad one to receive an attack."[2]

John Robert Shaw was a British infantryman in the 33rd Regiment posted at Camden at that time. He had been ill, but related Cornwallis's words to the troops "nearly to this effect"—

> Now, my brave soldiers, now an opportunity is offered for displaying your valour, and sustaining the glory of the British arms; —all you who are willing to face your enemies; —all you who are ambitious of military fame stand forward; for there are eight or ten to one coming against; —Let the man who cannot bear the smell [of] gun-powder stand back, and all you who are determined to conquer or die turn out.
>
> Accordingly, we all turned out except a few who were left to guard the sick and military stores.

Despite these words of war, Cornwallis still had monumental decisions to make in the next day or so that could impact not only his personal aspirations but, most importantly, the Crown's fortunes in North America.[3]

Gates renewed his advance south on August 12 and reached Clermont, home of the Loyalist Lieutenant Colonel Henry Rugeley, the next day. The Americans encamped there on the sprawling, hilly grounds around the house, Gates declaring it Camp Clermont. Still, this was enemy country, known as a regular staging area for rival militia. A large, stout log barn, situated about 75 yards from the house, was used in various stages as a barracks, council chamber and fortified position. Loyalist troops, including Tarleton's Legion infantry who had displayed their bayonet skills so expertly against Buford at the Waxhaws, camped there two or three days earlier as part of Rawdon's reserve at Little Lynches Creek. Rugeley operated a nearby mill on Grannys Quarter Creek, grinding grain for local residents. Brigadier General Edward Stevens arrived there the next day—Monday, the 14th—with 700 Virginia militia. These men were welcomed by Gates, but had no provisions with them, other than "a few articles of West India produce, principally molasses." In addition to being hungry, they also were exhausted, many ill. "The troops are much Fatigued, and are dropping sick in great numbers every day," Stevens had written Gates from the vicinity of Hanging Rock earlier that day. Already, he had left behind a number of ill soldiers at the Pee Dee River. "This, with great desertions, &c, has reduced my numbers very low ... and all my horses nearly given out...."[4]

Gates, meanwhile, had sent out several reconnaissance parties of staff officers from the afternoon of the 13th through the morning of August 14 to examine the countryside somewhat closer to Camden. They were to find "a well-selected defensive position" and "await developments" including possibly drawing the British out of Camden to fight Gates on ground of his choosing. By this point, Gates was reconsidering a direct assault on Camden, as he had little reliable information about the outpost's defenses, other than general troop strength. The deserter Langham had provided key details, but could he be trusted? Gates was certain that his army outnumbered the British, but also realized it was composed primarily of militia who had never before been in combat. One recon party, including the Virginian Porterfield and Colonel John C. Senf, the army's chief engineer, found an "advantageous position" north of Sanders Creek where Gates could dig in and await an enemy assault. The location was about seven miles from Rugeley's and five from Camden, along a rise about 300 yards from the creek. The terrain in this region is interlaced with sandy pine barrens, ravines and boggy, flood-prone lowlands, including Gum Swamp. The two officers even advised Gates about where to emplace a redoubt and abatis to bolster the position.[5]

The general was evaluating their information on the 14th when an incident occurred which prompted suspicion of treachery among some of Gates's officers, but apparently not in the general himself. An unidentified man supposed to a Camden resident "came as if by accident" to the American camp and was taken to Gates's headquarters. The man "affected ignorance" of the army's approach, "pretended very great friendship for his countrymen, the Marylanders, and promised" Gates that he would return from Camden in a few days with information about the enemy. "The suspicions of the officers about headquarters were aroused, but the General's confidant was allowed to go without restraint; and he went doubtless to Lord Cornwallis with a full report," said one account.[6]

Thomas Sumter, meanwhile, was at the Waxhaws where he and his command were resting, healing and regrouping after the Rocky Mount and Hanging Rock clashes. From Rugeley's, Gates sent word for the Gamecock to leave Waxhaws and, with reinforcements that Gates would provide him, move down the Wateree's west bank near Camden, intercepting any supplies bound for the Redcoats there. Sumter also was to try to block any more reinforcements from the British post at Ninety Six from reaching Camden. Certainly Wateree Ferry, was the primary crossing point, but there were others that Sumter would have to watch as well. On the night of the 14th, Gates dispatched troops to join Sumter west of the Wateree for this operation. This force consisted of 100 Maryland Continentals, 300 North Carolina militia and two brass three-pounders. The militia were commanded by Lieutenant Colonel Elijah Isaacs while the total force was led by Lieutenant Colonel Thomas Woolford of the Continentals and accompanied by Colonel Senf, the army's chief engineer. Woolford linked with Sumter during the night about 12 miles west of the main army. Gates was not worried that this detachment would seriously weaken his own strength since intelligence gathered since his arrival at Clermont indicated he greatly outnumbered the enemy. An aggressive strike down the Wateree, coupled with the main army threatening Camden would likely improve his chances of overall success.[7]

If Sumter and Woolford could seize Wateree Ferry, Elkins' Ford and Whitaker's Ferry on the river, the Redcoats in Camden might be choked off from supplies and reinforcements coming from Charleston or Ninety Six. In this scenario, the British would soon run short of food and other essentials, forcing them to attack Gates in an effort to reopen their supply routes.[8]

Sumter showed his efficiency early on the morning of August 15, his men seizing these "passways" including "Carey's Fort" the British redoubt near the west bank at Wateree Ferry about three miles from Camden. "The enemy had guards at many different places ... all of which were evacuated last night or this morning, and the guards ordered into Camden, except those at" the ferry, Sumter wrote to Gates. A party of the Gamecock's raiders, led by Colonel Thomas Taylor, surprised the Redcoats there, killing seven and bagging about 30 prisoners, including Colonel James Cary, the Loyalist commander and local landowner. The bigger prize, however, was 38 wagons of corn, rum, other supplies and "a number of horses" captured.

Enemy riflemen on the opposite bank peppered the Americans with "a constant fire, but I have received no damage yet," Sumter noted. "I intend to keep possession if I can...." From prisoners, Sumter appears to have obtained general information about the enemy's strength at Camden, telling Gates: "The number of troops, regulars I mean, do not exceed two thousand, and not as many as one thousand ... militia, who are generally sickly, and much dispirited...." Before Sumter could dispatch this jubilant message, there were more glad tidings: a small British wagon train from Ninety Six trundling unaware into Taylor's snare that afternoon. Sumter reported this in a post script to Gates: "I have ... this instant made about seventy prisoners, all British, six wagons, baggage ... many of the prisoners are sick." Sumter's marauders retreated about ten miles upriver after "the Enemy made motion to cross the river below to attack him." Senf returned to the main army overnight.[9]

Almost unnoticed on the morning of the 15th, a small party of unimpressive-looking South Carolina militiamen led by a diminutive but equally unimpressive officer rode out of Gates's encampment. Francis Marion had come to Gates seeking permission to move well south of

7. "I resolved ... to attack the rebel army"   81

Camden, take charge of militia in Williamsburg District and to begin a boat-burning strike along the Santee River which would help impede enemy communications and supplies coming inland from Charleston. Recalled Colonel Otho Williams:

> Col. Marion, a gentleman of South Carolina, had been with the army a few days, attended by a very few followers, distinguished by small leather caps, and the wretchedness of their attire. Their number did not exceed twenty men and boys, some white, some black, and all mounted, but most of them miserably equipped; their appearance was in fact so burlesque, that it was with much difficulty the diversion of the regular soldiery was restrained by the officers, and the General himself was glad of an opportunity of detaching Col. Marion, at his own instance towards the interior of South Carolina, with orders to watch the motions of the enemy and furnish intelligence.

"This was the commencement of Marion's brilliant career," wrote Edward McCrady, an early historian of the Revolution in the state. It also marked the beginning of Marion's exploits as the "Swamp Fox," one of the war's most feared but elusive and respected partisan fighters.[10]

A few miles away in Camden on August 15, Cornwallis was in the last stages of girding his army for combat. The "principal part of the King's troops had orders to be in readiness to march," Tarleton related. "The town, the magazine, the hospital ... were committed to the care of" Major Archibald McArthur of the 71st, "with a small body of provincials and militia, and the weakest convalescents of the army." Some infantry of the 63rd regiment, supplied with horses at Charleston, were expected to join McArthur overnight "for the security of Camden."

In his postwar account, Tarleton claimed that later in the day on the 15th, he and his troopers brought in three American prisoners who said they were "directed to join the American army ... that night, as General Gates had given orders for his troops to move from Rugeley's mill to attack the British camp next morning near Camden." According to Tarleton, the three had been "left in a convalescent state" at Lynches Creek before being sent to rejoin Gates. Tarleton continued, stating that he escorted the captives to Camden where they were questioned by Cornwallis. Their "story appeared credible, and confirmed all the other intelligence of the day," the Green Dragoon noted. This appears to be an exaggeration, since the three had not been in Gates's bivouac that day and would have had no knowledge of his plans, unless possibly informed by a courier urging them and others to rejoin the army.[11]

At least one other pro–British account states that "two of Burgoyne's soldiers" who had "enlisted in the rebel army" after being captured by Gates's forces at Saratoga, reached Camden on the night of the 15th, with information that "the whole rebel army was then in full march to attack his lordship." Gates appears to have had no intent of attacking on the morning of August 16, his troops marching to occupy the selected defensive position. If Cornwallis or his staff did interrogate prisoners on the 15th, he does not mention these rather dramatic revelations in his reports or correspondence. Still, spies abounded on both sides, and if British operatives did see the enemy army on the move toward Camden, it's possible they were unaware of Gates's intent to take a defensive posture. And Cornwallis likely would have not noted his covert activities in writing, such documents at risk of capture.

Amid this speculation and skullduggery, Cornwallis weighed his other options. Arithmetic from intelligence reports still told him that he would be outnumbered about three to one, Gates's army amounting to about 6,000 troops with Sumter leading another 1,000. Additionally, "almost the whole country [in South Carolina] seemed on the eve of a revolt," Stedman wrote, adding the "militia ... were in general faithless, and altogether dissatisfied in the British service." Stedman continued:

> The communication between Camden and Charleston appeared in danger of being cut by the enterprising movements of Sumter, whose numbers were daily encreasing [sp] ... The safety of the army depended upon preserving a communication with the sea coast; and something was necessary to be done immediately.... At this juncture, a retreat to Charleston might have been effected without much difficulty.

Cornwallis would have to leave behind the hundreds of ill Redcoats recuperating at Camden. He also would have to destroy or abandon the multitude of ammunition, provisions and other supplies stored there. To relinquish Camden, "the loss of the whole country would have necessarily followed, except Charleston" which was strongly garrisoned. It would also scuttle—or at least further delay—his planned thrust into North Carolina. The general also pondered the fact that his already "very small Army," as the Royal Governor Martin described it, was "exceedingly reduced and daily diminishing by sickness."[12]

Still, a British journal noted at the time, Cornwallis also realized that

> his troops were excellent, admirably officered, and well found and provided in all respects. The inevitable consequences of a retreat, were almost the heaviest evils which could befal [sp] him in any fortune. I had now my option to make, either to retire or attack the enemy, for the position at Camden was a bad one to be attacked in, and by.... Sumter's advancing down the Wateree, my supplies must have failed me in a few days.

Cornwallis later wrote to Lord Germain. "I saw no difficulty in making good my retreat to Charleston, with the troops that were able to march; but in taking that resolution I must have not only" had to deal with the ill soldiers and supplies "but I clearly saw the loss of the whole province except Charleston, and of all Georgia except Savannah, as immediate consequences, besides forfeiting all pretensions to future confidence from our friends in this part of America." Thus, Cornwallis realized the Empire's destiny in the Carolinas, as well as his own military career, hung on his decision whether to fight—at significant risk of a setback—or withdraw. "A defeat could not be much more injurious in its consequences than such a retreat," Stedman noted. "And where the motives for action so strongly preponderated, there was not much room for deliberation in the breast of an officer of so much enterprise as [L]ord Cornwallis."[13]

In the end, the general really had only one choice: "I resolved to take the first good opportunity to attack the rebel army." The Earl planned to strike Gates at Rugeley's Mill early on the morning of August 16 and "point his attack principally against the [C]ontinental regiments, whose position, from the information he had received, he knew to be a bad one," Stedman related. "His Lordship, whose mind and whose attention comprehends every object, was fully Master of the Crisis of our Affairs, and instantly discerned that an immediate meeting with the Enemy could alone retrieve them," added Governor Martin.[14]

Some of the events which transpired in the American camp on August 15 are muddled in the mists of time. "Certain intelligence" for Gates that day revealed that Cornwallis himself was in Camden "& a reinforcement had arriv'd that Day, but no certainty of the strength could be obtained," noted the engineer Col. Senf. Other accounts claim that Gates was unaware of Cornwallis's presence until information was obtained from at least one British prisoner taken early on August 16. Senf also claimed that Gates "consulted with all the General Officers on taking another Position for the Army, as the Ground where they were upon was by no means tenable" and that the officers were unanimous in agreeing to "march that night [the 15th] the Army to that Creek" based on the advice of Senf and Porterfield. Some accounts make no mention of Gates discussing the move with his generals.

Whatever the case Gates issued orders preparing the army to march from Clermont overnight on August 15–16 to this new location. Rations of a pound of flour and a gill of molasses were to be immediately issued to every soldier and officer on the morning of the 15th, and the Americans had a heavy repast of meat, cornmeal and the molasses that afternoon. "As there were no spirits yet arrived in camp" the molasses was supplied instead of the rum the troops were usually issued before combat or a forced march, Col. Williams noting "it was unluckily conceived that molasses would, for once, be an acceptable substitute." It would not, as will be noted a bit later. Stevens's Virginia militia, or at least most of them—were supplied with bayonets that day, but without any training on how to use them, found they made excellent spits to roast their beef. General Rutherford was designated officer of the day for August 16, when the army was expected to be posted at Sanders Creek. Gates also ordered a return of the seriously sick, or others unable to march.[15]

Gates believed his troop strength to be roughly about 7,000 men by his own estimation, sharing his marching orders and manpower totals with Williams, his deputy adjutant. From his own observations, Williams believed that Gates's calculation was inflated. To prove this, the colonel issued supplemental instructions for all the general officers, who were to attend a meeting with Gates that afternoon, to bring with them field returns of their commands. This would give Gates a more accurate count of how many soldiers were in his army. The conference was held in Rugeley's barn, assembled officers "to hear read the orders which the commanding general had prepared for their guidance and execution," stated one account.

The ill, extra artillery supplies, excess baggage and quartermaster stores not in immediate need were to leave that night for Waxhaws, along the Wagon Road. This movement would allow the Americans to open a line of communication north through Charlotte. After the conference, Williams gave Gates the totals of the field returns, showing that the army had 3,052 rank and file fit for duty. In a 1929 campaign study, U.S. Army historian Lieutenant Colonel H.L. Landers described what happened next: Gates "was much surprised at the small showing, but said to Williams, 'These are enough for our purpose.' What that purpose was Williams did not know, but he supposed that it was to march and attack the enemy. Allowing for a due proportion of officers ... and others, the total strength fit for duty was about 3,700."[16]

Tents were to be struck and the troops of the "Grand Army" as Gates styled it, formed to move about 10 p.m. that night. "We marched off the ground [at Rugeley's] the baggage following close in the rear," related Sergeant-Major William Seymour of the Delaware Continentals, "so confident was the General, and indeed it was every one's opinion, that we should drive the enemy, we being far superior to them in numbers...." The cavalry of Armand's Legion, about 60 horsemen, would lead with single-file columns of infantry and militia on each flank and about 200 yards off the road. Armand was far from happy in leading the army that night, believing that cavalry should not be in front when the "profoundest silence" was required on this march. The right column consisted of Colonel Porterfield's troops bolstered by about 70 of Stevens's Virginians "experienced in woodcraft." Continental Major John Armstrong, Jr., headed the left column, composed of light infantry and a contingent of North Carolina militia and woodsmen. The Pennsylvanian served as a staff officer for Gates at

Saratoga and was assigned adjutant-general of the Southern army when Gates took command. On the march south he took ill at the Pee Dee River and was temporarily replaced by Otho Williams, but returned to Gates at Clermont.[17]

Behind this "covering force" was a string of pickets in front of the main army, headed by Smallwood's Continentals and then the Second Maryland Brigade of Continentals led by Brigadier General Mordecai Gist, both with their artillery moving in front of their ranks. Caswell's North Carolina militia followed the Marylanders, the rest of Stevens's Virginians behind Caswell. Baggage wagons of each brigade followed their respective commands, and the artillery reserve under Lieutenant Colonel Elias Edmunds marched with the Virginia militia. The train of heavy baggage followed the troops and was guarded by a hodgepodge of volunteer cavalrymen, artillerists and other "supernumerary" soldiers.

In all, Gates had about 1,400 dependable troops, well officered. The rest were green militia, many of whom had never before been under hostile fire. On the march, the molasses given to the soldiers earlier in the day began to have a debilitating effect on the men. "You must observe that instead of rum we had a gill of molasses per man served out to us, which instead of enlivening our spirits, served to purge us as well as if we had taken jalap, for the men, all the way as we went along, were every moment obliged to fall out of the Ranks to evacuate," recalled William Seymour of the Delaware Continentals. The Marylander Otho Williams added: "The troops ... had frequently felt the bad consequences of eating bad provision[s]; but, at this time, a hasty meal of quick baked bread and fresh beef, with a desert [sp] of molasses, mixed with mush, or dumplings, operated so cathartically, as to disorder very many of the men, who were breaking the ranks all night, and were certainly much debilitated...." The army was to advance with the utmost silence "and any soldier who offers to fire without the command of his officer, must be instantly put to death."[18]

Gist, 38, was known not only for his individual leadership and fighting qualities but also for his family's military heritage. His father, Thomas, was a distinguished colonel in the Revolution while an uncle, Christopher, was a surveyor and scout for George Washington on the march to Fort Duquesne in 1753. Another relative, Nathaniel, would be killed at the battle of Kings Mountain. Several other Gists were spread through the ranks of Continentals and militia. Gist fought well at Germantown, but his reputation was forged at the battle of Long Island. There he commanded the Maryland Regiment, his Continentals matching the cold steel of British bayonets which to that point had been a brutal—and terror inducing—weapon for the King's regulars. The Marylanders' blood and gallantry there earned them the nickname "The Bayonets of the Revolution."[19]

Cornwallis

As the sun settled over the Wateree, Cornwallis, Rawdon and Tarleton made final preparations to make the 13-mile trek from Camden to Rugeley's Mill and serve Gates's rebels a bloody surprise for breakfast. "Confiding in the valour and discipline of his troops, however inferior in number, he [Cornwallis] resolved to move forward and attack the enemy, whose present situation" and positions at Rugeley's inclined Cornwallis to "execute his intention without delay." "At ten o'clock the King's troops moved from their ground, and formed their order of march on the main road," Tarleton related. The "front division" of the column was commanded by 37-year-old Lieutenant-Colonel James Webster, with an advanced guard of 20 Legion cavalry and about the same number of mounted infantry, "supported by four companies of light infantry" that had arrived from Ninety Six.

Next in line were the 23rd and 33rd regiments of foot, the latter noted for their pointed, bearskin headpieces. The 33rd's Webster, a Scot, was an especially bright star of the King's men. A minister's son, he entered the army in 1760 as a lieutenant in the 33rd, which Cornwallis then commanded. He had seen action in the New York campaigns and Philadelphia and excelled in combat at Monmouth. "There was no man in the whole of Cornwallis's army who proved more soldierly, more brave, more gallant, or more capable," wrote a regimental historian. "It was acknowledged that 'his skill as a commander and his bravery as a soldier was scarcely equaled among his contemporaries."[20]

Rawdon led the center "division" of the column, composed of his own Volunteers of Ireland, Tarleton's Legion infantry, Lieutenant-Colonel John Hamilton's corps of North Carolinians and Colonel Bryan's North Carolina "refugees" who were so roughly handled at Hanging Rock. Two battalions of the 71st Highlanders followed Rawdon's division as a reserve. Six guns, four moving with the divisions and two with the reserve, accompanied the army. A few wagons trundled ahead of the British Legion dragoons who formed the rear guard—or a strike force if victory appeared likely.[21]

Near midnight, the British advance was "somewhat broken" in trying to cross Sanders Creek, five miles from Camden. "A short halt remedied this inconvenience, and the royal army proceeded in a compact state with most profound silence," Tarleton recalled. A short distance away, the head of Gates's column was nearing the ford over Gum Swamp, beyond which lay the position Gates intended to occupy and defend. American scouts sent out ahead of the army, returned about 2 a.m., "nothing seen in the Road" ahead, related Colonel Senf, Gates's engineer. "The moon was at full and shone beautifully," related one of Porterfield's men, "not a breath of air was stirring, nor a cloud to be seen big as a man's hand. Consequently, we could see ... in the open piney wood plains, destitute of brush wood almost, as well in the night as in the day." "Not one, in those silent columns of more than 5,000 men, knew that the foe was approaching in full strength and with sinister purpose," the Army historian H.L. Landers added 149 years later.[22]

It was about 2:30 a.m. on Wednesday, August 16. Suddenly, the night flared with spasmodic gunfire, yells of alarm and the tinny clanking of rival cavalry rushing toward the foe through underbrush. Flashes of increasing musketry lit the pines, smoke wafting through the trees like ghosts rising from eternal slumber. The armies had collided in the blackness, near the Jasper Sutton farm.

"The first revelation of this new and unexpected scene, was occasioned by a smart, mutual salutation of small arms between the advanced guards," recalled Otho Williams. Armand's horsemen briefly held their ground but were soon overmatched by the mounted Redcoats in Cornwallis's vanguard. "The British Horse made a most violent onset, Huzzaing all the time...," noted Major Charles Magill, a Virginian on Gates's staff, Tarleton adding "the advanced guard of the British charged the head of the American column." Believing Tarleton was leading this detachment, another American recalled,

> Tarleton, sounding a charge, came on at the top of his speed, every officer and soldier with the yell of an Indian savage—at every leap their horses took, crying out, "charge, charge, charge," so that their own voices and the echoes resounded in every direction through the pine forest.

Quick to meet this threat, the infantry of Porterfield and Armstrong—primarily Captain Thomas H. Drew's Virginians leading Porterfield's troops and the North Carolinians of Captain Samuel Lockhart heading Armstrong's force—hustled forward from both sides of the road. Their flintlocks barked at the enemy horsemen, who appeared like silhouettes in the thin gloom, inflicting some casualties, including Lieutenant Jeremiah Donovan, the Legion officer leading the troopers, who was wounded. "Porterfield ordered 'halt, face to the road and fire,'" related one soldier. "This order was executed with the velocity of a flash of lightning, spreading from right to left" as the woods "resounded with the thunder of our musketry; whilst the astonished British dragoons ... drew up, wheeled their horses, and retreating with the utmost precipitation, were out of our reach before we could possibly ram down another cartridge." "The weight of the enemy's fire made the detachment of the Legion give way" after Donovan was hit, Tarleton related. The British horse "were bravely repulsed by Porterfield with considerable loss," Magill recalled.[23]

The unexpected shock of battle, meanwhile, also infected the Americans' column as some of Armand's wounded and disorganized men streamed to the rear. Smallwood's Marylanders, heading the main body, were somewhat disordered and there was "a general consternation through the whole line of the army" but the effects were short lived "as the advance guard of light infantry bravely and effectively held the ground in front...." There was "a very hot fire, in which the infantry and advance picquet [picket] suffered very much," recalled the Delawarean William Seymour.[24]

As the Redcoat cavalry recoiled, Webster deployed his division—the light infantry companies, the 23rd and 33rd Regiments—across the road. "The Enemy's Light Infantry next came up," related Major Magill, claiming that most of the Virginia militiamen in Porterfield's flank force "took to their heels." Still, the remainder of Porterfield's troops held their ground for about five minutes "in which a warm and incessant fire was kept up." A North Carolinian added that the foes "poured in upon each other the heaviest fire that (had) yet been exchanged during the conflict." "The enemy soon rallied," a British sergeant in the 23rd remembered, "and both they and we kept our ground...." "Musketry continued on both sides" for about 15 minutes when the armies "as if actuated by the same present feelings and future intentions, ceased firing," Tarleton recalled, the Brit officer Charles Stedman adding: "firing soon afterwards ceased as if by mutual consent." Porterfield and his men "executed their orders gallantly," noted the American Colonel Williams, "and the enemy, no less astonished than ourselves, seemed to acquiesce in a sudden suspension of hostilities."[25]

In the closing minutes of the firefight however, a Redcoat bullet did the most damage of any in the opening clash. Porterfield "in turning his horse about had his Leg shattered by a musket ball, which struck him upon his shin Bone." Guilford Dudley, a "private soldier" who served as a messenger for Porterfield, was nearby and saw that the colonel "received a horrid wound in his left leg, a little below the knee, which shattered it to pieces," Porterfield slumping "forward upon the pommel of his saddle." Porterfield was able to tell Captain Drew, who was next to him at this point, to order a retreat, Dudley said. Still under fire, Drew and Dudley steadied Porterfield in the saddle until another swath of musketry spooked the colonel's mount, causing it to rear and hurl Porterfield to the ground. In the confusion, Drew also fell, uninjured, but disappeared into the night, leaving the stricken Porterfield and Dudley in a virtual no-man's land.[26]

Gates, meanwhile, had ridden to the front of his column when the firing erupted, so that he could determine what was happening and what threat he faced. He described this initial encounter in a letter written four days after the battle:

Having marched about five miles ... [Armand's L]egion was charged by the enemy's cavalry, and well supported on the flanks, as they were ordered, by Colonel Porterfield, who beat back the enemy's horse, and was himself unfortunately wounded; but the enemy's infantry advancing with a heavy fire, the troops in front gave way to the first Maryland brigade, and a confusion ensued, which took some time to regulate.

Cornwallis also wrote about the violent first blood: "By the weight of the fire I was convinced they [the enemy] were in considerable force...."[27]

A "few shots only from the advanced centries [sp] of each army were fired during the night," wrote British Sergeant Roger Lamb of the 23rd Regiment. "A colonel Patterfield [sp] on whose abilities general Gates particularly depended, was wounded in the early part of this skirmish." An unidentified American recalled that "we remained in anxious expectation till near daybreak, nothing material occurring, but partial firings from the advanced and reconnoitering parties" of each side. While both armies had marched at the same time—10 p.m.—Gates's troops covered only five miles, compared to eight by the British. At least one account explains the disparity: Cornwallis wanted his men to reach Rugeley's and prepare for a dawn assault, while the Americans were merely moving, with baggage, to the new defensive position.[28]

Both sides suffered untold casualties and took a few prisoners. Cornwallis wrote that he was "assured by some deserters and prisoners that it was the whole rebel army on its march to attack us at Camden. I immediately halted and formed, and the enemy doing the same, the firing soon ceased." Rawdon rode forward in the dark with a small party to try to ascertain what enemy troops were engaged by touching the clothing and accoutrements on their corpses. "When we came to where their dead lay, I got off my horse to feel by the uniforms if they were the Continental infantry which I suspected them to be by the nature of their fire," he wrote years later. "I was immediately satisfied on the point."

In the American camp, a British captive told Colonel Williams that the Redcoats' force 500 or 600 yards away was Cornwallis's entire army of about 3,000 regulars, led by Cornwallis himself. Informed of this, Gates's "astonishment could not be concealed." He called a meeting of his generals, asking "what is to be done," Williams claimed. "All were mute for a few moments, when the gallant Stevens exclaimed, 'Gentlemen, is it not too late now to do anything but fight [?]'" Earlier, when Williams went to inform DeKalb of the conference, the Baron said, "and has the General [Gates] given you orders to retreat the army[?]" indicating what he believed to be the best course of action. In the meeting, DeKalb heard Stevens's comment, but did not oppose the Virginian's opinion to fight "and every measure that ensued was preparatory for action,"[29]

Gates, still at the front after the night skirmish, soon deployed his army, the troops resting on their arms for a brief time: DeKalb's corps—the two brigades of Maryland Continentals and the Delaware regiment—were posted on the right. Gist's Second Maryland Brigade and the Delawares, remained there, but Gates shortly afterward repositioned Smallwood's First Maryland to serve as a reserve and a second line across the road and about 200 yards to the rear. Caswell's North Carolina militia were in the center, and the Virginia militia on the left. Also on the left were Porterfield's troops, now apparently led by Captain Thomas Drew, with Porterfield wounded. Major Armstrong's North Carolinians, also bloodied earlier, were to protect a small area between some marshy terrain and Stevens's men. Six pieces of the American artillery were unlimbered in the center of the front line, while two other guns were positioned on the road to the rear with Smallwood's reserve. The remnants of Armand's Legion were assigned to support the militia. Swampy terrain bordered both of Gates's flanks, making it difficult for the enemy to penetrate behind him in those areas.[30]

Caswell's North Carolinians consisted of three brigades of about 400 men each, led by Brigadier Generals Griffith Rutherford, Isaac Gregory and John Butler. A Marylander by birth, 51-year-old Richard Caswell was a leader by nature—a politician, judge, soldier and one of North Carolina's delegates to the Continental Congress in 1774. As colonel of militia, he led a patriot force that defeated Scotch Loyalists at Moore's Creek, North Carolina, in February 1776, a small, but important battle that stifled early Loyalist ambitions to dominate the province. Later that year, he was elected the state's first governor, serving for about three years before buckling on his sword as a brigadier general. Ironically, Gregory, 43, was from Camden County, N.C., established on the Pasquotank River in 1777, also in honor of the British statesman. One of Gregory's regiments was commanded by Lieutenant Colonel Henry Dixon, a former Continental officer whose men called him "Hal." Dixon's militiamen were put into line next to Gist's Marylanders. Dixon was a combat veteran, having led a Continental regiment under Washington.[31]

Across the field, Cornwallis pondered whether to risk a night assault or wait for daylight, among other options. He was confident and satisfied that the terrain he and Gates occupied benefited him most and also about the mettle of the soldiers he commanded. He wrote,

> Confiding in the discipline and courage of his Majesty's troops, and well apprised by several intelligent inhabitants, that the ground ... being narrowed by swamps ... was extremely favourable for my numbers, I did not choose to hazard the great stake for which I was going to fight, to the uncertainty and confusion to which an action in the dark is so particularly liable. But having

taken measures that the enemy should not have it in their power to avoid an engagement on that ground, I resolved to defer the attack till day....

The Loyalist officer Charles Stedman added:

> The ground on which the two armies had accidentally met was as favorable for Lord Cornwallis as he could have wished. A swamp on each side secured his flanks, and narrowed the ground in front, so as to render the superiority of the enemy in numbers of less consequence. He therefore waited with impatience for the approach of day; and as soon as it appeared, made his last disposition for the attack.

A rural road leading to Camden and located beyond the marsh on the British left was of some concern, since it could potentially be used by the Americans to outflank him, but Cornwallis sent a small force to watch this bypass "and soon dispelled his anxiety."[32]

Satisfied with his field position and that he could not be outflanked, Cornwallis sent dispatches to his subordinates "to halt the troops upon this ground, and order them to lie down to wait the approach of day." These commands were executed soon after pickets were posted. "Except a few occasional shots from the advanced sentries of each army, a silent expectation ushered in the morning," noted Tarleton. Due to the Redcoats' success in the night combat, "we were eager for a general engagement," remembered the Brit John R. Shaw of the 33rd, "but Lord Cornwallis finding that the enemy were on bad ground, was unwilling to hazard in the dark, the advantages which their situation would afford him in the light." On the American side, Otho Williams added: "Frequent skirmishes happened during the night, between the advanced parties—which served to discover the relative situations of the two armies—and as a prelude to what was to take place in the morning."[33]

Somewhere in the pine woods, Guilford Dudley huddled in the underbrush with the severely wounded Colonel Porterfield. Throughout the rest of the early morning, the two had evaded capture from British patrols as Dudley desperately tried to bring Porterfield back to the American lines where he could receive medical treatment. The colonel's strength was ebbing by the minute due to his massive leg injury; both men were exhausted. Still, there was a faint glimmer of hope—they earlier had encountered two American militiamen whom Dudley implored to bring help for the colonel. They promised to do so, but who knew if they actually would? With the silver sky lightening to the east, Porterfield and Dudley heard a cannon blast well in the distance. In a "feeble voice," the colonel told Dudley this was a morning gun fired by the British in Camden near the break of day. Dudley believed it also could be Cornwallis's signal for his army to attack. Soon afterward, the two militiamen returned with a party to aid Porterfield. They had kept their word! Shortly, the colonel was being borne to the rear on a hastily-built litter. Dudley bade Porterfield a quick farewell "telling him at the same time, that I hoped to join him again in the course of an hour or two, which was in sincerity my expectation, so sanguine were my hopes of immediate victory, notwithstanding the disasters of the past night." The thunder of artillery crushed the stillness and Dudley turned his horse toward the awakening battle.

He would never see Porterfield again.[34]

8

"The most tremendous firing I ever heard"

Peering through the dull, first light of dawn, about 4:30 a.m., Captain Anthony Singleton of the Maryland Continental Artillery saw a scarlet-clad column of men on the move in front of him about 200 yards distant. Singleton told Otho Williams that "he plainly perceived the ... British uniform" in front of the American army's position. Williams related that he "immediately ordered.... Singleton to open his [two-gun] battery; and then rode to" inform Gates about the cannon fire and the Redcoats' advance opposite the position of Stevens's Virginians. Williams continued his account:

> The general [who was with Smallwood's reserve at the time] seemed disposed to [a]wait events—he gave no orders. The deputy adjutant general (Williams) observed, that if the enemy, in the act of [deploying] were briskly attacked by General Stevens's brigade, which was already in line of battle, the effect might be fortunate, and first impressions were important. "Sir," said the general, "that's right—let it be done." This was the last order that the deputy adjutant general received.

Years later, one of Gates's aides, Major Thomas Pinckney of South Carolina, recalled the brief conference between the general and Williams:

> I well remember Col. Williams riding up to him [Gates] just at daybreak, & giving him information of the movement of the Enemy's troops on their right.... I however observed no hesitation, but admired the promptness with which he ordered that.... Stevens should be directed to make an immediate attack while the Enemy were maneuvering....

Gates then told Pinckney to find DeKalb "and desire him to make an attack on the enemy's left to support that made by General Stevens on the [British] right." Anticipating Stevens's assault, Gates also instructed Smallwood's First Maryland to move forward and to the left front and occupy the line to be vacated by the advancing Virginians. Gates then rode to Gist, telling him to slowly move up with the Second Brigade of Continentals, "reserving its fire until close to the enemy, when it was to fire and charge with the bayonet." The immediate problem was that Rawdon's Redcoats were on the move as well.[1]

"As soon as day light appeared, we saw at a few yards distance our enemy drawn up in very good order," recalled Sergeant Roger Lamb, who was a flag bearer of the 23rd Regiment, also known as the Royal Welsh Fuzileers. Tarleton added: "At dawn the two commanders proceeded to make their respective arrangements for action." Indeed, Cornwallis was arranging his lethal chess pieces for battle. With the American Captain Singleton watching, Webster's division filed into position on what would be the British right flank. Campbell's four light infantry companies from Ninety Six—about 150 men in all—hustled into line on the extreme end near swampy terrain. The almost 300 troops of the 23rd Regiment were next and then the 33rd Regiment (also known as the West Riding Regiment) of some 240 soldiers. The left of the 33rd rested on the Camden-Waxhaw Road and was the link between Webster and Rawdon's division, the latter situated on the left, or west, of the road.[2]

The 300 or so Loyalists of the Volunteers of Ireland, Rawdon's own regiment, connected with Webster's left—the 33rd, at the road. About 125 infantry of the British Legion, led by Captain Patrick Stewart, were next in the battle line and on the extreme left of Rawdon's "division" were the 270 or so North Carolinians of Hamilton's regiment, their left protected by marshy woods. The remnants of Bryan's Loyalist force, about 200 men, were posted behind Hamilton's troops. Cornwallis's artillery consisted of two six-pounders and two three-pounders stationed on the left of the road and commanded by Lieutenant John McLeod of the Royal Artillery. The 71st Highlanders, along with two six-pounders, formed a second line reserve, the First Battalion—144 officers and men—about 200 yards behind Webster's troops and the Second Battalion—numbering 110—the same distance in rear of Rawdon's ranks. The 182 troopers of the Legion cavalry, led by Major George Hanger, remained in column due to the dense woods and were to the right of the road, close behind the Highlanders supporting Webster's line. Tarleton, who maintained overall command of the Legion infantry and cavalry, noted that Hanger's horsemen had "orders to act offensively against the enemy, or in defence of the British troops, as opportunity offered, or necessity required." McLeod's artillerists consisting of 19 men total, were shorthanded and had to rely on other soldiers to assist in working the guns. "The British, the provincials, and the militia of the royal army, officers and soldiers inclusive, amounted to something above two thousand men," Tarleton claimed.[3]

After his brief conversation with Gates, Otho Williams "hastened" to

Stevens with the attack order. The Virginian "instantly advanced with his brigade, apparently in fine spirits," but the assault was just as quickly stymied. Ahead, Webster's Redcoats—"the right wing of the enemy"—were "soon discovered *in line*—it was too late to attack them" deploying; "nevertheless, the business of the day could no longer be deferred." Sensing this danger point for the entire army, Williams asked Stevens to give him "forty or fifty privates, volunteers, who would run forward of the [Virginia] brigade, and commence the attack." In reality, Williams was trying to buy time before the expected devastating volley of Brown Bess flintlocks bloodily shredded the battle-raw Virginians. Williams led the volunteers forward, "within forty or fifty yards of the enemy," shouting for them to "take trees, and keep up as brisk a fire as possible." It was a valiant, but futile effort. "The desired effect of this expedient, to extort the enemy's fire at some distance, in order to rendering it less terrible to the militia, was not gained," Williams noted.[4]

The British units in front of Stevens had indeed just completed their deployment when Cornwallis, "observing a movement on their [Gates's] left, which I supposed to be with an intention to make some alteration in their order" and "instantly, in person," told Webster to attack. The Earl, at the same time, sent a staff officer to Rawdon, telling him to advance as well. Cornwallis apparently mistook the motions of Stevens's troops as a change of position rather than an assault, but it made no difference either way as Webster's Redcoats surged through the trees and underbrush with fixed bayonets and a chorus of war cries. "General Stevens, observing the enemy to rush on" desperately shouted for his militiamen to meet the enemy blades with their own cold steel: "We have bayonets, too! We can charge! Come on, men! Don't you know what bayonets are for?" The obvious answer was no, since these green militiamen had no instruction about bayonets other than as a cooking utensil, and Stevens's exhortations were lost on most of them as they saw the British line rushing toward them.

"We immediately began the attack with great vigor," noted the Redcoat Sgt. Lamb, adding that he and his comrades "either kept up a constant fire, or made use of their bayonets as opportunity offered." In minutes, momentum's fateful pendulum swung swiftly and lethally against the Americans as Gates's left flank collapsed in a contagion of panic. The Virginians triggered a few scattered shots before breaking ranks and fleeing, despite the exhortations of Stevens, Williams and other officers, Williams noting that "the impetuosity with which they [the enemy] advanced, firing and huzzaing, threw the whole body of militia into such a panic that they generally threw down their loaded arms and fled, in the utmost consternation."[5]

The fear fury ignited like an overturned lamp, most of Caswell's North Carolinians quickly following the "unworthy example" of the

Virginians and bolting for the rear. Williams added that "a great majority of militia (at least two-thirds of the army) fled without firing a shot." "The light infantry and the 23d regiment ... first broke the enemy's front line" of the militia, related Tarleton. General Rutherford "acted with distinguished gallantry" in attempting to rally his Carolinians, but crumpled when a musket ball ripped into his thigh. Likewise, General Butler tried in vain to hold his militiamen in line, but his troops, along with a portion of Gregory's soldiers broke in disorder. Gregory, however, remained with the regiment of his militia led by Lt. Col. Dixon, which was standing firm against the enemy onslaught. "Having their flank exposed by the flight of the other militia, Dixon's regiment joined the Marylanders [and Delawareans] of Gist's Continental brigade whose left they became, and vied in deeds of courage with their veteran comrades" stated one account. Dixon, by "his precept and example ... infused his own spirit into his troops, who, emulating the ardor of their leader, demonstrated the wisdom of selecting experienced officers to command raw soldiers."[6]

North Carolina militiaman Garret Watts claimed to have fired the first shot of the battle—highly unlikely—and also that he was among the first to flee. The British "appeared to maneuver in contempt of us, and I fired without thinking except that I might prevent the man opposite from killing me," he wrote. "The discharge and loud roar soon became general from one end of the line to the other. Amongst other things, I confess I was amongst the first that fled. The cause of that I cannot tell, except that everyone I saw was about to do the same. It was instantaneous."

Gates described this stage of the battle, noting that "to my astonishment, the left wing and North Carolina militia gave way." John Shaw, who was in the 33rd Regiment in this part of the British line noted that the militia "took to their heels [at] the first fire, and though their general did all in his power to rally them, he could not persuade them to make a single stand, and so getting to the wood as fast as they could, they totally dispersed, leaving the continental regular troops to oppose the whole force of the British...." Battle-tested as he was, Otho Williams later described the psychology of soldiers, even veterans, caught up in such wild alarm:

> He who has never seen the effect of a panic upon a multitude can have but an imperfect idea of such a thing. The best disciplined troops have been enervated and made cowards by it. Armies have been routed by it, even where no enemy appeared to furnish an excuse. Like electricity, it operates instantly; like sympathy, it is irresistible where it touches.[7]

Riding to join the battle after aiding Porterfield, Guilford Dudley listened to "the most tremendous firing I ever heard" as the foes engaged, the terrible symphony heightened by unrelenting cannon blasts. He reached the field, passing behind the ranks of the Maryland and Delaware Continentals and enduring "a shower of balls that whizzed incessantly around me" as he tried to find his company. Riding behind Dixon's North Carolina militia, Dudley noted how they and Gist's Continentals "maintained their ground with great firmness and gallantry, at one time driving the enemy opposed to them in front out of line…." His admiration abruptly changed. With "horror and surprise [I] saw the whole left wing falling back in the utmost confusion and dismay, throwing away their arms and all their accoutrements, in order to run the swifter…."[8]

DeKalb

The panic failed to stifle the grit and courage of DeKalb and Gist's Continentals, the Marylanders and Delaware Blue Hens fighting like cornered panthers. "The regular troops, who had the keen edge of sensibility rubbed off by strict discipline and hard service, saw the confusion [of the militia] with little emotion. They engaged seriously in the affair…," said one American. The Baron was on horseback and with Gist's troops who were already heavily engaged against Rawdon's wing and the 33rd regiment of Webster's division. These Redcoats were being pummeled by an accurate and destructive fire from the American artillery. "Lord Rawdon began the action on the left with no less vigour and spirit than Webster had done on the right," recalled the Loyalist officer Charles Stedman, "but here, and in the centre, against part of Webster's division, the contest was more obstinately maintained by the Americans, whose artillery did considerable execution."

"Our line continued to advance in good order, and with the cool intrepidity of experienced British soldiers," Cornwallis related, "keeping up a constant fire or making use of bayonets…." "The action became immediately general along the front, and was contested on the left and in the center with great firmness and bravery," Tarleton wrote. The British 33rd and the Continentals had advanced to within 100 yards of each other when the Marylanders' triggered a thunderous volley, the balls from their French-made Charlevilles bloodily scything much of the Redcoats' formation. The "Americans gave the first fire, which killed and wounded nearly one half of our number," wrote John Shaw of the 33rd. "We returned the fire, and immediately charged on them with the bayonet." "General Gist preserved perfect order in his brigade, and, with his small arms and artillery, continued a heavy and well-directed fire upon the 33d regiment and the whole of the left division" stated a British account. With the issue still in doubt, Cornwallis was observed riding calmly among the Volunteers of Ireland, rallying and exhorting them.[9]

"We advanced at the same time, and began the attack from both cannon and small arms with great alacrity and uncommon bravery," recalled William Seymour, the Delaware Continental, "making great havock [sp] among them, insomuch that the enemy gave way...." Gist's men seized a British cannon "and kept it for some time," stated another Continental's account. By this time and even earlier, as Webster's assault "was done with great vigour," Cornwallis and others recalled the morning mistiness, accented by waves of gun smoke smothering the battleground. Cornwallis wrote: "It was at this time a dead calm, with a little haziness in the air, which, preventing the smoke from rising, occasioned so thick a darkness, that it was difficult to see the effect of a very heavy and well-supported fire on both sides." Tarleton added: "The morning being hazy, the smoke hung over, and involved both armies in such a cloud, that it was difficult to see or estimate the destruction on either side. Notwithstanding the resistance, it was evident the British moved forwards...." John Shaw of the British 33rd also recalled the "thick cloud" settled over the armies.[10]

Smallwood's Plight

With hundreds of distraught and disorganized militiamen scurrying through and around their formations, Smallwood's Continentals were temporarily thrown into some confusion as they advanced. The very soldiers whom they were to replace in the battle line ahead were running in the wrong direction. Who knew why—or what the Marylanders were facing in their front. Despite the chaos and smoky conditions, these troops regrouped and moved forward through the sparse woods, going into position east of the road, generally in line with DeKalb and Gist. Their first issue was that a sizeable gap existed between the two Maryland brigades.

The second, and most dangerously immediate problem, was that they had marched into a hornets' nest of Webster's Redcoats, who had refrained from pursuing Gates's vanquished militia. Various elements of Webster's division—the 23rd, 33rd and light infantry, bolstered by one of the 71st Highlanders battalions—crashed into Smallwood's command, primarily on the Marylanders' left flank. Tarleton noted that these British forces—mainly the 23rd and the light infantry who were instrumental in crushing the rival militia—"judiciously" followed up their momentum "not by pursuing the fugitives, but by wheeling on the left flank of the [C]ontinentals, who were abandoned by their militia."[11]

Quickly, the First Maryland soldiers were "greatly outflanked, and charged by superior numbers," wrote Otho Williams, who went to their assistance. Forced to yield ground, at "this critical moment" the regimental officers "were reluctant to leave the field without orders" and "inquired for their commanding officer" General Smallwood, "who, however, was not to be found," Williams related. Smallwood was later said to have been swept up in trying to rally the panicked militia and was separated from his troops. But this was of little consequence as his subordinates dealt with his absence in that terrifying moment amid a pitched battle.

This group, including Williams, Colonel John Gunby, Major Archibald Anderson, Captain John C. Jones (one of Smallwood's aides), and "a number of other brave officers" were twice able to rally the brigade and continue fighting. It was a heroic, but forsaken effort. The opposite flanks of the Continental brigades were basically perpendicular to each other, but a critical gap of about two hundred yards existed between them. "The enemy having collected their corps, and directing their whole force against these two devoted brigades, a tremendous fire of musketry was, for some time kept up on both sides, with equal perseverance and obstinacy," Williams noted. With the thick smoke clutching the ground, there was little—if any—communication between the separated Continentals, as if they were fighting separate battles. Amid all this, the pressure on the First Marylanders intensified to the breaking point when Hanger's troopers charged into the mayhem with sabers flashing, Tarleton also attacking with the "remainder of his regiment."[12]

"At this instant I ordered the cavalry to complete the rout...," Cornwallis stated, a Redcoat in the 33rd adding, "We then opened to the right & left and let Tarleton's light horse pass through...." Otho Williams observed that "Cornwallis, perceiving there was no cavalry opposed to him, pushed forward his dragoons—and his infantry, charging at the same moment with fixed bayonets...."[13]

Combined with Webster's relentless infantry onslaught, and—to some degree—the absence of their general, Smallwood—the Continentals broke. "The First Maryland brigade ... repeatedly resisted the attack upon their left, until the British right wing overwhelmed them by numbers and forced them to retire," said one account. "It was just then that the British [L]egion ... joined" Webster's troops "and made the decisive charge upon the First Maryland."[14]

Gates

Gates and Caswell, meanwhile, were desperately trying to regroup the fleeing militiamen well to the rear of the fighting. "General Caswall [sp] and myself, assisted by a number of officers, did all in our power to rally the broken troops, but to no purpose...," Gates wrote a few days after the battle. Major Magill noted that Gates tried three times to halt the panicked men, all in vain. "I was there with Genl. Gates, who perceiving the militia run, rode about twenty yards in the rear of the line to rally them, which he found impossible to do there; about half a mile further, Genrl. Gates and Caswell made another fruitless attempt, and a third was made at a still greater distance with no better success." Magill also found himself aiding Major Thomas Pinckney, whose leg was smashed by a musket ball as he tried to deliver orders to DeKalb. Pinckney soon "becoming faint" from blood loss, noted that he was "supported on my horse" by Magill. Seeing an "Ammunition Wagon then endeavoring to escape," the majors made their way to it "into which I was thrown," Pinckney recalled.[15]

Simultaneously, DeKalb, Gist and their dauntless veterans were more than holding their own: "Upon Genl. Gates' Riding to stop the Militia, Gist's Brigade charged Bayonets, and at first made the Enemy give way, but they were reinforced." Gist's Marylanders and Delawares "were engaged with the enemy's left, which they opposed with very great firmness," Otho Williams wrote. "They [the Continentals] even advanced upon them, [Rawdon's soldiers] and had taken a number of prisoners," Magill related. The Delawarean Seymour added that Rawdon's troops who were repulsed, upon "observing that our militia were in great confusion the chief part of them without so much as firing a single shot" quickly rallied. The collapse of the militia "gave them [the British] an opportunity of coming round us, the militia having entirely left us at this time...."[16]

"I endeavoured, with General Caswall [sp] to rally the militia at some distance, on an advantageous piece of ground, but the enemy's cavalry continuing to harass their rear, they ran like a torrent, and bore all before them." Magill noted this effort was about "half a mile further" and was "another fruitless attempt.... Hoping yet, that a few miles in the rear they might recover from their panic, and again be brought into order, I continued my endeavor, but this likewise proved in vain." Of this effort, Magill related that it "was made at a still greater distance with no better success."[17]

Continental Captain Alexander Brevard watched in amazed horror as much of Gates's army disintegrated in front of him. A North Carolinian, he was a quartermaster officer and had ridden forward to see how the battle was developing. Brevard had been in action at White Plains, Trenton, Princeton, Brandywine, Monmouth and Germantown, but nothing had prepared him for the wild exodus he saw this morning. Realizing "that defeat was certain," he frantically galloped back to the rear to see if he could save the army's baggage train. Brevard arrived in time to get a few wagons started off, but the rout soon engulfed all, "so complete that everything was lost."[18]

DeKalb and Gist

The intense smoke and noise prevented DeKalb from realizing that the First Maryland was finished, but he remained the Continentals' Leonidas, leading Gist's troops against Rawdon's Redcoats. Three times he attacked and each time had to fall back due to being outnumbered, but "on the whole he maintained his advantage," related a biographer of the Baron. His horse was shot from under him at some point and he had suffered a saber blow "that laid open his head." Captain Peter Jaquett, adjutant of the Delaware troops, desperately bandaged DeKalb's wound and urged his chief to withdraw, but the Baron would have none of it; he had not received any such orders from Gates and would fight on. He had no way of knowing that Gates was miles to the rear by this point. "Long after the battle was lost in every quarter, the gigantic form of DeKalb, unhorsed and fighting on foot, was seen directing the movements of his brave Maryland and Delaware troops," stated one account. Charles-François, Le Chevalier Du Buysson, one of DeKalb's aides, added, "The Baron..., deserted by all the militia, who fled at the first fire, withstood with the greatest bravery, coolness and intrepidity, with the brave Marylanders alone, the furious charge of the whole British army."[19]

As the First Maryland crumbled and sensing that the struggle was about to get even further out of hand, Otho Williams had ridden to Gist's troops and called upon his own regiment, the Sixth Maryland, to hold its ground. Despite the smoke and confusion, he still clung to vague hope of uniting the Continental brigades, even if they did so in retreat, but through the combat haze, the Redcoats could be seen regrouping and massing to attack again. Thus, Williams's entreaty was answered by the Sixth's commander, Lieutenant Colonel Benjamin Ford, who replied with a shout: "They have done all that can be expected of them—we are outnumbered and outflanked—see the enemy charge with bayonets." The violence and cacophony reached a crescendo of bloodlust, the foes realizing that the next few minutes would likely decide the battle. The Continentals' blue jackets meshed with the British red, all tinted by the smoke and the glint of swords and bayonets doing their gory worst. The musketry bellowed deafening thunder and death, the stale air scorched by shrill screams, huzzahs and pitiful moans and pleas from the wounded.[20]

With the First Maryland gone, Cornwallis focused on the last men standing—DeKalb, Gist, their stalwart Continentals and the doughty North Carolina militiamen led by Gregory and Dixon. They had battled Rawdon's troops to a standstill, indeed had cracked his line with at least two bayonet charges, but now "fought alone until the whole British army enveloped them in fire." The Americans had put up "an obstinate resistance for three quarters of an hour" but the British's overpowering pressure "threw the enemy into total confusion, and forced him to give way in all quarters," Cornwallis recalled.[21]

DeKalb

Amid this final mayhem, it is unclear if DeKalb was mounted or not. As stated earlier, his horse was killed, but he may have remounted—even as the Continental line melted into the battle fog. Humphrey Hunter, a lieutenant in Rutherford's North Carolina militia who was captured earlier, claimed to have seen the Baron's fall from a horse. Hunter stated that DeKalb appeared to be alone and "apparently separated from his command, ride facing the enemy." British soldiers nearby "began clapping their hands on their shoulders, in reference to his [DeKalb's] epaulettes," and "shouted, 'a General, a rebel General!'" Momentarily, a Redcoat on horseback—not Tarleton—noted this account, met the Baron and demanded his sword in surrender. DeKalb, "with apparent reluctance, presented the hilt; but drawing back, said in French, 'Are you an officer, sir?' His antagonist, perhaps not understanding his question, with an oath, more sternly demanded his sword." DeKalb "dashed from him, disdaining, as is supposed, to surrender to any but an officer, and rode in front of the British line, with his hand extended." Along the scarlet ranks were yells of "'a rebel General,' speedily followed by a volley...." DeKalb rode another "twenty or thirty rods" before crumpling from the saddle, Hunter claimed.[22]

Hunter likely saw DeKalb fall when his horse was killed, since most sources maintain the Baron was fighting on foot when he suffered 11 wounds—three from musket balls and eight from sword and/or bayonet. The bloodied general was immediately surrounded by Redcoats, his aide Du Buysson trying to shield DeKalb with his body and shouting "Save the Baron DeKalb!" a plea to the enemy to spare his commander. Du Buysson himself sustained wounds to both arms and hands, at least some in protecting DeKalb. Due to the confused nature of the combat, the identity of the units to which the British troops encountering DeKalb belonged is unclear, although they were likely Loyalists from Rawdon's wing, they having been locked in fighting the Continentals in that sector. Whatever their units, they were likely in a frenzy, the tall "rebel General" having fatally slashed one of their comrades with his sword shortly before he collapsed. Some of these soldiers hefted DeKalb to his feet. He was then "stripped of his hat, coat, and neck-cloth, and placed with his hands resting on the end of a wagon." Most sources agree that DeKalb was standing or propped up in this position, "blood streaming from his shirt," when Cornwallis and his suite—or escort—reined to a halt and were told that the general was DeKalb. Cornwallis said to the Baron: "I am sorry, sir, to see you; not sorry that you are vanquished, but that you are so severely wounded." If there was any response from DeKalb it is not recorded. Cornwallis ordered an officer to provide medical treatment for the Baron before he and his entourage rode to other parts of the battlefield. "The brave.... DeKalb, fought on foot, with the second brigade, and fell, mortally wounded, into the hands of the enemy," wrote Colonel Williams, "who stripped him even of his shirt; a fate which probably was avoided by other generals, only by an opportune retreat." Tarleton gave this version of DeKalb's last minutes in the battle: The Baron "on the right of the Americans, being still ignorant of the flight of their left wing and center, owing to the thickness of the air, made a vigorous charge with a regiment of [C]ontinental infantry through the left division of the British, and when wounded and taken, would scarcely believe that General Gates was defeated." Of "the noble DeKalb," a North Carolinian noted that he was "covered with wounds and glory."[23]

"After an obstinate resistance for some time the Americans were thrown into total confusion, and were forced to give way in all quarters," related the British Sgt. Lamb of the Twenty-third. "The Continental troops behaved well," despite the rout of most of the enemy militia. "Almost all their officers were separated from their respective commands." From his position near the center of Webster's right wing, Lamb "had an opportunity of beholding the behavior both of the officers and privates; it was worthy of the character of the British troops. The recollection still dwells deeply in my memory." John Shaw of the British 33rd added: "The [C]ontinental troops indeed made a gallant stand, and merited the highest encomiums."

Lamb also praised Gregory's and Dixon's North Carolinians for their mettle. "In justice to the ... militia, it should be remarked, that part of" Gregory's brigade "acquitted themselves well.... They were formed immediately on the left of the Continentals, and kept the field while they had a cartridge to fire." Gregory himself had his horse killed under him and sustained two bayonet wounds in trying to regroup his men. "Several of his [Dixon's] regiment and many of his brigade, who were made prisoners, had no wound except from bayonets."[24]

Still, even if the battle was already a one-sided and significant triumph for Cornwallis, the fighting was ongoing after DeKalb's fall. Mordecai Gist "moved off with about one hundred [C]ontinentals in a body, by wading through the swamp on the right of the American position, where the British cavalry could not follow; this was the only party that retreated in a compact state from the field of battle. The [C]ontinentals, the state troops, and the militia, abandoned their arms, their colours, and their cannon, to seek protection in flight, or to obtain it from the clemency of the conquerors."[25]

Despite Tarleton's assertion about Gist's group being the "only party," there appears to have been other Continentals who banded together, as Otho Williams explained: "Every corps was broken and dispersed; even the boggs [sp] and brush, which in some measure served to screen them from their furious pursuers, separated them from one another." Continental Major Archibald Anderson, described as "a brave and valuable officer, whose grade was of the highest left on the field," rallied an untold number of Marylanders from different companies as he retreated, later commended for his "prudence and firmness" which afforded "protection to those who joined his party on the rout." Separate from Anderson, a few other Continental officers, including Colonel John Gunby, Lieutenant Colonel John Eager Howard, Captain Henry Dobson, all of Maryland, and Captain Robert Kirkwood of Delaware with some others, banded with 50 or 60 soldiers to make a somewhat fighting withdrawal. Howard was in the midst of the close-quarters combat. Even in retreat, however, he had not seen the last of Camden, as will be shown. Thrust into a greater leadership role due to the capture of his superiors, Lieutenant Colonel Joseph Vaughan and Major John Patten, Kirkwood also would travel the road of destiny back to Camden in a few months.[26]

The major battle was over in less than an hour, but the nightmare for hundreds of the Americans would stretch over many bloody miles.

9

"A perfect scene of horror and confusion"

If Gates's army had basically ceased to exist, the terrors of the rout were just beginning. "After this last effort of the [C]ontinentals, rout and slaughter ensued in every quarter" related Tarleton, adding that his dragoons "advanced with great rapidity" after the fleeing enemy. Indeed, his horsemen thundered down the road and through the woods in a frenzy of slashing, stabbing and shooting the Americans. Guilford Dudley was caught up in the masses, noting that "nothing saved me then but the crowds of soldiers a little in my rear, who literally choked up the road and its margins, who were, of necessity, to be disposed of before the enemy could come at me" adding that their green-jacketed tormentors were "hacking, killing or dispersing" the "unfortunate men" behind him.

Dudley soon guided his exhausted mount off the road and into a cluster of blackjack oak. He then rode ahead through the scattered thickets some two or three hundred yards before retaking the road at a less congested area, realizing the enemy horsemen would soon slash their way to that point as well. Dudley quickly realized that he had made the right decision, as from the rear "my ears were saluted with the savage yells and shouts of the enemy and the lamentable heart-rending cries and screams of their unfortunate victims. They spared none at this stage of their butchery that they could possibly reach, nor lost a moment in capturing and giving quarter to any individual."[1]

General Gist barely evaded death when a British cavalryman rumbled toward him with his saber raised. The general wheeled his horse to engage the oncoming Redcoat. Instantly, a nearby Maryland sergeant in Gist's command triggered his flintlock, sending the trooper tumbling dead from the saddle. The sergeant immediately grabbed and mounted the rider-less horse, spurring away from more pursuers. "The road for some miles was strewed with the wounded and killed, who had been overtaken by the legion in their pursuit," wrote the Loyalist officer Charles Stedman.

"The number of dead horses, broken wagons, and baggage, scattered on the road, formed a perfect scene of horror and confusion. Arms, knapsacks, and accoutrements found were innumerable; such was the terror and dismay of the Americans." Tarleton noted that his men captured North Carolina militia General Rutherford "with many other officers and men" on the road. Rutherford, already wounded in the leg, was roughly handled by his captors, "one of whom, after his submission, cut him in several places" stated one source. Based on another account, Rutherford was riding a "not very fleet" horse and "not dressed in military," meaning he wore essentially the same homespun as his militiamen.[2]

A dragoon attacked Rutherford, his saber cleaving through the general's beaver-pelt hat and "inflicting a severe wound across the top of his head." Seeing this, Major James Harris of Rutherford's command called out, "thats [sic] an officer." It is unclear if Harris was a prisoner at the time or merely within shouting distance, but whatever the case, the cavalryman yielded, likely sparing the general's life. By then, the attack and pursuit had "greatly dispersed the British" troopers who reined in just south of Grannys Quarter Creek to regroup and re-form with reinforcements coming up. North of the creek and along the road in the general vicinity of the Rugeley place, the Redcoats—based on Tarleton's account—saw Colonel Armand and his men, along with several other officers "employed in rallying the militia ... and in sending off the American baggage." The "quick junction of the scattered cavalry" soon overwhelmed this force and "counteracted the designs of the enemy," Tarleton related, adding "Armand's dragoons and the militia displayed a good countenance, but were soon borne down by the rapid charge of the [L]egion."[3]

Otho Williams had a sharply different take than Tarleton about Armand's force at the wagon train: "What added, not a little to this calamitous scene, was the conduct of Armand's Legion. Whether it was owing to the disgust of the colonel, at general orders, or the cowardice of his men ... they retired early, and in disorder, and were seen plundering the baggage of the army on their retreat." Williams also claimed that one of Armand's troopers cut a Maryland Continental Captain William Lemar on the hand when Lemar tried to retrieve his portmanteau from a wagon. Having broken his sword in the battle, the captain was unarmed and "was obliged to submit, both to the loss and to the insult." The Delaware Continental William Seymour added: "As for Col. Armand's horse, they thought upon nothing but plundering our waggons [sp] as they retreated off."[4]

The North Carolinian Guilford Dudley also claimed to have seen at least some of Armand's men looting wagons, a few of which contained the belongings of the Maryland officers. "Their trunks were broken open and rifled," he wrote, "their Holland gin cases ripped open and the case-bottles profusely handed about...." Still, Dudley noted that he approached a few of Armand's dragoons, entreating them to try to stem the overall rout of the soldiers "even if they had to cut them down with their sabers." The cavalrymen reluctantly did so, some facing about in a line, but Dudley noticed "that there was not a single musket" to be seen in the hands of these troops. "Not only the road but the whole plain to the East, as far as our line extended, was covered with the flying troops, some of whom were bearing towards the road, while others kept straight forward through the pine plain and over sand hills...," recalled Dudley. Another American, unidentified, noted: "The retreat now became general, and the militia by this time had got six or eight miles in the rear, some of whom, together with our camp women, wagoners, [sp] and some scattering light horse, plundered all our baggage."[5]

Amid his exhaustion and battle stress, Williams also confessed to giving in to the temptation of war's spoils. "The tent covers were thrown off the waggons [sp], generally, and the baggage exposed, so that one might take what suited him to carry off." He joined other soldiers gathered at Caswell's "mess waggon" which "afforded the best refreshment." The thirsty men were sharing some "good Madeira" and Williams had a taste of the booty, taking "a draught of wine, which was the only refreshment ... received that day." This sojourn appears to have been a brief break in the mayhem. Dudley was among the many who continued struggling north on the road. He likely spoke for all who survived, writing:

> Urged by the powerful principle of self-preservation, it seemed to be the order of the day that every man should take care of himself, and everyone appeared willing to avail himself of this common privilege, without regard to the laws of chivalry; and who can be blamed, in such a juncture of rout and disaster, for carrying himself off to a place of safety with all the dispatch in his power.

Fear and panic seemed to grip the fugitives, fueled by the incessant threat of Tarleton's horsemen rampaging ever closer with blades flashing death.[6]

Dudley soon came up with several wagons that were "filled with camp-women" sitting on piles of baggage belonging to the Maryland Continentals. In an instant, a ghastly portrait was created, as he noted: "The wagoners, having taken the alarm from the flying troops, drove on at full speed, and now and then coming in contact with a stump overset, when away went the camp-women, dashed twelve or fifteen feet, and some of them with new-born infants in their arms, a sight lamentable to view." Dudley also added this description of what he saw:

> wagoners ... throwing off the cover, and then strewing the baggage, marquees, tents, trunks, boxes and everything else in the road, in order to lighten

their carriage, and in full speed drove on, until a new alarm added to the panic already operating upon their minds, compelled them also to halt, cut out their saddle horses, and away in their best speed....

He noted that the contents of many wagons were dumped over "many miles up the Waxhaw road, and it was literally strewed with baggage, so that a man might almost walk upon it without touching the ground."[7]

Throughout the rest of the day on the 16th, the Americans who had avoided death, wounding or capture continued streaming north either by roads, through woods, swamps and thorny wilderness paths. Totally unfamiliar with the Carolina countryside, swarms of Stevens's disgraced Virginians simply reversed course from their march south from Rugeley's Mill and beyond. Fractured units of Caswell's North Carolina militia, meanwhile, were more dispersed, bent on taking the shortest routes to their homes "as their hopes led."[8]

The myriad British war trophies that day included the wagons of heavy baggage, quartermaster stores and excess artillery supplies which Gates had ordered sent to the Waxhaws the previous evening but, for whatever unknown reason, remained with the army. "The general order for moving off" these wagons "was not put into execution, as directed to be done," Otho Williams recalled. "The whole of it, consequently, fell into the hands of the enemy; as well as all that which followed the army...." The wagons with the baggage and personal effects of Generals Gates and DeKalb, "being furnished with the stoutest horses, fortunately escaped under the protection of a small quarter guard."[9] Major Hanger of Tarleton's command added this interesting tidbit from the rout:

> Flushed with victory, and eager in pursuit, my arm was too well employed to allow much time for observation; but overtaking the wagon of DeKalb, on which was seated a monkey, fantastically dressed, I ceased to destroy, and addressing the affrighted animal, exclaimed, "You, Monsieur, I perceive, are a Frenchman and a gentleman." *Je vous donne la parole.*[10]

Gates

Shocked and swept up in the backwash of this nightmare, Gates rode for Charlotte, accompanied by General Caswell and their aides on the 90-mile journey from the battleground where his career had so quickly cascaded into ruin. A few miles into the ride, Gates encountered Major Davie and some of his troops who had been heading from Charlotte to reinforce the army—too late. Before seeing Gates, Davie's force had encountered a fleeing American soldier and arrested him as a deserter. The soldier told Davie of the defeat, Gates confirming the disheartening news. The general also told Davie to fall back because Tarleton would soon be upon them, based on various accounts. The major replied to the effect that he and his men were accustomed to Tarleton and did not fear him. The generals' party continued on, leaving the astonished Davie to contemplate his next move. Shortly thereafter, the major sent a rider to overtake Gates, Davie offering to go to the battlefield and bury the dead. Gates's answer was, "I say retreat! Let the dead bury the dead!" The ever-steady Davie also had the presence of mind to dispatch a messenger to Thomas Sumter, informing him of the defeat. The Gamecock received the news that evening, Gates and Caswell reaching Charlotte later that Wednesday night.[11]

Cornwallis

Tarleton's cavalry, meanwhile, had ridden like vengeful demons, hunting down the panicked enemy as far north as Hanging Rock, some 22 miles distant from the main action, before calling off the savage chase. "Immediately after the action every possible assistance was given to the wounded of both parties," related Tarleton. "The loyal militia were ordered to explore the adjacent woods, and to collect the disabled. Waggons were afterwards assembled, in which they were placed with care, in order to follow the principal [sp] part of the British army, which fell back to.... Camden." The fate of Isaac Gregory, the wounded North Carolina brigadier, remained somewhat murky due to conflicting information after the battle. Sources vary, some stating that he was captured while Cornwallis himself reported that Gregory was killed, which was erroneous. Likely the most accurate account is that British troops saw the general fall when his horse was shot down. Gregory appears to have suffered his bayonet wounds at that time, the Redcoats assuming that he was mortally injured and later leaving—or paroling—him on the field.[12]

After consoling the fallen DeKalb and issuing orders for his army's withdrawal to Camden, Cornwallis rode north toward Rugeley's Mill. Little more than 12 hours earlier, Gates's troops had marched south on this same route, the victor of Saratoga careless but confident of more martial laurels. Now, Cornwallis moved through the carnage of his conquered foe. The sand road was churned up, often blood stained, littered here and there with twisted American corpses and wounded men begging for help, many of them victims of the Green Dragoon's sabers. Dead horses and mules, muskets, swords, canteens, blankets, kettles, shards of uniforms, and other military accoutrements of every assortment were also scattered along the way. Occasional gunshots, screams and yells resounded from the woods on either side of the road where many of Gates's fugitives were still trying to avoid death or capture. Otho Williams wrote of Cornwallis:

> His victory was complete. All the artillery, and a very great number of prisoners, fell into his hands—many fine fellows lay on the field—and the rout of the remainder was entire—not even a company retired in any order—every one escaped as he could. The pursuit was more fatal to the rebels than the action [a British account added], it continued ... with unremitted ardor, the whole of which distance was strewed with dead and wounded bodies.[13]

"It was a hard-fought battle, and the victory not very cheaply purchased on the side of the British," wrote the Redcoat soldier John Shaw. Cornwallis's casualties amounted to 68 killed, including two officers, 245 wounded, including 18 officers, for a total—including 11 men missing—of 324. Webster's 33rd sustained the worst losses of any of Cornwallis's regiments engaged, losing Captain Allan Malcolm and 17 rank and file killed; Captain Richard Cotton, Lieutenants George Wynyard, James Leigh Harvey, Ensign John W. Collington, four sergeants and 72 rank and file wounded and one man missing. Webster, slightly wounded, completed the total. The Volunteers of Ireland suffered heavily as well, with 87 casualties, including 17 dead and 70 wounded. Lt. Col. Hamilton of the North Carolina Loyalists was another of the more notable wounded. Both he and Webster would recover from slight injuries to fight again. "The destruction fell principally upon the center, owing to the well-directed fire of the [C]ontinentals, and the execution done by the American artillery," Tarleton related of the hardest-hit regiments.[14]

The number of American casualties—even now, more than two centuries later—is unknown and can only be estimated, due to the army's collapse that day and the scattering of the soldiers afterward, especially the militia. A dearth of records contributes to the void. Writing to Lord Germain, Cornwallis claimed 800 to 900 Americans killed and about 1,000 captured, many of whom were wounded. These statistics were discredited in the 1929 battle study by Lt. Col. H.L. Landers of the U.S. Army War College, who wrote: "These numbers are so far from correct that they are valueless as a guide." Landers, who spent considerable time on the battlefield and examining pertinent records and other documents, estimated the Continentals' casualties at about three hundred, but did not even attempt to give a total for the militia losses, writing these men "broke early in the day and scattered in so many directions ... that very few were made prisoners." Renowned military historian Henry Lumpkin—in his fine 1981 work *From Savannah to Yorktown*, wrote that American casualties ranged from 683 to 733 killed, wounded and captured. Author Lucien Agniel in his 1972 book *Rebels Victorious*, gives the battle tally as "about 900" American dead and 1,000 prisoners taken.[15]

Regardless, any Camden battle casualty tallies also have to include losses incurred in the early morning clash.

A mixed procession of victorious, begrimed and exhausted Britons mingled with an equally drained but defeated throng of hundreds of gloomy American prisoners on the road from the battlefield to Camden. Among them were an untold number of sullen, worn-out Continentals and almost 400 of Caswell's militia, the latter not including up to 80 other wounded North Carolinians. As for the proud men and boys from Delaware and Maryland, it was four months to the day since they had marched proudly from their camps at Morristown, N.J., on their grueling journey south, a trek that ended for many of them in the grim carnage of Camden.

Couriers and officers galloped up and down the column, carrying orders and dispatches updating the latest, glorious news of Cornwallis's magnificent triumph. A Highlander who was credited with killing as many as seven Americans, claimed that his bayonet was "twisted like a corkscrew." Dozens of wagons extended the cavalcade, many bearing the seriously wounded, others with cargoes of every description, the vast booty wrenched from an enemy army leaving its bloodied soul and everything else as it was chased from the field. Twenty ammunition wagons were taken with a "large supply" of ordnance, "2,000 stand of arms" and a number of colors were also in British hands. An array of captured horses and mules, some pulling seven seized artillery pieces—an eighth gun, disabled, wedged in a wagon—also were in the procession. Some of the cannon were believed to have been captured by Gates at Saratoga, now rightfully returned by the might of the Crown's military. In one of the wagons lay Baron DeKalb, the highest ranked prize taken by the British that day. He was alive, barely; 11 savage wounds from bayonet, saber and bullets, as well as months of strenuous campaigning, were a massive toll to overcome.

An unidentified and seriously wounded American officer recalled that he was in a wagon starting toward Camden from the battlefield when a British sergeant from the 33rd Regiment peered in at him with "an expression of generous sympathy," saying, "You appear, Sir, severely injured, and much exhausted by the loss of blood. Take my canteen, its contents may revive and strengthen you." The officer accepted the "gift" and found that the canteen contained "wine of an excellent quality." The American never forgot the "benevolent Sergeant" but also mulled "how great the contrast with the condition of *our* unfortunates, who for many days previous to the battle, had not, even under the pressure of their greatest fatigues, been cheered with a single glass of spirits," referring to Gates's march to Camden.[16]

Cornwallis encamped at Rugeley's, awaiting the return of his cavalry.

With him were the light and Legion infantry, and the 23rd Regiment, all of whom were bloodied and exhausted from almost continuous marching since the previous night and fighting since early that morning. The veteran fuzileer Sgt. Roger Lamb of the 23rd had one of the most compelling stories of the day. Almost three years earlier—subtracting two months and a day, he noted—Lamb was captured during Gates's victory at Saratoga. The sergeant noted that he had "at length, the satisfaction of seeing the same general to whom his majesty's forces under Burgoyne surrendered, sustain a signal defeat." Lamb continued: "What were his feelings at that eventful moment! How did he bless that Providence which inspired him" to escape "and preserved him to be a partaker of that triumph which the soldier feels, when his sovereign's troops are victorious over his enemies! More especially when that victory was obtained in the hard fought field over a general whose former success at Saratoga, had been trumpeted from one end of America to the other, and who had injured the British name...."

The exultant but spent Legion horse reined in at Cornwallis's bivouac that afternoon. They would have a few hours to rest, but the Earl would soon have them back in action. Sumter was reported to be moving slowly up the Wateree and if Cornwallis could "but crush the Gamecock, he would bring his campaign to a glorious end."[17]

10

"The firmest troops in the field"

From an upstairs window of their home later that Wednesday, Sarah Kershaw and her children watched "with sad hearts" as victorious British soldiers returned from the Camden battle. Among the children was nine-year-old Mary Kershaw, who never forgot the epic scenes unfolding beyond the glass pane. Below, American prisoners were "driven like sheep" into the Kershaws' backyard "where barrels of water were brought in and dipped out to them in tin cups." The cacophony in the yard did not cease until long after midnight on the 17th. Meanwhile, the mansion was filled with prisoners and some wounded from both armies. Mary recalled one American in particular who was a fine fiddler and who "managed by merry tunes to enliven the dreary tedium of illness and captivity. The guards were suffered to listen outside the door, but, if one of them dared show his face inside, he was met with a volley of brickbats ... supplied the lamed musician by the little rebel Kershaw children." Mary also saw "many a poor soldier" buried in long trenches near the house.[1]

The gravely wounded DeKalb was taken to the post's general hospital, apparently located near the corner of Meeting and Broad streets. There, he and many others were attended by Dr. Isaac Alexander, an American army surgeon who was captured in the battle. "The fall of [De] Kalb decided the fortunes of the day, for the Americans were now without a leader," claimed a 19th-century biographer of the Baron. "The work begun by the bayonets of the British infantry was finished by the sabers of Tarleton's horse, who met with no resistance, owing to the want of cavalry on the side of the Continentals."

Another prize prisoner was the wounded brigadier Rutherford, whom Cornwallis described as "that violent and cruel incendiary" for inciting rebellion in North Carolina, adding that Rutherford's capture "has been a lucky circumstance." Another Redcoat officer was even more blunt than Cornwallis, describing Rutherford as "a perfect savage" notorious for his hatred of Loyalists. The British had left another North Carolina general, Isaac Gregory, on the field, bayonetted and presumably dying there. The Virginian Lt. Col. Charles Porterfield, seriously wounded in the opening night action, also was a prisoner, but had yet to be moved to Camden.[2]

Dr. Hugh Williamson of North Carolina was with Gates's army on the 16th and was caught up in the hadean exodus. Overtaking General Caswell, he was given a truce flag to "return to the Enemies' Lines for the relief of our wounded." He would soon realize that he was facing the most daunting task of his career. "I wish I could say that our loss after the Battle, either by wounds or sickness, was inconsiderable; but we labored under many difficulties," he later wrote. Amid the grim "difficulties" was the fact that the injured soldiers "Laboured under at least 700 Wounds."[3]

From 60 to 80—the number varies by accounts—wounded and captured North Carolina militiamen were taken into Camden compared to only two or three from Virginia. One North Carolinian made the point that Dixon's men "were the firmest troops in the field" and that "the whole of her militia would probably have stood their ground had it not been for the example of their neighbors"—the Virginia militia.[4]

Among the other captive wounded was 29-year-old Thomas Pinckney, who had been unable to escape after Major Magill placed him in a fleeing army wagon. Described as "one of the noblest of South Carolina's noble sons," the Charlestonian's younger brother Charles also was a well-known patriot, soldier, and judge. Thomas's wife of about a year was Elizabeth Motte, better known as Betsy, oldest daughter of Rebecca Brewton Motte, who would become one of South Carolina's most prominent Revolutionary War heroines. The Mottes owned a plantation, Mount Joseph, on the Congaree River near present-day St. Matthews, S.C. Thomas had previously served as an aide to General Lincoln at the siege of Savannah and fought well at Stono Ferry. In that battle he distinguished himself in fierce combat against the Seventy-first Highlanders.

In the Redcoats' ranks was Captain Charles Barrington McKenzie who had been a schoolmate of Pinckney in England before the war. Fate had soon brought the old friends together in another battle—Camden. It is unclear what happened to Pinckney between the time he was put in the wagon and when he was left on the field, possibly still in the wagon. At least one account states that McKenzie found the major "insensible, and had him removed to Camden with the wounded British soldiers."[5]

That night, Pinckney was taken to the home of a Mrs. Clay, described as a "patriotic lady," and was quietly laid in her piazza, the major refusing to disturb her sleep. In the morning, Mrs. Clay discovered what appeared to be a corpse at her door, but Pinckney soon revived, having earlier fainting from exhaustion and his injuries. McKenzie, meanwhile, obtained permission from Tarleton to bring the latter's regimental surgeon to treat Pinckney's wounds. "Something in the prisoner excited Tarleton's generous feelings," Pinckney's grandson, the Rev. Charles C. Pinckney, wrote in a biography of his grandfather. "He [Tarleton] ordered every attention to be paid him, sent him wine and other delicacies, proffered his purse" and, incredibly, offered to return four "fine bays" which he had confiscated from the Mottes' plantation.[6]

Cornwallis issued orders on Thursday, August 17, probably from the Kershaw House after returning from Rugeley's Mill, praising his army for the Camden triumph:

> My sense of gratitude and admiration for the behavior of the troops which I had the honour to command in the action of yesterday, is so great, that words cannot express my feelings. The determined intrepidity with which every soldier fought in that glorious field, proved his sincere affection to his king and country, and his resolution to maintain their rights, and revenge their injuries.

He went on to give special thanks to Rawdon and Webster for their "great assistance" and "for the courage and ability which they shewed in conducting their respective divisions." The Earl added accolades for Tarleton and Lt. John McLeod of the artillery "for the great service they performed on that important day." More compliments went to Lt. Col. Hamilton and his soldiers whose "ardour which was shewn by the young troops under his command, will, in future, be productive of the best consequences to the cause of Britain." McLeod was a rising star of the Crown's long arm, but Cornwallis's praise was bittersweet that day, as McLeod's second in command, Lieutenant William Marquois, was struggling to survive wounds sustained on the 16th. Sergeant Roger Lamb of the British 23rd was an Irishman who took great pride in the battle mettle of the sons of Erin: "In all the various engagements, which the safety, the honor, the interests of the empire have demanded, the Irish soldier has seldom, if ever, lagged behind in the career of glory." He added that after the Camden triumph, Rawdon was so proud of his own regiment, the Volunteers of Ireland, that he ordered a silver medal cast "and presented to several of his men who had signalized themselves in the action."[7]

None of this martial splendor was evident in the overcrowded hospital areas where the exhausted and overwhelmed Dr. Williamson labored over the dozens of suffering Americans. The stark fact that the battle was a humiliating disaster and rout for Gates's army—despite the gallantry of the Continentals and Dixon's North Carolinians—earned disrespect and disdain among the victorious Redcoats, he claimed; he related:

> It was our misfortune that the Countenance we showed immediately after the Battle was not calculated to Command that respect which is due to an army of

the United States. The Enemy was disposed to neglect us, and a victory which they greatly overrated did not seem to increase their Humanity. For eight or ten days after the Battle our people suffered under great neglect. We were also weak in Medical Help ... Our Militia Surgeon disappeared after the Battle, and the Commander-in-Chief [apparently meaning Cornwallis] had not yet turned his attention to the Wounded Prisoners. After the Bitterest Complaints and most urgent importunity our supplies became more liberal.[8]

Also aiding the American casualties was Dr. Thomas Charlton of Camden who had also assisted the wounded after the Waxhaws battle. In the coming days or weeks, Charlton continued his work in the British hospital, but was eventually accused of spying, the British burning his home. One of the Camden prisoners, Lieutenant Colonel Joseph Vaughan of the Delaware Continentals, also recognized the immediate need for more medical personnel and supplies. He wrote to Gates on the 17th:

> The situation of our wounded officers and Soldiers makes it necessary that Surgeons should be sent in to take care of them, and if the Medicine Chests should not be all taken, some medicine should be sent also. Not less than two surgeons will be sufficient to give the necessary attendance, and I intreat [sp] you to send them as soon as possible....[9]

British medical personnel were equally inundated in treating about 250 of the King's soldiers wounded in the battle. Their tasks, like those of their American counterparts, was complicated due to the ongoing and ominous smallpox infestation at Camden. "The British Camp generally contains the Seeds of Small Pox [sp]," Williamson related. "It had been in Camden for some time. We were not suffered even to inoculate those Men whose wounds would admit of that operation with safety." Days after the battle, Cornwallis told Clinton that the army's "sickness was very great, and truly alarming." He added that many of his officers were ill and his chief surgeon—Dr. John M. Hayes—and most of his assistants were stricken as well.

In addition to the Camden casualties, the Redcoats lost two officers who died of their wounds from the Hanging Rock battle. A Capt. Hewlett of the New York Volunteers "universally lamented as a brave and gallant officer" succumbed on the 15th, while Capt. Kenneth McCulloch of the British Legion infantry died on the 16th, the latter described as being "esteemed and beloved by his company, a tender and indulgent master, a polite gentleman and a dear friend...."[10]

William Allman was a wounded Virginia militiaman from Col. George Stubblefield's regiment who was captured in the battle and made some observations of what he saw in the British encampment. The time frame is unclear, but Allman escaped from Camden on or about September 9 and made his way to Hillsborough where he was questioned by army authorities 11 days later. Allman claimed that Cornwallis was in Camden when he fled and that three regiments of regulars—the 23rd, 33rd and the 71st—were in garrison, along with some 500 Loyalist soldiers "who all were wearing red rags in their hats for distinction." Allman also contended that Rawdon's Volunteers of Ireland were sent to retake Ninety Six, which had been seized by Pickens's partisans—totally inaccurate intelligence—and that most of Camden's artillery had been sent to the Charleston defenses. The American prisoners in Camden were issued one gill of "unsifted" meal with seldom any meat, "the wounded were very much neglected, and when they died, were suffered to lay until they stunk horribly, in the yard with the other prisoners," the Virginian noted. Some of the captured officers complained about this neglect of the dead, he added. A party had been sent to the Waxhaws to "thrash wheat and procure provisions" due to a lack of flour and a low supply of "Indian meal." The wounded general Rutherford "was recovering fast" and likely would be sent to the British post at Orangeburg with other officers, Allman reported, adding that he was "confident the enemy are very much in want of provisions, particularly of the bread kind."[11]

Cornwallis, meanwhile, also was bent on destroying the remnants of Gates's army as soon as possible. On the 17th, he dispatched orders from Camden to Loyalist leaders in North Carolina "with directions to our friends there to take arms and assemble immediately; and to seize the most violent people and all military stores and magazines belonging to the rebels, and to intercept all stragglers from the routed army." In this August 21 letter to Lord Germain, he added: "And I have promised to march without loss of time to their support. Some necessary supplies for the army are now on their way from Charleston; and I hope that their arrival will enable me to move in a few days." On a more ominous note, the Green Dragoon and his Legion rested a few hours overnight on the 16th-17th, preparing for their seek-and-destroy mission to annihilate Thomas Sumter's force.[12]

Gates

While the British celebrated in Camden on the morning of the 17th, the scene was vastly different in Charlotte, where Gates and Caswell had halted after their flight. Of the generals reaching Charlotte, Otho Williams wrote: "The ... morning presented nothing to them but an open village, with but few inhabitants, and the remains of a temporary hospital, containing a few maimed soldiers of Colonel Buford's unfortunate corps, which had been cut to pieces on the retreat, after the surrender of Charleston." Gates did not linger, riding out within hours for Hillsborough where the North Carolina Assembly was gathered. Gates and his little entourage stopped briefly in the Moravian village of Salem on Saturday, August 19; a local wrote, "General Gates and several officers breakfasted with us (at the home of a 'Mr. Kleinert') this morning, but seemed in haste."

When he arrived in Hillsborough that night, Gates had covered about 200 miles on his circuitous route from the Camden battlefield. On at least a portion of his retreat—if not all—the commander was astride a powerful horse sired by the famous racer *Fearnought*—irony noted. Caswell briefly remained in Charlotte to round up as many survivors of the mangled army as possible. For days after the Camden battle, the scattered remnants of Gates's army made their way north toward Charlotte, Hillsborough, Salisbury or anywhere else to escape either a continued pursuit or an anticipated enemy attack from Cornwallis's victorious forces.[13]

Thomas Pinckney felt well enough on August 18 to write to Gates, taking advantage of a truce flag to have the message delivered. The major, his leg wound still serious, requested that his "Servant, horse and Cloaths [sp]" be sent to him at Camden if possible. He noted:

> My Wound was dressed at [British] Head Quarters on the Day of the Action, where I received every Mark of kindness and Attention. I am likewise under great obligation to the officers in General ... for their Civility and Care of me. My wound is, as nearly as I recollect, in the same part of the Leg in which Genl. Lincoln receiv'd his; & tho' the bone is entirely shattered, I have hopes of retaining my Leg....

On the side of the letter was written: "A Private Soldier rode my Horse when I was put into a waggon." Fearing that this note had not reached Gates, Pinckney penned a similar letter to the general on August 24: "My Treatment has been humane, Politic & attentive from the British officers into whose Hands I have fallen, and my wound bears as favorable an aspect as could be expected...." Amid the other wounded Americans whom we are able to identify at Camden on the 18th was Lieutenant John Blair of the First Continental Artillery, struggling for his life. Blair's fellow Virginian, Lieutenant Samuel Coleman, also of the First, was killed in the battle, and Blair did not survive the day. Another artillerist in the First, Lieutenant William Wallace of Maryland, lay somewhere among the other wounded prisoners.[14]

11

"A prisoner of war ... with one of my legs quite broke by a musket ball"

"The fatigue of the troops rendered them incapable of further exertions on the day of the action [Camden on the 16th]; but.... I saw the importance of destroying or dispersing, if possible...." Sumter's force, "as it might prove a foundation for assembling the routed army...." Cornwallis wrote. Tarleton noted: "Though the late victory was complete ... there yet remained in South Carolina some troops under ... Sumter, well furnished with arms, and provided with cannon. The vicinity ... to the late scene of action ... afforded them opportunity to give refuge to the fugitives, and to augment their own numbers."

Thus on August 17, Cornwallis sent Tarleton and his Legion, along with Captain Charles Campbell's light infantry detachment—about 350 troops and a field gun—to attack Sumter wherever he could be found. A detachment led by Lt. Col. Turnbull and Major Patrick Ferguson was at Little River and was also sent to hunt down the Gamecock and his partisans. Riding from Rugeley's Mill early that morning, the Green Dragoon and his command were still exhausted from their combat exertions the day before, but Tarleton "executed this service with his usual activity and military address," Cornwallis noted of the operation against Sumter.[1]

His Legion soldiers plunging through lush woods and murky swamps east of the Wateree River, Tarleton pondered his best options to find, surprise and obliterate Sumter. His troops picked up 20 or so scattered Continentals along the way, and by that Thursday afternoon "gained intelligence" that Sumter was retreating on the river's west side. Learning of Gates's defeat, Sumter had immediately begun moving out of striking distance of the British in the Camden vicinity. His column was encumbered by about 250 prisoners and a number of enemy supply wagons, most, if not all, seized in the Wateree Ferry raid on August 15. The Gamecock marched with "so much dispatch, that, thinking himself already out of danger" encamped his exhausted troops on the north side of Fishing Creek, near Rocky Mount—about 30 miles from Camden—early on the 18th to rest the men and horses "with some repose during the heat of the day." His force consisted of about 800 soldiers and two cannon, still including Woolford's Continentals and North Carolina militia sent to him from Gates's army before the Camden battle.

Like Buford at the bloody Waxhaws in May, the Gamecock vastly underestimated the speed, raw determination and naked aggression of a pursuer hell-bent on his destruction—this was Tarleton. With his characteristic "forced and concealed marches," the Green Dragoon closed in on Sumter, but as had been the case in his chase of Buford, physical punishment and heat had affected more than half of his force which was "overpowered with fatigue." Thus, with some 160 of his strongest troops, he surprised and attacked the Gamecock's camp about 2 p.m. on the afternoon of Friday, August 18.[2]

The British slashed into the "extensive" bivouac where most of Sumter's men were literally caught napping, cooking or washing in the creek, their muskets stacked. Another British account stated that at the time of the assault, some of Sumter's men were gathering peaches in an orchard and that the Gamecock himself was generously doling out a gill of captured rum and other provisions to the prisoners. There was a brief, weak resistance, a few Americans firing at the rampaging horsemen from behind the wagons, before being overwhelmed. In an orgy of savagery, about 150 of the Gamecock's troops were killed or wounded "on the spot" and another 300 or so prisoners were taken, including Woolford and the militia Lt. Col. Isaacs. The Redcoats seized Sumter's two brass fieldpieces and recovered 44 of the British wagons, taking 1,000 muskets and two ammunition wagons as well. Tarleton also freed about 100 Brits taken in Sumter's various actions and released another "150 of our militia-men or friendly country people seized by the rebels." Sumter himself narrowly escaped death or capture, his force "totally destroyed or dispersed," the Gamecock reaching Charlotte two days later.

Cornwallis described the British casualties as "trifling,"—nine killed and six wounded—other than the significant loss of Captain Campbell, slain in the latter stages of the fighting. Little more than 48 hours earlier, Campbell had led his troops through the deadliest brambles of combat at Camden. "His death cannot be mentioned without regret," wrote Tarleton. "He was a young officer, whose conduct and abilities afforded the most flattering prospect that he would be an honor to his country." Cornwallis also mentioned Campbell's demise in his August 21 letter to Germain, describing him as "a very promising officer" who was "unfortunately killed in this affair."[3]

The American captives, including a number of wounded, were soon on the march. "The prisoners were conducted to Camden, and there treated with civility," wrote the Brit soldier John Shaw, who apparently was not engaged at Fishing Creek. In the long column was Colonel Thomas Taylor, slightly wounded, and his brother, Captain James Taylor, both from the Camden region. Col. Taylor had led Sumter's raid on Wateree Ferry. Capt. Taylor wasn't expecting any of the "civility" mentioned by Shaw. The captain was paroled when Charleston fell in May. Having violated his terms by returning to service, he likely faced the hangman's noose if he was taken before Cornwallis at Camden. The Taylors managed to escape at some point in the slow, three-day trek, the Colonel smearing blood from his wound on his hands and face making him appear less likely to bolt from the column. Still, the arrival of the Fishing Creek captives further strained the already overcrowded British facilities in Camden, including the prison pens and medical units.

The number of wounded prisoners brought into Camden after the fighting on August 16 and 18—the latter from Fishing Creek—was 240, related Dr. Hugh Williamson, the North Carolina physician. Of these, there were 162 Continental soldiers, 12 South Carolina militiamen, three of Stevens's Virginia militia, and 63 of Caswell's North Carolinians. Fearing that these additional prisoners—wounded as well as uninjured—might further aggravate the rampant malaria and smallpox already savaging the post, Cornwallis made immediate plans to transfer numbers of them to Charleston. "I therefore sent them off as early as possible, by Divisions of 150 each," he wrote to General Clinton. One of the first—if not *the* first—procession to leave Camden for the coast consisted of 150 Maryland Continentals, a mix of whom were captured at Camden and Fishing Creek.[4]

Sumter's catastrophe at Fishing Creek was slightly offset that same day by a minor American triumph at Musgrove's Mill on the Enoree River near present-day Cross Anchor, S.C., but this action by backwoods militia from the Carolinas and Georgia was certainly overshadowed by Tarleton's rout of the Gamecock. Sumter and his escort "were amusing themselves in a wood on a nutting party," before Tarleton struck, "killing or securing most of the enemy's detachment," a derisive article in the pro–British *Rivington's Gazette* stated.[5]

Within hours of the Fishing Creek fight, a Redcoat officer reached Charleston that Friday afternoon—the 18th—with news of the "most complete and decisive victory" of Cornwallis at Camden.

> At sunset, the troops in garrison were paraded, the cannon in the batteries and a feu de joy fired, attended with the acclamations of the soldiers and numerous spectators; joy beamed in every countenance but those of the adherents to the late usurpation, whose lengthened visages denoted their inward grief. In

the evening there was as general an illumination as the shortness of the notice could admit; but on the following one [Saturday] it was more universal, notwithstanding the badness of the weather.[6]

The crushing conquests at Camden and Fishing Creek convinced Cornwallis that he was well on track toward quelling the rebellion in the Southern provinces. He wrote on August 21:

> The rebel forces being at present dispersed, the internal commotions and insurrections in the province will now subside. But I shall give directions to inflict exemplary punishment on some of the most guilty, in hopes to deter others in [the] future from tampering with allegiance, with oaths, and with the lenity and generosity of the British Government.

Cornwallis was right in the sense that major resistance by the Americans had been snuffed out, but he had yet to realize that the partisans, particularly under Marion, Davie and even Sumter, despite Fishing Creek, were strengthening, while Loyalist recruitment was waning. Deciding that an iron fist was his best reaction, he issued this directive to his post commanders a few days after Camden:

> I have given orders that all inhabitants of this Province who have subscribed and have taken part in the revolt should be punished with the greatest rigour [sp]; and also those who will not turn out that they may be imprisoned and their whole property taken from them or destroyed. I have likewise ordered that compensation should be made out of their estates to the persons who have been injured or oppressed by them. I have ordered in the most positive manner that every militiaman who has borne arms with us and afterwards joined the enemy shall be immediately hanged. I desire you will take the most rigorous measures to punish the rebels in the district in which you command, and that you obey in the strictest manner the directions I have given....

Among the unknown number of unfortunates hanged at Camden during this period were Samuel Andrews, Richard Tucker, John Miles, Josiah Gayle and Eleazer Smith. Others were executed at the various British outposts, slaves encouraged and permitted "to accuse their masters."[7]

Gates, DeKalb and Porterfield

As Gates rode for Hillsborough, DeKalb finally succumbed to his wounds on August 19. Du Buysson was at his bedside, "assisted by the English officers in soothing the last moments of the dying hero." Based on many accounts, the Baron weakly expressed his gratitude to these former enemies, whom he had battled so fiercely: "I thank you for your generous sympathy, but I die the death I always prayed for: the death of a soldier fighting for the rights of man." Even as his life faded, the Baron's thoughts were with the courageous, defiant Continentals whom he had led with cold steel and an iron will three days earlier, telling Du Buysson to relay his admiration and appreciation to Gist and Smallwood. One of the Baron's biographers noted:

> [DeKalb] was buried by his victorious adversaries, among whom there were many free masons, with military and masonic honors. [His] loss was felt, and much lamented, by the American army; and, during his short intercourse with the British officers, though wounded and a prisoner, he made a very favorable and deep impression on them, by the amiability of his character, his patience and magnanimity in suffering, and the excellence of his heart.

Seven-year-old Mary Kershaw claimed to witness "the interment of Baron DeKalb, who, she said, was buried with his sword beside him, between two British officers."[8]

The general was buried along what is now Meeting Street near its intersection with Church Street and near the site of the Old Presbyterian Meeting House and Burying Ground. Du Buysson, meanwhile, recovered enough from his own wounds to be released by his captors a few days after the Baron's passing. He was in Charlotte by August 26, and that day wrote a letter to Gist and Smallwood based on DeKalb's dictation to him.

> Dear Generals:
>
> Having received several wounds in the action of the 16th instant, I was made a prisoner with the honorable Major-General the Baron DeKalb, with whom I served as aid-de-camp and friend, and had an opportunity of attending that great and good officer during the short time he languished with eleven wounds, which proved mortal on the third day.
>
> It is with pleasure I obey the Baron's last commands in presenting his most affectionate compliments to all the officers and men of his division; he expressed the greatest satisfaction in the testimony given by the British army of the bravery of his troops, and he was charmed with the firm opposition they made to superior force when abandoned by the rest of the army. The gallant behavior of the Delaware regiment and the companies of artillery attached to the brigades, afforded him infinite pleasure, and the exemplary conduct of the whole division, gave him an endearing sense of the merit of the troops he had the honor to command.
>
> I am, dear generals, with regard and respect,
>
> Your most obedient humble servant,
> LE CHEVALIER DU BUYSSON[9]

About this same time, the severely wounded Lt. Col. Porterfield lay in increasingly desperate need of medical attention, still at the rural home of a woman named Judy Brown near Rugeley's Mill. His urgency and helplessness are starkly evident in a letter penned to General Gates on August 20:

> Sir: I am now at this place a prisoner of war on parole, with one of my legs quite broke by a musket ball, & without any surgeon to attend me. I have been here since Wednesday last [the day of the battle] being only once visited by a surgeon from the Maryland line, a prisoner. The British officers [at Rugeley's] have treated me with the utmost attention & politeness, & have furnished me with such necessaries as in their power; also have wrote To Camden in my behalf, but I expect no surgeon can be spared. As my life in this season depends on speedy relief, I have to pray a surgeon skilled be sent To attend [me] for some Time. This, I hope, will be granted, as every indulgence seems to be the wish of those under whose direction I am.

The Virginian's torturous journey was only beginning.[10] Even as Porterfield pleaded for help that day, Gates remained at Hillsborough, crafting his own letter that would likely be the most difficult of his military career. "In the deepest distress and anxiety of mind, I am obliged to acquaint your [E]xcellency with the defeat of the troops under my command," he wrote to Samuel Huntington, President of the Continental Congress, on August 20. He went on to offer a brief description of the battle (earlier incorporated into this narrative) before continuing:

> The militia having taken [to] the woods in all directions, I concluded, with General Caswall, [sp] to retire towards Charlotte. I got here late in the night; but reflecting there was no prospect of collecting a force at that place adequate to the defense of the country, I proceeded with all possible dispatch hither, to endeavor to fall upon some plan of defense, in conjunction with the legislative body of the state. I shall immediately dispatch a flag to Lord Cornwallis, to know the situation of our wounded, and the number and condition of the prisoners in his hands.

The report was first taken to Virginia Governor Thomas Jefferson, then relayed to Huntington in Philadelphia, Colonel Senf and Major Magill being the messengers. These officers were chosen due to their loyalty to Gates and because they could "answer any questions and clear up any doubt" from Congress. Notwithstanding his manpower losses, Gates painted a bleak picture regarding the army's equipment situation, noting that his artillery was captured, entrenching tools were lost and "most assuredly the small arms are gone, for those that the enemy did not take are carried off by the militia." Gates also pointed out the titanic difficulties his troops suffered for weeks—even months—before even going into battle on the 16th: "Famine, want of tents for the militia, and of every comfort necessary for the troops in this unwholesome climate, has, no doubt, in a degree, contributed to our ruin."[11]

> Gates was under no illusions that he would be retained in army command; the few hours of demoralizing and wholesale defeat at Camden certainly offset the glories of Saratoga, the repercussions of the former quite possibly resulting in

the Americans losing the war, even with the French intervention. Yet while he still held the sword of leadership, Gates vowed to do what he could to reconstruct the army. He wrote to Caswell on August 22:

While I continue in office, [I] will exert my utmost to serve the public interest, but as unfortunate generals are most commonly recalled, I expect that will be my case, and some other Continental general of rank sent in my place to command. When he arrives, I shall give him every advice and information in my power; in the meantime, I doubt not, Sir, that the candor and friendship that has subsisted between us, will continue, and that you are infinitely superior to the ungenerous custom of the many who, without benefitting themselves, constantly hunt down the unfortunate.[12]

A faint glimmer of hope seeped from the clouds of defeat on August 25 when Marion and his partisans surprised an enemy party escorting more than 150 American prisoners from Camden to Charleston. The Loyalists' bivouac was in and around Thomas Sumter's main home (the other burned by Tarleton in May) at Great Savannah near the Santee River and a few miles from Nelson's Ferry. The raiders noisily pounded into the British camp at dawn, trying to make the startled Redcoats believe they were being attacked by a superior force. The ruse worked, the guards dropping their muskets. The prisoners—most of them Maryland and Delaware Continentals—were thankful to be freed, but even this minor victory was sullied. Some of the soldiers were sick; others wanted to try to rejoin their comrades with Gates in North Carolina. Still others insisted that as prisoners of war they should be allowed to continue on to Charleston.[13]

Moravian settlers in Salem, N.C., watched a seemingly endless column of Gates's men trudge through the town on August 21. "All day soldiers and wagoners [sp] were passing, who had been in the battle near Pinetree," an unidentified Moravian—possibly Bishop Graff, mentioned earlier—noted, using Camden's former name. "Most of them were on foot, hungry and without money, and bread was given to some." Word had spread through the village two days earlier that the "English" had routed the American army, capturing 400 wagons. This caused great concern among the Moravians since wagons from the nearby settlements of Bethabara and Bethania had been trying to reach Gates's troops with a supply of meal, leaving on or about August 9. "The Daily Texts during these days have seemed to suggest trouble and difficult circumstances, such as they may be obliged to undergo," the writer related. The soldiers retreating on the 21st also brought news of Sumter's Fishing Creek disaster. Continental Major John Armstrong, Jr., so heavily engaged in the overnight skirmish opening the Camden battle, arrived with other officers in Salem on the 22nd. They offered more details of the Camden defeat, including the capture of Griffith Rutherford, the North Carolina militia brigadier. "An attempt will be made to gather the scattered troops, and half the militia are to be called out," the Moravian scribe noted. "The people are in the extreme of fright because of the English. In the meeting for communicants Br. Reichel spoke on the Text: 'In the world ye shall have tribulation, but be of good cheer, I have overcome the world.'"[14]

In Camden six days after the battle, Dr. Williamson remained in woeful need of even the most basic supplies, including clothing, for his patients. The British physician general, Doctor MacNamara Hays (also called the Inspector of Rebel Hospitals), had apparently ordered supplies but they had not yet arrived, prompting Williamson to write him on August 24:

> Sir: The Articles you was [sp] so kind as to order have not been received. Our ... patients are near 250, many of them dangerously Wounded. They are lodged in six small wards, without straw or Covering. Two of them have not any Cloaths besides a Shirt and pair of trowsers. In the six Wards they have only 4 small Kettles, and no Canteen, Dish, or Cup, or other Utensil. We have hardly any Medicine, not an ounce of Lint, Tow, or Digestine; not a single Bandage or Poultice Cloath, nor an ounce of meal to be used for Poultices. In a word, nothing is left for us but the painful Circumstances of viewing wretches who must soon perish if not relieved.[15]

The awful conditions for the wounded Americans had not improved much, if at all, five days later when partisan Major William Davie received intelligence of their plight. Davie had led a force of about 100 men on a foray a few miles below Hanging Rock toward Camden and wrote to General Caswell on the 29th about conditions in the town. "Our poor wounded ... are in a most wretched situation. Colonel Wilson told me General Rutherford had no surgeon but himself, and that many of them had never been dressed. Something should be done for them—it is cruel." Davie described Rutherford as "a valuable officer of the most extensive influence over the North Carolina militia...."[16]

Camden was still so overwhelmed with prisoners, including the wounded and sick, that Cornwallis continued transferring many of them to Charleston and also to at least one of his other posts in the interior. He related that Camden was "so crowded and so sickly, I was afraid that the close place in which we were obliged to confine them might prove some pestilential fever during the excessive hot weather." To this end, Lt. Humphrey Hunter and about 50 other captured officers were transferred to the British post at Orangeburg after spending seven days in the Camden prison yard. Hunter was the North Carolina militiaman who claimed to have witnessed DeKalb's fall and treatment by the Redcoats on the battlefield. Without a hat or coat, Hunter spent almost three months imprisoned at Orangeburg before he was paroled on November 13. Thomas

Woolford the Continental colonel captured at Fishing Creek, wrote to his brother, James, from Camden on August 24, telling him of his unfortunate circumstances.

> I take this opportunity to inform you that I was on the 18th ... made Prisoner of war whence I received Four wounds none of which are mortal. I Had the misfortune to loose [sp] all of my baggage and no money will replace it but Hard [coins.] You will please therefore to Colect [sp] what hard money you can and send it by Cap[t] Gassaway who is Come For that purpose. I send you 1900 Dollars which you will please to Exchange For Hard money. Should be glad you would send me as Large a Sum as you can. No more at present only my Love to all friends....[17]

Still, Cornwallis remained intent on moving into North Carolina as quickly as possible after the Camden victory, but "the weakness of his army, and, above all, the want of transport, greatly delayed him," noted Charles Ross, one of his staff officers. Ross blamed General Clinton for this shortage, claiming that Clinton took "most" of the wagons and heavy horses with him when he sailed for New York from Charleston in June, "without even informing Lord Cornwallis of what he had done." At least one 19th-century historian advanced the opinion that Cornwallis's decision not to immediately move in to North Carolina was a mortal blow to the Crown's Southern campaign. Had "Cornwallis followed up his victory by marching at once into North Carolina the last of the Southern States ... might have been overrun, but in the exuberance ... over the defeat of the conqueror of Burgoyne ... and the subjection of South Carolina, he lost his energy and judgment and sat down to secure and organize the territory he had won, rather than add to his conquests," wrote David Schenck, author of an 1889 history of the Carolinas military operations, primarily in North Carolina. "Tardiness was the weakness of Cornwallis."[18]

It is hard to make this argument hold water, since Cornwallis on August 17 dispatched messengers to the North Carolina Loyalists to finally take action against "rebel" storehouses and magazines and seize stragglers from Gates's defeated force at Camden. By August 23, he had not received any response to these directives. "I have not yet heard any accounts from North Carolina," he penned to Clinton from Camden that day, "but I hope that our friends will immediately take arms, as I have directed them to do.... The troops here have gained reputation, but they have lost numbers.... It is difficult to form a plan of operations, which must depend so much on circumstances...."[19]

There also was little "tardiness" in Cornwallis's execution of the Camden battle. Outmanned and with some 800 soldiers ill, he also realized that retreat from his vital inland outpost was not an option and would, indeed, blunt British momentum in securing the province after the stirring capture of Charleston. In need of supplies, equipment, horses and with troops sick or otherwise affected by hard marches and fighting in the Carolina furnace, Cornwallis also had to consider the always fluctuating sentiments of the local people and if he could depend on the Crown's North Carolina "friends" to rise in arms or help feed his army on the move. Knowing all this, it is hard to criticize Cornwallis for not being more aggressive on the heels of a major triumph at Camden and then taking the offensive—as he eventually did—as will be seen.

On August 17–18, about 150 exhausted, hungry soldiers of Gates's army straggled in to Charlotte, but this was no solace to any of them. Gates was gone—again—riding for Hillsborough. There were few, if any, supplies or provisions in the town and no defenses constructed to prevent a knowingly relentless enemy from attacking and destroying them. With Charlotte untenable, it was decided that the army should retreat to Salisbury, some 40 miles distant. "We assembled at Salisbury, the few that were left, Genl. Smallwood having taken command of them, this being the first place we made any halt since the action" at Camden, the Delaware soldier William Seymour noted. He had seen firsthand some of the grim results of Cornwallis's August 17 orders for Loyalists to apprehend Gates's soldiers fleeing after Camden: "Here was a most shocking scene to behold, our poor scattered troops everywhere dispersed through the country, and the Tories, every day picking them up, taking everything from them which was of any value." Many of the exhausted and demoralized Americans were in awful shape, hungry, a great number almost naked and others who had lost or discarded their weapons. Seymour also lamented the sacrifice of his fellow Continentals who had been assigned to Thomas Sumter on August 15 only to be caught up in the Fishing Creek calamity. "Here was another scene of misery to see about one hundred and thirty of our Continental troops ... all killed, wounded and taken prisoners...."[20]

Kershaws

With Joseph and Ely Kershaw aboard, the schooner *Savannah* reached the Bahamas in late August or early September after a three-week voyage from Charleston. The brothers were detained by the British at Nassau for several more weeks, waiting to be sent to Bermuda where they were to be exiled. Ely's health was no better and in fact had been aggravated by the long sea journey. In Charleston, their other brother William continued to prosper as a merchant in the British-held provincial capital. The coming four months would forever alter the fates of the three, all immersed in the cauldron of the Revolution.

Despite the Camden victory, the addition of French military might in the war made the overall situation in the colonies slide from bad to worse for the British. General Clinton wrote as much in an August 25 message to Lord George Germain:

> At this new epoch of the war, when a foreign force has already landed, and an addition to it is expected, I owe it to my country, and I must in justice say to my own fame, to declare ... that I become every day more sensible of the utter impossibility of prosecuting the war in this country without reinforcements.... We are, by some thousands, too weak to subdue this rebellion.[21]

Cornwallis, however, remained adamant and optimistic in his goal of advancing north: "I hope to move my first division in eight or nine days into North Carolina by Charlotte and Salisbury," he wrote to Clinton from Camden on August 29;

> the second [division] will follow in about ten days after, with convalescents and stores. I shall leave the New York [V]olunteers and [Lt. Col. Alexander] Innes's corps [of the South Carolina Royalists] to take care of this place [Camden] until the sick and stores can be removed. Our sickness at present is rather at a stand [standstill], the recoveries nearly keeping pace with the falling down. I dread the convalescents not being able to march; but it is very tempting to try it, as a move of forty or fifty miles would put us into a much better climate.

In this same dispatch Cornwallis's optimism dimmed even more in describing the overall response from North Carolina Loyalists to his August 17 orders to openly oppose the rebels. "We receive the strongest professions of friendship from North Carolina," he told Clinton. "Our friends however, do not seem inclined to rise until they see our army in motion." Another worry for the British was that Thomas Sumter was active again, regrouping after his disaster at Fishing Creek. At least one Loyalist newspaper reported the Gamecock killed in the battle, but this was wrong, sadly for the Redcoats. The "indefatigable Sumter is again in the field, and is beating up for recruits with the greatest assiduity," Cornwallis wrote to Clinton.[22]

In Camden about this time, a group of some 300 to 400 uninjured North Carolinians from Caswell's command who were captured on August 16, were sent to Charleston, Dr. Hugh Williamson concerned about their susceptibility to smallpox. "There is, I presume, the utmost danger of those Men taking the Disease in the Natural way, unless they are inoculated," he wrote on August 30 to Major Richard England, Cornwallis's acting deputy adjutant general. "Be so kind as to inform me whether Lord Cornwallis is willing those Troops should be inoculated, and by whom he wishes it should be done. You will excuse the mention I have made of this subject, but having the chief Medical Care of the Troops of that State, I conceive it is my duty." Williamson received a brief but polite response on September 1: "Sir: I have Lord Cornwallis's orders to acquaint you that, with respect to the American prisoners sent to Charleston being inoculated, his Lordship will give proper orders." Of this correspondence, Williamson recalled, "nothing could be expected." On September 7, 18 other North Carolina militiamen were recovered enough from their Camden wounds to be transferred to Charleston, Williamson related. Nine others healed enough to escape "at different times" At some point, possibly in late August or early September, Williamson was aided by an unidentified Continental surgeon captured by the British and sent to Camden, but Williamson remained inundated. "It may be supposed that with his assistance, tho' he was indefatigable, I found it impossible to give the desired help" to so many. More help arrived, however when after "three weeks we were happily reinforced by Dr. Johnson, a Senior Surgeon of great skill & Humanity in the Continental Service."[23]

The victories over Gates and then Sumter at Fishing Creek seemed to awaken the British to the threat of future enemy attacks on Camden. Realizing most of the town lay on open ground with very few natural barriers, Cornwallis ordered construction of perimeter defenses to protect the outpost. The engineer officer Haldane was tasked with this project, using troops and slaves requisitioned from the area. Many of the laborers were laid low by sickness thus slowing the work and supply issues undoubtedly plagued Haldane's efforts as well.[24]

Stunned by Gates's debacle, George Washington placed blame for the Camden disaster squarely on the reliance on the militia in a front-line combat role. "The shock was the greater as the operations a few days preceding the action were much in our favor," he wrote. "The behavior of the Continental troops does them infinite honor." His criticism of the American militia in general and especially at Camden, however, was blistering. "I solemnly declare I never was witness to a single instance that countenances an opinion of Militia or raw troops being fit for the real business of fighting," he noted in a letter to New York Governor George Clinton on October 18, 1780.

> I have found them useful as light parties to skirmish ... but incapable of making or sustaining a serious attack. This firmness is only acquired by habits of discipline and service. I mean not to detract from the merit of the Militia. Their zeal and spirit upon a variety of occasions have entitled them to the highest applause, but it is of the greatest importance we should learn to estimate them rightly. We may expect everything from men that Militia is capable of, but we must not expect from [them] any services for which Regulars alone are fit. The late battle at Campden [sp] is a melancholy comment on the

doctrine. The Militia fled at the first fire, and left the Continental troops, surrounded ... and overpowered by numbers, to combat for safety instead of Victory. The enemy themselves have witnessed to their valor.

What Washington did not mention was that Gates made the decision to post the Virginia and North Carolina militiamen in his front line, facing Cornwallis's Redcoats.[25]

"We owe all our misfortune to the Militia," Major Magill, one of Gates's staff officers, wrote in a similar vein, "had they not run like dastardly cowards, our Army was sufficient to cope with theirs, drawn up as we were upon a rising and advantageous ground." While much disdain over the years has been heaped on the militia, especially Stevens's men, for the Camden debacle, Otho Williams, however, seems to spread the blame: "If in this affair the militia fled too soon, the regulars may be thought as blamable for remaining too long on the field; especially after all hope of victory must have been despaired of." Surprisingly, since he was there, Williams failed to take into account the weather conditions, coupled with the suddenly billowing clouds of black powder smoke from hundreds of muskets and small arms, as well as artillery, and the likely dripping humidity of South Carolina in mid–August. Officers and soldiers on both sides noted this very real fog of war. DeKalb himself fought in confusion, believing the Americans were winning the battle despite the militia's loss. Plainly speaking, he couldn't see what was happening around him other than in the violent pocket where he, Gist and their steely Continentals were engaged.[26]

There was a much different—and lighter—take on the other side, an impish wag with the British-backed New York *Royal Gazette* offering this satirical piece about the Camden battle:

> Millions! Millions! Millions! Reward, strayed, deserted or stolen from the Subscriber on the 16th of August last near Cambden [sp] in the State of South Carolina a whole Army, consisting of Horse, foot, and Dragoons, to the amount of near 10,000 as has been said—with all their Bagage, Artillerie, Waggons, and Camp Equipage. The subscriber has very strong Suspicions from Information received, from his aid de Camp, that a certain Charles Earl Cornwallis was principally concerned in carrying off the said Army with their Bagage etc. Any Person or Persons civil or military, who will give information either to the Subscriber, or to Charles Thompson Esq. Secretary to the Continental Congress, where the said Army is, so that they may be recovered and rallied again, shall be entitled to demand from the treasurer of the united States the sum of three Millions of Paper Dollars as soon as they can be spared from the public funds, and another Million for apprehending the Persons principally concerned in taken the said Army of proper Passes will be granted by the President of the Congress to such Persons as incline to go in search of the said Army—and as a further Encouragement, no Deduction will be made from the

above Reward on account of any of the Militia who composed Part of the said Army—not being to be found or heard of, as no Dependence can be placed on their services and nothing but the most speedy flight can ever save their Commander. Horatio Gates, M.-General and late Commander-in-Chief of the Southern Army.[27]

Rivington's Gazette added: "Mr. Gates was, at the above disastrous crisis, in an indifferent state of health, his complaint a diarrhoea [sp]; his person was disguised in the retreat," adding that his officers were likely requesting a court-martial for "their commanding officer on the ever-memorable but calamitous 16th of August." The American statesman Alexander Hamilton viciously piled on as well, writing: "Was there ever such an instance of a general running away … from his whole army? And was there ever so precipitous a flight? … It does admirable credit to the activity of a man at his time of life."[28]

12

"We made our retreat like lost sheep"

Horatio Gates was still in the early stages of trying to reassemble his army at Hillsborough in early September, many of his strewn soldiers first making their way to Charlotte and Salisbury, the latter about 90 miles to the southwest. Fortunately for him, the British had cooperated, so to speak, in not embarking on any aggression against the Americans, the "Enemy remaining still and the Disaffected doing nothing of Consequence to disturb us," he wrote to George Washington on September 3. By August 27, there were 234 Continentals at Hillsborough and two days later about 700 Marylanders, among other soldiers, had returned to the army. Additionally, some 1,400 new North Carolina militia were operating in the territory between Salisbury and Charlotte, the latter place serving as a base for Thomas Sumter's force, "which occasionally acts upon the West Side of the Wateree, and has hitherto given such a jealousy to the British in Camden as to keep them at Home."

A detachment of 300 "Virginia riflemen" were also on the move and Brigadier General Stevens "with what have not run home" at the outset of the battle of Camden, was at Guilford Court House with his regrouped Virginians. Still, many of Stevens's troops were nearing the expiration of their enlistments and soon afterward discharged. The valiant Marylanders and Delaware Continentals who had managed to claw their way out at Camden were at Hillsborough as well, refitting and being reorganized, as was the artillery. Due to losses, however, the two brigades were combined into one regiment of two battalions.

Major Archibald Anderson would lead the First Battalion consisting of the First, Third, Fifth and Seventh Maryland. Major Henry Hardman's Second Battalion was composed of the Second, Fourth and Sixth Maryland, along with the Delaware Regiment. The Blue Hens were divided into two companies headed by captains Robert Kirkwood and Peter Jacquett. Colonel Otho Williams, who had performed so admirably in the Camden battle, commanded the regiment.[1]

Gates also had received word that about 500 Virginia Continentals were on the march from Petersburg, Virginia, to Hillsborough, telling Washington that these men, along with the Maryland and Delaware contingents, "will make us stronger in Continental troops than I was before the action" at Camden. The cavalry arm—basically non-existent at Camden, other than a handful of horsemen in Armand's Legion—also was being upgraded and equipped under the direction of lieutenant colonels William Washington and Anthony White. Washington commanded the cavalry troop, although it remained a small contingent. Gates also added two fieldpieces to the other few guns in his artillery park. The Americans' ranks were soon augmented from other avenues, including some Virginians of Abraham Buford's ill-starred command who had escaped the bloody nightmare at Waxhaws in May. Other Virginia troops—light infantrymen who had fought at Camden—also came in, still unsure about the fate of their commander, Lt. Col. Charles Porterfield, who had been severely wounded there and possibly dead or captured.[2]

The late DeKalb's loyal aide Le Chevalier Du Buysson also was on scene and soon on his way north to see General Washington. Gates described him as a "most amiable young officer" who, recovered from his wounds, had been paroled by Cornwallis and permitted to travel to Philadelphia. "All the Baron's baggage and Papers are saved; they are delivered to Colonel Dulyson [sp] who will be responsible for them," Gates wrote. "Too much honor cannot be paid by Congress to the Memory of the Baron DeKalb, who was everything an Excellent Officer should be, and in the Cause of the United States has sacrificed his life." Washington would later write to Du Buysson in praise of the Baron: "The manner in which he died fully justified the opinion which I ever entertained of him, and will endear his memory to the country."[3]

Gates had done an admirable job in piecing together his broken army in these initial stages, but the howling shadows of Camden hung over him like the Sword of Damocles, his battle laurels from Saratoga, long ago withered into so much wind-stirred dust.

By early September, Major General Nathanael Greene had received enough information—including a letter from Gates—to piece together an account of the Camden battle, and wrote:

> Our militia gave way [at] the first fire, and left the Continental troops to bear the brunt of the whole of the enemy's force, which they did with great spirit and bravery.... General Gates made several unsuccessful attempts to rally the militia, but they were so panic struck, it was all to no purpose, and the general was borne away ... and had the mortification to leave the Maryland line bravely engaged, without having it in his power to assist them, or even to tell what was their fate, but as the firing ceased after he had got eight to ten miles

in the rear, he supposes they must have been cut to pieces. This is a great misfortune.... It is high time for America to raise an army for the war, and not distress the country by short enlistments....

Greene, it will be recalled, was George Washington's choice to replace General Lincoln after Charleston was captured. Without consulting Washington, Congress appointed Gates, and the rest, as they say, is history. Within a few weeks of writing this letter, Greene would be blazing his own path in the saga of Revolutionary War Camden.[4]

McCalla

Possibly the most amazing woman in Camden's colonial epic was Sarah McCalla, who stood up to Cornwallis and Rawdon at the risk of her own life. Marital devotion and love fueled her courage and heightened her risks; her amateur spying added to the odds of facing the hangman's noose.

Born in rural Pennsylvania, Sarah's mother was a first cousin to Brig. Gen. "Mad Anthony" Wayne. Sarah's husband, Thomas, served in the Pennsylvania militia and Sarah had treated the wounded after the battle of Brandywine. The McCallas moved to Chester District, South Carolina, in late 1778, and Thomas joined Sumter's partisans, fighting in the summer 1780 engagements. Incredibly, he was granted leave to visit his family on the evening of August 17, within hours of Sumter's disastrous defeat at Fishing Creek the next day. He escaped death or capture then, but was taken prisoner a day or so later and sent to Camden. Sarah, meanwhile, was unaware of his plight, knowing only that he was missing. It was an "agony of anxiety" as she talked to the wives and daughters of Thomas's comrades, seeking information but getting none. She went to the Fishing Creek battleground, looking for traces of him, but in vain.[5]

Amid all this strife, the McCalla children were stricken by smallpox, as were other families in the area, with many lives lost. Sarah's most seriously ill child was her son John, who was at death's brink for nine days before slowly recovering. As soon as he was out of danger, Sarah made preparations to go to Camden in September 1780. There she hoped to learn something about her husband's disappearance, or perhaps to determine if he was one of the prisoners in British captivity. "With her to resolve was to act, and having set her house in order, she was in the saddle long before day, taking the old Charleston road leading down on the west side of the Catawba River," said one account. By 2 p.m., she had been allowed past the Redcoats' strongpoint at Wateree Ferry and the village's inner defenses, bolstered by her "fearless determination." Learning of her intent, Major

John Doyle, Rawdon's second-in-command, escorted her through the British camp to Rawdon's headquarters at the Kershaw home. An 1856 account of Mrs. McCalla's exploits described the mansion as

> a large, ancient looking house on the east side of the main street (present-day Broad Street) [adding that the home was] left standing alone some four hundred yards from any other, as if the memories associated with it had rendered the neighborhood undesirable. It was here that the haughty and luxurious nobleman fixed his temporary residence, "sitting as a monarch," while so many true-hearted unfortunates whose fate hung on his will, were languishing out their lives in prison, or atoning for their patriotism on the scaffold.

Shortly afterward, Sarah found herself face-to-face with Rawdon himself; her first impression was favorable: "he was a fine looking young man, with a countenance not unprepossessing."[6]

From Doyle, Sarah had learned that Thomas was indeed a prisoner there. She told Rawdon of her family's desperate plight and sufferings due to her husband's absence, asking for mercy and praying that he might come home to care for his loved ones. As tears wet her cheeks, Rawdon turned to Doyle, saying, "I would rather hang such damned rebels than eat my breakfast." His shocking reply suddenly turned Sarah's subservience to anger and she glared at the colonel with "a look of the deepest scorn." She then requested to see her husband. There was a fiery duel of words before Doyle interceded—the major and Rawdon, both close friends and comrades in arms who together recruited the Volunteers of Ireland—talking in hushed tones. Finally, Rawdon relented, allowing Sarah to spend ten minutes with her beloved Thomas, but only in Doyle's presence.

> The sight of the prison-pen almost overcame the fortitude of the resolute wife. An enclosure like that constructed for animals, guarded by soldiers, was the habitation of the unfortunate prisoners, who sate [sp] within on the bare earth, many of them suffering with the prevalent distemper, and stretched helpless on the ground, with no shelter from the burning sun....

Overwhelmed by emotions, she exclaimed to Doyle, "Is it possible that you shut up men in this manner, as you would a parcel of hogs!"[7]

Sarah's reunion with Thomas was painfully brief. She told him about their children and asked what he needed, promising to return soon with such provisions she could bring and clothing. As she departed, she shook hands with prisoner John Adair and others she knew, telling them, "Have no fear; the women are doing their part of the service." Leaving Camden, she was home by midnight after an exhausting roundtrip of about 100 miles. Sarah later noted that other than Rawdon the British officers she encountered gave her "kinder treatment" as they were "favorably impressed by the courage and strength of affection evinced by her." Other Redcoats also "paid her marks of respect," but the Loyalists were a much different matter, showing "no sympathy or pity for her trials; it being constantly observed that there was deeper hostility towards the [W]higs on the part of their countrymen of different politics, than those of English birth."

In another instance, Sarah noted that the British soldiers were "uniformly polite and respectful to women, and frank and manly in their deportment" while the Loyalists she encountered were "coarse, vulgar, rude and disgusting in their manners." She also singled out the New York Volunteers as "pilfering, thievish, contemptable scoundrels." "She generally spoke well of the British officers, some of whom she thought an honor to the service; but in her praise always excepted Lord Rawdon." Sarah was soon ready to return to Camden after preparing food, and mending and sewing clothes for Thomas. On this second trip she was accompanied by Mrs. Mary Nixon, a sister of the prisoner John Adair. Both women had a pack horse with supplies for their loved ones and others. After another meeting with Rawdon, who treated Sarah with "much haughtiness," the two were allowed to deliver their care packages to the prison. Over time, she made more journeys to Camden, often accompanied by other women taking bundles to their beloved captives there.[8]

By September's first week, Isaac Gregory, the North Carolina militia general left for dead by the British on the Camden battlefield, was back home, still recovering from his bayonet wounds, but would survive. On September 11, the state legislature passed a resolution stating that he should be "furnished at the Expense of the State, for immediate service, with a gelding of the first Price ... in consideration of the one by him lost in the late action near Camden. Gregory's horse was killed in the battle."[9]

There was a change in the Crown's leadership at Charleston in early September, Brigadier General James Paterson taking sick leave and replaced by Lieutenant Colonel Nisbet Balfour as commandant of the city. The transition had little or no bearing on Cornwallis's final preparations to move north after stockpiling the necessary supplies. "We lay in Camden until our wounded recovered and then marched ... in close pursuit of the enemy," related John Shaw of the British 33rd. Cornwallis intended to "establish a strong post" at Charlotte—some 90 miles distant—possibly trying to weave together a line of strongholds across that province as he had done in South Carolina. It would be a three-pronged effort. The Earl and his main army—the first prong—marched from Camden on September 8, leaving behind the small garrison and medical personnel for those too sick to move. In the ranks were a number of "convalescents," men recovering from illness but believed strong enough for a return to active duty. The second prong, Tarleton, his British Legion and a detachment of light infantry were to proceed up the west side of the Wateree.[10]

The third prong consisted of Major Patrick Ferguson and his 1,100 or so Loyalist militia on the extreme western flank. Cornwallis's march was through the Waxhaws and other areas hostile to the Crown, in what was likely a show of force. "This march was no doubt projected with a view of bearing down all opposition," stated a British account. Cornwallis's force was halved into two divisions led by Rawdon and Webster. Marching about a day apart as a "covering party" for each other as well as to guard the army's foragers and "cattle drivers. This measure was rendered necessary from the hostile disposition of the inhabitants" related the Loyalist officer Charles Stedman. "This was a 'dark and doleful' period of American History," John H. Wheeler, a North Carolina historian, penned in 1851. "The British flag floated in triumph over Charleston and Savannah. The troops of Cornwallis, with all the pomp and circumstance of glory, advanced from the field of Camden" toward Charlotte. "The brave had despaired, the timid took protection under the enemy."[11]

Unopposed, the march was going smoothly on all fronts before Tarleton was stricken by a serious and violent wave of illness, possibly yellow fever, based on some accounts. His men conveyed him to White's Mill on the upper reaches of Fishing Creek where the Green Dragoon struggled for his life over about two weeks. Tarleton was bloodily infamous by now, his reputation as a fierce and often brutal warrior marking him as a prime target to be killed or captured by the Americans. Thus, he had to be guarded by a sizeable force as he lay on his sick bed. "Tarleton's illness is of the greatest inconvenience to me at present," Cornwallis wrote to Balfour on September 21, "as I not only lose his Services, but the whole Corps must remain quite useless in order to protect him." The next day—the 22nd—Cornwallis decided to resume the march, leaving at least a portion of McArthur's 71st Highlanders regiment to guard Tarleton, who was showing signs of vast improvement. Additionally, some of the convalescent soldiers also "relapsed into their former state of illness, and were left behind" with McArthur's force which also was protecting mills along the route as well as "preserving the communication with Camden."[12]

From his camp at the Waxhaws, Cornwallis also wrote to Clinton on September 22, updating him on his plans. The Earl wanted to continue his advance toward Charlotte "as soon as … Tarleton can be removed." He would proceed with the 23rd, the 33rd, the Volunteers of Ireland and some elements of the British Legion to Charlotte, McArthur's Highlanders posted there (at Waxhaws) "until the sick can be brought on to us." Cornwallis intended to establish and fortify a "fixed post" at Charlotte. "To that place I shall bring up all the sick from Camden, who have any chance of being serviceable before Christmas, and trust to opportunities for their joining the army." The post at Charlotte "will be a great security to all this frontier of South Carolina…." The British reached Charlotte on September 26, taking the town after slight resistance, Tarleton back in the saddle by then. Cornwallis viewed Charlotte as a link between Camden and possibly Salisbury, when the Redcoats proceeded further north. But he himself was unwell, in the early stages of illness that would incapacitate him for several critical weeks.[13]

Williamson and Pinckney

About this same time, Dr. Hugh Williamson received permission to give smallpox inoculations to some prisoners who had "hitherto escaped," been recaptured and returned to Camden. By now, the physician had been in the town for more than a month, treating the wounded and sick since the August 16 battle. Williamson also found himself ordered to care for "State Prisoners" held in the jail, many of whom were quite ill. Those who appeared healthy were inoculated and "suffered very little by the Small Pox, [sp]" he noted. Still, most of the soldiers he treated at Camden were victims of "the Flux"—a medical condition "which prevailed in" the place and was essentially a malady of diarrhea and dysentery. Williamson was proud of the fact that "we did not lose a single Man by that disease, unless of those who had broken thighs or Legs" adding that "small Boys" were the most susceptible to this illness. Shortages of victuals, however, plagued the prisoners. "That the sufferings of our men were greatly increased by the want of Sugar, Tea, Coffee, Vinegar, and such other palatable antiseptic Nourishment as is best suited the Sick" was an ongoing problem, the doctor related. "The cry for these Articles was constant, while our supplies were so scanty as hardly to deserve the name, nor was any thing [sp] of the kind to be purchased … unless in trifling Quantities."[14]

Major Thomas Pinckney of Gates's staff was still in Camden during September, continuing to recover from his serious leg wound. His wife, Betsy, had given birth to a baby boy in August and was still too weak to come to his aid, but Pinckney was attended by one of Betsy's relatives, Mrs. Robert Brewton. When Pinckney was strong enough to travel a few weeks later—about mid–October—he was transferred from Camden to Mount Joseph, the home of the recently widowed Rebecca Motte, his mother-in-law. Cornwallis had granted the parole permit "authorizing Mrs. Motte to remove Major Pinckney to her plantation on the Congaree, until convalescent." Betsy and the baby were both recovering from not only the birth but at least some symptoms of smallpox still savaging the colony, but would survive. At Mount Joseph, a healthier Betsy now "proved a faithful wife, and skillful nurse" and "became both nurse and surgeon" to her husband. Her grimmest task almost certainly was the removal of shattered bone fragments "which continued to exfoliate from his wounded leg." It is likely that Pinckney's parole and trip to Mount Joseph was the first time the major had seen his weeks-old son.[15]

As autumn brilliantly colored the Southern wilds, major catastrophe soon loomed for Cornwallis. On October 7, Ferguson's force suffered a crushing defeat at Kings Mountain on the Carolinas border about 35 miles west of Charlotte. A large body of frontier militia surprised Ferguson there, killing him, a good portion of his men and capturing most of the others. It was a devastating blow not only to Cornwallis's immediate plans but to the Crown's overall strategy in the provinces. Henry Clinton wrote that the debacle "unhappily proved the first Link of a Chain of Evils that followed each other in regular Succession until they at last ended in the total loss of America." Based on the short-term ramifications, Charles Ross of Cornwallis's staff added: "This defeat was not only fatal to the attempt on North Carolina, but it dispirited the Loyalists and proportionately elated the Americans." More personally "vexatious" at the time was that Cornwallis had placed his trust in the advice and assurances of Ferguson and Tarleton before embarking on the operation.[16]

"The blow was severely felt" and, likely, aggravating illness plaguing Cornwallis at the time, caused him to retreat from Charlotte and back into South Carolina. "This retrograde march was attended with some loss, and his [Cornwallis's] difficulties were increased by the bad state of his health…," Ross wrote. Tarleton added: "The plan for the winter's campaign being abandoned, the next object was to look out for a proper position to cover South Carolina. Immediate attention" was given to the region between the Catawba and Broad rivers and "of a situation" to allow "safe and direct communications" with Camden and Ninety Six. The gloomy retreat began on October 14, which was as soon as "the army could be put in motion" after receiving word of Ferguson's defeat, related the Loyalist officer Charles Stedman.

With Cornwallis sick "and continued ill for some time," Rawdon assumed command, but no matter who led, the Redcoats, already dispirited by this short-lived offensive, were about to endure a hellish retreat due to suddenly wicked fall weather and a lack of equipment and rations. Stedman related that

> the king's troops suffered much, encountering the greatest difficulties; the soldiers had no tents; it rained for several days without intermission; the roads were over their shoes in water and mud. At night, when the army took up its ground, it encamped in the woods, in a most unhealthy climate; for many days without rum. Sometimes the army had beef, and no bread; at other times bread and no beef. For five days it was supported upon Indian corn, which was

12. "We made our retreat like lost sheep"

collected as it stood in the field, five ears of which were the allowance for two soldiers for 24 hours. They were to cook it as they could, which was generally by parching it before the fire.[17]

"We made our retreat like lost sheep," recalled British soldier John R. Shaw—who fought in the Camden battle—and by others, "not knowing where to go—no forage—no provisions for our men, though marching day and night. I saw an English guinea offered for a bit of corn-bread not larger than my two fingers—Hard times with us indeed—16 days without a morsel of bread." Stedman continued:

> The water that the army drank was frequently as thick as puddle. Few armies ever encountered greater difficulties and hardships; the soldiers bore them with great patience, and without a murmur. Their attachment to their commander supported them in the day of adversity; knowing, as they did, that their officers' and even lords Cornwallis and Rawdon's fare was not better than their own.... The continual rains had swelled the rivers and creeks prodigiously, and rendered the roads almost impassable. The waggon [sp] and artillery horses were quite exhausted....[18]

At one roiling creek, with steep clay banks "as slippery as ice," Loyalist militiamen replaced horses and mules in the wagon harnesses, struggling to pull their burdens through the roaring waters and along the treacherous creeksides. During the march the militia, most of whom were mounted, had played a crucial role in finding cattle and rooting out other scant food supplies to feed the troops, Stedman—Cornwallis's chief commissary officer—stating "that it was impossible to have supplied his majesty's army in the field without them" and that "without whose assistance he could not possibly have found provisions for the army." That being said, Stedman watched in stark abhorrence as some of the Loyalists in the wagon traces were whipped and yelled at by officers: "We are sorry to say, that, in return for these exertions, the militia were maltreated, by abusive language, and even beaten by some ... in the quarter-master-general's department...." He added that several of these Loyalists left the army the next morning, choosing "to run the risque [sp] of meeting the resentment of their enemies rather than submit to the derision and abuse of those to whom they looked up[on] as friends."

Major Hanger—Tarleton's second in command—and five other officers were among troops at Charlotte stricken with yellow fever. In the retreat, these six were conveyed in wagons with straw for their bedding. Hanger alone survived—subsisting only on "opium and port-wine"—the others dying in the first week of the exhausting march. Their bodies were "buried in the woods as the army moved on," the major related. The straw in his wagon soaked from crossing swollen brooks and creeks, Hanger's health continued to deteriorate.[19]

Writing from Charleston in spring 1782, the South Carolina Loyalist officer Robert Gray offered his perspective on this phase of the British campaign:

> A universal panic seized the rebels after [the battle of] Camden and had Lord Cornwallis had a sufficient army to have marched into North Carolina and have established posts in his rear at convenient places to preserve his communications with South Carolina and to prevent the rebels from assembling in arms after he passed along, North Carolina would have fallen without a struggle, but the smallness of his numbers soon turned the tide against him.[20]

McCalla

Sarah McCalla continued her treks bringing food and clothing to her husband and other prisoners held in Camden. She was about to embark on one of these trips in early October when she learned of the American victory at Kings Mountain. Sarah was excited to share the good news with Thomas, but when she reached the village, the sentries denied her permission to enter. Perplexed, she unloaded her pack horse and sat under a tree to think about what to do. Before long, however, a man who lived in the town came out and escorted her to his house, helping her carry in her supplies. "This piece of kindness called forth her feelings of gratitude, and was often mentioned by her in after life as an unexpected and gratifying instance of good will." The next day she had another unpleasant encounter with Rawdon, but Major Doyle again intervened such that Sarah was able make her delivery to her husband. She also told Doyle about the Kings Mountain battle, of which he was unaware. The major replied that Rawdon apparently already knew of the British defeat, since he had almost instantly become so surly and stern that "scarce anyone dared to speak to him."[21]

Sarah's frequent travels to Camden did not go unnoticed by American sympathizers, and she "often had secret interviews" with them, including operatives John McWaters and Thomas Steel. "Her eye was keen and penetrating as the glance of the eagle," the Americans having "high respect for her opinions on military affairs." In one meeting, Sarah communicated all she knew of "the position of the British in the town, and the guard stationed at the river...." That being said, this spy work was a very low priority for her as she tried to free her husband.[22]

During Cornwallis's strike north, the British and Loyalists at Camden and other South Carolina outposts strengthened their defenses, "attentive to the security of their respective commands." Lt. Col. George Turnbull of the New York Volunteers was left in charge of the Camden garrison and the ongoing effort to build up the perimeter fortifications there. His troops "with the assistance of the inhabitants, and by the labour of the provincials and the [N]egroes, had commenced, and almost completed" a series of redoubts "which would greatly remedy the badness of the position," Tarleton noted. Other posts, including Ninety Six, Nelson's Ferry and Georgetown were bolstered as well "to secure the communications" with Charleston, where defenses were also being improved.[23]

Looking for the "most convenient position on the frontier," the exhausted British force reached the village of Winnsboro, South Carolina—about 65 miles from Charlotte—on October 29. Cornwallis, by then "fortunately recovered from his indisposition," decided to establish an outpost there, some 33 miles northwest of Camden over steep and hilly roads. The Earl set up his headquarters in a house on what is now North Zion Street across from the Mt. Zion Institute, a preparatory school whose classes were disrupted by the British occupation. Many of the Redcoats bivouacked on the campus grounds. Tarleton related that a

> proper encampment was discovered [and] after minute inquiry and examination, [Winnsboro] presented the most numerous advantages: Its spacious plantations yielded a tolerable post; its centrical [sp] situation between the Broad river and the Wateree afforded protection to Ninety Six and Camden; and its vicinity to the Dutch forks, and a rich country in the rear, promised abundant supplies of flour, forage, and cattle.[24]

"As soon as the army arrived on this ground, the sick were conveyed to the hospital at Camden," Tarleton continued, "rum and other stores were required from that place, and communication was opened with Ninety Six." Charles Stedman described Winnsboro as "an intermediate station between Camden and Ninety Six. The army thus encamped, was at hand" to assist either of these outposts "and covered from the enemy's incursions all the country behind to the sea-coast." Cornwallis also was in communications with Major General Alexander Leslie and his British force on the Virginia coast. Clinton had sent Leslie's troops there shortly after the Camden battle, to coordinate with Cornwallis's anticipated thrust into North Carolina. With this operation now blunted—at least temporarily again—Cornwallis ordered Leslie to bring his corps by sea to Charleston and then join him at Winnsboro. He did not plan on lingering at Winnsboro, his expectation being that these reinforcements "would allow him to prosecute his further designs," of again marching northward. A Winnsboro tradition goes that when the British were gathering food and other supplies in the area, an old farmer was told that the general in charge was Cornwallis. The farmer asked "if he was any kin to the Wallis's up the road."[25]

The King's troops at Camden were buoyed by news of Cornwallis's recuperation and by the elan' of the rest of their comrades, despite the ordeal of their retreat. "Lord Cornwallis is perfectly recovered (he had had an attack of bilious fever), and his army in high spirits," a Redcoat wrote. Still, there was somber news circulating that Lt. William Marquois of the Royal Artillery had died in Camden on October 15. Marquois was second in command of the British guns in the August 16 battle, but was too badly wounded there to survive. Two months after the Camden fight, the American surgeon Hugh Williamson remained in the village, his patients including ten North Carolina militiamen wounded in the battle who by then were "chiefly well." In an apparent reference to other, less fortunate, North Carolinians, Williamson wrote that five privates had died of their wounds, nine others from smallpox, one by "a putrid fever" and four more "by the flux." Two officers succumbed to wounds and two others to smallpox. Williamson was then called to examine two sick "State Prisoners" both South Carolinians incarcerated by the British in Camden. He found the pair suffering from smallpox and held "in a small Room" with 17 other men who were not yet infected. "I wrote Lord Cornwallis on so pressing a Tryal [sp] of Humanity, Stated the Cases fully, and assured his Lordship that Confinement in such a Room, putrescent as the Atmosphere there was, must be followed by death, equally certain as immediate execution," Williamson wrote. His appeal resulted in the two ill men being removed, but the others were still detained. Of the 17, "they were not inoculated; most of them died."[26]

13

Dance of the Devils

Kershaws

On New Providence in the Bahamas, Joseph and Ely Kershaw were put aboard the schooner *Nassau* in mid-October bound for Bermuda and exile. They had already been away from Camden for some two months and Ely's health continued to wane. Stormy weather and the threat of privateers delayed the journey, the vessel forced to shelter at Eleuthera—another Bahamian island—for almost a week. Finally, the *Nassau* was nearing Port Royal, Bermuda, on November 10, 1780, but Ely would never see the island, dying that night. He left behind his wife, Mary Cantey Kershaw, and three children.[1]

Cornwallis and Rawdon

From Winnsboro in early November, Cornwallis sent Rawdon and his Volunteers of Ireland back to Camden where Rawdon would oversee the six British "stations" in the South Carolina interior. These soldiers arrived in Camden on November 13, Rawdon relieving Lt. Col. Turnbull in command of the outpost. The young lord was not pleased with what he saw, especially with winter's embrace fast approaching. Turnbull had used his time to continue construction of the perimeter redoubts—as Cornwallis had ordered—but had neglected basic shelters for the troops to withstand an even more formidable enemy—the cold. "Matters are in so backward [a] state here that we shall have difficulty to get the fort into a proper state before bad weather sets in, [but] we shall make it moderately convenient and pretty secure," Rawdon wrote to Cornwallis from Camden on the 15th. Four days later Rawdon noted that his command "had no hopes of being able to complete regular barracks, but I shall convert barns, stables, etc., into tolerable quarters and shall take huts contiguous to them for the officers."

Still, at least one unidentified Redcoat in the garrison appeared confident that they were under no immediate threat from the enemy. "We are under no apprehensions of having a visit paid us by the Americans," he wrote from Camden on the 13th. "They have nothing for miles round to subsist on; and their only incitement for coming into the country, is plunder." At Winnsboro, Cornwallis remained satisfied with his choice of the town as a temporary post. "Winnsboro, my present position, is a healthy spot, well situated to protect the greatest part of the northern frontier, and to assist Camden and Ninety-Six [sp]," he wrote to Clinton on December 3, 1780. The British army in South Carolina and Georgia—including provincial troops—numbered between 7,400 and about 8,000 at this time.[2]

Gates

By October 1780, Gates was still engaged in rebuilding the Southern army, but Congress ordered a court of inquiry to be held regarding his conduct in the Camden disaster. Washington, authorized to appoint members of the court, ordered that "only those officers should sit who were not present at the battle, or such as were unobjectionable to General Gates." With the war still raging, and with Washington's ever burgeoning fame and mandate in place, the proceedings were postponed indefinitely. Still, Congress requested that Washington choose another general to supplant Gates in command of the Southern Army and Department. Washington's choice, confirmed on October 14, was Major General Nathanael Greene, an obvious selection since Greene was a trusted friend and confidant. Greene started south in late November after spending several weeks in Philadelphia dealing with logistical and strategic issues, as well as myriad problems in putting the army back into fighting trim. Also on the 14th, Congress passed resolutions to honor Baron DeKalb and others from the battle of Camden. One measure called for a monument to DeKalb to be erected in Annapolis, Maryland, with a fitting inscription describing his gallantry and sacrifice to the American cause.

It was also resolved "That the thanks of Congress be given to Generals Smallwood and Gist, and to the officers and soldiers of the Maryland and Delaware lines; the different corps of artillery; Colonel Porterfield's and Major Armstrong's corps of light infantry, and Colonel Armand's cavalry; for their bravery and good conduct, displayed" in combat at Camden. A third resolution offered "the thanks of Congress ... to such of the militia officers and soldiers who distinguished themselves by their valor on that occasion." Despite these honors being bestowed in the wake of a catastrophic defeat, the politicians were voicing their optimism, not only for

Greene but for the fractured forces he would need to rebuild the Southern army, as well as revering the supreme sacrifice of DeKalb, who had given his life for the American cause.[3]

McCalla

Sarah McCalla claimed to have met with Cornwallis at Camden in November which, at first blush, seems unlikely. But Cornwallis and his troops were encamped at Winnsboro by October 29 after retreating from Charlotte. It is totally believable that Cornwallis likely traveled the 30 or so miles to Camden during this time to inspect his main outpost in the province's interior. "Treated with kindness" by the general in their November encounter, Sarah also claimed to have met with Cornwallis at Camden in early December. Again, for the reasons noted above, the time frame could be construed to support her story. During this conversation, however, the Earl was "reserved and silent," his bad moodiness attributed to a small-scale defeat at Rugeley's Mill.

This setback was a successful ruse carried out by William Washington and his cavalry against the Loyalists' outpost, basically the fortified home and barn of Henry Rugeley, the prominent local leader and colonel of militia who had aspirations of becoming a general in the Crown's service. Rugeley was with more than 100 other Loyalists when Washington's force approached his home on December 4, 1780. With no artillery, Washington did not want to make a possibly bloody frontal assault. Instead, he and his men fashioned a pine log to resemble a cannon and demanded a surrender. With the threat of this "artillery" looming, Rugeley capitulated, his career doomed. Cornwallis wrote to Tarleton: "Rugeley will not be made a brigadier."[4]

Amid the wintry gloom, there was a bright spot for the Patriots on November 20, 1780, when Thomas Sumter roundly defeated Tarleton in a clash at Blackstock's Ford on the Tyger River near present-day Cross Anchor, S.C. Yet other than about 150 British casualties (contrasted to seven Americans) and a boost to morale, arguably the most significant result of the battle was Sumter himself being seriously wounded by enemy buckshot. He would survive, but would be out of action for some two months. After the battle, Tarleton captured Colonel Benjamin Roebuck, Sr., an older gentleman, who brought his family from Virginia to settle along the Tyger in 1777. His son, Major Benjamin Roebuck, Jr., served with Sumter and other American forces, in combat at Stono Ferry, Savannah and Hanging Rock. The senior Roebuck was jailed in Camden where he eventually died of smallpox. In another development about this time, Griffith Rutherford, the militia brigadier wounded and captured in the August 16 battle, was recovered enough to be transferred to Charleston. By November, he and Lt. Col. Isaacs of his brigade, who was captured at Fishing Creek, were imprisoned at St. Augustine, the capital of British East Florida. Both were exchanged in June 1781.[5]

Greene

By early December, Gates had established his headquarters at Charlotte, using the momentum of the Kings Mountain victory to continue piecing together his shattered army. Ferguson's shocking utter defeat had demoralized British sympathizers in the Carolinas while energizing "the friends of independence," as an officer in Cornwallis's army recalled. Still, Gates was steeled to hand over the sword of leadership, the Pandora's box of the Camden rout too much for him to retain command or even possibly salvage his career. Still, his successor was far from exuberant—and indeed melancholy—about his upcoming new endeavor. Noting to a colleague that the Southern army "is shadow rather than substance, having only an imaginary existence," Nathanael Greene already realized the many obstacles he faced when he replaced Gates on December 3, 1780, after arriving in Charlotte the previous day. "What I have been dreading has come to pass," he wrote his wife about the seemingly ill-fated command, but he did not want to disappoint Washington.[6]

Greene, 38, was a combat-wizened officer and natural leader whose battle laurels were forged at Trenton, Brandywine, Germantown and Monmouth. He also had distinguished himself in the American army's retreats in New Jersey and Rhode Island. "Greene is as dangerous as Washington," noted a British officer who fought against him in New Jersey; "he is vigilant, enterprising, and full of resources. With but little hope of gaining any advantage over him, I never feel secure when encamped in his neighborhood." The officer was Lord Cornwallis.[7]

Washington himself, who had endured the snake pit of high-command jealousies and backstabbing, held Greene in the highest regard, writing of him:

> There is no officer in the army more sincerely attached to the interests of his country than General Greene. Could he but promote those interests in the character of a corporal, he would exchange, without a murmur, his epaulette for the knot. For, although he is not without ambition, that ambition has not, for its object, the highest rank, so much as the greatest good.

The Loyalist officer Charles Stedman noted that Greene "was supposed to enjoy the esteem and confidence of Washington more than any other officer...."[8]

The son of a Quaker preacher and farmer, Greene's ancestry was deeply rooted in the rocky soil of Rhode Island, where four generations of his family had lived. Born in July 1742 at Potowomut, his parents, Nathanael and Molly Mott Greene, owned a large farm where six-year-old Nathanael soon earned his keep tending sheep and cattle and cutting and hauling wood, among many other chores. His schooling was limited, but the seemingly endless hard work molded him physically and mentally. The family prospered to a degree that his father had an ironworks constructed on their property, the business adding to their income.

By his early teens, Greene had some rudimentary reading and writing skills, along with some basic math, but he thirsted for more knowledge. He became a voracious reader, and by about age 18, his self-education found him immersed in various topics of law, philosophy, languages and other subjects. Meanwhile, his backbreaking labors on the farm and at the forge sculpted his 5'10" physique. He had a strong chin, a ruddy complexion and an "easy manner," said one account, and a permanent injury to his right knee gave him "an unmilitary gait." He also sometimes suffered from asthma. Somewhat like his adversary Cornwallis, Greene had a "blemished eye," caused by a fever apparently brought on after a smallpox inoculation.[9]

By 1770, Greene was running his father's new ironworks at Coventry and was further making a name for himself by being elected to the Rhode Island general assembly. He was later mired in some controversy in the *Gaspee* affair in June 1772 when falsely accused of being involved in the destruction of the British revenue schooner by a party of Patriots. Though later shown to be innocent, the accusations embittered him against the Crown and heightened his fervor for rebellion. It was also during this period—1773—that Greene was straying ever further from his faith by organizing and joining in militia drills, running afoul of the Quakers' tenets of pacifism.

Despite his business, Rhode Island politics, military involvement and rebellious activities, Greene found time to marry the beautiful Catherine Littlefield—his "Kitty"—who was 13 years his junior, in July 1774. That winter, however, he was engaged in forging cannon for the colonials, as well as continued efforts to ready the militia for possible war against the mother country. Meeting three days after the fighting at Lexington and Concord, the Rhode Island assembly appointed Greene a brigadier general, based on his leadership, patriotic zeal, soldierly and organizational qualities. He was placed in command of about 1,500 militia. Over time, his reputation spread throughout the New England colonies and beyond, including the fact that he was among the first to call for a declaration of independence from the Crown, opining that hopes of a peaceful reconciliation were gone. As the conflict unfolded, Greene soon became one of Washington's most trusted and competent generals.[10]

At Charlotte, Greene noted that Gates "was in great distress," having heard shortly before that his only son, Robert, had died in the weeks after the Camden battle. Gates issued his last order to his command on the 3rd; in fact, it would be his final communication to any troops, as his military tenure was basically over, other than some formalities. In this swan song at Charlotte, he wrote in part:

> General Gates returns his sincere and grateful thanks to the Southern Army, for their perseverance, fortitude, and patient endurance of all the hardships and sufferings while under his command. He anxiously hopes their misfortunes will cease therewith, and that victory, and the glorious advantages attending it, may be the future portion of the Southern Army.[11]

After a few days with the army, Greene also had gained respect and sympathy for the despondent leader he replaced. "General Gates sets out tomorrow for the northward," he wrote to Washington on December 7. "Many officers think very favorably of his conduct, and that whenever an inquiry takes place, he will honorably acquit himself." Of a more immediate—and massive—problem for Greene was what he had experienced in his new role. "To give your Excellency an idea of the state and condition of this army, if it deserves the name of one...," he wrote in the same dispatch before describing the soldiers:

> Nothing can be more wretched and distressing than the condition of the troops, starving with cold and hunger, without tents and camp equipage. Those of the Virginia line are, literally, naked; and a great part totally unfit for any kind of duty, and must remain so until clothing can be had from the northward.... Lord Cornwallis lies, with his principal force, at a place called Weymsborough [Winnsboro], about half way between Camden and Ninety Six; at both of which places the enemy have a post, and are strongly fortified.

Greene added that Camden had "seven redoubts." One bright spot was that Washington in December had dispatched Lt. Colonel Henry "Light Horse Harry" Lee's Second Partisan Corps—better known as Lee's Legion—to assist Greene. The army had received some reinforcement by Virginia Continentals, but as mentioned, these troops were deficient in uniforms and equipment. "I have written to Governor [Thomas] Jefferson not to send forward any more until they are well clothed, and properly equipped," Greene told Washington. To Jefferson, Greene wrote in part, "There must be either pride, or principle, to make a soldier. No man will think himself bound to fight the battles of a state that leaves him to perish for want of clothing, nor can you inspire a soldier with the sentiment of pride while his situation renders him more an object of pity than of envy...."[12]

Despite the many obstacles in his own ranks, Greene also realized he was facing a tenacious, formidable and confident foe well anchored in a string of forts in South Carolina, and coiling yet again to strike into North Carolina, very likely destroying his command in the process. "On his [Greene's] arrival in Carolina, he found a country everywhere marked with outrage, desolation and blood, and an enemy bold in enterprize [sp] and flushed with success, prepared to crush him," noted Alexander Garden, a Charlestonian in Lee's Legion who later served as an aide-de-camp to Greene.

> The prospect was truly appalling. The remnant of the army, delivered up by Gates, consisted not only of inferior numbers, but was mostly composed of militia, dispirited by misfortune, and entirely destitute of every adequate means to sanction the hope of effectual resistance. Their provisions were exhausted—the comfort of decent clothing was unknown—and the want of arms and ammunition so great and deplorable, as to render impracticable, every attempt to commence active operations. Yet, beneath such an accumulation of difficulty, his resolution sunk not.[13]

Still, in addition to Lee's reinforcements, another monumental positive for Greene was the presence of Brig. Gen. Daniel Morgan, a grizzled, frontier warrior nicknamed the "Old Wagoner" who was known for his unorthodox, but successful combat tactics. His nickname was derived from his days as a teamster during the French and Indian War. Morgan had joined Gates in September, soon taking charge of a newly established corps of light infantry. Despite the army's deficiencies, Greene had some 2,000 troops fit for duty and knew he was greatly outnumbered by Cornwallis. Yet within weeks of relieving Gates, he decided to split his force and menace the enemy simultaneously at several points. It was a bold—perhaps foolhardy—gamble, especially since British Maj. Gen. Alexander Leslie and his troops landed at Charleston on December 13, 1780, despite "hard Gales, and contrary Winds" lashing the fleet. Ashore, he received orders to "march up the Country" with about 1,530 men to reinforce Cornwallis as soon as possible. A shortage of horses and wagons delayed his advance from Charleston until December 19.[14]

Morgan's detachment of about 600 men was to deploy west of the Catawba River and operate against the enemy "either offensively or defensively as your own prudence and discretion may direct," were Greene's purposely vague orders based on his trust of Morgan's judgment and leadership. Greene would lead the rest of the little army—about 1,400 troops—southeast toward Cheraw. In so doing, the Americans would generally be on both flanks of Cornwallis at Winnsboro. The possibly disastrous downside was that these movements would leave Greene and Morgan about 140 miles apart, inviting destruction for either or both forces, if the enemy was aggressive enough. Hindered by bad winter weather, including rain-gorged rivers and the resulting mud-bogged roads, Greene's actions were delayed until just before Christmas, but were unmolested by the British.

With Morgan poised to menace Ninety Six and Greene in position to threaten Camden from the vicinity of Cheraw—which he reached on December 26—Cornwallis held his ground in Winnsboro, unsure of the Americans' intent. Gates was vanquished, but Greene was a much different adversary, as the Earl well knew from their chess-game combat in New Jersey. Caution, vigilance and patience had to guide his decisions with so much at stake, the Crown's fate in the Southern provinces possibly hanging in the balance amid the dreary, miserable cold cloaking the British encampment and the wild, silent country beyond.[15]

Gates

A despondent Gates rode out of the army camps at Charlotte, departing for "Traveller's Rest," his home in northeastern Virginia. "On his route no countenance shed the balm of condolence, all were gloomy and scowling," noted Colonel Henry Lee. This response changed when Gates reached Richmond. Lee wrote:

> Great and good men then governed the state. They appointed a committee of their body to wait upon the vanquished general and to assure him of their esteem, that the remembrance of his former glorious services was never to be obliterated by any reverse of fortune, but ever mindful of his great merit, they would omit no opportunity of testifying to the world the gratitude which Virginia owed him.

Still, however, the specter of a court of inquiry hovered over Gates.[16]

Rawdon

At Camden, Rawdon completed the perimeter defenses in late November, the works bristling with six redoubts, one at each corner of the outpost and two others at equally key points. These mini-forts were earthworks, manned by infantry, each with a light fieldpiece and guarded by abatis, a wall and ditch. They were the outer defenses for the post and were of different designs based on the terrain and position they occupied.

The northern redoubt straddled the Wagon Road just north of the village and enclosed the jail. The U-shaped southwestern redoubt protected the road (present-day Wateree Street) linking Camden to Wright's Ferry, a crossing a short distance south of Wateree Ferry. Situated near the site of the dismantled Presbyterian meeting house, the southwestern redoubt was bolstered by the western redoubt, an E-configured work located at the entrance to the Quaker cemetery near the intersection of today's Campbell and Meeting streets. The northeastern redoubt was constructed just north of the Kershaw house, near the corner of present-day Bull and Lyttleton streets; the northwestern redoubt erected at what-is-now the intersection of Campbell and Bull. The southeastern redoubt stood to the south of the Kershaw house.

The fortified magazine south of the Kershaw mansion remained the southernmost stronghold of these defenses. "A retrenchment was thrown up Round the Jail with an Abbatis [sp] ... another work and Abbatis in form of a half Moon was also thrown up near the road ... and a new work just begun at the lower end of the Town," an American spy reported in November, adding that the construction was proceeding rapidly as the redoubts were nearing completion late that month.[17]

The redoubts bulwarked the defenses, but Rawdon soon realized that practically any assault could be made successfully at any point between these independent forts, leaving his munitions and supplies—as well as his garrison—open to possible catastrophe. Construction soon began on a palisade of sharpened wooden posts to enclose the town. When completed in early 1781, this defensive Hadrian's Wall, so to speak, ran east and west across the Wagon Road, paralleling it with two north-side walls to form a basic square. The only variation to this design was at the southwest corner where the palisade was extended to protect the brewhouse. All of the new redoubts were situated outside of the walls. In today's terms, the wall ran parallel to and just south of Bull Street, south from Bull and just west of Church Street and across Meeting Street to the southwest corner where the brewhouse and the site of the Presbyterian meeting house which the Redcoats had dismantled. DeKalb's gravesite also was in the enclosure. From that point the palisade continued east across Broad Street toward the southeast redoubt and then north to Bull at the south end of Market Street.

The area around the Kershaw House was also fortified to function independently in the event of attack. Surrounded by a separate wooden palisade contoured based on the terrain, the British headquarters was guarded by light artillery as well as a detachment of troops billeted, apparently in tents or huts, behind the mansion. The stockade also enclosed a barn and other outbuildings on the grounds. The headquarters defenses served as an anchor for both of the eastern redoubts.

Additionally, the small British post at Wateree Ferry—Carey's Fort—was also strengthened as was Henry Rugeley's home and Loyalist stronghold at Clermont, briefly abandoned when Gates's army occupied the area. Other British posts in the province were bolstered as well.[18]

There were other developments at Camden during this time. Weeks earlier, the seriously ill Major Hanger of Tarleton's legion had reached Camden, "safe, and all but dead" while "reduced to something very like a skeleton." The cavalryman slowly recuperated, thanks in some degree to Rawdon's generosity, as well as the British medical personnel there. Rawdon daily sent Hanger "many comfortable and nourishing things ... from his own table, which my servants could not make, and were not to be purchased; and the butcher's meat killed at that time of the year, is absolutely little better than carrion at Camden," the major noted. In this same account, Hanger wrote that "If I do not actually owe my life to Earl Moira [a title Rawdon acquired after the war] I certainly am indebted to him for the more speedy recovery of my health."[19]

After more than two months in Camden, caring for the American wounded and ill—and likely the enemy as well—Dr. Hugh Williamson had returned to his home in Edenton, N.C., by December 1, the day he wrote to Thomas Benbury about his experiences at the British outpost. Indeed, he had some stark recommendations for further war operations from a medical perspective:

> From a transient view of our misfortunes it is clear that we should save many Lives by any kind of Military establishment which would admit of the Troops being inoculated before they took the Field. It is also clear that a moderate supply of Sugar, Rice, Tea, Coffee or such other wholesome Nourishment for the sick and invalids of our Militia would tend greatly to reconcile them to the hardships of a Campaign & would save the lives of many.[20]

McCalla

In late December, Sarah McCalla made yet another journey to Camden, this one likely the most desperate of her many trips there. Imprisoned since about mid–August, her husband Thomas's health had been deteriorating for weeks and Sarah knew she would likely have to appeal to the compassion of his captors to bring him home if he was to live. Her old antagonist Lord Rawdon refused her petition to have Thomas released, but told her that if she went to Winnsboro, Cornwallis might possibly consider her request. Undaunted, Sarah soon set off north through the rugged hill country in the midst of winter to find the British general who might save her ailing husband's life.[21]

The wounded Major Thomas Pinckney remained at Mount Joseph, the Motte plantation, into December, but his battle injuries were not healing well. By early January 1781 he, Betsy and their baby, were permitted to travel to Charleston, possibly to obtain better medical care from the

Crown authorities there. It proved to be an arduous journey, the major's condition worsening to the point that he seemed to be on the brink of death. His health gradually improved, however, when the family reached the city, Pinckney reuniting with friends and comrades he had not seen since Charleston fell to the British the previous May. Among them was his brother, Colonel Charles C. Pinckney. The brothers were eventually shipped to Philadelphia where Thomas was freed in a prisoner exchange.[22]

As the curtain fell on 1780, Great Britain's troubles extended vastly beyond the South Carolina wilds and the northern provinces to the farthest reaches of the Empire. France and Spain were allied against the British, their fleets menacing the Crown's territories in the West Indies. A French invasion of the home isles was a real possibility. The Spanish also were besieging Gibraltar and rebellion flamed in the East Indies. Additionally, the "peace with America" faction in Parliament was strengthening, these advocates willing to grant independence to the colonies. To the Redcoats at Camden and at any other post in the New World, all this meant that reinforcements and supplies would be scarce; the King's mailed might was stretched thin around the globe.[23]

Thus, to some degree, Cornwallis and Rawdon were left to their own devices. On the other side, the devils in South Carolina were only beginning to dance.

14

"The late affair has almost broke my heart": 1781

The lack of sufficient housing and other buildings needed in Camden continued to frustrate Rawdon as the year dawned. The "village is by no means capable of holding the number of persons who require quarter in it," he wrote to Cornwallis on January 1. "I have therefore sent [for] a quantity of plank and boards with which I hope we shall fit up some kind of barracks and use huts for officers." Rawdon's force totaled 1,410 at the time, the outpost also holding about 200 prisoners, likely including some men captured at the Camden battle, Fishing Creek, and lesser engagements and situations since then.[1]

Desertion,—and related frustration and desperation—also plagued the Redcoats over the waning days of 1780 and into January. Lt. Col. John Hamilton of the First Royal North Carolina Regiment, which had fought so well at Camden in August, had notices placed in newspapers offering pardons to those fugitives who returned to his ranks and money to anyone bringing in a deserter:

> "I DO HEREBY GIVE NOTICE to all deserters from the regiment ... that if they will return to their duty, by joining their corps at Camden or elsewhere, on or before the first day of March next, that they will be pardoned for all past offenses. And I do hereby offer a reward of TWO GUINEAS for every deserter who shall be taken up and brought to the regiment after that date."

In Charleston on December 20, Loyalist Charles Atkins offered a reward for a runaway slave named "Fortune," who belonged to his son, an officer in Hamilton's regiment at Camden.[2]

McCalla

Sarah McCalla, meanwhile, arrived at Winnsboro on the morning of January 1, Cornwallis observing the New Year with his troops on parade as he reviewed them. It was an "imposing scene" but she was more focused on an audience with the general than anything else. After waiting several hours Sarah was allowed to see Cornwallis, who was readying the army for yet another thrust into North Carolina. She was received with "courtesy and kindness," the Earl listening to her plight. Still, the result was the same—the general saying that his duties and policies would not allow him to free her husband. Cornwallis did, however, tell her that he was willing to enter into a prisoner exchange with General Sumter, releasing Thomas McCalla for any British or Loyalist held by the Gamecock. As an alternative, Cornwallis also said he would accept a pledge from Sumter that McCalla should not serve again until exchanged. On that promise he would release her husband.[3]

Thus, Sarah headed home from Winnsboro with a dim flicker of hope. She was only there long enough to prepare for a journey to Charlotte, where Sumter was still recuperating from his wounds suffered at Blackstock's Ford in November. Reaching Charlotte, Sumter was agreeable to the terms regarding a pledge that Thomas McCalla would not take up arms until properly exchanged. He gave Sarah a note to this effect and in her excitement, she again started for home. After crossing the Catawba River, she encountered Daniel Morgan's force and, suspected of being a Loyalist, was brought before the general to be questioned. Showing Morgan Sumter's hand-written message, she also told him of her visit to Winnsboro on January 1 and of the troop review she had witnessed. The "Old Wagoner" thanked her for the information and allowed her to proceed homeward.[4]

Cornwallis

Cornwallis wrote to Clinton from Winnsboro on January 6:

The difficulties I have had to struggle with have not been occasioned by the opposite army, they always keep at a considerable distance, and retire on our approach. But the constant incursions of refugees, North Carolinians, Back Mountain men, and the perpetual risings in different parts of this province, the invariable successes of all those parties against our militia, keep the whole country in continual alarm, and render the assistance of regular troops everywhere necessary.... I shall begin my march tomorrow.... Events alone can decide the future steps.... I have the pleasure to assure your Excellency that the army here is perfectly healthy and in good order.[5]

Cornwallis actually marched from Winnsboro on January 8, his army having spent almost ten weeks in the village. The troops were slowed by ongoing rainy weather and perpetually sloppy, bad roads. The column also was burdened with guns, baggage and supply wagons and other equipment needed for an expected long campaign, but the men were buoyed by the expectation that Leslie and his reinforcements would soon be joining them. Tarleton also was on the move, Cornwallis ordering him to find and attack Morgan if he was "anywhere within your reach," adding "No time is to be lost...." Morgan, meanwhile, wanted to avoid a fight with the Green Dragoon, believing that he was outnumbered, possibly in danger of being trapped by Tarleton and Cornwallis and with Greene too far away to offer any assistance.

Still, by January 16, Morgan was brought to bay by Tarleton at the Cowpens, so named as an area of rolling meadowland near the Broad River where local farmers grazed their cattle over the years. January 17 would be a monumental day, not only in the war in South Carolina, but in the crucible of the Revolution as well. In the cold, orange dawn, Tarleton's force crashed through the gloomy woods, the wily Old Wagoner Morgan awaiting in the distance. Both sides were about equal in number with some 1,000 troops engaged. Tarleton, however, not only had his vaunted British Legion on hand but some 500 British regulars and two artillery pieces. In stunning fashion, Morgan used his withdrawing lines of militia to pull the surprised Redcoats into a killing field anchored in part by his Maryland Continentals with William Washington's cavalry doing stellar work as well. It was as much a crushing defeat for the British—Tarleton's force almost annihilated—as a glorious triumph for Morgan.

Most military historians concur that Cowpens was among the most significant battles of the war in that it was a decisive American victory over British regulars. It also was, other than Kings Mountain, the only major battle won by the Americans in the Southern campaign and helped shift the tide of momentum in favor of the Americans while deflating the Crown's cause. Possibly the most immediate handicap for the British were the combat losses of so many troops—perhaps 900—which would seriously handcuff Cornwallis in the coming weeks and months.[6]

On the day of the battle, meanwhile, Cornwallis encamped at Turkey Creek on the Broad River, some 25 miles from Cowpens, Leslie and his troops joining him on the 18th. Cornwallis had been out of contact with Tarleton for several days and was unaware of the battle. Thus, news of the disaster stung the Earl like no other defeat to this point. "The late affair has almost broke my heart," he wrote to Rawdon on January 21. "I was never more surrounded with difficulty & distress, but practice in the school of adversity has strengthened me..." "The defeat at Cowpens was the most serious calamity which had occurred since Saratoga, and crippled Lord Cornwallis's movements during the remainder of the war," added the British officer Charles Ross. Cornwallis assembled his army at Ramsour's Mill, along the south fork of the Catawba River, on January 25 to rest the troops and consider his next move. Throughout the ranks there was a burning desire to avenge not only Cowpens but Kings Mountain as well, the Redcoats—on Cornwallis's orders—destroying much of their equipment and other supplies as they girded to hunt down Greene. "...Without baggage, necessaries, or provisions of any sort for officer or soldier, in the most barren, inhospitable, unhealthy part of North America, opposed to the most savage, inveterate, perfidious, cruel enemy, with zeal and with bayonets only, it was resolved to follow Greene's army to the end of the world," related the veteran fighter Brigadier General Charles O'Hara.[7]

The next day Cornwallis "with great pleasure" relayed a special communique to the troops congratulating them for the victory at Camden more than five months earlier. The message was an extract of a letter from Lord George Germain dated November 9, 1780. It read:

"It is particularly pleasing to me to obey his Majesty's [King George III] command by signifying to your Lordship [Cornwallis] his Royal pleasure, that you do acquaint the officers and soldiers of the brave army under his command, that their behavior on the glorious 16th of August is highly approved of by their Sovereign...." Rawdon, Lt. Col. Webster and Tarleton were also singled out for "his Majesty's approbation of their judicious and spirited conduct." Tarleton "has, indeed, a double claim to praise for his great alertness in overtaking and destroying" Sumter's force at Fishing Creek "thereby rendering the victory at [Camden] still more decisive."

It is unclear or unrecorded how this tribute was received by the troops, especially since so many of the soldiers who fought at Camden such a seeming eternity ago were dead from combat or disease, incapacitated by wounds or just worn out by the severity of campaigning in such an unforgiving, foreign climate. What *is* related are the meager rations issued for that day and the next: "Two days flour for the officers, and two days meal for the men ... will be issued immediately."[8]

McCalla

Shortly after Cornwallis marched from Winnsboro, the British moved through Chester District, the area where the McCallas lived. Seizing this chance, Sarah went to the Redcoats' camp, where they had halted for the night, and again was able to see Cornwallis. The Earl recognized her when she entered the bivouac and was courteous; but he also was inquisitive, asking about her movements in the countryside and having several questions about Morgan and Sumter. The questions made her uneasy and she offered as little information as possible before showing Cornwallis the note she had obtained from General Sumter. Her long suffering patience and optimism at that moment were quickly crushed. Cornwallis referred her back to Lord Rawdon at Camden! "The very name was a death-blow to her hopes, for she well knew she could expect nothing from his clemency."[9]

Porterfield

The sad saga of Lt. Col. Charles Porterfield, severely wounded in the opening minutes of the Camden battle, was nearing a heartbreaking end by January's second week. He had struggled with his injuries and related ailments since being incapacitated, remaining in or about Camden and "entirely dependent on the generosity of the Enemy"—in particular, Rawdon—since his "papers, money" and "baggage" were lost when he was captured. Porterfield's brother, Captain Robert Porterfield of the Virginia Continentals, was made a prisoner when Charleston surrendered and remained in confinement there. When Charles was "permitted to go to Charleston on parole" Robert was allowed to go to Camden and assist him in the journey. Charles was apparently deemed well enough to travel; in reality he was not. On January 10, 1781, the Porterfields were somewhere "on the banks of the Santee River" when Charles died, cradled in his brother's arms. Robert was soon returned to confinement in Charleston and wrote to Virginia Governor Thomas Jefferson on February 1, 1781:

> Sir, I think it is my duty to inform Your Excellency, That on the morning of the 10th ult: I had the misfortune to loose [sp] my brother (Lieut—Col. Porterfield) on his way from Camden to this place [Charleston]. I have also to beg leave to mention to Your Excellency, That during my brother's almost five months [of] extreme illness, The consequence of a wound he received ... near Camden, His necessary expenses amounted to a considerable sum; for the purpose of defraying which, he borrowed of Lord Rawden, [sp] thirty guineas, which I have made myself answerable to his Lordship for, as soon as may be in my power. My present situation will point out to Your Excellency the impossibility of raising such a sum... [since the captain was a prisoner].[10]

Porterfield went on to praise Rawdon for assisting his brother: "Should Your Excellency conceive an impropriety in the State paying such debt.... I should esteem the loan of thirty guineas a particular favor, in order that my faith with a gentleman (who granted not only that, but many other favors to my brother while in great distress) may not be broken...." Jefferson ordered that "a heavy hogshead of tobacco" be sent to Charleston on a vessel already soon to be bound there under a truce flag. Robert Porterfield was to use funds from the sale of the tobacco to repay Rawdon. Porterfield was also complimentary of Rawdon in an August 9, 1781, letter to the new governor, Thomas Nelson Jr., calling Rawdon a "gentleman whose great degree of humanity and politeness to my brother and others, while ill, not only claims every exertion in my power to comply with my promise for the payment of the ... debt, but merits the friendship of every good man."[11]

McCalla

Unaware of the Cowpens battle and the resulting American triumph, Sarah McCalla embarked on yet another trip to Camden a few days later to try to win her ailing husband's freedom. Her old adversary Lord Rawdon she knew would be waiting there and despite any discouragement she felt for past failures, she was steeled to meet him again and lobby for Thomas McCalla's release. Reaching Wateree Ferry, she noticed that the British guard there was doubled, which struck her as unusual. Entering the village she saw her friend Major John Doyle, Rawdon's second in command, who had assisted her on multiple other visits. Doyle told her of the Cowpens defeat, which had angered Rawdon. The commander had apparently been further enraged by an escape attempt by some of the prisoners who had injured one of the jail keepers in the effort. As she expected, Rawdon was in a fury when Sarah appeared before him, railing at her, "Enough! You go from one army to another, and Heaven only knows what mischief you do! Begone!" Their meeting was over and Sarah turned homeward once again, defeated, but not broken.[12]

Jacksons

After Cornwallis's army speared north from Camden in September 1780, Elizabeth Jackson and her sons left their Waxhaws home and hurried north, away from the British advance. They stayed with friends and relatives in the Charlotte area until it seemed safe enough to return to the Waxhaws in February 1781. Still, however, the region seethed in rebellion, beset by rampaging Tories and Patriots with an occasional foray from Rawdon's garrison at Camden.

Within weeks of their returning home, Andrew and Robert Jackson, along with their militia lieutenant cousin Thomas Crawford and about 20 others, were captured in a British cavalry raid at the Waxhaws. At the Crawford family's home occurred probably the most famous event of Andrew Jackson's early life. Both Jackson boys were surprised and seized there that morning by the raiders, Crawford's wife and young children also being in the house. The enemy troopers—it is unclear if they were

British, Tories or a mixture of both—"began to destroy, with wild riot and noise" basically everything in the house. Amid the chaos, the officer leading the party ordered Andrew to clean his boots, caked and splashed with mud. Andrew refused, telling the officer in so many words: "Sir, I am a prisoner of war, and claim to be treated as such." Infuriated by the teen's reply, the officer "glared at him like a wild beast" said one account, and raised his sword to deal a massive strike at the boy's head. Andrew blocked the blow, somewhat, with his left arm and hand, but the blade gashed him deeply on the head and hand. The officer then turned to Robert Jackson, repeating his demand to have his boots cleaned. But Robert also refused, the officer's already bloody steel slashing him heavily on the head so badly as to "prostrate and disable him."[13]

Bleeding from their injuries, the Jacksons and Crawford—who had suffered a severe head wound while resisting capture the day before—and all of the other 11 or so captives were put on horses seized in the raid. The column was soon on the road to Camden, some 40 miles distant. At least one account describes the journey as an episode of cruelty by the guards, who didn't provide any food and would not allow the captives any water, even as they crossed streams on the way. Reaching Camden, the conditions were of "utter wretchedness," wrote a 19th-century Jackson biographer. The three relatives found themselves crowded in the jail with about 250 other prisoners, the building surrounded by a "contracted enclosure," or stockade. The captives were without beds and medicine, forced to subsist on a mainly meager supply of bad bread. Some of the prisoners were robbed of pieces of their clothing, and all endured jeers and insults from Tories passing the compound. The brothers and Crawford were separated when their keepers found that they were related. "Miserable among the miserable; gaunt, yellow, hungry and sick; robbed of his jacket and shoes; ignorant of his brother's fate; chafing with suppressed fury, Andrew passed now some of the most wretched days of his life," wrote James Parton, who penned a three-volume biography of Jackson.[14]

As it had since the early days of the British occupation of Camden, smallpox soon broke out in the jail, many of the weakened prisoners helpless to resist it. The healthy, the sick and the dying remained clustered together in a putrid chamber of horrors. Incredibly, Andrew avoided illness, and one day an incident happened that not only benefited him but his prison mates. Warming in the sun outside the jail entrance, he was approached by the officer of the guard, who stopped to talk to him. Andrew used the possible opportunity to describe the awful conditions among the prisoners, including the rancid food and their clothes being taken. The officer apparently was shocked and otherwise moved by the teen's strong plea, so much so that the prisoners' treatment improved almost immediately, including some rations of meat, better bread and overall care.[15]

Meanwhile, Thomas Sumter—somewhat recovered from his wounds—was operating in the vicinity of Friday's Ferry—near-present-day Columbia, South Carolina—and was wary of being attacked by Rawdon from Camden. The Gamecock showed his respect for his adversary in a February 20 dispatch to Francis Marion:

> Everything hitherto favourable [sp] and have no doubt but I shall succeed, if not interrupted by Lord Rawdon, who, I know, will strip his post as bare of men as possible to spare, to obviate which, as far as may be in your power, it is my wish that you would be pleased to move in such a direction as to attract his attention, and thereby prevent his designs....[16]

From his headquarters at Newburgh, New York, George Washington "with great satisfaction" issued a general order on February 14 congratulating the army for the recent victories—Kings Mountain and Cowpens—in South Carolina. Washington singled out General Daniel Morgan, Colonel John Eager Howard and Colonel William Washington for their gallantry, Congress eventually awarding gold medals to each of them for their conspicuous service. Such accolades were not on the mind of Nathanael Greene, however, who was forced to deal with the loss of Morgan about this time due to health issues. The seemingly relentless hardships of campaigning and combat over the past months had weakened the Old Wagoner, who suffered from sciatica, to the point that he could no longer ride a horse and had to ride in a carriage. Greene granted him a leave of absence on February 10, "until he recovers ... as to be able to take the field again." This was a major blow to Greene, who depended greatly on Morgan's stellar leadership, common-sense advice and battle intuition. Morgan traveled to his home near Winchester, Virginia, to recuperate, but his tenure in the Carolinas campaign was over.[17]

McCalla

Thomas Sumter soon proved to be the hero of the day for the intrepid Sarah McCalla and some of the other women whose husbands, sons and brothers were held at Camden. His partisans, including some of the McCallas' neighbors in Chester District, captured two of Cornwallis's officers. The Gamecock shortly after negotiated an exchange of prisoners, the two British to be given up for captives from the Chester area who were jailed in Camden and Charleston. Unfortunately for the Camden prisoners, a snafu tangled the deal for their release, meaning they would spend several more weeks incarcerated. When the matter was resolved and compiled in a letter, Sarah McCalla was chosen to convey the document to Rawdon. But not wanting her hostilities with the Briton to possibly taint the prisoners' possible freedom, her friend, Mrs. Mary Adair Nixon, delivered the letter, Sarah going along but waiting near the stockade gate at British headquarters. Mary was a widow, her late husband, Capt. John Nixon, having been a scourge to the enemy as a partisan officer before being mortally wounded in a skirmish. She met with Rawdon for the first time on a March day in 1781, the commander polite and gracious. He wrote a discharge for 11 of the prisoners, handed it to her and said, "You can get them out, madam. I am very sorry they have been confined so many weeks longer than they should have been." He also gave Mary a guinea, telling her that it "will bear your expenses." Rawdon accompanied Mrs. Nixon outside and immediately recognized Sarah McCalla standing nearby. Approaching her, his voice rose in anger: "Did I not order you, madam, to keep out of my presence?"

Sarah's pent-up emotions burst forth: "I had no wish, sir, to intrude myself on your presence; I stopped at the gate on purpose to avoid you." Her long hardships, pain and suffering further fueled her words: "I might turn the tables on you, sir, and ask, why did *you* come out to the gate to insult a woman? I have received from you nothing but abuse. My distresses you have made sport of, and I ceased long since to expect anything from you but ill treatment. I am now not your supplicant; I come to *demand*, as a right, the release of my husband!" With that, she bowed, wheeled and walked away, not waiting for Rawdon to reply. Horrified, Mary trotted after her, exclaiming, "You have ruined us, I am afraid! Why, he may put us both in jail!" Sarah was past the point of caring by now, laughing and replying, "It is not the first time, Mary that I have given him to understand I thought him a villain!"[18]

Returning to the jail, they waited for a blacksmith to arrive, the sharp clang of his tools soon telling them that the prisoners' manacles were being removed. Many of them had been chained to the prison floor as a precaution after the attempted escape. In time the 11 staggered outside into the sweet air of freedom. Sarah finally reunited with her husband Thomas and Mary Nixon reveled in the release of her brother, John Adair. Among the other newly freed captives were Thomas Gill, William Wylie, Joseph Wade, and Nicholas Bishop, the latter 80 years old and completely deaf. Bishop's "crime" was that he was the father of eight or nine sons then fighting the British. His 13th child, John Bishop, remained jailed in Camden. The two courageous women led the group of ragamuffins out of the village, their songs of the "liberty-men" sung with as much gusto as they could muster.

A mile or so out of town, the party decided that those who were the healthiest should go on ahead, leaving the weakened McCalla and

Adair—the latter having survived smallpox—with the women, along with the horses and baggage. Wade, "a stout, able-bodied man," stayed to assist this last party. He had suffered greatly from the British, and was said to have survived a thousand lashes for taking up arms while under parole. Wade also was involved in the attempted jailbreak in Camden, shackled to the floor as punishment and telling the guards we would have preferred "a pair of stockings." He also was known to jingle his chains to the tune of "Yankee Doodle," much to the amusement of the other inmates and to the chagrin of the jailers.[19]

With Adair barely able to walk, Wade hoisted him on his much-scarred back, telling him, "Never mind, my boy, you are not quite so heavy as a thousand lashes! My back is a little rough, so hold on tight!" Nevertheless, the little party made it home to Chester District. With Thomas taking some time to regain his health and Sarah having to sacrifice so much in her many journeys to free him, the McCallas worked for years to repay debts and loans the war thrust upon them. The widow Mary Nixon, meanwhile, later married David McCalla, who had served with her late husband. David was Thomas McCalla's brother, as will be recalled. Mary was the mother of eight children, some by her first marriage.[20]

Kershaws

In Charleston during this time, William Kershaw wrote to his brother, John, in Yorkshire, England, telling him of the latest news, some of which the Kershaws there were likely already aware. He noted Ely Kershaw's death and Joseph being sent to Bermuda. In the first weeks of the year, William had chosen to remain loyal to the Crown after months of indecision, including his service as an American officer in the siege of Charleston. He had "joined my own countrymen and became once more a Loyalist," he penned. Of Joseph he wrote

> I soon expect him returning to Carolina where I doubt not we shall enjoy many happy days after we are restored to peace and fully convinced of the errors mankind sometimes fall[s] into when they [sp] get ensnared in an unnatural war which I must confess the present one is and God only knows when or how it will end; God grant us peace and that soon....[21]

15

"To the plains of Zama"

Cornwallis and Rawdon

After a weeks-long, lethal waltz across the North Carolina countryside, Greene and Cornwallis collided at Guilford Court House on March 15, 1781. The Earl won the day, but at a cost of some 600 casualties, a hollow victory that would further weaken his army. It took some two weeks—toward late March—for Rawdon to receive word from Cornwallis regarding this triumph over Greene. Indeed, news of the "Glorious Victory" at Guilford reached Camden on March 24, Rawdon's men erupting in celebration. "A feu de Joie was fired, by all the artillery & troops in the Garrison," noted Loyalist soldier Henry Nase of the King's American Regiment.

Obviously, this was great news, but Rawdon likely realized it had little if any effect on the Camden garrison or other outposts struggling with supply shortages and other problems due to increasing raids by Sumter, Marion and Pickens. To Rawdon, Cornwallis's prolonged absence and lack of communications meant that the burden of holding the province rested squarely on his shoulders. By the time Rawdon received Cornwallis's victory dispatch the Earl already had embarked on a decision that would alter the course of the war. He had monumental choices to make after bloody Guilford. If he attempted to rejoin Rawdon, it meant another maddening retreat to South Carolina, complicated by no promise of rations, a difficult march over bad rural roads and crossing rivers already being swollen by ongoing spring rains. Compounding the issue were the 400 or so wounded or ill soldiers who would encumber the column, whatever course he chose.

Cornwallis's other main option was to move the army overland about 200 miles east to Wilmington near the North Carolina coast, which had been a British base since January. There his troops could recuperate, reorganize and be resupplied while the wounded and sick could receive proper medical attention. From Wilmington, his rejuvenated men could advance into Virginia and continue the campaign there, linking with other British forces. This would shorten his line of communications with Clinton in New York and also be a healthier climate for his troops.[1]

On the 18th, three days after the battle, Cornwallis set his army on the grueling march from Guilford to Wilmington. He hoped to reach Cross Creek, the pro–British Scottish settlement, at the halfway point of the trek, and obtain supplies there, but there was little to be had.

The Camden garrison was heartened on April 1 by the return of a detachment led by Lt. Col. Welbore E. Doyle—John Doyle's younger brother—who had set out on a search-and-destroy mission against Francis Marion on March 22. Doyle's men had decimated the Swamp Fox's base camp on Snow's Island and reached Camden with 14 prisoners after days of sporadic hard marching, fighting and skirmishing.

Elsewhere, Cornwallis's tortuously slow march to the coast lasted over more than two weeks and by the time the tattered column neared Wilmington on April 7, the Redcoats were even more in rags, exhausted, battle shocked and most of them shoeless. The Earl also was shaken by the loss of one of his best and favorite officers, Lt. Col. James Webster, seriously wounded at Guilford and then who died on the march. Webster had been the pride of the British lions at the battle of Camden, his right wing crushing Gates's militia and then ripping into the flank of DeKalb's desperate Continentals to help secure a decisive victory.

As his troops rested and recovered, Cornwallis wrote to Lord Germain explaining that the long distance to reach Camden, the "difficulty of subsistence on the road and the impracticability of the passage of the Pee Dee against an opposing enemy" would have made such a move useless to Rawdon as well as his own troops and that his (Cornwallis's) "corps might be lost in the attempt." Cornwallis also believed that Greene would follow him, thus drawing the American army farther away from South Carolina, Rawdon and the British-held posts. The proverbial elephant in the room was the question of whether Greene would actually give chase or embark on a different course of action. The answer was yes on both counts.[2]

Greene

Greene indeed did give chase, but halted his pursuit on March 28 at Ramsey's Mill on North Carolina's Deep River, turning his attention back to South Carolina. He sent two detachments to follow Cornwallis, as if his entire force was committed to that effort. On the 29th, he wrote to Washington, explaining his reasoning: his army was "remote from re-enforcements, inferior to the enemy in numbers" and had "no prospect of support." Despite being unsure of his decision—especially in light of Daniel Morgan's departure—it proved to be a brilliant chess countermove brought on by Cornwallis's desperate situation in the Carolinas. By spearing south on April 6, Greene would likely force Cornwallis to make a choice that could decide the outcome of the Southern campaign. If Cornwallis pursued him, the Briton would have to abandon his ambitions in North Carolina and Virginia. If the Earl decided not to follow him, Greene intended to lash out at the British outposts in South Carolina, including Camden, some 130 miles from his camp on Deep River. Major William Pierce, one of Greene's aides, noted that the Quaker general's tactic "was the same that actuated Scipio when he led the Carthaginian hero [Hannibal] out of Rome to the plains of Zama" where Hannibal met crushing defeat in the Second Punic War. After some Virginia militia were discharged due to expiration of their enlistments, "the whole army was put in motion for Camden," Pierce related, "with views either to draw ... Cornwallis after us, or dispossess the British of all their interior posts in South Carolina." "General Greene finding it impracticable to follow Lord Cornwallis any farther, and seeing he could not come up with him, he therefore bent his course towards" Camden, wrote the Delaware soldier William Seymour.[3]

Certainly, there were difficulties for Greene to consider. Cornwallis's army was on the move, his intent and direction unknown to the Americans, but he was drawing further distant from his other troops remaining behind in South Carolina and Georgia. Still, Charleston remained strongly defended and the major inland outposts at Camden and Ninety Six, along with smaller strongholds at Georgetown, Orangeburg, Forts Watson, Motte and Granby all still bristled with Redcoat bayonets, as did Savannah and Augusta. Rawdon had a total of about 8,000 troops, most of whom were on garrison duty, in all of these places. At Camden were about 1,400 soldiers. News of Greene's return reinvigorated the partisan activities of Sumter, Marion and Pickens fueling their aggressiveness especially the elusive Swamp Fox. "General Greene, being obliged to retreat from before the King's army, turned his view towards this province, as the most vulnerable point, in the absence of Lord Cornwallis," related Lt. Col. Balfour in Charleston.[4]

With all this in mind, Greene ordered Sumter to reinforce him when the army eventually neared Camden; Pickens was to assail Augusta; and Marion—strengthened by "Light Horse Harry" Lee's Legion and a detachment of Maryland infantry, sent by Greene—was to operate against the lesser British posts and lines of enemy communication between Charleston, Camden and Ninety Six. After a four-day delay at the Pee Dee River due to a lack of boats, Greene was moving almost blindly when he wrote to Marion on April 17, asking for intelligence reports from the Swamp Fox:

15. "To the plains of Zama"

We are on our march for Camden, and shall be there next day after tomorrow. I am greatly in the dark respecting the enemy's strength and situation in South Carolina, and also of Lord Cornwallis's motions. This last circumstance is of the highest importance to the safety of our army.... Don't spare either time or pains to get the earliest information, and to forward it as soon as possible....

The Gamecock—based on a Loyalist officer's account—had mustered his partisans, telling them that "Cornwallis has gone into North Carolina—to seek a grave for himself and his army."[5]

In the meantime, Sumter was pounding off on a retaliatory strike against two Loyalists settlements along the Broad River. Greene's reaction to this offers a vividly stark view of the civil war storming in mad bloodshed across South Carolina that spring. "The animosity between Whigs and Tories of this State renders their situation truly deplorable," he wrote to Washington and the Continental Congress:

> There is not a day passes but there are more or less who fall a sacrifice to this savage disposition. The Whigs seem determined to extirpate the Tories, and the Tories the Whigs. Some thousands have fallen in this way in this quarter, and the evil rages with more violence than ever. If a stop cannot be put to these massacres, the country will be depopulated in a few months more, as neither Whig nor Tory can live.

More important in the moment, however, was that the independent-minded Sumter did not feel compelled to link with Greene, who needed his manpower as well as provisions gathered locally.[6]

The Americans arrived in the Camden vicinity late in the day on April 19, encamping about four miles from the town. Many of the troops were "marching over the same ground which our army went the last summer along with General Gates," William Seymour wrote of crossing the Camden battlefield where he and so many others fought the previous August: "This is a poor barren part of the country. The inhabitants are chiefly of a Scotch extraction, living in mean cottages, and are much disaffected, being great enemies to their country.... We took this day eleven of the enemy prisoners, who were straggling through the country."

That evening, Greene sent Captain Robert Kirkwood and his light infantry company of Delaware Continentals forward about 8 p.m. in an attempt to seize Logtown, then "a group of six or eight cabins in a rather extensive clearing on a slight elevation" less than a mile north of Camden. Kirkwood's company reached Logtown about 10 p.m., finding some enemy pickets and a small force posted among the houses. Despite the element of surprise, the Marylanders soon found themselves in a sharp firefight. Muskets flared and echoed in the blackness as the foes fought at close quarters in and around the little village until almost midnight. By then, Kirkwood had wrested the position from its stubborn defenders, but there was intermittent fighting until sunup on the 20th. The exhausted and bloodied Blue Hens who held Logtown were heartened hours later by the "Very agreeable Sight" of Greene's main force marching to their support.[7]

Rawdon

Seeing American troops assembling about Logtown and the low ridge just to the north, were troubling but not unexpected developments for Lord Rawdon in Camden. Over the previous week or more he had received dubious and unreliable reports of Greene's approach, but then had gotten "clear information" regarding the enemy advance although he remained ignorant of the foe's strength. Perhaps more frustrating, Rawdon was "equally in the dark" about Cornwallis's situation "and having no particular instructions for his guidance, he thought it his duty, at all events, to maintain his post," a British account stated. "The communications were so entirely cut off, that.... Rawdon had no manner of knowledge" of the Crown's army after the battle at Guilford,

> much less could he have the most distant idea, of the hard necessity which compelled Lord Cornwallis to fly from the arms of victory, abandon the line of operation and by a most difficult march ... retire ... to Wilmington. He could not therefore but be astonished at receiving intelligence, that Greene, whom he looked upon as ruined, or at least as having fled to Virginia, was in full march to South Carolina, with a view of attacking him at Camden.

Whether Rawdon was "astonished" is debatable since he was aware—by about April 12—that Greene was not pursuing Cornwallis. But he also had to be highly frustrated with the sparse information from Cornwallis, especially with the gravity of his situation in holding the British line in the province. As the Americans spread out "in full view," Rawdon also realized he did not have the strength—only a few hundred soldiers—to cope with this threat, since so many defenders were needed to man Camden's fieldworks surrounding the town. "The paucity of troops and the extensiveness of the posts which they had to defend, were sufficient motives with the British commander for not risking the loss of men by any attempt to harass the enemy in their approach."[8]

It was also about this time that Rawdon was advised by Balfour at Charleston that the Commander-in-Chief—General Clinton—had ordered that Camden be abandoned, but the aggressive activity of Greene, Sumter, Marion and Lee had "rendered such a movement impracticable," said one account. Still, the garrison he had on hand was formidable in spirit and tenacity if not in numbers. Rawdon's force was composed of the 63rd Regiment of Foot, led by Major Alexander Campbell; his own

15. "To the plains of Zama"

Volunteers of Ireland, the King's American Regiment, organized in and around New York and commanded by Lt. Col. George Campbell; George Turnbull's New York Volunteers, and a small number of New York Dragoons—also identified as the South Carolina Loyalist Dragoons—under Captain John Coffin. With Rawdon in overall charge, his Volunteers of Ireland were led by Major John Doyle, his second in command at Camden.

The garrison was strengthened somewhat on the 19th when a contingent of Loyalist militia from across the province approached the outpost. Rawdon praised these volunteers for their "great zeal and fidelity" since many had come "from considerable distances to offer their services." Amazingly—with Greene sitting on his doorstep—Rawdon had to turn away some of these badly needed men since he could not feed them. His supply of rations "was but scanty" and he could only accept "those who would otherwise have been exposed to suffer from the enemy."[9]

Reaching Camden's outskirts with his main force on April 20, Greene spent some time in Logtown, sizing up the British works from afar. Deciding that Rawdon's defenses were too strong to assault—at least on that side of the village—he withdrew about a mile north to the heights along Hobkirk Hill to await events and decide on a course of action. Considered a stronger position, the hill was actually a narrow, sandy ridge—some half-mile in length—and about 80 feet in elevation running east to west and blanketed with pine trees and underbrush.

The hill was named for Thomas Hobkirk, or one of his relatives, who owned about 100 acres in that area as of about 1769. Carved through the middle was the Waxhaw road—present-day Broad Street. The east end of the ridge sloped down to the fringe of a swamp bordering Pine Tree Creek, the swamp and creek south past Camden's defenses. The southern base of the ridge was far less wooded, consisting of a plain dotted by thickets and sloping to Logtown. There was more open, flat ground to the south and to the edge of Camden's fortifications, the British having cleared some terrain for a better field of fire and to remove anything that an enemy force could use for cover. A number of trees had been left where they fell to obstruct the movements of enemy cavalry.

For Greene, there was one very dangerous complication: from the top of the hill there was no unobstructed vantage point of its approaches due to contours of the land, the woods and the thickening spring greenery. On a few occasions, some of Greene's officers ventured out to get a better look at the enemy defenses, attracting a few cannonballs from the Redcoats in the redoubts. Some officers narrowly escaped death or injury when a round hit a small brick oven behind which they had sought refuge.[10]

Greene's Virginia brigade was commanded by Brigadier General Isaac Huger, while his Maryland brigade was led by the stalwart Colonel

Otho Williams. Meanwhile, the Americans had learned that an enemy force of about 500 under Lt. Col. John W.T. Watson was endeavoring to reach Camden, returning after their unsuccessful strike against Marion in the Pee Dee region. This prompted Greene on April 22 to move his army southeast of the town from Hobkirk Hill. From this position, the Americans could possibly block Watson from entering Camden and also prevent Rawdon from sending reinforcements to Fort Watson, the British outpost on the Santee River that was besieged by a combined command under the Swamp Fox and Henry Lee. To allow his men more mobility in this march over boggy, wild terrain, Greene sent his artillery and baggage to the rear.[11]

Another development stung Greene at this time. British Major Thomas Fraser had cobbled together reinforcements for his South Carolina Royalists regiment of cavalry and militia—also known as the South Carolina Provincial Regiment—from various detachments in the region and had managed to slip into Camden on or about April 21 after marshaling at Ninety Six. The Quaker general was clearly irritated with Sumter, writing to the Gamecock on April 23:

> Since I wrote you I have critically examined the fortifications of this place and find them much superior to what I expected. The garrison from the best intelligence I can get is also much stronger than I expected; and I have had the mortification to hear yesterday [the 22nd] that the South Carolina royalists had the Day before thrown themselves into the place [Camden] from Ninety Six.

Greene had no way of knowing that Fort Watson had fallen that same day, the 23rd, after an eight-day siege—although he learned of this victory the next day—or that Rawdon couldn't spare any troops if he was to hold Camden. Also, why did Rawdon allow Fraser's men to remain in the outpost when he had turned away other Loyalist militia only two days before, due to his ration shortages? Perhaps the best answer is that after he saw Greene's army nearing Camden on the 20th, Rawdon realized he would need every man he could muster, no matter his supply issues. Rawdon also learned about this time that John Watson had diverted his Redcoats to Georgetown instead of further risking his force in trying to reach Camden. Watson's soldiers temporarily bolstered the Crown's garrison in that coastal town. Since he no longer expected Watson, Rawdon welcomed Fraser's reinforcements. The fact that Fraser had veterans who had seen action at Musgrove's Mill the previous August likely also factored into Rawdon's decision.[12]

Greene's troops spent much of April 22–23 toiling through trackless swamps to reach a point near MacRae's mill pond and Paint Hill where the Americans hoped to intercept enemy troops coming from or entering Camden. The effort was backbreaking, even if in short duration. The men had to build a log road and a bridge across Pine Tree Creek as well as struggling through the backwater morass of nearby Little Pine Tree Creek in order to gain their objective. Unknown to Greene, all was in vain, since Watson's troops had gone to Georgetown, Fraser's were already in the town and no other British reinforcements were coming. As always, Greene's soldiers were desperately short on rations, but this was allayed somewhat by the arrival of Zach Cantey, whose family had a plantation near Camden. Cantey had been Greene's assistant commissary in Virginia and had a supply of bacon and corn—hidden in the swamps—brought to the army. A few skinny cattle also were herded in and slaughtered. On the 24th, Greene ordered his troops to retrace their muddy slog through the swamps and back to the slopes of Hobkirk Hill, with nothing to show for their efforts.[13]

During the army's movements over April 20–24, Greene had sent out several patrols to probe the strength of the enemy defenses around the town's entire perimeter and to perhaps entice Rawdon to launch an assault. Parties of foragers were also active, trying to bring in more supplies for the army. On the 21st, Colonel Washington's cavalry and some infantry struck an enemy outpost on the Wateree River, destroying a house and some fortifications, returning to camp with 350 captured horses and cattle. The next day, a sharp skirmish erupted at a mill the Redcoats were using near the village. "The efforts made by the enemy [Greene's force] to examine the British works, and particularly an attempt to destroy their mill, necessarily brought on some skirmishes," stated a British account. "By the prisoners taken in these excursions, Lord Rawdon had the satisfaction to learn that…. Greene's army was not by any means so numerous as he had apprehended" but was expecting more reinforcements at any time.[14]

Jackson

For days, rumors of Greene's presence had energized the overcrowded prisoners in the Camden jail compound, including Andrew Jackson, all cautiously hopeful of being liberated by the American army. As Greene edged ever closer to Camden, the captives at one point were herded out of the stockade, the complex possibly being within range of enemy artillery along Hobkirk Hill. This precaution soon ended, the men hustled back inside when it was learned that Greene had no cannon. A few more days passed with no action, but by April 24 the inmates sensed something was imminent. Troops moving about in the town and whispered bits of conversation suggested that the British were girding to attack the Americans. A board fence had recently been built atop the wall enclosing the jail grounds, and Andrew—now 14 after his March 15 birthday—knew that any view of the expected battle would be obscured if he didn't find—or make—a hole to see from. He looked for a crevice in the fence on the afternoon of the 24th, but found none. Overnight, however, he used "an old razor blade" given to the prisoners to use as a meat cutter, and hacked away at a knot in the wood. By sunup on the 25th, he had carved a hole to watch any upcoming action. Lord Rawdon and his troops would not disappoint.[15]

Greene's troops were settling back into the lines along Hobkirk Hill later in the day on April 24 when the commander issued this directive to discourage desertions and try to keep the troops combat alert:

> The general orders respecting passes are punctually to be observed. None are to be granted but by commandants of corps. The rolls are to be called at least three times a day and all absentees reported and punished. Officers of every rank are to confine themselves to their respective duties. And every part of the army must be in readiness to stand at arms at a moment's warning.

Indeed, Greene posted his regiments in line of battle, expecting to draw Rawdon into attacking him on terrain of his choosing. "The sally [from Rawdon] was what we wished for, and had taken a position about a mile from the town for the purpose, on a very advantageous piece of ground," he wrote to Henry Lee days later. His soldiers were strong and hearty souls, but they were exhausted, starving and muddy from the exertions of the past three days, as well as the trials of the arduous march even to reach Camden. Still, they were eager for the coming day—the 25th—when rations and grog were expected, orders stating: "The troops are to be furnished with two days provisions, and a gill of spirits per man, as soon as the stores arrive." Greene's artillery was also on the way to Hobkirk Hill.[16]

In Camden that night, a drummer of the Maryland Continentals "whose fidelity had for some time been questioned," deserted to the British. There are varying accounts about this shadowy youngster, who was identified only as Jones. Whatever his background, he was brought before Rawdon, telling him that the Americans were without artillery or provisions and had not been reinforced by Sumter. Word also possibly reached Rawdon on the 24th of Fort Watson's surrender and that Marion was marching to join Greene's army before Camden. The timing and facts are vague about this situation, but Rawdon was decisive based on the information he had on hand. Like Cornwallis against Gates the previous August, he would not wait to be attacked, but would be the aggressor against a numerically superior force. Rawdon would hammer Greene with everything he had in a surprise assault on the morning of Wednesday, April 25, in an effort to seize momentum and "evade much greater, and not far distant, evil and danger" from his stronger foe.[17]

15. "To the plains of Zama" 175

"Nothing could exceed the joy manifested by the whole garrison on these orders being made known," a British officer wrote. "Every arrangement was made...." Could Rawdon replicate the stunningly epic conquest Cornwallis won along Sanders Creek eight months earlier? Another question arises: Knowing the artillery was on its way, could Greene have intentionally allowed the deserter drummer to "slip" through his lines and tell Rawdon that the Americans had no guns as part of his attempt to entice a British attack? Even if Rawdon was unaware of Greene trying to lure him into making an assault, the decisions—basically deadly gambles—by both commanders would be decided by the soldiers in the ranks. Only an hourglass of hours would tell the bloody tale.[18]

16

"In the flush of victory and pursuit": Hobkirk Hill

Well after sunrise on the 25th, a "comfortable supply of provisions," along with three six-pounder artillery pieces, arrived under escort in the American camp. As the rations were soon distributed, the men stacked arms and prepared to cook their breakfasts, the only disappointment being that the spirits were still en route. It was after 9 a.m., the day already warming under a bright sun and clear skies. Many of the first soldiers to eat their meals then headed down to several springs on the northeast side of the hill to wash themselves, clothes, kettles and other mud-caked equipment. Despite the possibility of an imminent assault and Greene's restriction on leaves, other men "were out in the country on passes," noted a Delaware Continental. The bulk of Greene's troops were posted on the east side of the road, facing southeast, while Huger's Virginians were encamped to the west and looking south, the route being the most direct and obvious point of a British assault. From left to right were the Fourth Virginia Continentals, led by Lt. Col. Richard Campbell, which anchored Greene's right flank, and the Fifth Virginia of Lt. Col. Samuel Hawes whose flank rested beside the road. Greene's artillery, commanded by Col. Charles Harrison, were positioned on the road in the middle of the American line, aimed south toward Camden.[1]

The addition of the six-pounders and 40 cannoneers was important not only to Greene's firepower, but also could be a sanguine welcome if the British attacked. With Harrison was artillery Capt. Anthony Singleton whose guns had inflicted much damage on the Redcoats in the battle of Camden. Troops were to be posted in front of the guns to hide them from the enemy's view. As stated earlier—but possibly unknown to the Americans—Rawdon's intelligence, including information from the deserter drummer, indicated that Greene had no artillery. To the east of Harrison were Williams's two Continental regiments, composed of Colonel John Gunby's First Maryland and the Fifth Maryland led by Lt. Col. Benjamin

Ford. Greene's reserve, some 250 North Carolina militia commanded by Col. James Read—or Reade—were to the rear of the Marylanders, while Greene had situated his men in a line curving generally south to southeast, especially strong on the east end of the ridge.

The army bivouacked in positions which it would hold if attacked. "The horses were tethered nearby to graze" to be in readiness, accounts varying on whether their saddles were on or off. Along the southwest end of the ridge, patrols were alert for any enemy incursions in that area. Lt. Colonel William Washington's 60 or so horsemen—about 30 other cavalrymen had no mounts—were to be in reserve behind Williams's line. Apparently realizing that the area in front of the Marylanders' positions might be vulnerable to attack, Greene posted a strong line of pickets commanded by Captains Perry Benson of Maryland and the Virginian Simon Morgan, about a mile ahead of their position. The pickets were supported by Kirkwood's light infantry—whose ranks were thinned after the Logtown fighting overnight on April 19–20—a short distance behind them.[2]

Gunby's Continentals were Greene's shock troops "ever ready to encounter danger at the word of command, and ever ready to lead in battle, under the most discouraging circumstances," said one account. These veterans were stalwarts in defeat at Camden, savored victory at Cowpens and "acquired the highest distinction" at Guilford Court House, thus marking their path to Hobkirk Hill with their blood and valor. Lt. Col. John Eager Howard, 28, was Gunby's second-in-command but had already possibly ascended to the zenith of his career at Cowpens, leading a devastating bayonet charge that was one of the keys to the victory. At some point that day, Howard held the swords of seven British officers who had surrendered to him. Earlier, in the northern campaigns, he was in combat at White Plains, Germantown—where he was wounded—and Monmouth. At Camden, where he was with the Second Maryland, Howard fought gallantly, banding a few of his troops together during the rout and reaching Charlotte some three days after the battle. He also had distinguished himself in action at Guilford Court House. Weeks before Greene reached Hobkirk Hill, the Continental Congress on March 9 voted to award a silver medal to Howard as the "Hero of Cowpens."[3]

Gunby's command also included a light infantry company under Captain John Smith, about 45 Irishmen all under age 30. Smith himself was known for his fearlessness, not only as a leader, but also in close-quarters combat. At Guilford, he led his boys in a charge against the enemy lines, encountering and killing a British lieutenant colonel with his sword in one-on-one action. Smith also was believed—at least by the British—to have slain two or three other Redcoats after they surrendered at Guilford, an accusation that would later haunt him—violently. On this

April 25, however, Smith and his company were detached from Gunby's troops, assigned to protect the American artillery from a position in the rear.[4]

Also in Gunby's ranks was Captain William Beatty, Jr., a popular officer who was fated to play a pivotal role in the upcoming battle. Beatty, 23, was from Frederick County, Maryland, described as "the pride and stay of his command" and also as a "promising youth, engaged to marry an amiable girl." He had been away on a recruiting mission and missed the Camden battle in August, he and his recruits reaching the army shortly after Greene took command. A few weeks before this spring morning on Hobkirk Hill, he had written his father, Colonel William Beatty, from the army's camp at Buffalo Creek in North Carolina. "Should be extremely glad to hear how You & all the family are..." he noted in this excerpt of the letter, also expressing his interest in Maryland's ongoing recruiting efforts and in being sent news "articles ... for I am in the greatest Want of them.... Please to remember my best respects to all the Family Who I hope with Yourself are all in perfect Health[.] I have been in Very good State of Health ever Since I left Home[.] Believe me Sir to be with the Sincerest respect your most obt [obedient] & Dutiful Son." Ford's regiment was an entirely different story. His Sixth Maryland had suffered severely at Camden. Now, after the army's reorganization, the Fifth Maryland's ranks consisted of a large number of raw recruits. Matters were much the same with Huger's troops. The Virginia brigade had served in action under Greene in Pennsylvania, but most of its veterans had been discharged after three years of service. Thus, Hawes's and Campbell's regiments also were composed primarily of inexperienced soldiers. Greene's army on Hobkirk Hill totaled 1,200 to 1,500 troops.[5]

Rawdon

In Camden, Rawdon had ordered his troops ready to move about 9:30 a.m. but was delayed due to "part of the cavalry being then out aforaging" which "prevented the march ... at the hour appointed," a British officer noted. By arming every available man who could trigger a Brown Bess, including musicians, Rawdon pieced together a force about 900 to 950 strong with two six-pounders. "His Lordship immediately had the Redoubts all manned with Negroes and Tories, and every man of his whole Army, in the most silent and secret manner without any Drum, Fife, Horn or any noise ... all went off...." These soldiers marched out the south side of their outpost about 10 a.m. and proceeded north, along the west bank of Pine Tree Creek, staying on the edge of its bogs and concealed by woods.

16. "In the flush of victory and pursuit": Hobkirk Hill

The Redcoats then turned generally to the northwest toward Hobkirk Hill, intent on flanking the left of the American position in an area where the slope was gentler, thus easier for the soldiers to ascend. It was a bold, desperate risk, since Rawdon was "committing the redoubts, and every thing [sp] at Camden, to the custody of the militia, and of a few sick soldiers." A British officer wrote that "our little army marched ... taking a circuitous rout[e] through the woods, and always avoiding the publick [sp] road."

On the heights a short distance away, Greene had settled into his tent with a cup of coffee, a "rare luxury" at this point in the campaign. The calm was suddenly fractured by a gunshot, then another and then an ever heightening staccato of musketry, all coming from the direction where the pickets fronting the Maryland Continentals were posted. Hobkirk Hill, from its opening moments, would be mainly a battle of rival colonials, like Kings Mountain and later Augusta and Ninety Six, noted the renowned historian of the Southern campaign, Henry Lumpkin.[6]

Leading the British column, a light infantry company of the Volunteers of Ireland, first clashed with enemy pickets on the left of Greene's position near the intersection of the Camden-Cheraw road. These Redcoats had "emerged from the rocky creek bottoms prematurely" about 11:05 a.m. and exchanged scattered fire with Benson's Marylanders. The Volunteers, part of Rawdon's own regiment, "suddenly poured in upon their pickets," said a British account. "As soon as the sentinels [the Maryland pickets] discovered them, they fired on them, and gave the alarm...." Benson's riflemen briefly held their ground, but were gradually pushed back toward the northwest, although a British report contended the Marylanders "though supported, were almost instantly driven in and pursued to their camp." Morgan's Virginia pickets were also engaged by then, and in short order Kirkwood was assailed by the British 63rd Regiment. Kirkwood's Delawares staved off these Redcoats for a few minutes, buying critical time for Greene to scramble his troops into their pre-set battle line along the crest. "Although the enemy were in much visible confusion," related an English account, "yet they formed with expedition, and received the British column bravely."[7]

After gaining ground in brushing off the pickets and Kirkwood's infantry, Rawdon's troops hustled into a compact battle line across the Waxhaw road and at the southern foot of Hobkirk Hill. The New York Volunteers were in the center with the 63rd Regiment on the right and the King's American Regiment on the left. The rest of the Volunteers of Ireland were posted behind the 63rd, while a detachment of "Convalescents"— possibly composed of the musicians, other non-combatants and walking wounded under a Captain Robertson—was situated in support behind the King's Americans. Fraser's South Carolina Provincial Regiment and the

New York Dragoons were held in reserve. Loyalist sharpshooters crept in among the trees on both flanks, ready to pick off enemy officers, a tactic Rawdon undoubtedly learned while fighting in the South Carolina swamps and woods. The majority of Greene's men were now in action. "By now our main army was drawn up, and engaged them" with musketry and other small arms, related the Delaware soldier William Seymour, a British officer adding that minutes earlier the Americans in "their hurry and surprise ... flew to their arms, most without their coats, and a considerable body had formed...." "The whole line was soon engaged in close firing," Greene wrote.[8]

To the lethal shock of the British in the vicinity of the road, the Americans in the center parted a few steps in front of Harrison's and Singleton's six-pounders, which then belched grapeshot into the massed Redcoats. Unprepared for this, Rawdon's men paid the butcher's bill, the iron sleet searing down the slope and through their ranks with bloody accuracy. "Captain Singleton ... very much signalized himself in levelling [sp] his pieces so well and playing with such impetuosity, that they put the enemy in great confusion, having killed and dangerously wounded great numbers of them...," noted Seymour. A Redcoat officer wrote: "they gave our troops a very heavy fire of musketry and grape shot, but could not check their ardour [sp]. The fire was immediately returned...." Both sides were "in the midst of a very smart fire, as well from our small arms as from our artillery...."[9]

Seeing the enemy's narrow front and that the scarlet ranks were staggered by the cannon fire, Greene went for the jugular, ordering an all-out attack downhill. On each end of his extreme lines, Campbell and Ford were sent forward, both to wheel and assail the British's exposed flanks in their respective sectors. In the middle, Gunby and Hawes were to launch a bayonet charge without firing a shot. Washington and his cavalry were instructed to ride west of the ridge, turning south to come in behind Rawdon's soldiers and attempt to bag the whole lot. It was a masterful and instantaneous plan made by a general amid the hell of combat; and in a few critical, precious minutes, Rawdon's gallant sortie would have been blunted, his force obliterated and Camden taken. Greene's assault "seemed to promise the most conclusive finish to the grateful beginnings of the day."[10] And yet...

There were too many working parts to coordinate in such a short time and communications by messengers were sporadic with no remote chance of synchronization. Additionally, the rival commander watching from below had become a wily, battle-savvy tactician and leader after almost a year of campaigning in the Southern wilds. Seeing Greene's deployments underway, Rawdon summoned his reserves—Robertson's detachment to the left of the King's American Regiment, and the Volunteers of Ireland coming up on the right of the 63rd Regiment, thus extending his flanks. In so doing, Rawdon was able to "counteract this movement of the Americans" and "to expose their wings to the very disadvantage to which Greene had proposed to subject his," stated one account. As a result of Rawdon's quick action, both Campbell's Virginians and Ford's Marylanders, who had "started forward under an impetus at once swift and steady" suddenly began taking a withering fire of British musketry in their flanks.[11]

Still, the American wave rolled down the slope to the southern base of the ridge and beyond.

The maneuvering by both sides brought the brunt of the British attack against Greene's left-center, where Gunby's crack First Maryland Continentals were posted. In fact, the movements also resulted in Rawdon's best—the 63rd Regiment and the King's American Regiment—coming up against the Marylanders' bayonet charge. But an engagement between these elite troops was not to be.

Some of Gunby's men opened fire as they advanced, contrary to orders and not expected of experienced troops. It is unclear if these Continentals halted to deliver a volley or fired individually, but whatever the case, the men's formation and/or momentum, was interrupted. Shortly thereafter, Captain Beatty, leading the right company of the First Maryland, slumped dead, a bullet slamming into his forehead. Beatty's fall "caused those nearest to him to check their progress"—in plainer words, they faltered or paused—"and the halt was rapidly communicated" from right to left, disrupting the advance of two other companies "before the cause [Beatty's death] was understood." With these Continentals temporarily confused and somewhat disorganized, "some hesitation ensued when the men were urged to regain the line." Instead of trying to re-form these Continentals and resume the assault, Gunby sent Lt. Col. Howard with orders to the rest of his regiment to withdraw to the base of the hill, some 60 yards to the rear, and regroup there.

Seeing the Marylanders' withdrawal, the Redcoat veterans of the 63rd Regiment and the King's Americans smelled blood and plunged ahead with huzzahs and glinting blades. Gunby's repositioning quickly became a retreat and then a rout. Describing these events as a "stroke of fortune," Greene noted that Gunby's order "gave the whole regiment an idea of a retreat, which soon spread...." As Williams, Gunby and Howard desperately tried to rally the First Maryland there was suddenly massive trouble on the other flank. Leading the Fifth Maryland's assault, Lt. Col. Ford was unhorsed when a musket ballet splintered his left elbow. Their commander down and untethered from their link with Gunby's broken regiment, Ford's Continentals soon "faltered and retired." The center of Greene's position was caving in.[12]

Greene, meanwhile, had been focused on "the vital importance of rapidity" involving his flank units—Campbell and Ford—and, with Huger, was personally leading Campbell's Virginia Continentals when he received word of the chaos in the center and left of his line. Riding amid these men the General "vainly tried the influence of his voice and presence to bring his panic-stricken soldiers once more into action," stated one account. By this point many of the Marylanders had fled over the top of the ridge and down the opposite slope where they halted, due to Greene's admonitions and likely those of Williams, Gunby and Howard as well. Shouts from the enemy drew the general back to the summit where "the whole extent of his misfortune opened upon his view."

Except for the dead and wounded scattered about, his battle line had disintegrated. Campbell's troops were gone, overwhelmed by the flank fire and enemy pressure to their front. The only American unit still intact was Hawes's Fifth Virginia, these Continentals still fighting west of the road and in the general vicinity of Harrison's artillery, which appeared to be in immediate danger of being captured. The Virginians had descended the south slope a short distance, but with their flanks laid bare, "the enemy immediately doubled upon them and attacked them both on the flank and in front," Greene related.[13]

Desperately, Greene flung Smith's light infantry forward to help defend the guns. Also about this time his officers had been able to pull elements of Campbell's troops and Ford's Continentals into a makeshift line on both sides of Gunby's men, who had rallied to some degree, at the base of the ridge's northern slope. Hawes's Virginians were also posted with the jumbled main body and would cover the retreat, unless Greene decided to renew the battle. The central issue then was whether the cannon would be lost, Smith's Marylanders bracing to prevent such a catastrophe. Some of the artillerists were toiling with the drag ropes to pull the guns out of danger, assisted by Smith's soldiers, but men were crumpling from the fire of the Redcoat infantry and John Coffin's Loyalist dragoons. At one point, Greene himself dismounted and grabbed the ropes, "thus inspiring his men with a zeal which could not be resisted."

Smith "had a stout heavy *Cut and Thrust* and a very strong arm with which he did great execution" with his sword in the close-quarters combat that ensued. It was a heroic effort, but it was not enough. The repeated enemy thrusts gradually whittled down Smith's Irishmen until the captain, slightly wounded, and 14 others were all that were left. Their comrades already killed, wounded or captured, Smith and his survivors were overwhelmed and taken prisoner. Still, the Americans had been able to wheel the cannon into underbrush on the hill's back slope—or north—where they were overlooked by victorious Redcoats pushing over the crest.[14]

16. "In the flush of victory and pursuit": Hobkirk Hill

So where was the dashing William Washington and his small band of cavalry during this overall action, which some accounts incorrectly state lasted only fifteen minutes? Washington was late to the waltz, having arced wide around the armies, to assail the enemy right flank but coming in too far behind the British to apply critical pressure to Rawdon's main force. Instead, the Americans surprised and fell on a variety of rear echelon personnel, including doctors, quartermasters, teamsters and "all the loose trumpery of an army" who had come out of the Camden defenses and were in the area between the village and Logtown, observing the battle. Washington captured about 200 of these unfortunates, mounting some of them behind his troopers to be carried to the American lines. At some point he realized that a brief but desperate struggle was underway on the hill and changed course, paroling a number of the prisoners in quick order and riding hard back toward Hobkirk. Still, valuable time was lost in taking the prisoners. Essentially Washington and his men were galloping into the rear of Rawdon's attack force, but the British were well advanced in pushing back Greene by then, both armies disorganized in various degrees amidst the combat smoke and forested ground. Whatever the case, Washington troopers were able to avoid a firefight on the hill, locate the concealed six-pounders and get them safely off the field, pulled by the cavalry horses.[15]

"To accident only, they [the Americans] were indebted for saving their guns, which being drawn into a hollow, out of the road, were overlooked by our troops in the flush of victory and pursuit, so that their cavalry, in which they greatly exceeded us, had an opportunity of taking them off," Lt. Col. Balfour in Charleston wrote to Lord Germain, based on Rawdon's reports. In the same dispatch, Balfour noted that Rawdon had made "the most marked decision" to attack the enemy and "with that spirit ... prevailing over superior numbers, and an obstinate resistance, compelled them to give way...." Despite the bitter lost chance to seize the enemy cannon, Rawdon's rugged fighters were the kings of Hobkirk Hill. A frustrated Greene was done for the day, *undone* by the collapse of his vaunted Marylanders as well as the supposed trap into which he had lured the outnumbered enemy.

"The cup of victory had been snatched from his lips while the draught was most grateful and ready for the taste...," wrote a 19th-century Greene biographer. "The victory was already in his grasp." The Americans retreated about two miles, the withdrawal covered by Hawes's Virginians and Washington's horse against a feeble pursuit. There Greene regrouped and tried to gather his stragglers, before renewing the march that afternoon to Sanders Creek, where he encamped for the night. Ever active, Washington pushed back toward Camden on a reconnaissance after the army halted, surprising and routing John Coffin's Loyalist dragoons on or near the battlefield.[16]

The battle carnage—though nothing to compare with the 1780 Camden combat—spread for acres, dotted by corpses, dying and wounded soldiers of both sides, carcasses of horses and all the equipage of war, personal belongings, splintered muskets, bloody pieces of uniforms and myriad other items littering the pine woods, slopes, sandy depressions and ridge top of Hobkirk Hill. "The enemy's killed and wounded were scattered over such an extent of ground, that their loss could not be ascertained," said a British report. Although the "field was kept by neither party," there was intermittent skirmishing—or "the repetition of partial strokes," as Otho Williams described it—at various points on the field until about 5 p.m., including Washington's rout of Coffin. Greene's troops took 55 enemy prisoners who were soon sent to the American post at Salisbury along with two paroled British officers. As many as ten other of Rawdon's officers were paroled by the Americans on the battlefield. Based on at least one source, Rawdon himself was nearly taken when he was briefly surrounded by Washington's cavalrymen before onrushing British soldiers drove off his potential captors.[17]

Jackson

From his knothole in the jail fence, Andrew Jackson watched the battle, relaying news of developments to a group of fellow prisoners on the ground below him. The outcome, with the British holding their own, left the captives in even deeper despair. "Andrew's spirits sank under this accumulation of miseries, and he began to sicken with the first symptoms of the small-pox," wrote Jackson biographer James Parton. Robert Jackson was in even worse shape. His head wound was never properly treated and wasn't healing. He also was in the grip of disease, burning with fever or shivering with chills. "Another week of prison life would have probably consigned both of these boys to the grave."[18]

Within hours of the battle, an exhausted Rawdon penned a message to Cornwallis informing him of his victory:

> My Dear Lord, General Greene arrived before us on the 19th. As Watson had not joined me, I remained on the defensive; but hearing that Lee, Sumpter [sp], and Marion were coming to Greene, and the South Carolina regiment [Fraser's] having got safe to me from Ninety-Six [sp], I thought it best to risk an action.... After a severe action we routed him [Greene] totally; his cannon escaped by going off very early, and the enemy's superiority in cavalry prevented our making many prisoners. I cannot yet tell the loss on either part;

but I think the enemy's treble ours. Excuse this scrawl, my dear Lord, for I am overcome with fatigue...."[19]

American casualties were about 264, including killed, wounded and missing, although Otho Williams, two days after the battle, estimated Greene's losses at about 130 killed and wounded, plus some 50 officers and men—most of them privates—missing, for a total of 180. Beatty's death was much lamented, one account describing him as "one of the best of officers, and an ornament to his profession." Col. Ford of the Maryland Continentals was "dangerously wounded" and sent to a hospital in Charlotte to recover. Also "very slightly wounded" in the thigh was Lt. Col. Richard Campbell of the Fourth Virginia Continentals. He soon returned to duty, but his luck ran out at Eutaw Springs on September 8, 1781, where he was killed in action.

British losses vary by different accounts. Rawdon claimed his casualties did not exceed 100, "in which are included one officer killed and 11 wounded," Lt. Col. Balfour at Charleston wrote to Secretary George Germain on May 1. Rawdon, according to Balfour, also "states the loss of the enemy, on this occasion, as upwards of 100 made prisoners, and 400 killed and wounded," the latter figure almost certainly inflated. Historian Henry Lumpkin places British losses in total at between 257 and 269.[20]

The day after the battle, Rawdon wrote to Greene—who had retreated to Rugeley's Mill on April 26—regarding the well-being of casualties on both sides. He asked Greene for the return of three captured British surgeons "who were dressing your wounded as well as ours, upon the ground where we fell in with your advanced guards" and that the doctors' efforts in "their situation should have exempted their capture." Rawdon added that the American wounded he held were "received into our general hospital" and urged Greene to release the surgeons so they could return to Camden and treat the fallen of both armies. In return, Rawdon would request the release of an equal number of American surgeons being held in Charleston. Greene replied the same day, thanking Rawdon for his humane treatment of the captive wounded and noting that he had ordered "the same act of generosity and humanity" to the British casualties in his custody. *Five* Redcoat surgeons were allowed to go into Camden on April 27, Greene apparently sending the additional men to augment the care for all of the wounded in the enemy outpost.[21]

In a "cipher" message written to Cornwallis on May 2, Rawdon stated: "Greene is still at Rugeley's—I suppose waiting for succor. Lee and Marion, I believe have joined him. Sumpter [sp] is collecting provisions for him.... Be assured every exertion shall be made, but nothing done rashly. I have provisions for a fortnight, and horses plenty. Our action cost us 220 men. Greene lost at the very least 500...." A British officer who left Camden that same day and fought at Hobkirk Hill had nothing but praise for Rawdon:

The gallantry and good conduct displayed by Lord Rawdon on this occasion are spoken of in the highest terms by the whole army, and particularly entitle him to the grateful acknowledgments of every loyal inhabitant in this province. His Lordship enjoys good health, the troops under his command are in high spirits and amply supplied with provisions.

The Briton's assessment of Rawdon is somewhat believable, but the rest of his claim is utter propaganda, unless the post received a shipment of supplies between April 26 and May 2, which is unknown and unlikely. Rawdon indeed deserved accolades for Hobkirk Hill. Conducting an offensive operation uphill, against a numerically superior enemy seemingly waiting to be attacked and led by Greene, who was, next to Washington, considered the Americans' best general are not factors usually associated with winning a battle, yet Rawdon did just that.

The condition of the Camden garrison, however, is another matter entirely. The outpost was short on provisions, especially if it had to endure a siege of any length, and Greene knew of this deficiency. During the battle or in the few days leading up to it, the Americans captured prisoners, eight of whom were deserters from Greene's army. One of the condemned was also accused of being a spy who had given critical information to the British at the siege of Savannah. All were hanged. "This execution, according to the information given him [Greene] almost bred a mutiny in the garrison, which was composed very much of deserters," claimed a 1788 account. Whatever the case, the men who followed Rawdon that April morning deserve as many accolades as their commander.[22]

The tone of messages was much different in the American camp, especially shortly after the fighting. One of Greene's aides penned to Sumter on April 25,

> General Greene wishes you to collect all your forces and join him immediately. His army is too small to maintain his ground before Camden, and therefore it becomes necessary that we should form a junction of our forces. The Enemy advanced out this Morning and gave us Battle. They drove us some little distance from the field, but we saved our stores and took a number of Prisoners.

Recognizing the severity of the action, Greene later wrote: "The action of Camden [Hobkirk Hill] was much more bloody, according to the numbers engaged, than that of Guilford [Court House] on both sides."[23]

The day after the battle, Greene wrote to Francis Marion: "We are now within five miles of Camden, and shall closely invest it in a day or two again." In another dispatch, apparently penned the same day, he noted: "We fight, get beat, rise and fight again." On the 27th, "parties were sent to bury our dead," related the Delawarean William Seymour, Otho Williams wrote to his wife two days after the clash:

The unfavorable consequences were that the army lost a glorious opportunity of gaining a complete victory, taking the town and biasing the beam of fortune greatly in favor of our cause. The action was at no time very warm, but it was durable. Our troops, by the gallant exertions of their officers, were rallied frequently, but always fought at long shot; ... none, or very few of our men, were wounded with buckshot or bayonet [indicative of close-quarters combat]. The loss was nearly equal on both sides, if we do not consider the loss of opportunity....

Williams also wrote that some Americans would pay with their lives for this botched chance to crush Rawdon and seize Camden. "Many of our officers are mortally mortified at our late inglorious retreat; I say mortally, because I cannot doubt but some of us must fall in endeavoring the next opportunity to re-establish our reputations."[24]

Additionally, the reliable Col. William Davie contended that William Washington's halt to capture the rear echelon enemy personnel consumed "precious moments" which cost him the chance to swing in behind Rawdon's troops as they realigned to attack. Without this delay, the cavalry could have "made actual contact with the [British] second line ... either before it moved up to extend the front or while this maneuver was performing, and in either case the charge would have been decisive, and the battle would not have lasted fifteen minutes." It remains debatable whether Washington's 50 or so mounted troopers could have had such an impact on the battle.[25]

Among the American prisoners herded into Camden just after the battle was Captain John Smith, Rawdon ordering the Marylander held in "close confinement" due to the murderous allegations against him from Guilford Court House. After his command was decimated in helping save the American cannons, Smith was seized by the British soldiers and "stripped of everything he had on him except his Shirt and his Commission which hung round his Neck in his Bosom," said one account. At one point Smith was told that he would be hanged the next morning for his supposed atrocities at Guilford. Still, there were communications under truce flags on both sides about the captain and the charges against him. The time frame is unclear, but the accusations "having been disproved by the united testimony of" Greene, George Washington and John Eager Howard of the Maryland Continentals, Smith was paroled by the British and sent to Charleston on foot. A few miles from Camden, Smith was surprised and seized by "persons connected with the British army, in disguise, calling themselves whigs [sp]," said one account that appeared in several other 19th-century publications about the war. Smith was at least partially stripped and bound, his assailants whipping him with "switches" on his bare back. The assault was likely prompted by British and/or

Loyalists looking to avenge Stuart's death at Guilford, the alleged atrocity by Smith at the same battle or both.[26] Greene wrote to Rawdon on May 3, 1781, regarding Smith:

> Nothing can be more foreign to the truth than the charge. I have only to observe upon it, that had such a charge been made against any of your officers, whom the fortune of war had thrown into our hands, before I should have treated them with any peculiar marks of indignity, I should first have made the inquiry and had the fact better established. It is my wish that the war should be conducted upon the most liberal, national and generous principles; but I will never suffer an indignity or injury to be offered to our officers without retaliation.

Whatever the intent and whoever the assailants, Smith survived and resumed his trek to Charleston. In the capital, Smith's "character for bravery being known, he became intimate with a number of British officers of kindred spirits—equally honorable and equally brave." Dining with some of them one day, Smith was introduced to a Redcoat officer whom he "immediately recognized as one of those who had treated him so ignominiously. Smith took occasion to say, that their [his British companions'] whole deportment to him had been so honorable, that it was a pity any dishonorable fellow should intrude among them." After some explanation, he pointed out the man, describing how he had suffered from the attack from this officer and the others after he was paroled. "Then kick him, Smith," was the general reply; and "Smith had the gratification of kicking the rascal out of the company." In later years, Smith was known as "the hero of Hobkirk."[27]

Jackson

Greene and his army had failed to liberate them, but the Jackson brothers had an even more powerful ally. Learning of her sons' desperate plight, Elizabeth Jackson journeyed to Camden from their Waxhaws home after the battle, intent on freeing them. Conversing with a "Waxhaw captain" on the American side, she prompted negotiations with the British for a prisoner exchange. The agreement resulted in the release of 13 captured Redcoats in return for Andrew and Robert Jackson and five other Waxhaws men. When the Jackson brothers were reunited with their mother in Camden, Elizabeth Jackson "could but gaze upon her boys with astonishment and horror—so worn and wasted were they with hunger, wounds, and disease." Indeed, Robert was unable to stand or to sit on a horse "without support."[28]

Elizabeth procured two horses—one which she rode and the other bearing Robert, held in place by the other five released prisoners. Andrew walked behind them, Parton noting that the teen "dragged his weak and weary limbs, bare-headed, bare-footed, without a jacket; his only two garments torn and dirty." The small party were within about two hours of completing the 40-mile trek home when a cold, heavy rain set in, soaking them all. Still, the Jacksons made it to their cabin, where both boys fell into bed. Elizabeth could do little for Robert, who died two days later. Andrew's ordeal could have been just as deathly serious, but with his mother's stamina, persistence and nursing skills, he slowly recuperated, although he was invalided for several months. With a grim dash of humor, Jackson later recalled his imprisonment and ordeal: "They kept me in jail at Camden about two months, starved me nearly to death and gave me the small-pox.... When it left me I was a skeleton—not quite six feet long and a little over six inches thick!"[29]

17

"Camden" Has "an evil genius about it"

By May 1, Greene learned that Cornwallis's army, with Tarleton leading, had left Wilmington on April 25—the day of the Hobkirk Hill battle—but it was unknown which direction the British were moving. Greene reasoned that Cornwallis would likely return to South Carolina, probably either to Camden or Charleston. And the lightning speed and ferocity of Tarleton were his most imposing concerns. "Keep a good lookout for Tarleton," Greene advised Francis Marion on the first. "Should Tarleton get into Camden, Lieutenant-Colonel Lee with his force [Lee's Legion] must join us immediately." The possible threat of being trapped between Rawdon and Cornwallis caused Greene to react cautiously and limited his offensive plans while he tried to determine Cornwallis's whereabouts.

After Guilford Court House, the Earl had rested and healed his army at Wilmington for 18 days while he mulled his next move. Whatever his decision, it would be monumental. If he withdrew to South Carolina, his longtime plan for the Southern campaign would be dealt a serious blow and ruin his timetable for subjugating the Carolinas. It also would be the second time he had withdrawn to South Carolina with very little to show for his efforts, possibly a critical setback to his military career. One positive would be that the army could regroup at Camden—about 175 miles from Wilmington—bolstering Rawdon's force there, and possibly attempt another foray north, although it would likely have to be made in the toasty embrace of late summer. The problem in this was that Camden remained a haven for pestilence. Also, Cornwallis's troops were rapidly wearing out due to hard campaigning—including long marches—the toll of fierce combat, various maladies and the ever-tormenting heat, and dripping humidity.

The Earl also had only a vague idea of what was happening to the south. His communications with Rawdon were sparse at best and even rarer were dispatches to or from Charleston. Obviously, Cornwallis was unaware of the Hobkirk Hill battle, since his army left Wilmington the same day. Despite all this he had made his decision to move into Virginia, consulting his officers in a council of war as part of the process. The fading, tattered hope of reviving the Crown's military glories in the Southern provinces rested there, where Major General William Phillips with a "sizeable corps" occupied the Chesapeake Bay area, near the coast. Linking with Phillips would shorten Cornwallis's line of communications with General Clinton in New York. Virginia also offered a more temperate climate for his soldiers. The Redcoats marched north—Cornwallis leaving Camden and South Carolina, never to return.[1]

Also on May 1, there was a grim scene in the American camp as five more prisoners were executed, William Seymour explaining that they "were deserters from our army, who were taken prisoners in the late action." Word of the hangings apparently added to the sobering effect on many of the men in Rawdon's ranks, "composed very much of deserters," said one account. Greene, meanwhile was still chafing over his lost battle, writing on May 4: "Camden seems to have an evil genius about it," he told President Joseph Reed of Maryland. "Whatever is attempted near that place is unfortunate." Two days earlier, a court of inquiry, composed of Greene's senior officers, was conducted regarding Gunby's performance at Hobkirk Hill. There were harsh words—Gunby ordering his regiment to retire was deemed "extremely improper and unmilitary," an "error in judgement" that likely cost the Americans a "complete victory." It was a hot-aired scolding of the highest order that scapegoated Gunby—with no other action taken against him—for Greene being embarrassed, out-generaled, out-fought and out-foxed by Rawdon.[2]

In Camden, Rawdon on May 7 was finally joined by Lt. Col. John Watson's detachment, returning from its strike against Marion. Watson's force—originally about 500 men—reached Log Town early that morning. It is unclear how many troops actually came in or were fit for duty, Rawdon noting that Watson's troops were "much reduced in Number, through Casualties, Sickness, and a Reinforcement which he had left to strengthen the Garrison" at Georgetown. Even worse, Watson gave Rawdon "the unwelcome intelligence that the whole interior country had revolted" although Rawdon was savvy enough to know this, at least to some degree, based on his isolation, supply and command issues. A few miles away, Greene was obviously displeased about Watson's arrival, writing that same day to Marion of this "unfortunate circumstance, as the enemy will begin to be impudent and to show themselves without their works, which they have never ventured upon since the morning of" the Hobkirk Hill battle.

Although still outnumbered, the "impudent" Rawdon was quick to prove Greene right. Allowing time for Watson's troops to rest a few hours, he led a force crossing at Wateree Ferry on the night of the 7th, intent on assailing Greene's flank along Sawney's Creek. But Greene refused to be drawn into another engagement at this point, and Rawdon, believing his foe occupied a formidable defensive position, did not want to risk "suffering such loss as must have crippled my force for any future enterprise" Rawdon also had to worry about Greene "slipping by me to Camden" if he ventured too far from the town, allowing the Americans to overwhelm the weak garrison there. Greene "was still so superior to me in Numbers, that had I left such a Garrison at my Post as might enable it to stand an Assault, my Force in the Field would have been totally unequal to cope with the Enemy's Army."

With these and other factors in mind, Rawdon withdrew to Camden on the afternoon of May 8. A British officer who fought at Hobkirk claimed that during three days after the battle, 70 deserters "amongst whom were several of Lee's dragoons, with their horses and accoutrements, came into Camden.... They all agreed in saying, there were in Green's [sp] hospital from two to three hundred men dangerously wounded, besides those who could walk about." Not much of this actually mattered in the big picture.[3]

By Wednesday, May 9, 1781, Rawdon decided that it was no longer tenable to hold Camden and made the difficult decision to abandon the town. He realized the loss of the British's key inland base would doom the lesser outposts, but he had little choice. Watson's "unwelcome intelligence" about a countryside aflame in rebellion was sound, since that officer's force had just trudged through backwaters to reach Camden. After Hobkirk Hill, Rawdon had been unable to lure Greene's force into another battle on his own terms, possibly eliminating that enemy threat, as Cornwallis had destroyed Gates in August. Thus, the wily Greene still lingered, in South Carolina, waiting to pounce again. The fall of Fort Watson was another major blow to the already grave condition of the British inland supply routes—both land and water—from Charleston. Additionally, Sumter's troops were assailing Fort Granby on the Congaree and the Crown's garrison at Orangeburg was threatened, as was the post at Fort Motte.

The destruction and aggression wrought by Greene, Sumter, "Lighthorse Harry" Lee, the intrepid "Swamp Fox" Marion and others had decimated the British strength in the interior. The crushing defeats at Kings Mountain and Cowpens—and even Cornwallis's costly victory at Guilford Court House—also had not only weakened the British army due to casualties, but also had further aroused American sympathies while dousing enthusiasm among Loyalists in both Carolinas. "The situation of Affairs in this Province has made me judge it necessary for a Time to withdraw my Force from the Back Country, and to assemble what Troops I can collect...." near Charleston, Rawdon wrote to Cornwallis shortly after the evacuation.

Years later, he would write to his old adversary Henry Lee:

Camden had always been reprobated by me as a station, not merely from the extraordinary disadvantages which attended it, as an individual position; but from its being on the wrong side of the [Wateree] river and covering nothing; whilst it was constantly liable to have its communication with the interior district cut off.

Rawdon on May 9 issued orders to his "Troops and to the Militia" informing them of "my Design of evacuating Camden…" offering "to such of the latter as chose to accompany me every Assistance that we could afford them."[4]

So much had happened over the past year. On May 9, 1780, Charleston and the broken, starving American army defending it, were within days of a cataclysmic fall that could have been a back breaking setback for the infant republic. A proud and confident British force led by the stately Cornwallis had marched into Camden in June, in what now seemed an eternity ago. Days after the Redcoats' occupation, a jubilant Tarleton and his green-jacketed dragoons had pranced through the village with their war trophies seized from Buford's luckless Continentals at the Waxhaws bloodbath. Camden was to have been the linchpin of the Crown's army outposts in the South Carolina interior, allowing the British to regain momentum and possession of that province, as well as being a base to return the Empire's influence and control of North Carolina, vital portions of Virginia and possibly beyond. But it was not to be, and none of those lost-on-the-breeze imperial ambitions mattered now as Rawdon prepared to leave Camden and obliterate much of it in the process.

"I sent off all our Baggage, &c. under a strong Escort, and destroyed the Works…." Rawdon wrote of his troops' operations overnight on May 9–10. "We brought off all the Stores of any Kind of Value, destroying the rest," he noted, meaning that much of Camden was put to the torch. The British left Camden "with great precipitation," Greene wrote to George Washington a few days later, "after burning the greater part of their baggage, and stores belonging to the inhabitants. … They also burnt the jail, mill, and several other houses, and left the town little better than a heap of rubbish."

Loyalists who operated businesses in Camden during the occupation saw their ventures vanish in the flames. The store of Thomas Hopper and Thomas Charlton inside the palisade was destroyed, as was the dry goods business and storehouse of Michael Egan, Robert and Joseph English. The Loyalist only identified as Major Downes lost his property, including the blacksmith and turner's shop. The Loyalist soldier Henry Nase was among the troops who marched out of Camden. "The town was evacuated," he wrote in his diary, "the Ks. A. Regt. [King's American Regiment] being detached in front with the sick & baggage. [W]e continued our march … without being molested."[5]

Unaware of what was happening in Camden that same day, the *Royal Gazette* in Charleston published a ditty mocking Greene and the Americans for the Hobkirk Hill defeat as well as Gates's disaster at Camden:

To General Greene, requesting a Return of killed, wounded and missing, to submit to the Publick.

> To Camden, so fatal to Rebels, we're told
> That Greene with his forces so bold,
> Promis'd laurels to each, who fought under his banner.
> On the 25th ult. fatal day! what a hardship?
> Without the least warning, out sallied his Lordship;
> Kill'd, wounded and took, alas! my poor Tanner,
> How many of those lost who fought under your banner?[6]

Rawdon himself remained in the smoldering remains of the village until about 10 a.m. on Thursday, May 10, leaving with a rearguard "in order to cover the March." In the retreating British column were an untold number of their sick and wounded, but another 30 or so soldiers were in no condition to be moved and were left behind. "I left an equal Number of Continental Prisoners in Exchange," Rawdon told Cornwallis. Greene added: "Upon the enemy's evacuation, we immediately took possession of the place," his totals on ill and wounded soldiers of both sides remaining in the town varying somewhat from Rawdon's numbers. Thirty-one Americans along with 61 Redcoats, including three officers, all seriously wounded at Hobkirk Hill, were left to the mercies of the American troops. "It is confidently asserted, by several people of the place, that the enemy suffered, in the late action [at Hobkirk], not less in killed and wounded, than three hundred men,"[7]

Amid Rawdon's retreat were about 500 blacks—likely most of them freedmen or escaped slaves–"who had flocked to his camp from the surrounding country." There also were an untold number of Loyalists, including some of the merchants whose stores were destroyed, and the "most noted royalists" in the area who "left their farms and followed the British army," stated an 1877 newspaper account.

> The scales, they saw, had begun to change. Heretofore, the poor Whigs from all sections of the State, had been dragged to Camden and tortured. Some were hanged like dogs, multitudes were starved to death or suffered to die of sheer neglect, and all were grossly insulted. During all this time, the tories [sp] and loyalists in and around Camden had been feasting on the luscious dainties of the earth and supinely reclining beneath the folds of the British flag.

When Rawdon withdrew, "a cold tremor ran through the bodies of every tory and loyalist in the region. The day of rejoicing was done, and phantoms of future misery frightened them." Among the civilians in the column was Mary Bartlam, whose husband, John, was the renowned potter who had flourished in Camden before the war and had joined Joseph Kershaw's patriot militia in the conflict's early stages. Little is known of Bartlam's military record, but it appears that he switched sides at some point and fought with the British force at Hobkirk Hill, based on research by the Historic Camden Foundation. Bartlam was apparently killed or mortally wounded in the battle or at some point prior to Rawdon's evacuation. Mary was accompanied on the march by the couple's two daughters, Honour and Betty.[8]

At Camden and still recuperating from yellow fever, Major George Hanger of Tarleton's command saw firsthand the maturity and leadership of Lord Rawdon, especially as Greene's army threatened the outpost. It also appears that Hanger was there when Rawdon decided to evacuate the village. "I was witness to the arduous task to which this nobleman, young in years, but a veteran in abilities and military science, was appointed, and from which he extricated himself with so much honour [sp] to his talents and advantage to his country," Hanger wrote after the war. With Cornwallis out of the immediate picture, Rawdon had been "left to protect South Carolina, with a feeble force, against the whole power which General Green[e] could assemble in both the provinces...."[9]

Greene sent a detachment to occupy the village soon after the last of the enemy troops departed, and Continental Army medical personnel assumed care of the patients in the military hospital. They immediately contended with a shortage of staff, supplies and medicine. Among the physicians was Dr. Thomas Charlton, the Camden resident who treated wounded men at the Waxhaws and Camden battles. As was noted previously, Charlton had been accused by the British of being a spy in 1780 and history nearly repeated itself at Camden in summer 1781. A fellow doctor, Robert Johnston, had Charlton arrested on charges of "neglect of Duty, Desertion, & taking an active part with the Enemy." Charlton pleaded his case to Greene, claiming the charges were false, although he had administered smallpox inoculations to some British soldiers at the request of a Loyalist officer who had been a prewar friend. The matter was dropped and Charlton eventually returned to Camden to rebuild his home and practice.[10]

Incredibly, the Kershaw mansion escaped the torch, but not the indignities of vandals, whether among the withdrawing British units or otherwise. Yet when Mrs. Kershaw and her children returned to town within days of Rawdon's withdrawal, they found their own very personal devastation. Furniture and other household goods—including fine crockery imported from China and a punch bowl from which Cornwallis drank, lay shattered on the ground, having been hurled out of the windows. Among the few things saved was a previously buried grandfather clock, still ticking away years after the war.[11]

Still, the British left their marks in the house. The Kershaws likely remembered Cornwallis, Rawdon, Tarleton and other officers gathered in the dining room where they planned operations and strategy while the family was confined upstairs. In a southeastern room was a bloodstain where a British officer fell, shot through an open window by a patriot rifleman somewhere in the thickets along Pine Tree Creek. The story goes that some Redcoats were playing cards in the room when the ill-fated officer was killed. Another tale handed down was that for years after the war, older residents of the town told of American prisoners hung on beams from second-floor windows in a northwest room—supposedly haunted ever since.[12]

The North Carolinian Col. William Davie intimated that Greene knew of the British leaving the town even as the enemy preparations were underway. He claimed that the commander summoned him to his headquarters tent about sunrise—what date is unclear—but possibly May 10. Davie recalled: "On entering the General's tent I soon perceived some important change had taken place. 'I have sent for you,' said Greene, his countenance radiant, 'to inform you that Lord Rawdon is preparing to evacuate Camden … all will now go well…,'" including the collapse of the enemy outposts. Regardless of Davie's account, Greene was frustrated that he had been unable to capture Camden and Rawdon's force intact, blaming the tardiness of expected Virginia militia in reinforcing him. "Had the … militia arrived in time, the garrison would have fallen into our hands, as they would have enabled us to have invested it on all sides, and the garrison had neither provision nor stores to hold out a siege," he wrote to Washington.[13]

With Camden abandoned, the Americans wasted little time in capitalizing on their momentum—and Cornwallis's other strongholds in the interior began toppling like so many bayonet-studded dominos. Rawdon had ordered Orangeburg evacuated, but before it could be done, Sumter's partisans swooped in on May 11 and captured it, along with 350 of its garrison. Marion's raiders—using flaming arrows to set Mrs. Motte's house ablaze—overwhelmed Fort Motte on May 12; Fort Granby on the Congaree fell on the 15th. Thus, all of the inland posts, other than Ninety Six and Augusta, were in American hands five days after Rawdon left Camden in charred shambles. "We marched from Camden the 12th, leaving a guard to destroy the works, and proceeded on our march for Ninety Six," wrote William Seymour of the Delaware Continentals.

Greene kept Camden's hospital facilities operational under the direction of Dr. Charlton, still caring for the ill and wounded of both sides. This was a wise move, as the coming weeks would show. Despite the damages to the Kershaw mansion, Greene's wife, Kitty, was a guest of Mrs. Kershaw for several days during this time. Said an 1851 account,

> Mrs. Greene was represented to have been a very handsome woman, and as elegant in her manners as in her person. She was dressed in a rich military jacket and skirt, for her riding dress. She travelled on horseback, with a numerous retinue [including a cavalry detachment]—her decorations were richly plaited, and she lived in much style.[14]

Rawdon

To fully illustrate the vast gulf of 18th-century communications, Cornwallis was at Petersburg, Virginia, on May 20, when he penned a dispatch congratulating Rawdon for his Hobkirk Hill triumph: "My Dearest Lord, I cannot describe my feelings on your most glorious victory, by far the most splendid of this war. My terrors for you had almost distracted me, but served to heighten, if possible, my heartfelt satisfaction." Even though he was writing nearly a month after the battle and knew little about events in South Carolina since then, Cornwallis was skeptical that the province could be held. He noted to Rawdon:

> As to the extensive frontier which we have hitherto endeavored to occupy, I am not certain whether we had not better relinquish it, even if Greene should move this way. But this I leave to your discretion, or eventually to that of Balfour, promising my most hearty support… The weakness and treachery of our friends in South Carolina, and the impossibility of getting any military assistance from them, makes the possession of any part of the country of very little use, except in supplying provisions for Charlestown [sp]. The situation of the province renders it impossible for us to avail ourselves of its rich produce, and a strong garrison in Charlestown [sp], with a small corps in the country, will prevent the enemy from reaping any advantage from it--unless they kept a strong force of Continentals in the interior.

Cornwallis was a bit less pessimistic in a letter, also written on the 20th, to Henry Clinton regarding Rawdon's victory and conditions in South Carolina.

> There is now great reason to hope that we shall meet with no serious misfortune in that province; if, however, General Greene should persevere in carrying on offensive operations against it, we must, I think, abandon Camden, and probably Ninety-Six [sp], and limit our defense to the Congaree and the Santee; this will only be giving up two bad posts, which it is difficult to supply with provisions, and quitting a part of the country, which for some months past we have not really possessed.

Of Rawdon, Cornwallis wrote: "His Lordship's great abilities, courage, and firmness of mind, cannot be sufficiently admired and applauded."[15]

Thus, in a time-lapse-way of thoughts and messaging, Cornwallis on May 20, had agreed with Rawdon's decision to leave Camden ten days after the actual operation.

Rawdon's column, meanwhile, continued toward the coast, reaching the Santee River at Nelson's Ferry on May 13, shadowed by Marion's partisans. During the march, his troops "brought off not only the Militia who had been with us at Camden, but also all the well-affected Neighbors on our Route, together with the Wives, Children, Negroes and Baggage of almost all of them." The trek from Camden had been uneventful, other than the rear guard being assailed by some mounted militia, "but a Party of them having fallen into an Ambuscade, the rest of them gave us no further Trouble," Rawdon wrote to Cornwallis. The British force and the refugees began crossing the river on the night of the 13th, and by the evening of the next day, "every Thing was safely across."

It was also at this time that Rawdon received word of the fall of Fort Motte, the officers from the captured post arriving at Nelson's on the 14th. Rawdon had earlier considered trying to relieve Fort Motte and possibly the British posts at Orangeburg and Granby, but now realized he was powerless to do so. At the ferry, Rawdon was met by Colonel Balfour, commander of British forces in the capital. Balfour wanted to discuss his "circumstances" and told Rawdon that "revolt was universal" across the province. Balfour had other grim news: Charleston's defenses were weak, his garrison was inadequate to oppose any force of substantial size and the city's townspeople were defecting in masses. Rawdon wrote: "I agreed with him in the conclusion ... that any misfortune happening to my corps might entail the loss of the province." There was more "misfortune" soon to follow for the British. Lee and Thomas Sumter combined forces to besiege Augusta, whose defenders capitulated on June 5. Even as the struggle for Augusta was underway, the Americans also were concentrated on capturing Ninety Six.[16]

Jackson

For 14-year-old Andrew Jackson, the war was over as he slowly regained his health at his Waxhaws home in summer 1781. Still, the conflict that had killed his two brothers, almost taking him as well, would soon claim his dearest loved one. With her son healing, Elizabeth Jackson turned her attention toward aiding soldiers from the area who had been captured by the British and were being held in prison ships off Charleston. These vessels were floating hellholes of pestilence, filth and famine for hundreds of hopeless American captives. Elizabeth knew that her sisters, friends and neighbors had men—husbands, brothers, sons—in these ships. Thus, she and a party of other women set out on the 160-mile journey to Charleston. With them they carried "a precious store of gifts and rural luxuries and medicines for the solace of their imprisoned relatives, and bearing whole hearts full of tender messages and precious news from home," wrote Parton, the Jackson biographer.

The women safely reached Charleston and were allowed aboard the somber vessels where they "emptied their hearts and saddle-bags, and brought such joy to the haggard prisoners as only prisoners know, when angel women from home visit them." A happy ending soon soured. Leaving Charleston, Elizabeth stopped at the home of a relative who lived about two miles from the city. There, she was overcome by the "ship fever" as it was called—possibly a myriad of contagious ailments. She died there after a brief illness. Young Andrew Jackson was suddenly an orphan of the American Revolution. It is beyond the scope of this work to examine his rise from this point to the presidency, but Jackson's life-altering experiences at the hands of the British in Camden, Waxhaws and beyond helped forge the persona of "Old Hickory" as a soldier, statesman and commander-in-chief.[17]

Washington

George Washington was headquartered at Newburgh, New York, when he learned of the British evacuation of Camden and Greene's other recent victories in at least one—possibly two—dispatches from the latter delivered on or about June 14. Washington confided in his diary on that date: "Received agreeable accts from General Greene, of his successes in South Carolina—viz—that Lord Rawden [sp] had abandoned Cambden [sp] with precipitation, leaving all our wounded and taken in the action of the 25th of April last, together with 58 of his own too bad to remove—that he had destroy'd his own stores—burnt many buildings and in short left the town little better than a heap of rubbish...." On June 15, Washington congratulated the army on the "glorious news" of Greene's triumphs in South Carolina.[18]

18

"He conquers by magic"

Rawdon's last huzzah in South Carolina came in a valiant attempt to relieve Ninety Six with British reinforcements just arrived in Charleston from the mother country. Ironically, Rawdon had ordered the beleaguered stronghold abandoned when he evacuated Camden, but the messenger was intercepted. A needless siege ensued, scores of men paying with their lives and blood. Among them were a number of Irish Redcoats fresh off the ships and almost immediately marched into the seething jaws of a torturous summer in a strange land. Many perished from heat stroke and others fell by the wayside unaccustomed to the steamy climate. American attempts to take Ninety Six had been underway since May 22 and stretched into June. At some point in this period, Greene likely received word regarding the June 15 death of Lt. Col. Benjamin Ford of the Maryland Continentals. Ford led his command amid the hottest combat at Camden and Hobkirk Hill, his arm shattered by a wound in the latter fight. For weeks, he had been in a military hospital in Charlotte since shortly after Hobkirk Hill, but was unable to rally. One account described Ford as a "worthy little friend" of Col. Otho Williams.[1]

Meanwhile, Mary Bartlam and her daughters, along with the other Loyalist refugees from Camden, settled into squalid camp conditions outside Charleston. The location would soon be known as "Rawdon Town." Sometime apparently in July, Mary was appointed executor of her husband John's estate, basically confirming that John—the master potter and soldier—was dead.[2]

By June 11, Greene received word from Sumter about Rawdon's approach and on June 18 ordered a massive assault to try to take Ninety Six before these reinforcements arrived. It stalled with heavy American casualties and, two days later, Greene abandoned the siege and withdrew to avoid being pinned between Rawdon's force and the Ninety Six defenders. The British evacuated the post on July 3, Greene's battered little army settling into camps in the High Hills of Santee to rest and recuperate. By this time, Rawdon was done, physically and mentally worn down by the hardships of this campaign and from exhaustive active service for more than a year since he took over at Camden. On July 20, he relinquished command to Lieutenant Colonel Alexander Stewart of the Third Regiment of Foot and marched with some 500 troops into Charleston. Soon afterward he departed for England, but his woes would continue. The ship upon which he sailed was seized by a French privateer and he was taken to Brest, France, as a prisoner of war. Soon, however, he was exchanged and returned to England.

Rawdon was hardly alone among the Redcoats in being laid low by the sauna-like heat and humidity, ravenous insects along with the herculean exertions suffered by soldiers who lacked sufficient rations. Tarleton himself described the cruel adversities the British endured that South Carolina summer:

> During renewed successions of forced marches, under the rage of a burning sun, and in a climate at that season peculiarly inimicable [sp] to man, they were frequently, when sinking under the most excessive fatigue, not only destitute of every comfort, but almost of every necessary which seems essential to his existence. During the greater part of the time they were totally destitute of bread, and the country afforded no vegetables for a substitute. Salt at length failed; and their only resources were water, and the wild cattle which they found in the woods.[3]

Greene

Accompanied by Colonel Williams, Greene rode down from the High Hills to explore the Camden battlefield in late July or early August 1781. He approved of the position chosen by the "judicious and gallant" Gates to fight Cornwallis, according to Williams. Greene confirms this in an August 8 letter written to an unidentified "friend in Philadelphia" in which he vigorously defended Gates's conduct at Camden: "Gen. Gates left this country under a heavy load; and I can assure you he did not deserve it. If he was to be blamed for anything at all, it was for fighting, not for what he did or did not do in or after the action. I have been upon the ground where he was defeated, and think it was well chosen, and the troops properly drawn up; and had he halted" at Charlotte during his exodus after the battle "I am persuaded there would have been as little murmuring upon that occasion as in any instance whatever, where the public meet with a misfortune of equal magnitude."

Historian John Austin Stevens in 1880 added his thoughts to Greene's comments about Gates:

> By common accord Greene stands at the head of the military men developed by the war and his unsupported testimony is alone sufficient to outweigh the

censorious criticisms of civilians or historians of whatever grade. He commanded the very troops who had been defeated under Gates, was surrounded by their officers, acquainted with their opinions, and his practical eye had measured the route of the army and the scene of its contests.[4]

That being said, Greene was still seething over the lost opportunity of the Hobkirk Hill debacle more than three months earlier, still targeting Gunby for the setback. "The troops were not to blame in the Camden affair," he wrote to President Reed of Maryland:

> Gunby was the sole cause of the defeat; and I found him much more blameable [sp] afterwards, than I represented in my public letters.... Depend upon it, our actions have been bloody and severe, according to the force engaged, and we should have had Lord Rawdon and his whole command prisoners in three minutes, if Colonel Gunby had not ordered his regiment to retire, the greatest part of which were advancing rapidly at the time they were ordered off. I was almost frantic with vexation at the disappointment. Fortune has not been our friend.[5]

Ruined Camden, meanwhile, was being converted into a base for Greene's army. Military supplies were stored in the town and the quartermaster general's department for the army operated from there to feed and equip the troops. Greene appointed Camden merchant Samuel Mathis—Sarah Kershaw's brother—as quartermaster there in fall 1781. The general hospital was still functioning under Dr. Charlton's direction, smallpox and other sicknesses still a major menace. Greene's army, numbering some 2,000, remained in the Santee hills for about six weeks, but there was a problem to be dealt with: the British Lt. Col. Stewart, who had replaced Rawdon, was an aggressor, moving inland from Charleston with about an equal number of men and operating in the area of Fort Motte, which had been abandoned by both foes.

Realizing that his work was not done, Greene marched on August 23, crossing the Wateree at the Camden ferry and had established his headquarters in the town by the 26th. It is not recorded where Greene stayed during this brief sojourn in Camden, but a good guess would be the Kershaw House or in a tent on the grounds. It will be remembered that the general's wife had been a guest of Mrs. Kershaw and some of her children shortly after Rawdon evacuated and torched much of the village. Weeks earlier, one of the most incendiary incidents of the war in South Carolina occurred on August 4, when Colonel Isaac Hayne, commanding a patriot militia regiment, was captured by the British and hanged in Charleston. In a conflict brimming with years of sanguine atrocities by both sides, it is unclear why this incident attracted such attention and venom. Nevertheless, Greene issued a proclamation from Camden on the 26th about

Hayne's execution, vowing immediate retaliation. "Every officer in the line of the Southern army, that was present, has addressed General Greene on the late execution of ... Hayne, praying that the Lex Talionis [Latin, basically eye-for-an-eye] shall follow," an unidentified "correspondent" in Camden wrote on August 29.

The retaliation would be aimed at regular British officers, but not Loyalist militia leaders, Greene referring to the latter as "deluded inhabitants" who chose to join the wrong side. The declaration obviously rattled three British officers being held as prisoners at Camden, the men "quaking in fear" but "not of sufficient rank to become objects" of the intended revenge, the correspondent noted. Governor Rutledge was in Camden on September 2–3, 1781, and issued orders to General Marion on several topics, including rooting out civilians with hidden British sympathies. Again, it is not known where Rutledge lodged in Camden at this time, but it was likely the Kershaw home.[6]

Eutaw Springs—September 8, 1781

After days of maneuvering, Greene—with the partisans of Marion, Sumter and Pickens included in his ranks—caught up with Stewart's force at Eutaw Springs, near present-day Eutawville on the south banks of Lake Marion. Many of the officers and soldiers, who had survived the bloodlettings at Camden and Hobkirk Hill, now eyed each other across the fields and woods once again. Much of the scattered, savage combat centered on a two-story brick house and garden near the British camp with Redcoat riflemen picking off American artillerists from the windows. Both sides were equally maimed—casualties approaching 700 for each—and Stewart held the sanguine ground long enough to bury many of the slain. Still, he retreated toward Charleston, with Greene's troops following, slowing shoving the British into a small defensive ring around the city. Scores of wounded from both armies—at least those able to be moved by wagons—were taken to the Camden hospital, overwhelming Dr. Charlton's small staff and resources. Lt. Col. John Eager Howard of the Maryland Continentals had escaped serious injury at the battles of Camden, Hobkirk Hill and Guilford Court House, but his good fortune ran dry in the brutal combat at Eutaw Springs. As he had done on other fields, Howard led his Marylanders in a bayonet assault, but this time he was severely wounded. The four hours of slaughter at Eutaw Springs would be the last major battle of the war in South Carolina.[7]

Kershaws

Joseph Kershaw, meanwhile, was released from custody in Bermuda as part of a general prisoner exchange and reached Philadelphia in late August 1781. There he attended an event in company with George Washington, Rochambeau, Henry Knox and other American and French luminaries of the Revolution. He was trying to make his way home to Camden on September 25—apparently in Maryland—when he wrote to his friend Henry William Harrington, congratulating him on the "happy prospect of our affairs" with the hope that

> soon we may all return to our possessions to the Southward & enjoy them in Peace. I have gone through various sceens [sp] since the British entered Camden.... You will probably have heard of the death of my brother Ely on our passage from [New] Providence to Bermuda.... I fear his affairs are in great confusion. It is probable that you at some future day inform me what have come of his Books, &c. at Cheraws. We have heard his Stores and Houses there were burnt. I understand Ld. Rawdon left me pretty bare at Camden....

Kershaw rejoined his family at the big house on Magazine Hill on October 3, but nothing would be the same the conflict sapping him physically and financially. Ely had been taken from him as well, buried in Bermuda and among the uncounted victims who never returned to what had become the United States of America. Joseph had also been dealt a major monetary blow in Bermuda, mortgaging his land holdings to local merchants in order to aid the South Carolinians. With these funds he obtained a ship and had it stocked with supplies for the war effort, but the vessel was captured by the British. Still, he was rejoining Sarah and five of their seven children, the other two, John and James, remaining in England for the war's duration.[8]

As Kershaw was savoring his freedom and return to his family the war was roiling toward a dramatic climax about 400 miles to the northeast from Camden at Yorktown, Virginia. A year and some six weeks after striking north from Camden in September 1780, Cornwallis surrendered at Yorktown on October 19, 1781, after a siege of almost three weeks by American and French forces—commanded by Washington and Rochambeau respectively. His capitulation effectively blunted the Crown's efforts to retain the American colonies, but the war lumbered on for more than a year, Camden remaining very much in the Revolutionary picture.

General Greene and his army were refitting and resting in the High Hills of Santee when they received word of the Yorktown triumph. Jubilation and celebrations reigned in the camps. The war was over! In reality, however, it wasn't.

The British still held Charleston, Savannah, New York, and other outposts, sporadic hostilities ongoing as they would be well into 1782.

No peace documents had yet been signed. The question arose: might the Crown still marshal its considerable military resources to crush the revolution, even at this late hour? To that end, Washington divided his forces—including Greene's troops in South Carolina—in several strategic locations should the British try to rekindle hostilities. Thus, even after Yorktown, Greene relied on Camden as a key point for his army.

In November, Col. Otho Williams was at Fort Motte when he dispatched Capt. James Field—or Fields—to escort a number of British prisoners to Camden. Apparently, there were no longer facilities to hold POWs in the village since Fields was instructed to care for and secure them until "something better can be done." Some arms and ammunition were expected to come through Camden from Salisbury and Field was to draw some weapons and a "few dozen cartridges" per man for any "convalescents as may be able to do guard duty." The military hospital in the village remained fully active, perpetually dealing with the various shortages. "The want of a Proper Diet and the necessary means of accommodation" were essential to the patients, Dr. Samuel Vickers wrote to Greene from Camden on November 20. "It is easily perceivable what vast superiority these conveniences have over the boasted effects of Medicine." Greene was already well aware of these deficiencies, observing on the 14th: "Our hospitals have been in the greatest distress ... and if they fail us our situation will be truly deplorable ... if you could but behold the unfortunate sufferers who have bled in their Country's cause suffering for want of hospital stores it would melt your heart with pity."[9]

1782

The year 1782 saw the newly minted American states enacting harsh retribution against known Loyalists who had been active in the British war effort, legal channels being used rather than bullets or swords, for the most part. Based in some degree on recommendations made by Congress, the states passed laws allowing banishment of these residents, seizure of their land, homes, businesses and other "property" including slaves, and possible charges of treason. Massachusetts and South Carolina had some of the sternest of these laws and Camden was the focus of some enforcement for which a number of Loyalists paid dearly.

After the British victory at Camden, at least 13 pro–British supporters—not all necessarily from Camden—presented Cornwallis with their congratulations on his triumph. It is unclear if these Loyalists expressed their sentiments in person or in a document or documents, but these unfortunates were soon in the bulls-eye after Yorktown. Labeled as

"Congratulators" of Cornwallis, their "estates" were confiscated and they were banished from the new country. All South Carolinians, the men were James Brisbane, Samuel Carne, Dr. James Clitherell, Basil Cowper, Jacob Deveaux, Edward Fenwicke, Dr. Alexander Garden, John Glen, Patrick Hinds, Charles Johnston, Robert Perroneau, Alexander Rose and John Scott.

Additionally, two Camden men, John Dounie and William Valentine, had their property seized. Dounie was "in commission under the crown after the surrender of Charleston" while Valentine held "an office under the crown." A similar process was carried out against Loyalists who had congratulated General Clinton after he captured Charleston. The Crown still clung to its rapidly fading presence in the Southern states in 1782, but this also soon vanished like campfire smoke in a hurricane of change. The Redcoats evacuated Savannah in July; Charleston abandoned on December 14.[10]

Gates

The court of inquiry regarding Gates's conduct at Camden was never held, due to Washington's indefinite postponement of the proceedings. Greene, who had treated Gates with great respect when relieving him, worked in tandem with Washington, claiming that his few generals could not be spared to participate in the hearing. In August 1782, Congress reversed its call for the inquiry and Gates was ordered to rejoin Washington and the main army. Somewhat vindicated, Gates arrived at Verplanck's Point, N.Y., on October 5, meeting Washington for the first time since his Camden defeat. A force of Continental and French soldiers were posted in the area at the time. "The interview excited the curiosity of the officers ... and all admired the courage with which Gates bore his misfortunes, and the remarkable freedom from restraint of both gentlemen," said one account. Washington's main force was encamped at New Windsor near Newburgh, New York, where Washington was headquartered. There Gates served in various capacities and, next to Washington, was the army's senior general.[11]

Greene

Greene and his army remained near Charleston until after the last British sail disappeared over the horizon in December. He eventually returned to his native Rhode Island "where he was received in a manner highly honorable to himself, and to the citizens, who exhibited their attachment and regard, by every demonstration of welcome and joy" an 1847 account stated. More elaborate praise came during wartime from the Chevalier de la Luzerne, the Minister of France who wrote of Greene's Southern campaign:

> Other generals subdue their enemy by the means with which their country or sovereign furnishes them; but Greene appears to subdue his enemy by his own means. He commenced his campaign, without either an army, provisions, or military stores. He has asked for nothing since; and yet, scarcely a post arrives from the South, that does not bring intelligence of some new advantage gained over the foe. He conquers by magic. History furnishes no parallel to this.[12]

Kershaws

For a few postwar years the Kershaw mansion "was the scene of much hospitality and gayety," said one account. "But earnest work was now necessary" for Joseph Kershaw to resuscitate his "crippled fortunes...." Still, Kershaw "set about this task with characteristic pluck and energy" one project during this time being the "cutting of a private canal" connecting his town home with some of his property outside of the village. He also quickly revived his civic leadership, was elected to the state legislature in December 1781 and appointed a justice of the peace for Camden District a few months later. Kershaw also was a strong advocate for the Catawba nation, lauding their wartime service and lobbying for state aid to pull them out of their postwar poverty.

Financially, however, Kershaw was almost ruined by the war, one of the major blows being the capture of the supply ship he and business partners in Bermuda had intended for the Americans. Kershaw was forced to liquidate his estate to settle some of his debt, but the destruction, theft, neglect and confiscation of his holdings in Camden and beyond were too much to overcome. The Kershaws' two oldest sons, John and James, returned to Camden from England with peace on the horizon. John reached Camden in early 1783 and James in 1784, both, especially John, becoming immersed in the family's financial efforts to stay afloat. Infant Samuel Geoffrey—or Godfrey—was the Kershaws' eighth child, born in 1782. His world was still dawning when the Treaty of Paris was signed in September 1783, officially ending the conflict, but the Kershaws' trials were far from over.[13]

Joseph was in Charleston on February 24, 1784, when he wrote to then former Governor John Rutledge about his tenuous state of affairs and his efforts to seek reimbursement for monetary losses due to the war.

Early on in Camden's occupation, the British destroyed many of his financial records, but he had had the forethought to send away his "principal books of accounts & land titles to the mountains of Virginia & my bonds & notes" to a business associate in Philadelphia. This was

> nearly the whole property I saved except my dwellings house, the British having destroyed not less than from 17 to 20,000 pounds of my rich property, besides cutting me out of an income of at least 2,000 [pounds] sterling per annum, which my mills, brewery ... distillery and farms yielded me, so that I am very near, if not entirely ruined.

Kershaw wrote to Rutledge again the next day, further detailing his losses: "A great proportion was the produce of my mills, farms and stock or taken for old debts as specie currency. My brew house & out houses were much injured, as was [sp] several of the stores belonging to my brother's [Ely's] Est., and the old store burnt to the ground ... made use of as barracks &c...." Within a few weeks Kershaw received a state reimbursement of 3,593 pounds, a drop in the well for the time and treasure lost and other sacrifices he had made to establish Camden and South Carolina in a new land of independence. The bad blood between Joseph and William Kershaw never went away, Joseph no longer considering his brother a part of the family after William became a Loyalist in 1781. William died in Charleston in November 1785.[14]

Meanwhile, Camden District was subdivided into Lancaster, York, Chester, Fairfield, Richland, Claremont and Clarendon counties in 1785, Camden itself in the early stages of forming a municipal government. A new Presbyterian church rose from the ashes of the previous sanctuary, demolished by the Redcoats, who used the wood and other material to construct shelters for their troops. These crude structures were consigned to the flames during the evacuation.

Kershaw's business troubles could not be alleviated by the growing populace of a wounded town, itself recovering from the charred, bloody but illustrious history of its role in the Revolution. What mattered more was the man who had steered the course for a rough, backwoods community in the Carolina wilderness to slowly blossom. What mattered more was the man who—with his business partners—believed in this tiny, rustic settlement in the 1760s becoming a flourishing inland trade and crossroads outpost on the muddy Wateree. The British pinpointed the man and his town as well, Clinton and Cornwallis noting its strategic location and the latter labeling Kershaw as "violent" in his zest and zeal for the rebellion. Thus, it was that the area around Camden was named "Kershaw County" and when Camden was formally incorporated in 1791, Kershaw was elected "the first intendant," essentially the first mayor.[15]

Kershaw died in the Great White House on December 28, 1791, buried within sight of his home. He had lived long enough to meet George Washington a few months earlier when the country's first president visited Camden. Kershaw was survived by Sarah and their eight children, whose "descendants are numerous," said an 1851 account.

> Among the ancestors at that latter time were Charles and Benjamin Perkins and family, Mrs. Alexander Johnson and family, all of Camden; Mrs. Henrietta Powers of Virginia; Samuel Wilds DuBose and family, of Darlington; Mrs. Mary R. Young of Jackson County, Florida; and Colonel Joseph Brevard Kershaw, of Camden, who acquired honorable distinction in the Mexican War, as first lieutenant of the Kershaw Volunteers in the Palmetto Regiment.

Joseph B. Kershaw became one of the most distinguished and finest brigadier generals in the Confederate army during the Civil War.[16]

A 1921 book by Harriette Kershaw Leiding about South Carolina's historic homes provides more information about the Kershaws' lineage during that period:

> The Kershaws have intermarried with the Langs, Shannons, deLoachs and deSaussures and are descended from the Canteys, Douglas and Debose families. Rev. John Kershaw, of Charleston, and his son, Dr. T.G. Kershaw, of North Augusta, South Carolina, and several grandsons are the only descendants of General Joseph Brevard Kershaw now bearing the name.

The Kershaw House passed out of the family's hands a few years after the patriarch's death. James English likely bought it during a sale of Kershaw's properties and later sold it to the Camden Orphan Society, which operated there from 1805 to 1822. Other owners from that time until the War Between the States were John Workman, James C. Doby, and John Meroney. The house was mute witness to much history even after the Revolution. The wide Common in front of it, across which the proud Redcoats of Cornwallis, Rawdon and Tarleton drilled and paraded, was the scene of regular community and military events, a nearby spring the centerpiece of "many a big barbeque" and other social gatherings.[17]

Still, Camden's crucial role in the Revolution and the sacrifices of DeKalb, Greene and even Gates—as well as the hundreds of men who followed them—were so important that Washington and General Lafayette separately journeyed to the town years after the war, as will be discussed.

An 1858 history of South Carolina stated that Camden

> languished for a considerable time after the peace. It now appears to be in a flourishing state. It was incorporated ... and has ever since had a regular city police. There are about 150 dwelling houses in it.... Camden is one of the largest inland cities in Carolina, and bids fair to become a considerable place of trade and business. It has an easy and quick communication with Charlestown

[sp] through the Santee canal—has the support of an extensive back country in both Carolinas—possesses many advantages for the erection of labor-saving machinery in its vicinity—and ample materials of the best kind for boat and ship building....[18]

Armed conflict savaged Camden again in the Civil War. From 1861 to 1864, the destruction was grievous, personal and bloody but on faraway fields, local men and boys falling at previously unknown places like Bull Run, Shiloh, Antietam, Gettysburg and Chickamauga. Still the thunder of guns crept ever closer as the Confederacy began to writhe in its own death agony. The Kershaw House was used by the Confederates as a supply storehouse. The Union XV Corps swept through Camden in February 1865 during Major General William T. Sherman's blazing march through the Carolinas. At the time, a *New York Herald* reporter described it as "a beautiful town" with "some very pretty private residences, and ... a very healthy and fashionable resort."

Sherman's troops burned the depot, a railroad bridge and some stores of cotton and tobacco. The Kershaw mansion was also torched; whether by Confederates trying to save the supplies from capture or by Yankee troops remains unclear. It really didn't matter since the damage was done. The town was assailed again in April during "Potter's Raid," a strike by a force of Federals led by Brigadier General Edward E. Potter aimed primarily at destroying Confederate railroad assets in the state's interior.[19]

By 1897 Camden was earning renown as a winter resort and later as a golf, polo and horse racing destination. In the early 1900s and possibly even before, the Common in front of the Kershaw House site was farmland, plowed for cotton or corn crops. Any of the "historic trees" about the mansion site, "long since fallen by the ax." On the afternoon of Friday, June 4, 1909, dignitaries and a large crowd assembled for the dedication of a battlefield monument to Baron DeKalb. The "imposing granite boulder" was placed on the spot believed to be where DeKalb fell mortally wounded. The local chapter of the Daughters of the American Revolution "with characteristic patriotism, has patiently labored to mark this historic spot and ... saw the rewarding of their noble efforts," stated a newspaper report. A "large number of patriotic citizens drove out and witnessed the exercises" and listened as "Mr. Bratton DeLoache delivered a stirring address." The monument, "firmly set in concrete and rock" bears the inscription: "Baron DeKalb, mortally wounded on this spot, at battle of Camden, Aug. 16, 1780."[20]

Camden today is a vigorous and bustling community, renowned for its Southern-accented refinement and gentility. In a state steeped in history, it is South Carolina's oldest inland city. Its equine scene is crowned by the Carolina Cup, a spring celebration of horse racing laced with seersucker, bourbon, and Technicolor fashion pageantry. First run in 1930, "The Cup" as locals called it, is a mini Kentucky Derby with a huge "y'all" in every tailgate conversation.

Yet beyond all this, the city has never forgotten its historic roots and its uniqueness in the vast tapestry of South Carolina's vibrant and amazing story. The Historic Camden Foundation, the Camden Archives & Museum (I actually saw John Dillinger's straw boater and bullets from the St. Valentine's Day Massacre at the latter!) and the Palmetto Conservation organization have been instrumental in keeping the life-blood of Camden and Kershaw County's saga in the forefront. An impressive Revolutionary War Visitor Center was recently opened.

A full-scale replica of the Kershaw House was completed by 1977 and stands on the foundations of the original structure. Various archaeological projects have uncovered remnants of colonial-era buildings, the British entrenchments, military relics and other artifacts from Camden's Revolutionary period.

Hobkirk Hill has been an upper-scale residential neighborhood for many decades and is dotted with historical markers detailing the 1781 battle. Greene Street honors General Nathanael Greene while Captain Robert Kirkwood who fought so heroically here, is memorialized by Kirkwood Common—a peaceful park on the battlefield—and nearby Kirkwood Lane. The grand and lavish Kirkwood Hotel on west Greene Street opened in 1903 and reigned over this area for almost half a century, but was lost to time and development.[21]

The battle of Camden site is about a ten-minute drive away and is relatively undisturbed since Gates and Cornwallis clashed there in 1780. It was certainly more remote when a teen with a metal detector—me—unearthed a handful of musket balls there in the 1970s. Today the site is crisscrossed by a series of walking trails with signage explaining different aspects of the fighting. The 1909 DeKalb monument remains the centerpiece of the battleground, much like the tragic hero of its namesake who forlornly made his last stand here.

The discovery of skeletal remains of 14 soldiers who fell in the battle of Camden was announced in November 2022. Buried in shallow graves on the battlefield, 12 of the men were Continental troops from Maryland or Delaware, units of which stood with the gallant DeKalb. The others were a North Carolina Loyalist and a soldier in the 71st Highlanders. Data about the soldiers was gleaned from uniform buttons and other artifacts found with the remains.

Today, if you walk through those quiet woods and listen closely, you might hear a faint staccato of muskets, a Redcoat's huzzah, the steely clang of crossed swords, or feel the earth tremble beneath you as warhorses thunder toward glory or defeat more than two centuries ago. All are whispers seared on the timeless winds of Revolutionary War Camden.

19

The Leaders in the Postwar Period

Gates

In early 1783, Gates remained with Washington's troops in the vicinity of Newburgh, N.Y, but soon found himself embroiled in the "Newburgh Conspiracy" in which some army officers, disgruntled over their lack of government pay, the provision shortages and other unkept promises, challenged the legitimacy of Congress, threatening possible action. Among the officers was Major John Armstrong, Jr., Gates's aide who had performed so well at the battle of Camden. As tensions rose, Washington calmed the waters in an impassioned March 15 speech to his officers, promising to work with Congress to address the army's concerns. As this crisis faded, Gates soon found himself facing a much more personal catastrophe. Elizabeth, his wife of almost 30 years, had become seriously ill, causing him to take leave to go to her bedside. She lingered until June 1 when she died, the ever-haunting loss of their only child Robert in October 1780 only aggravating Gates's grief.

Gates never returned to the army, retiring in November 1783 and settling into life at "Traveller's Rest" in Virginia. In 1784 he proposed to Janet L. Montgomery, widow of Major General Richard Montgomery, killed in the war, but she declined. Still, Gates found hope and love with 46-year-old Mary Vallance, a wealthy widow and Liverpool native who had immigrated to Maryland. They were married in July 1786.[1]

Gates and Mary lived at "Traveller's Rest" until 1790, when they sold the plantation—the eventual freeing of his slaves being part of the agreement—and moved to Manhattan Island, New York, not a part of New York City at the time. There he was "received with honors" and "the freedom of the city was tendered to him." The couple resided at "Rose Hill Farm," since overtaken by 23rd and 30th Streets and Second and Fourth Avenues in midtown Manhattan. Gates served one term in the state assembly, "elected by a large majority" as a Jeffersonian Republican. "Although firm and decided in his political views, this did not separate him from the many personal friends who entertained different opinions," stated a 19th-century account. "He possessed a handsome person; was courteous and agreeable in his manners; amiable and benevolent in his disposition; of warm social habits, and a kind and sincere friend."[2]

Gates was 78 when he died at Rose Hill on April 10, 1806, nine days before the 31st anniversary of Lexington and Concord. He was buried in Manhattan's Trinity Church cemetery. "General Gates possessed many excellent qualities, but he was deficient in the necessary qualifications for a successful commander," a critic stated, "and his vanity generally misled his judgment. He was a gentleman in his manners, humane and benevolent, but he lacked intellectual cultivation and true magnanimity." All of this may have been true to varying degrees, but Gates had the last word in a portion of a letter written to a friend a few weeks before his death: "I am very weak, and have evident signs of an approaching dissolution. But I have lived long enough, since I have lived to see a mighty people animated with a spirit to be free, and be governed by transcendent abilities and honor."[3]

Cornwallis

Cornwallis was neither scorned nor praised upon his return to Britain after Yorktown. Centuries of wars had taught the populace some sense of their soldiers doing the best they could under difficult circumstances and this was the atmosphere he experienced. Still, Cornwallis was renowned as an excellent administrator and was soon being considered for the dual role of governor-general and commander-in chief of India, a troubled Crown possession that needed a firm hand. He accepted the assignment in February 1786 and soon went to work to repair a corrupt civil service system as well as a military diluted by disorganization and weak discipline. He instituted reforms to improve both of these services over several years, but eventually found himself back on the battlefield, immersed in various Indian civil wars and rebellions lasting into 1792.

His conduct in India was so successful that he was honored as Marquis Cornwallis that same year—but his service to the Crown was far from over. By 1798 the Irish were in rebellion and Cornwallis was called upon again. As viceroy and commander-in-chief, he was able to suppress the outbreak with some military action, and arrests of the ringleaders. Cornwallis was in his retirement in 1804 when the Empire once again needed him. India was aflame with in-fighting factions and the 66-year-old

Marquis arrived in Calcutta in July 1805. Intent on mediating between the antagonists, Cornwallis sailed up the Ganges, but became ill during the voyage. He was taken ashore at Ghazipore, but never recovered, dying there on October 5, 1805.[4]

In South Carolina, Cornwallis is remembered as the British general whose troops occupied Camden, along with Charleston, Ninety Six and other outposts strung across the colony. The conqueror of Gates at the battle of Camden was ultimately thwarted in subduing the rebellion in the Carolinas for a variety of reasons, such as manpower and supply shortages, the inability to rally Loyalists to the Crown's banner, the ferocious resistance and disruptions caused by Marion, Sumter and Pickens and outdated intelligence due to communications woes. All of this was capped by the disasters at Kings Mountain and Cowpens plus Guilford Court House, where the field was soaked with victorious British blood.

In the years after the war, Cornwallis feuded in print with his former superior, Sir Henry Clinton, about the conflict and the minutiae of strategy and decisions shaping the struggle. Clinton had become the ultimate armchair general by then, never holding another army command after the Revolution. The nit-picking in postwar books by both old warriors soon lost its edge. But while Clinton faded into obscurity, dying in 1795, Cornwallis overcame the humiliation of Yorktown, his service in India and Ireland cementing a proud legacy recognized in monuments still standing across the old Empire to this day.

Rawdon

In February 1782 Rawdon was caught up in the controversy over the execution of Isaac Hayne, the South Carolina militia officer. Hayne was from an influential and prosperous Low Country family who had previously sworn allegiance to the British, but was later captured while bearing arms against the Crown, a possibly capital offense. In July 1781, Hayne was being held in the Provost Dungeon in Charleston when he received the worst news imaginable: a court of inquiry had found him guilty of the charge and condemned him to death. Despite the fact that other Americans had been hanged at Camden and other locations for similar "crimes" there was an outpouring of public opinion that Hayne's sentence was too harsh. The British authorities, however, felt the need to make an example of the colonel and he was executed on August 4, becoming "a shining martyr to the cause of American liberty," said one account.[5]

In Parliament months later, opponents of the war seized on Hayne's hanging, accusing the army of using "methods of barbarism" and targeting

Rawdon specifically, although he was in the process of relinquishing his command in South Carolina and returning to England at the time of the execution. In the House of Lords, Rawdon was verbally attacked during the introduction of a motion to condemn Hayne's execution. The motion failed, Rawdon later demanding and receiving a public apology from the politician who offended him. By 1783 the 28-year-old lord had risen to colonel of an infantry regiment and appointed aide-de-camp to the King. An uneventful ten years followed before Rawdon succeeded his father as Earl of Moira in June 1793.

Promoted to major general a few months later, Moira—as he was afterward referred to—was dispatched to Flanders as commander of 10,000 troops joining allies against the French in the War of the First Coalition the initial conflict of the French Revolutionary Wars. The general's brief record in this conflict was unremarkable. Over the next few years, Moira—by then in his early forties—appears to have spent much time and money in the social circles of the Prince of Wales as well as dabbling in politics. He caused a stir in 1797 when he wrote a letter stating that some members of Parliament were supporting him for prime minister and that he was ready to form his administration. Hearing of this, his former mentor Lord Cornwallis noted: "It is surely impossible that Lord Moira's letter can be genuine; if it is, excess of vanity and self-importance must have extinguished every spark of understanding, and I am sure there was a time when he had sense." The years had obviously dampened the friendship the two had enjoyed while serving at Camden. Despite this diversion, Moira's military star still ascended, rising to lieutenant general in 1798 and general in 1803.[6]

Moira married Flora Muir Campbell—the Countess of Loudoun—in 1804, their union eventually resulting in six children. On October 4, 1813, he reached Calcutta, to assume his latest position, governor-general of India, as Cornwallis had done years earlier. Moira's military skills and experience were tested in the Anglo-Nepalese War and the Third Anglo-Maratha War. During this time abroad, he was honored as the Marquess of Hastings, Earl of Rawdon and Viscount Loudoun, all in February 1817. After almost ten years of service, he left India in January 1823 to return to Britain.[7]

In March 1824 Moira was appointed governor and commander-in-chief of Malta. His somewhat-charmed life was nearing its eclipse, however. A fall from his horse aggravated a hernia and he died aboard the ship *Revenge* near Naples, Italy, on November 28, 1826. He was buried in Malta. In an odd twist, he requested that his right hand be cut off and kept until it could be placed with his wife when she died. "His manners were peculiarly striking," said an 1828 account of his passing. "The dignity of his appearance, and the polished urbanity of his address, marked him at once as a gentleman of the highest order, but his good-breeding, although perfectly refined, seemed the natural impulse of a kind disposition." Somewhere in time, Sarah McCalla screamed in full-throat disagreement, Charles Porterfield quietly disagreeing with her.[8]

Tarleton

Cornwallis's infamous cavalry chieftain was treated with disdain and raw contempt by the Americans in the days after the Yorktown surrender. His victories at Waxhaws and Fishing Creek and in other incidents were tarnished by his merciless bloodlust—at least in the minds of Washington's officers—who shunned him while socializing and dining with many of their British counterparts after the capitulation.

Historian Lucian Agniel related an encounter between Tarleton and the South Carolina Colonel John Laurens, the Green Dragoon inquiring if the snubbing was accidental. Laurens bluntly replied, "No, Colonel Tarleton, no accident at all, intentional, I can assure you and meant as a reproof for certain cruelties practiced by the troops under your command in the campaigns in the Carolinas." Tarleton riposted, "What, Sir, and is it for severities inseparable from war which you are pleased to term cruelties, that I am to be disgraced before junior officers? Is it, Sir, for a faithful discharge of my duty to my King and my country that I am thus humiliated in the eyes of three armies?"

Laurens interrupted him: "Pardon me. There are modes, Sir, of discharging a soldier's duty, and where mercy has a share in the mode, it renders the duty more acceptable to both friends and foes." Tarleton eventually was allowed to dine with the French, who had little or no involvement in the Carolinas battles and thus had not encountered Tarleton's men there. "Bloody Banny" as he was nicknamed by many Americans, also told the French that he was concerned about being killed by some seeking revenge for his wartime actions. The French obliged in moving his quarters and found the next day that his fears were well founded, "the bed upon which he was to have slept" having been "stabbed in several places." Rochambeau had assisted Tarleton in escaping the would-be killer(s), but had little respect for Ban in general, writing, "Colonel Tarleton has no merit as an officer, only that bravery that every grenadier has, but he is a butcher."[9]

Returning to England after Yorktown, Tarleton—unlike Cornwallis—was embraced as a hero, throngs of excited admirers lining the road from Dover to London, many shouting "Brave Tarleton!" as he passed by.

The Prince of Wales called on him the next day at his hotel, Ban dining that night with an assortment of royals and courtiers. Hours later he was graced by a private audience with King George at St. James Palace and soon thereafter was presented to Queen Charlotte at Buckingham Palace. Tarleton quickly resumed his gallivanting habits, romancing and gambling his way through the city's pubs, vice dens and faro parlors. He was hard to miss, parading about in his uniform, complete with green tunic and black-feathered helmet, posing for a portrait by Sir Joshua Reynolds. The artist was careful not to show that Ban had been shot and lost much of his right hand at Guilford Court House, but the wound endeared him even more to many.

At Reynolds's studio, Tarleton met Mary Robinson, an attractive leading lady on the London stage, who was nicknamed "Perdita," for her role in Shakespeare's *A Winter's Tale*. Their encounter evolved in a prolonged, very-public affair, giving much juicy fodder for the myriad society gossips. Among those attracted to Tarleton's gaudy sideshow was statesman and writer Horace Walpole who also noted the response of Tarleton's former schoolmate, playwright Richard Brinsley Sheridan. "I must tell you a saying of Sheridan too sublime to be called a *bon mot*," Walpole wrote to the Rev. William Mason in February 1782. "Tarleton boasts of having butchered more men, and lain with more women than anybody—'*Lain with*,' said Sheridan, 'what a weak expression; he should have said, *ravished*—rapes are the relaxation of murder.'"[10]

Elsewhere, the controversial cavalier could not resist becoming embroiled in the blame game and second guessing of many British officers who turned on each other to embellish their wartime images in the English press and in personal memoirs. Tarleton found himself sparring in ink with Clinton, Cornwallis and others, including his former Legion second-in-command Major George Hanger, who had operated so well in tandem with him in the rout at Camden.

Hanger seems to have been just as notorious a womanizer and just as tough a fighter as Tarleton, but the huge egos of both clashed after the war. These teapot tempests for Tarleton climaxed with the 1787 publication of his book *A History of the Campaigns of 1780–1781 in the Southern Provinces of North America*. With time and age, his tarnished stardom weakened, the unapologetic warrior marrying and taking a seat in Parliament, where he was a strong advocate for the British shipping industry, particularly the sea barons sending African slaves to America. Still, if Ban's fame faded elsewhere, he remained popular to many in his home city. His book, war service and the "untiring activity of his disposition, procured for him considerable popularity, particularly among his townsmen at Liverpool," stated a 19th-century account. Tarleton was 78 when he died on January

16, 1833, ever the most flamboyant, colorful, and—arguably despicable—Revolutionary War titan in Camden's history.[11]

Greene

After the war, Georgia and South Carolina offered the General large plantations in appreciation for his military service and sacrifice in the Southern campaign, Greene accepting Georgia's offer. By fall 1785, Greene and his family were preparing to leave their Rhode Island home and journey to Mulberry Grove plantation about 12 miles from Savannah. The estate's previous owner was John Grahame, the British lieutenant governor of Georgia and consisted of more than 2,000 acres. The Greenes planned to winter down south and spend their summers in the north after getting situated in Georgia. They endured a 16-day, somewhat stormy voyage, in which a man was lost overboard, Greene throwing a chicken coop for him to cling to, but in vain. At another point, the general called his five children to the quarter-deck to watch a whale swimming close by.

Reaching Mulberry Grove, the Greenes found there was work to be done in making the main house "thoroughly comfortable," but overall, the estate was beautiful and bucolic, the general's grandson, George Washington Greene, related. The tasks done, the words of Greene himself conveyed the excitement he felt for this new-life beginning in a letter to his friend Ethan Clarke of Newport, R.I.[12] Greene wrote after their Georgia arrival:

> We found the house, situation, and out-buildings, more convenient and pleasing than we expected. The prospect is delightful, and the house magnificent. We have a coach-house and stables, a large out kitchen, and a poultry-house nearly fifty feet long, and twenty wide, parted for different kinds of poultry, with a pigeon-house on the top, which will contain not less than a thousand pigeons. Besides these, are several other buildings convenient for a family, and among the rest, a fine smoke-house. The garden is in ruins, but there are still a great variety of shrubs and flowers in it.

When he was not supervising the plantation operations, Greene traveled to Cumberland Island off the southern Georgia coast, where he "had purchased a large interest," for timber production. Reading and playing with his children also occupied his time, one of them recalling to G.W. Greene that his father was "a tall man, who used to take him on his knee and teach him funny songs." A game called "Puss in the Corner" was among the favorite pastimes, Kitty Greene joining in the fun and frolic. "All the humor and freshness of his [Greene's] youth came back to him through their youth," his grandson noted. A frequent visitor was retired Major General Anthony Wayne, better known to his soldiers as "Mad

Anthony," who had served with Greene and was a close friend and neighbor. Wayne had relocated to Georgia from his native Pennsylvania after the war.[13]

Still, this was in no way a perfect world; far from it. A daring soldier and relentless commander, Greene was flawed in civilian endeavors, a mediocre businessman who amassed substantial debt and had also been accused of misusing army funds. That being said, by April 1786, the Greenes were busy with planting season, but were missing some of their Rhode Island friends. The general was known for his outspoken anti-slavery views and had some difficulty in hiring laborers, but about 60 acres of corn had been planted while some 130 acres were to be seeded with rice. Greene told Clarke,

> The garden is delightful. The fruit trees and flowering shrubs form a pleasing variety. We have green peas almost fit to eat, and as fine lettuce as ever you saw. The mocking birds surround us evening and morning. The weather is mild, and the vegetable kingdom progressing to perfection.... We have in the same orchard apples, pears, peaches, apricots, nectarines, plums of different kinds, figs, pomegranates, and oranges. And we have strawberries which measure three inches around. All these are clever, but the want of our friends to enjoy them with renders them less interesting.

One wonders if the general perhaps thought how such a rich bounty of nature would have been appreciated—and devoured—by the destitute soldiers he led after replacing Gates that grim December of 1780.[14]

Even if he did, his life's time—at age 44—was running out. Greene and Kitty traveled to Savannah for a business meeting on Monday, June 12, 1786. Afterward, they were in no hurry to return home, visiting with friends and staying with them overnight. The next morning the Greenes left early, planning to spend the day with their neighbor, William Gibbons, at his plantation just below Mulberry Grove. Gibbons had rice fields and Greene was eager to see them, since he intended to plant his own crop. It was a tortuously hot, sunny day and after looking over Gibbons's spread, Kitty and the general headed toward home.[15]

That afternoon, Greene complained of a headache, which gradually worsened. The pain lingered and intensified through Wednesday and Thursday, June 15, the General's forehead swollen. A friend noted Greene's seeming depression and "unwillingness to engage in conversation." A physician was called, drew some blood and administered "a few common remedies" before leaving. No one at the time diagnosed that Greene was apparently suffering from severe heat stroke, thus, the "disease was left almost free to do its fatal work," noted G.W. Greene. As the general's health continued to deteriorate, another doctor was summoned, but could do little to help him. "The sick man sank into a stupor for which science could do nothing" and the Greene children were sent to a neighbor's home, "too young to feel the calamity that was impending over them," the grandson related. Near dawn on June 19, 1786, the general's heavy breathing grew fainter. At 6 a.m. he died.[16]

"My dear friend General Greene is no more," Anthony Wayne wrote to a colleague later that Monday after being at Greene's bedside through the night and early morning. "He was great as a soldier, greater as a citizen, immaculate as a friend.... Pardon this scrawl; my feelings are but too much affected because I have seen a great and good man die." After a hastily planned but grand funeral with military honors in Savannah on June 20, the General's remains were apparently placed in a brick family vault built by John Grahame—the Crown lieutenant governor—but obviously not used after the British left Georgia. Nineteenth-century Georgia historian Charles C. Jones, Jr., noted that "the proof is not conclusive" but "the tradition lives and is generally accepted" that Greene's wooden coffin was put in the vault.[17]

George Washington was shocked and deeply saddened on learning of Greene's demise. "General Greene lately died at Savannah in Georgia, the public as well as his family and friends has met with a severe loss," he wrote to Rochambeau. "He was a great and good man indeed." Washington also described Greene as "our much lamented friend" and his own "keenest sorrow" in a letter to former general Henry Knox. Writing to Lafayette almost a year later, Washington was still stung by Greene's loss. "General Greene's death is an event which has given such general concern, and is so much regretted by his numerous friends, that I can scarce persuade myself to touch upon it, even so far as to say that in him you have lost a man who affectionately regarded and was a sincere admirer of you." Even "Bloody Ban" Tarleton, one of Greene's most feared enemies in the Carolinas, described the general as "the most able and accomplished commander that America had produced...."[18]

By 1820—more than three decades after the general's death—Savannah was in the midst of a campaign to raise funds for a monument to Greene. City officials appointed a committee to locate the general's remains—still believed to be in the brick vault—so that they could be placed beneath the memorial when it was eventually erected. To their amazement, the members found "no trace of the coffin" in the vault or elsewhere. There were rumors that friends and/or supporters of Grahame, the British official, were angered when Greene's body was placed in the Grahame vault, and that they removed the casket, burying it elsewhere. The mystery remains to this day.[19]

Greene's story resumes almost 40 years after his death when, after his Camden visit, Lafayette was entertained in Charleston before departing on "an elegant steamboat" south-bound for Savannah on March 17, 1825. The Frenchman did not know it at the time, but he would soon be asked to participate in two ceremonies honoring two American Revolutionary heroes, one of whom was Greene.

En route, the vessel anchored for two or three hours at Edisto Island, residents there packing their celebration, including a brief carriage tour, and "all the festivals they had prepared for several days" into the allotted time, Lafayette honored at the baptism of a "charming little infant" named for the illustrious hero. After the travelers marveled at alligators—foreign creatures to at least some of the Europeans—sunning along the shores of the barrier islands, Lafayette's ship was within sight of Savannah on the morning of March 19, soon greeted by "all the population on the shore and the militia assembled, who had waited during several hours" his secretary, Auguste Levasseur, noted. Georgia Governor George Troup welcomed Lafayette amid artillery salutes and martial airs. "The triumphal car and arches, the acclamations of the people, the wreaths and flowers scattered by the ladies, the sound of bells and cannon, every thing [sp] proved to Lafayette that though he had passed into another state, he was nevertheless among the same friendly and grateful people."

The proceedings culminated that night with a grand banquet, the celebration renewed on Sunday the 20th. At some point the local dignitaries approached the general about laying the cornerstones for planned monuments to Nathanael Greene and Casimir Pulaski in the city. Lafayette readily agreed, both ceremonies to be held on Monday, March 21, his last day in Savannah before departing that night for Augusta. "The citizens of Savannah had for a long time cherished the intentions of paying a tribute of gratitude to the memory of General Greene, justly considered as the southern hero of the revolutionary struggle," Levasseur related, adding that Pulaski was equally revered for sacrificing "his life in the cause of American independence."[20]

As usual, the elaborate procession and services at both monument sites were steeped in Masonic ritual and majesty, also including school children "uniformly dressed, and carrying baskets filled with flowers, which they scattered beneath the steps" of Lafayette. A large and "attentive crowd" of Savannahians were also present as the French luminary reached the location where the Greene memorial would be erected—present-day Johnson Square. Lafayette described Greene as a "great and good man to whose memory we this day pay a tribute of respect, of affection and profound regret, acquired in our revolutionary war a glory so true and so pure, that even now the name alone of GREENE recalls all the virtues, all the talents which can adorn the patriot, the statesman, and the general...." After more speeches and prayers, Lafayette stepped forward into the excavation where the cornerstone had been lowered. In it among other items were several medals, portraits of George Washington, Greene and Benjamin Franklin and some U.S. currency—paper money and coins. Lafayette then used a mallet to strike it three times, symbolizing that he had laid the cornerstone. It was sealed "while the music played a national air," Levasseur related. "The whole was terminated by a triple volley" from a contingent of American troops on hand.[21]

More than a decade passed before sufficient funds were raised to construct the obelisk in Johnson Square in 1837. Additional money was needed for the Pulaski memorial, so the cornerstone for the Polish hero was moved to that site, the structure initially known as the Greene-Pulaski monument. Pulaski's cornerstone was eventually moved to Monterey Square where the Pulaski obelisk was erected in 1853.[22]

Today, Johnson Square is one of the most popular and busiest of Savannah's beautiful squares, situated in the heart of the city. It is a shady oasis for thousands of people who live and work downtown and the myriad others who come from all over the world to experience Savannah's charms. The Greene monument remains the crown jewel of the square, still an impressive tribute to an American icon who contributed mightily, not only to the story of Revolutionary Camden, but to the extraordinary birth of the nation as well.

20

"Loud and long were the cheers of the multitude"

Washington, in the second year of his presidency, made a tour of the South. He embarked from Philadelphia in March 1791 and made stops in Fredericksburg, Richmond, Wilmington and Savannah, the southern-most point of his tour. On the return journey he visited Augusta and then Columbia—"the pretty little Carolina capital on the Congaree," said one account.

About 4 a.m.—the President's customary start time—on Wednesday, May 25, his entourage left Columbia bound for Camden, escorted by the old patriot Joseph Kershaw's son, Captain John Kershaw, and his troop of light cavalry. "His retinue was stately, as befitted so august a personage," noted one report. "First came the great white chariot in which his Excellency rode, drawn by four stalwart horses.... Next was a two-horse baggage wagon, followed by two mounted servants, leading an extra saddle horse." Kershaw's riders "with a number of mounted men from the adjacent country" brought up the rear. Most of the President's horses had served throughout his long journey, but one was injured after "foundering" and had to be led along slowly, thus lengthening the trip to Camden. Of this 36-mile segment of his journey, Washington noted in his diary:

> The Road from Columbia to Camden, excepting a mile or two at each place, goes over the most miserable pine barren I ever saw, being quite a white sand, & very hilly.—On the Wateree within a mile & [a] half of which the town stands the lands are very good,—they Culture Corn, Tobacco & Indigo.—Vessels [with cargos of tobacco] come up to the Ferry at this place at which there is a Tobacco Warehouse.

At the Wateree, "there was an exceptionally large concourse of people including almost the entire population" of Camden, stated one account. "Loud and long were the cheers of the multitude; and the throng quickly joined Washington's train as it moved on" into the town. The jubilant procession halted in the public square about 2 p.m., where "Colonel Joseph

Kershaw" as he was now titled, greeted the President on behalf of the local committee of leaders.[1]

On the morning of the 26th, Washington rode his stallion, Prescott, to DeKalb's grave "where he reverently paused for a few moments in respect for the fallen hero," said one account. "Your grateful remembrance of that excellent friend and gallant officer, the Baron De Kalb, [sp] does honor to the goodness of your hearts," he remarked to those gathered at the site. "With your regrets I mingle mine for his loss and to your praise I join the tribute of my esteem for his memory." Shortly thereafter, the President examined what was left of the redoubts and other defenses constructed by Cornwallis and Rawdon in 1780–1781.

He then resumed his journey toward Charlotte, halting to examine the Hobkirk Hill battlefield. "The ground [held by Greene] was well chosen—but he [was] not well established in it before he was attacked; which ... was, in some measure by surprise...." Washington penned in his diary. About six miles beyond, the President crossed Sanders Creek to the battle of Camden site "where Genl. Gates & Lord Cornwallis had their Engagement wch. [sp] terminated so unfavorably for the former," he noted. Washington also added a hindsight opinion of how Gates could possibly have emerged as the victor that terrible morning:

> As this was a night meeting of both Armies on their March & altogether unexpected each formed on the ground they met without any advantage.... Had Genl. Gates been ½ a mile further advanced, an impenetrable Swamp would have prevented the attack which was made on him by the British ... and afforded him time to have formed his own plans; but having no information of Lord Cornwallis's designs, and perhaps not being apprised of this advantage it was not seized by him.

Of Camden itself, Washington closed this portion of his tour with this description: "Camden is a small place with appearances of some new buildings—It was much injured by the British whilst in their possession."[2]

Lafayette

Lafayette's visit to Camden in 1825 came during a grand 14-month tour of America for the wildly popular French hero of the Revolution, and was in reverent honor of his friend and fellow soldier Baron DeKalb. The general would also journey to Savannah (mentioned in Chapter 19) where he would memorialize the late Nathanael Greene, whose war record included the battle of Hobkirk Hill.

In 1777 DeKalb and Lafayette, along with ten companions, sailed from Bordeaux to America, intent on joining the patriot cause. Lafayette and DeKalb landed on the South Carolina coast near Georgetown, both soon earning renown and generalships in Washington's army. For their service, they also found the everlasting gratitude of the American people, Lafayette savoring this affection in coming to Camden to lay the cornerstone for DeKalb's monument and final resting place in the front yard of Bethesda Presbyterian Church, a few miles from where he was mortally wounded in battle. Lafayette had been America's most famous postwar guest during a five-month stay in 1784. He returned in July 1824, making stops in 24 states, visiting many of the Revolution's more notable battlefields and whetting his "canine appetite" as a celebrity, wrote Thomas Jefferson. On this second tour Lafayette was accompanied by his son, George Washington Lafayette, and his secretary, Auguste Levasseur. Among myriad offers from across the young nation, Lafayette had accepted an invitation to visit Camden, the message signed by some of the town's foremost citizens, including Benjamin Carter, Thomas Salmond, Edward H. Anderson, William Blanding, Lewis Ciples, Abraham De Leon, John Doby, John Kershaw, Benjamin Bineham, James S. Deas and James Chesnut, Sr.[3]

A last chance to honor his compatriot and close friend in this way, plus the fact that DeKalb's remains had been exhumed (see Appendix) and were to be reinterred beneath the monument, were obviously great factors in attracting the illustrious Frenchman to Camden. Congressman John C. Carter's recently built home on Broad Street was selected to accommodate Lafayette during his visit. As was the custom of that time, "the various households of the community vied with each other in furnishing it with their best plate and mahogany," said one account. From their "Mulberry" home, the Chesnut family sent their "accomplished Philadelphia housekeeper, Miss Baldwin, to preside over the establishment. A set of china was made especially for the occasion...." At "Mrs. Levison's Millinery Store" a variety of "LaFayette [sp] Ladies' or Gentlemen's Ball gloves" were for sale along with "Badges for soldiers and private gentlemen.... Ladies Belts" and sashes. Some of the badges were made of "white silk, with a heavy gold fringe" and "stamped with an excellent likeness" of the 68-year-old Lafayette at the time of his Camden visit. As added enticement for these souvenirs, a newspaper ad claimed that the "above articles has [sp] been greatly admired at the North."

The town had continued to flourish during this period, despite the ravages of a malaria epidemic in 1816. Two years later members of the Kershaw family turned land they owned on Hobkirk Hill into 14 one-acre residential lots. They planned to develop the area into a summer retreat where locals and visitors could escape the hot months and accompanying illnesses by enjoying their time at the generally cooler, higher elevation. The Kershaws called their endeavor "Kirkwood Village," honoring Captain Robert Kirkwood and his heroism in the battle of Hobkirk Hill.[4]

That being said, Lafayette and his entourage journeyed from Fayetteville, North Carolina, through the "pretty little town" of Cheraw before being delayed by damage to the carriage that conveyed the general. The roads at times were "long and difficult" and "almost impassable" noted Levasseur, adding that in some places the party was "entirely cut off, by the overflowing of streams; in others, we were able to cross the swamps, only by moving slowly over a causeway formed of the trunks of trees, badly enough placed, side by side." Despite these hardships, Lafayette reached Camden on the morning of Tuesday, March 8, 1825, cannon salutes heralding his arrival.

"On approaching Cambden [sp] where we saw a considerable number of well cultivated gardens, we were a good deal surprised to find the trees in flower, and the balmy air perfumed by the plants, as in France during the month of June," Levasseur wrote. At the edge of town, Lafayette was greeted by Thomas Salmond, the "Intendant"—or mayor—and others, the general joining Salmond in a carriage provided by the town. An "expectant multitude," including some Revolutionary veterans, gathered on "the Green" in front of the Kershaw-Cornwallis house loudly welcomed Lafayette while "a national salute was fired from the old star redoubt, in plain view from the Green" the general reviewing the troops.[5]

With "great pomp" the column proceeded along Broad Street to the Carter house, known since that memorable day as "Lafayette Hall." There the procession halted, the marchers opening the way for Lafayette to enter the gate to the grounds. The committee of arrangements issued a welcoming address and young girls from Camden's Female Academy scattered flowers on the brick walkway. The lone boy in this contingent was ten-year-old James Chesnut, Jr., who alone had the white trousers and black coat required by the Rev. Jonathan Whitaker, principal of the town schools. Camden "is not a large town, containing only about two hundred inhabitants," Levasseur recalled. "We nevertheless found there a very numerous population, collected from more than eighty miles around...."

Colonel Henry G. Nixon, described as "Camden's gifted young orator," gave an eloquent speech "with remarkable warmth of feeling," telling the general "that his visit to the United States had added a new page to history, and that the splendor of Greek and Roman triumphs faded before the unanimity and harmony of this popular ovation," Levasseur recorded. Lafayette offered an equally lavish response to Nixon's comments, closing with: "Now gentlemen, I find myself in your good town of Camden, surrounded by beauty in its youngest bloom; by my old Seventy-six friends [the Revolutionary veterans] as it was the year of my enlistment in our noble cause...." One of the flower girls was Mary Young, who described the memorable pageantry at some point before her death in 1901. "She thought

Lafayette one of the homeliest men she had ever seen," said one account, "he was still red-haired and quite lame, leaning heavily, as he walked, on the arm of his son, George Washington." The only unpleasantness was the ejection of an "old Tory" named Jones by a Captain Starke, she recalled.[6]

Lafayette, like Washington and DeKalb, was a Mason and about 4 p.m. an escort of past masters accompanied him to the Kershaw Lodge of Freemasons where he was honored by "a large concourse of members and visiting brethren." Worshipful Master Abraham De Leon, whose family was originally from France, welcomed the guest of honor. In reply, Lafayette stated: "Amidst the gratification and favors which have been heaped on me at every step of my happy visit to the United States, the welcome of the Masonic Fraternity has been particularly pleasing." Lafayette was so overcome by his reception by the Camden lodge that he removed his Grand Masters Jewel of France and placed it around the neck of De Leon, based on a Masonic account. The elegant piece became known as the Lafayette Jewel.

After a lavish banquet, the Masons paraded the general back to the Carter home about 8 p.m., but his evening was far from over. Two hours later he was feted in a "brilliant ball" in the Long Room of the Camden Hotel. Joseph B. Kershaw, grandson of the famed local patriot, was only three at the time, but in years later relished telling about Lafayette at the gala: as gentlemen were introduced to him, the Frenchman asked, "Married?" If the answer was yes, Lafayette exclaimed, "Ah, happy fellow, happy fellow!" If no, he answered with a wink, "Lucky dog, sir, lucky dog!"[7]

The monument was dedicated in a noon ceremony the next day—Wednesday, March 9—at the stately brick sanctuary located on what is now DeKalb Street. The church was designed by renowned architect Robert Mills, who also created the monument and was on hand for the ceremony. "The Portico of the Presbyterian Church, during the ceremony, was crowded with a brilliant assemblage of ladies, who witnessed with profound attention the interesting scene that was passing before them," said a newspaper account. The procession to the churchyard was led by a group of "volunteer soldiery," followed by members of Camden's Masons. A hearse containing DeKalb's ashes came next. Six Revolutionary veteran officers bore the pall, or coffin cover, and a "war horse" was led after them. Lafayette and his entourage, other Revolutionary veterans, a variety of civil officials and local business leaders completed the groups of marchers. At the burial site, the Rev. Robert McLeod offered the opening prayer. The remains were then interred with Masonic rites, after which Abram Blanding, the superintendent of Public Buildings, made brief remarks to Lafayette, formally requesting the general to place the cornerstone over the grave. "To no hand can this office be so properly assigned as to yours,"

Blanding said. "You reached our shores together, brethren in arms and friendship ... and, as fellow soldiers, supporting in the field the cause of freedom, when our country, struggling for independence, most needed your aid...." Lafayette replied:

> The honor now bestowed upon me I receive with the mingled emotions of patriotism, gratitude, and friendship, and like other honorable duties which await me in the more northern part of the Union, I consider it as being conferred on the revolutionary army in the person of a surviving general officer. In that army.... Major general Baron DeKalb has acted a conspicuous part. His able conduct, undaunted valor, and glorious fall in the first battle of Camden, form one of the remarkable traits of our struggle for independence and freedom. He was cordially devoted to our American cause, and while his public and private qualities have endeared him to his contemporaries, here I remain to pay to his merits on this tomb, the tribute of an admiring witness, of an intimate companion, of a mourning friend.[8]

Lafayette then solemnly placed the cornerstone, using a trowel with a solid-silver blade and ivory handle. The monument, consisting of a white-marble obelisk, 15-feet high, was not completed until 1827. The base was composed of 26 large granite blocks, 24 of which bore the individual names of the states then in the Union. The 25th block was inscribed "*Foedus esto perpetuum*," and the 26th covered the Baron's remains. Levasseur described how Lafayette's hand rested upon the cornerstone as it was positioned, "whilst the multitude, in religious silence, contemplated the French veteran, after almost half a century, rendering the last offices to the German soldier, in a land which they both had moistened with their blood, and which their arms had contributed to set free." Tradition has it that Lafayette was also entertained at the Lausanne mansion, described as "the show place of the neighborhood" and "famous for its hospitality as well as for its beautiful rose gardens and stately magnolia trees."[9]

The Lafayette Trowel

The historic trowel used by Lafayette in the monument was made for the occasion by Alexander Young of Camden. It was engraved: "Made for Brother LaFayette to lay the cornerstone of DeKalb's monument, 1825." Young apparently was a fellow Mason with Lafayette, based on his used of the term "brother." The trowel was later used in memorial dedications to South Carolina Revolutionary heroes William Jasper and William Moultrie and William Gilmore Simms, one of the state's most noted literary figures—all in Charleston—as well as battlefield ceremonies at Cowpens and Kings Mountain and to Confederate soldiers buried in Camden.

The Salmond family owned it for many years before it was sold in 1893 to the Grand Lodge of Masons of South Carolina for a reported price of $400. Even today, the relic remains a treasured artifact of the state's Grand Lodge.[10]

21

Women "Reapers" of the Camden Region: 1780

As Gates's army marched ever closer to its date with destiny at Camden in summer 1780, the wheat fields in the region along nearby Fishing Creek were ready for the annual June harvest. A critical problem was that all of the men were away, either bearing arms or imprisoned after the fall of Charleston weeks earlier. Thus, it fell to the young women in the area to bring in the crop on which so many families relied. With "spirit equal to that of their gallant brothers" they formed a "company of reapers" to cut and gather the grain. The company consisted of Mary, Margaret and Ellen Gill, Isabella and Margaret Kelso, Sarah Knox, Margaret, Elizabeth and Mary Mills, Mary McClure and Nancy Brown. Day after sweaty day for five or six weeks, they toiled under the same savage sun that broiled the soldiers on both sides, going from one farm to another. Sometimes they were aided by the homestead matriarchs, sometimes by "a few old men"; sometimes not. The "reapers" only asked "Is the owner out with the fighting men?" before taking to the fields. "It seemed that Providence smiled on the generous enterprise; there were no storms during that period to ravage the fields…" said one account.[1]

Little more is known about most of these stalwart women, but at least two had strong connections to Camden during the war. Mary Gill was about 22 years old in June 1780, her family having moved to South Carolina from Pennsylvania shortly after her birth. The Gills made their new home on the south fork of Fishing Creek where many "Pennsylvania Irish" had settled, cultivating the fertile acreage there for wheat and other crops. Her father Robert, a deeply religious man, was active in establishing a church there. When the war came, Robert was too old to fight, but encouraged his sons, Thomas, Robert, Archibald, John and James, to join the rebels. Thomas and Robert the younger entered the fray, but were captured and taken to Camden after Sumter's debacle at Fishing Creek. Learning of her brothers being held at Camden, Mary and other women made several trips there, bringing pack horses with various goods for the captives.

Mary had a "figure of majestic height and proportions, and there was much dignity in her bearing," said one account. At one point, the British suspected her of being a male spy in women's clothing and she had difficulty in convincing them they were mistaken. Indeed, she did serve as a guide and spy for Sumter and possibly other partisans. Of her brothers imprisoned at Camden, Robert Gill died there, while Thomas was released after seven months in custody. With the war winding down after Cornwallis's surrender at Yorktown in 1781, Mary Gill married her longtime boyfriend, John Mills, a close neighbor and officer in Sumter's ranks and later in the state troops. They exchanged vows in May 1782, other soldiers in the Catawba region also taking advantage of brief furloughs about this time to marry their wartime sweethearts. Mrs. Gill-Mills, as she likely would be known in the 21st century, was 83 when she died in 1841.[2]

Isabella Kelso also was one of the "reapers" her family living adjacent to the Fishing Creek church in 1780. Her father, Samuel, made swords for the Americans and served in Sumter's force, along with sons Samuel Jr. and George Kelso. George was seriously wounded when Tarleton surprised and routed the Gamecock at Fishing Creek in August 1780, Samuel Jr. having some of his whiskers taken off by a musket ball in the action. Isabella was among the women who journeyed to Camden to aid and comfort loved ones imprisoned there. She was romantically involved with William Wylie, a veteran fighter in some of the lesser-known actions in South Carolina before his capture. Wylie was released in the prisoner exchange instigated by Sarah McCalla and Mary Nixon in March 1781. A few weeks later, Isabella and William were married, but he continued in military service until the war's end.[3]

22

African Americans at Camden and Beyond

Blacks, both free and slave, played an important role not only at Camden, but in the rest of the Revolution as well.

More than 500,000 African Americans lived in the 13 provinces—or colonies—during the conflict. While blacks fought on both sides, the overwhelming majority of them, roughly between 80,000 and 100,000, aided the British. Blacks "secretly wished that the British army might win, for then all Negro slaves will gain their freedom," stated an account during this time. "It is said that this sentiment is almost universal among the Negroes in America."[1]

African Americans served in various capacities in either army including combat soldiers—infantry, cavalry and artillerymen—to scouts, guides, spies, teamsters, cattle wranglers, cooks, laborers, hospital aides and other assignments. Undoubtedly, black women also served in many of these same non-combat functions and were among the camp followers—wives and sometimes even children—who often trudged along behind the armies on the march. To say that the contributions of all of them have been overlooked or neglected over more than two centuries is a vast understatement which hampers modern day historians—like me—in attempting to bring their contributions to light, especially in such a narrow focus as the Camden saga.

We do know that many black workmen were crucial in constructing the magazine near the Kershaw House before the British occupation. Their sweat and labor likely ranged from actual brickmaking to building the stout enclosure used to house munitions—not only for the Americans, but later for Cornwallis and Rawdon. When Cornwallis chose Camden as the keystone of his interior outposts in South Carolina in summer 1780, numerous African Americans were put to work erecting outer fortifications and some makeshift shelters for the British troops, especially in the coming months as winter neared. Later they would be instrumental in raising the log palisade around the village. This important story actually began a few months before Cornwallis's arrival. After Charleston's capture in May 1780, the conquering army found itself inundated with escaped slaves. "Most blacks came to equate the sight of a soldier in a red coat with liberty," related historian Gregory J.W. Urwin.[2] The British cavalry chief Banastre Tarleton wrote of this period:

> Commissioners were appointed to arrange the differences which subsisted in Carolina concerning the [N]egroes," "It is here necessary to observe, that all the [N]egroes, men, women, and children, upon the approach of any detachment of the King's troops, thought themselves absolved from all respect to their American masters, and entirely released from servitude. Influenced by this idea, they quitted the plantations, and followed the army; which behavior caused the neglect of cultivation, proved detrimental to the King's troops, and occasioned continual disputes about property of this description. In a short time, the attention of the commissioners produced arrangements equally useful to the military and inhabitants.[3]

"There can be no doubt that [N]egroes, bond and free, were in the ranks of the American army during the entire period of the war, or that they continued to be enlisted or enrolled in most of the States, especially as the pressure for recruits increased in the later years of the struggle," stated another account. "Swamp Fox" Marion's command varied from a few hundred to a few dozen, including former black slaves, and he was strongly resentful of landowners trying to reclaim slaves from his ranks, refusing to "suffer blacks to be removed from my brigade." This obviously put Marion at odds with South Carolina law against slaves bearing arms.[4]

Thomas Sumter recognized the active role African Americans played for the British, writing to Marion in early 1781: "The enemy oblige the [N]egroes they have to make frequent sallies." Sumter also embodied the prejudices of the time, adding "This circumstance alone is sufficient to rouse and fix the resentment and detestation of every American who possesses common feelings."[5]

Charles Stedman was the Pennsylvania Loyalist and commissary officer with the British army in South Carolina. As an outsider, he offered this interesting view of race relations in the Carolinas: The "planters['] property consisted chiefly in cattle and [N]egroes, there not being white inhabitants sufficient to cultivate the land; the planters asserting, that, without [N]egroes, indigo and rice could not be cultivated, the whites not being able to bear the heat of the climate. The [N]egroes in general followed the British army."[6]

George Washington's most trusted and able commander, Major General Nathanael Greene, was a New Englander who fought in the northern campaigns as well as in South Carolina, leading his troops in the battle of Hobkirk Hill near Camden. The Rhode Islander had been an outspoken critic of slavery before the war and amid its duration. Even in retirement, he refused to use slave labor at Mulberry Grove, the plantation near Savannah that the state of Georgia gifted him in gratitude of his military service.[7]

David Ramsay, an 18th-century historian of South Carolina in the Revolution, stated: "It has been computed by good judges that, between the years 1775 and 1783…" "the state lost twenty-five thousand [N]egroes." Based on these numbers, George Moore concluded: "This was a fifth part of all the slaves in the State at the beginning of the war, and equal to more than half the entire white population."[8]

23

DeKalb's First Grave: "in the 'custom of knighthood'"

For weeks after the Camden battle, General DeKalb's death was mourned across Maryland, he having led so many of her sons to martial glory. Sentiments ran so deep that the state legislature in October 1780 passed an act granting citizenship to his sons. At the same time, the legislators also approved a resolution for a monument to DeKalb to be erected in Annapolis, the provincial capital, even settling on an inscription for the memorial. Sadly, it would take more than a century to make the resolution a reality, the Baron's resting place at Camden, meanwhile, overgrown and forgotten for years after the war.[1]

Edwin J. Scott was a young boy living in Camden in 1811, later writing a book titled *Random Recollections* in which he recalls playing "frequently on the grave of Baron DeKalb, in the middle of a lonely old field...." The grave "was surrounded by a plain brick structure three or four feet high, covered by a white stone slab, with an inscription eulogizing his [the general's] character and services." In their invaluable two-volume *Historic Camden* work, initially published in 1905, authors Thomas J. Kirkland and Robert M. Kennedy claim that they found the original white slab in 1901 in the Presbyterian Church basement, where it had likely "lain forgotten during the past seventy-six years," since the 1825 ceremony. The stone's inscription, written by the historian David Ramsay—who died in 1815—was identical to the one on the DeKalb monument erected in the churchyard. It was unclear when the stone slab was initially placed on the general's burial site—Washington referring to it only as a grave during his 1791 visit—but Kennedy and Kirkland asserted that it was done between 1805 and 1811, based on their research. The duo also discovered much more with their investigative talents. Utilizing old newspaper accounts from the 1880s, they found that the Masonic Fraternity was responsible for placing the brick enclosure and inscribed stone over DeKalb's resting place in Camden. Possibly aiding the two authors in solving the mystery was the fact that a fine bronze monument to DeKalb was to finally be placed on the grounds of the Maryland state capitol at Annapolis on August 16, 1886—the 106th anniversary of the battle and the Baron's mortal wounding.[2]

Attention about DeKalb was renewed due to the monument excitement, resulting in more information—some inaccurate—about his funeral and burial. In an 1886 issue of the *Baltimore Sun*, an anonymous writer claimed there were six American officers who were Masons—like DeKalb—including several who were Maryland Continentals. These men were apparently captured during Gates's disastrous defeat and at least some may have participated in the Masonic and military honors at DeKalb's burial. Years later, the unknown writer continued, some South Carolina freemasons began a project to locate the Baron's unmarked gravesite so as to identify "the spot with some memento of a Mason's appreciation of a brother who gallantly fell in the cause of freedom."

In a separate 1886 letter to the *Baltimore News*, Dr. E.M. Boykin of Camden noted that "Miss Hettie Cummings, an old English lady, who had remained when the British army left" had been instrumental in finding the general's remains. Cummings, it may be remembered, was a staunch Loyalist who had stayed with Joseph Kershaw's family during the war, possibly even witnessing DeKalb's burial or visiting the site during the British occupation of Camden. Based on her information and the digging of several "rectangular ditches" the freemasons were able to proceed with construction of the brick enclosure and slab.[3]

By the early 1820s, an effort was underway across the Palmetto State for a more elaborate monument to DeKalb and fundraising was rushed so that Lafayette might lay the cornerstone during the portion of his national tour through the South. Fourteen wagonloads of granite were brought from a quarry at White Oak, on the old Ciples plantation about 16 miles from town. Abram Blanding, the landowner at the time, contributed the granite free of charge and "planters of the vicinity" contributed the wagons to haul it to Camden.[4]

Lafayette's visit to Camden and the churchyard ceremony would be unforgettable spectacles in honor of the gallant Baron, but there is more to this backstory. He had to be exhumed before Lafayette's arrival. Wash Carlos, an old former slave of Lewis Ciples, was present at the unearthing and related his observations to Dr. Boykin: "He [the Baron] lay, it seems, in the 'custom of knighthood,' as last of his race, buried in his armor; that is to say, his helmet, his sword and his spurs were in the grave with him." Included in those supervising the event were Ciples, Carlos, and a Captain Carter, who supposedly fought under DeKalb and was lame due to a war wound. Carter was allowed to take the helmet, later described as "old Kalb's muster cap."

DeKalb was reinterred at Bethesda with his sword and spurs, Boykin added, based on an account by Dr. James A. Young, who was at the reburial and the ceremony. After Carter's death, the helmet became the possession of Lewis Ciples, who was then living in a house on Hobkirk Hill just north of the Hobkirk Inn. After Ciples's passing, "the helmet was knocked about as a piece of old iron" before Dr. A.W. Burnet, a new owner of the property, found what was left of the headpiece—the visor—in an outbuilding on the grounds. Burnet later presented the visor to Dr. Boykin, and upon the latter's death, it became the possession of his widow and later his son, John Boykin. He sent the relic to be displayed at the Charleston Exposition in 1902, but it never reached the city and has never been found. In earlier years there were claims that the prominent Middleton family in Charleston had pieces of DeKalb's "armor" from shortly after the Baron's death in 1780, until spring 1865 when it was stolen from "Middleton Place," their beautiful estate on the Ashley River. This was during the last weeks of the Civil War, Charleston having been evacuated by Confederate forces on February 17–18, and Union troops were in the immediate vicinity of the estate. Still, this claim appears unfounded since DeKalb's sword, spurs and helmet were in his first grave when the remains were exhumed in 1825.[5]

24

DeKalb, Major Benjamin Nones and the "Hebrew Legion"

Untold numbers of Jews served with distinction and bravery on both sides in the American Revolution. One of the more notable was Benjamin Nones, who figured prominently in the Camden story during and after the war.

Nones was a 20-year-old Sephardic Jew when he came to America from France in 1777 and enlisted in the Continental Army. Over the next three years he made a name for himself in the military although records about him are scarce and often erroneous. Nones apparently served under Continental Maj. Gen. Benjamin Lincoln, as a volunteer in the South Carolina militia and also in Pulaski's Legion, seeing action in the siege of Savannah and other combat, earning a citation for bravery. Various accounts also state that he was on the staffs of Washington, Lafayette, DeKalb and Pulaski, all questionable claims at best. Possibly the biggest exaggeration about Nones is that he led a command of about 400 Jewish soldiers in the "Hebrew legion," a detachment of Gates's army which fought at Camden in August 1780. Other accounts claim that when DeKalb was mortally wounded, Nones, along with Captains Jacob de la Motta and Jacob De Leon, bore the Baron from the battlefield.[1]

The giant fly in the ointment here is that Nones, by his own admission, could not have been anywhere near Camden when the battle was fought, since he had been in British custody since May 1780. Writing to Thomas Jefferson in 1801 from his home in Philadelphia, Nones penned: "At the fall of Charleston [May 12, 1780] I became a prisoner of war and continued so till the surrender of Lord Cornwallis [October 19, 1781]." Regarding the saga of the stricken DeKalb being carried from the field, the Baron's aide Du Buysson—wounded in shielding DeKalb and at the general's bedside when he died—doesn't mention such a dramatic event. In his 1905 book, *The Jews of South Carolina*, author Barnett A. Elzas, a Jewish rabbi, physician and scholar, described the episode as "mythical on its

239

very face," especially since DeKalb fell and was almost immediately captured by the British, Cornwallis himself addressing his bloodied adversary on the battlefield. Elzas reached this conclusion apparently unaware of Nones's letter to Jefferson, which is not cited in his work. Similarly, DeKalb biographer Friedrich Kapp also has no record of it in his 1884 book, *The Life of John Kalb*.[2]

Little is known of the other two officers who supposedly assisted DeKalb from the field. Elzas, "after the most diligent inquiry and research, continued for many months," concluded that the "story of Captain Jacob De Leon is one of the many myths of the Jews of South Carolina." Elzas eventually did find De Leon's grave in an "old, abandoned cemetery" in Columbia, S.C., the tombstone stating that he died in September 1828 at age 64. Thus, Elzas speculated that De Leon *could* have been at the battle of Camden "but that he was a captain on DeKalb's staff is hardly imaginable." The rabbi also noted that Dr. Abraham De Leon was the leading Camden dignitary in organizing Lafayette's visit and the cornerstone ceremony, but stopped short of trying to make a connection between the physician and Jacob De Leon, based on their common last name. Elzas left the whodunit this way: "From Abraham De Leon, who took part in the ceremonies ... to Jacob De Leon, who carried DeKalb from the field at Camden, is not an unintelligible transition." Elzas does not give further mention to Jacob De La Motta, the third officer.[3]

But what of the "Hebrew legion?" None of the myriad sources examined for my work mentions such a command, other than Henry Morais's book, *The Jews of Philadelphia* in 1894, and a 1926 article about Nones in the *Jewish Daily Bulletin* of New York. Thus, since Nones did not participate in the Camden battle, he could not have led this body of troops even if it existed, which is doubtful, to say the least. A search on google.com turns up minimal hits for the "Hebrew legion"—linked to the above publications—but many for the "Jewish Legion," a volunteer force that fought with the British against the Turkish army in World War I.[4]

Still, at least two decades after DeKalb's death, Nones again surfaced in Camden's saga, this time in the search for the Baron's grave. As stated earlier, South Carolina freemasons began a project in the early 1800s to locate the general's resting place and to have it properly marked in honor of DeKalb's exploits and achievements as a fellow Mason. Also as mentioned earlier, six American officers, apparently captured in the Camden battle, were present when DeKalb was buried with Masonic and military honors. For unknown reasons, the project committee, believing that Nones was one of the officers at the burial, contacted him at his home in Philadelphia. An article in an 1886 issue of the *Baltimore Sun* further explained:

24. DeKalb, Major Benjamin Nones and the "Hebrew Legion" 241

The chairman of the committee, Dr. A.H. De Leon, of Camden ... addressed a letter of inquiry upon the subject to Mr. Nones of Philadelphia, who, as one, and perhaps the only one, of the survivors, might be supposed ... to have some recollection of ... where the body had been interred. Mr. Nones, who still retained a vivid recollection of the circumstances in his memory, dictated a letter describing the spot as nearly as possible, and, within a few feet of the place designated by him, the remains were found.

Even Elzas, author of *The Jews of South Carolina*, wrote that Nones "was present at the first burial."[5]

Nones and his wife, Miriam, raised a large family in Philadelphia after the war, the former soldier rightly proud of his combat service with Pulaski's Legion and as a South Carolina militiaman. He rose as a respected leader of the city's Sephardic Jewish community over the years as well as an "Interpreter for the United States," working with the Board of Health in Philadelphia in 1818 and 1821. Still, he remains an enigmatic figure, his 1801 letter to Jefferson about his confinement as a prisoner of war forever shadowing his military legacy.[6]

Appendix
Beyond the Battles: Camden Military Lore

An Incredible Relic Story

"Revolutionary Relic" was the headline of an article in the *Camden Journal and Southern Whig* on January 24, 1835, more than half a century after Cornwallis crushed Gates. A deteriorated musket which belonged to Levi, "a French negro" who came to America with Lafayette and who had fought throughout the Revolution, was found "bedded" in the mud of Gum Swamp on the Camden battlefield. Wounded in the battle, Levi had hidden the flintlock in the swamp. No details were given as to how or when the musket was found or by whom, but Levi was said to have lived in the Camden District for some years after the war and was "a servant for the Whitaker family," the article stated. "The barrel is badly eaten with rust, the bayonet beaten and broken." The relic was in possession of Dr. William Blanding, a longtime Camden resident, when the story was printed, but Blanding died years later in Rehoboth, Massachusetts, the musket seemingly disappearing. Levi's "gun would be a prize today, could it be rediscovered," said a 1905 account.[1]

Congress Thanks the Camden Heroes

Congress passed a measure in October 1780 calling for a DeKalb monument to be erected.

DeKalb's immortality in bronze at Annapolis would have to wait for more than a century, however—the American Revolution still in doubt, followed by the War of 1812, myriad other history-shaping events and the volcano of the Civil War and Reconstruction taking precedent over all. In February 1883, Congress finally appropriated funds for the Baron's Maryland monument, which was dedicated three years later.[2]

Agnes of Glasgow

One of the enduring enigmas of colonial Camden is the saga of a young woman known only to us as "Agnes of Glasgow."

A long-forgotten grave near the site of old Camden provides the scant information we have about her, a decrepit headstone carved "Here Lies The Body of

Agnes of Glasgow, who departed this life Feb. 12, 1780. Aged 20," the inscription done with the point of a bayonet, some claim. "It is said that she still roams the streets of Camden ... in hopes of finding her lost love," a South Carolina tourist brochure whispers spookily.[3]

The most widely accepted tale is that Agnes was in love with a Scottish soldier—sometimes identified as Lt. Angus McPherson—who sailed to the provinces with the British army during the Revolution. Hearing little if anything from him and obsessed with joining him or learning his fate, she found passage aboard a vessel and came to America. The story varies from that point on.

One version is that she had no way of locating him and wandered from "camp to camp," making her way from the New England provinces to South Carolina. At Camden, she found her lover buried in a churchyard and soon died of a broken heart. Earl Cornwallis was so touched by her story that he had her buried and the grave marked. Another version claims that Agnes was actually Cornwallis's mistress, but that his neglect of her resulted in a broken-hearted demise. As in the first version, a sad Cornwallis had her buried.[4]

The most obvious response to any of Agnes's stories is that Camden was not occupied by the Crown's troops in February 1780. The British fleet transporting Clinton's army, including Cornwallis—which ultimately captured Charleston in May—was just arriving off the Georgia–South Carolina coast in February.

That being said, there was a British presence along the seaboard much earlier, including Scottish troops. Redcoats, the 71st Highlanders among them, were landed near Savannah and seized that city in December 1778. In the coming months, the British established a post at Beaufort, S.C., where the 71st Scots were stationed, their stellar history later starred with many encounters in Georgia and South Carolina, including the battle of Camden. The 71st also earlier fought at Stono Ferry in June before reinforcing the Redcoat defenders who defeated American and French forces besieging Savannah in September-October 1779. Could one of these gallant lads have been Agnes's heartthrob? In another twist, a historical marker near the gravesite states that Agnes was "buried here at night by King Haigler [sp] and his men," referring to the Catawba chief. Since King Hagler was killed in 1763, this would have been at least 17 years before the year on her gravestone.[5]

If she even existed, Agnes could have been drawn to Camden due to the fact that Scottish, Irish and Welsh immigrants had settled there, the town's establishment rooted in their history. Could she have had relatives or friends in Camden? Could these folks have known her exact age and death date as they placed her in the ground and inscribed the grave marker? What does the Zapruder film show?

Perhaps it's just best to bid Agnes adieu, leaving her to float in the ethereal and romantic realm of an 18th-century soap opera of ill-fated love—or was it?

A Fanciful Account of Combat Action at Camden

A colorful—but highly fabricated—description of close-quarters fighting at Camden in 1780 made the rounds in 1853 and was published in at least one South Carolina newspaper, the *Lancaster Ledger*. The report likely was printed elsewhere as well, but whatever the case, here is an exciting excerpt:

With equal fury the rank-sweeping cannon and musket were employed on both sides, till the contending legions were nearly mixed. Then quitting this slower mode of slaughter, with rage-blackened faces and fiery eye-balls, they plunge forward on each other, to the swifter vengeance of the bayonet. Far and wide the woods resound to the clash of steel, while the red racking weapon—like stings of infernal serpents, are seen piercing the bodies of the combatants. Some, on receiving the fatal stab, let drop their useless arms, and with dying fingers clasp the hostile steel that is cold in the bowels. Others, faintly crying out, "Oh! God, I am slain!" sank pale and quivering to the ground, while the vital current had gushed in hissing streams from their bursted bosoms. Officers as well as men, now mingle in the ... strife, and snatching the weapons of the slain, swell the horrid carnage....

The account continues with a larger-than-life-or-death narrative about Baron DeKalb's last stand. Here is another excerpt: "Glorying in his [C]ontinentals the brave DeKalb towers before them like a red star guiding their destructive course—his voice as the horn that kindles the young pack in chase of blood."[6]

A closer look at this passage reveals that it came from an 1848 book, *The Life of General Francis Marion, a Celebrated Partisan Officer in the Revolutionary War*. This work was written by Peter Horry, one of Marion's most trusted lieutenants, and then edited, modified and embellished by Mason L. Weems, better known as "Parson" Weems. The latter is most remembered for an early biography of George Washington in which Washington's legendary boyhood cherry-tree and "I cannot-tell-a-lie" episode is first mentioned—and possibly fabricated—by Weems, although the controversy over the supposed event lingers even today.

What is *beyond* controversy is that neither Weems nor Horry, for that matter, were at the battle of Camden. Thus, the combat described above likely emanated from the fertile creativity of Weems's imagination.

Tarleton's Critque of Gates's Performance in the Camden Battle

This excerpt is from Tarleton's *A History of the Campaigns of 1780 and 1781, in the Southern Provinces of North America*, published in London in 1787:

On reviewing the striking circumstances preceding and during the battle, the conduct of Earl Cornwallis cannot be placed in a clearer light than by contrasting it with that of his opponent. The faults committed by the American commander, during his short campaign at the head of the southern army, were neither unimportant in themselves, nor inconsiderable in number. The first misconception imputable to General Gates, was the not breaking in upon the British communications as soon as he arrived near Lynche's [sp] creek. The move up the creek, and from thence to Camden, was practicable and easy before the King's troops were concenterated at that place; or he might, without the smallest difficulty, have occupied a strong position on Saunders' [Sanders] creek, five miles from Camden, before Earl Cornwallis joined the royal forces.

His second error was moving an army, consisting of young corps and undisciplined militia, in the night; a maneuver always to be avoided with troops of that description, in the neighborhood of an enterprising enemy; and only to be hazarded, when regiments are perfectly officered and well trained. His third mistake was in the disposition of his army before the action: If the militia had been formed into one line in front of the [C]ontinentals, they would have galled the British in the wood, when approaching to attack the main body. Or, if the militia had been kept totally separate from the [C]ontinentals, and too much confidence had not been placed in them, perhaps that confusion in part of the Maryland line, owing to the early flight of Caswall's [sp] brigade, had never happened.

His last and greatest fault, was attempting to make an alteration in the disposition the instant the two armies were going to engage, which circumstance could not escape the notice of a vigilant enemy, who by a skillful and sudden attack threw the American left wing into a state of confusion, from which it never recovered. The favorable opportunities which presented themselves to Earl Cornwallis during the march and the action, were seized with judgement, and prosecuted with vigor; a glorious victory crowned the designs of the general, and the exertions of the troops.[7]

Hobkirk Hill—Could Washington Have Taken Camden?

The question arises as to whether Col. William Washington could have made a quick strike into Camden itself rather than taking prisoners of the British rear echelon when he emerged behind Rawdon's lines after his flank movement. Certainly, it would have been contrary to his orders, but it is intriguing to think of this "what if" possibility. There had to be only a handful of British personnel in the village during the battle and many of these had ventured out of the palisade to watch the fighting.

If the palisade gate was open for the personnel to be outside the post when Washington struck, he and his only 50 or so cavalry could conceivably have galloped into the town, causing untold havoc, including the possible destruction of the magazine. Such a scenario—even if the Americans held the place for only a few minutes—would have left Rawdon's force temporarily without its base and possibly caused Greene—already contemplating retreat at this point—to renew the offensive. On the other end of this "what if" is whether a brief raid into Camden would have left Washington out of position to ride back north to Hobkirk Hill, likely meaning his horsemen would have been unable to find and bring off Greene's hidden artillery pieces.

Would any of these actions have altered the war—much less the Southern campaign? Definitely not. The British in South Carolina were already at a tipping point, Cornwallis's little army gone forever from the colony and the partisans of Marion, Sumter, Pickens and others on the rampage.

Still, a little woulda, coulda, shoulda, is always fun.

Hanger and Rawdon Reunite

A few years after the war, George Hanger, who had been a major in Tarleton's British Legion, attended a dinner party at the home of Lord Moira, formerly Lt. Col. Francis Rawdon of Camden fame. The soiree was an elegant affair, guests including the Prince of Wales, Sir Henry Clinton, other generals and officers who had served in the Revolution. Still, Rawdon's thoughts, at least at one point, returned to wartime Camden and Hanger's greatly emaciated condition there while recovering from his near-death illness. Hanger wrote that "his Lordship could not refrain from observing how surprising it was that a man should be sitting in his company, whose bones he had absolutely seen at Camden come through his skin...."[8]

The Waxhaws Flags

When Tarleton's British Legion rode away from the Waxhaws after the May 29, 1780, bloodletting, his victorious troopers carried three captured flags among the military equipage taken from the defeated Americans.

Little else is known about these banners during the war's duration, but Tarleton used them to famous effect as the conflict was winding down. Posing for his 1782 portrait by Joshua Reynolds in London, the Green Dragoon is depicted in full jade-jacketed splendor, with two excited war steeds and a cannon behind him. Under Ban's boots and symbolizing his victories are the Virginia flags from Waxhaws and another standard he seized from the Continental Second Light Dragoons in an engagement at Pound Ridge in New York State.

Tarleton had brought the four banners home with him to Great Britain. Despite his notoriety as a womanizer, Ban had no children other than an illegitimate daughter who died before him. Still, for more than two centuries the flags stayed in the Tarleton family, handed down over generations.

By 2005, the banners were owned by Christopher Tarleton-Fagan, a retired British army captain who was the great-great-great-great-nephew of Banastre Tarleton. Deciding to finally sell the flags, Tarleton-Fagan contacted Sotheby's, the prestigious and international auctioneers of fine art, to put them on the market. "I am very sad to sell them," he said. "They are an important part of our family history. However, there comes a time when their value is such that one can no longer afford to insure them." Since the three Waxhaws colors were the only intact set of American battle flags surviving the Revolution, they were sold as a group when the four banners were auctioned by Sotheby's in Manhattan on Flag Day, June 14, 2006. The most valuable of the three was the Third Virginia's main battle flag, made of "gold-yellow silk" with a painting of a beaver gnawing at the base of a palmetto tree. Underneath was the motto "PERSEVERANDO" while above was a painted-blue canton with 13 silver stars. The banner was blood stained, apparently from the flag bearer who was killed or wounded while defending it. The other two in the set were regimental standards—one blue, one yellow—each consisting of three silk strips sewn together and with a white-painted, scrolling ribbon with the word "Regiment" on it.

The Waxhaws flags sold for $5,056,000 to a bidder who wished to remain anonymous, but this was not the biggest sale of the day, by far. The same bidder earlier obtained the Dragoons' banner for $12,336,000, its rarity stemming from the fact that it was the earliest known surviving American flag with 13 red-and-white stripes, a precursor to the "iconic 'Stars and Stripes.'"[9]

Chapter Notes

Prelude

1. Thomas J. Kirkland and Robert M. Kennedy, *Historic Camden: Part One: Colonial and Revolutionary* (Columbia: The State Printing Company, 1905), 104.

Chapter 1

1. Richard Carney, *Catawba Indian Nation*, Charlottemuseum.org; Edwin L. Green, *The Indians of South Carolina* (Columbia: University Press, 1920), 9–10.
2. *Ibid*. The strongest tribes in the lower—or southern—portion of the province were the Savannahs, Westos and Yemassees.
3. George Howe, *History of the Presbyterian Church in South Carolina*, 2 vols. (Columbia: Duffie & Chapman, 1870), 1:214; David Duncan Wallace, *The History of South Carolina*, 4 vols. (New York: American Historical Society, 1934), 1:356; *Camden* (SC) *Weekly Journal*, May 15, 1855. An obvious misprint in Wallace's account states Fredericksburg was settled in "December, 1773, or January, 1734."
4. Peter G.D. Kershaw, *A Kershaw Family, 1670–1970* (Port Charlotte, FL: n.p., 1974), 18–19; Howe, 1: 495; Joseph Johnson, *Traditions and Reminiscences, Chiefly of the American Revolution in the South* (Charleston: Walker & James, 1851), 463; Archibald Henderson, *Washington's Southern Tour* [hereafter cited as *WST*] (Boston: Houghton Mifflin, 1923), 261; Lance Player, *Ely Kershaw: A Patriot Remembered*, Historic Camden Foundation, November 2021; Leila Sellers, *Charleston Business on the Eve of the American Revolution* (Chapel Hill: University of North Carolina Press, 1934), 89. Some sources place Joseph Kershaw's arrival in the colonies as 1755, which is erroneous. Ancestor and historian Peter G.D. Kershaw noted that accounts stating that the three brothers came to America at the same time are inaccurate, since Ely Kershaw was five and William Kershaw was one when Joseph set foot in Charleston in 1748. Peter Kershaw surmised that Ely and William likely arrived in the colony in 1763 when Joseph was married. Ely would have been twenty, William sixteen that year. However, a Historic Camden Foundation account claimed that Ely came to Pine Tree Hill in 1761.
5. Samuel A. Ashe and Edward McCrady, Jr., *Cyclopedia of Eminent and Representative Men of the Carolinas of the Nineteenth Century*, 2 vols. (Madison, WI: Brant & Fuller, 1892), 1:43; Howe, 1:43; Howe, 1:495; *Camden Weekly Journal*, May 15, 1855; Alexander Gregg, *History of the Old Cheraws* (New York: Richardson and Co., 1867), 104; Kershaw, *Family*, 67. From this point on in the narrative, "Cheraw" will be used unless the other names are used in quoted passages.
6. Robert L. Meriwether, *The Expansion of South Carolina: 1729–1765* (Kingsport, TN: Southern Publishers, 1940), 104.
7. Lance Player, "The Colonial Catawba of the Carolinas," Historic Camden Foundation, August 2020; Camden Timeline, Cityofcamden.org. The Catawbas also weathered a smallpox outbreak in 1738 which was not as widespread. Some accounts spell Catawba leader's name as "Haiglar" or "Haigler."
8. Howe, 1:495–96; Sellers, *Charleston*

Business, 90; Kirkland and Kennedy, *Historic Camden: Part One*, 90, 94; *South Carolina Gazette*, March 17, 1768; Camden Timeline; Player, *Ely Kershaw*. Logtown was situated on both sides of Broad Street between DeKalb and Chesnut streets. Some may observe that I use "DeKalb" in my narrative while "De Kalb" is used in other accounts. Either is considered correct. St. Mark's Parish, also identified as the Parish of St. Mark in some texts, was established in 1757. The Camden District included parts of the present-day counties of Kershaw, Clarendon, Lee, Richland, Fairfield, Chester, York, Sumter, and Lancaster.

9. Henderson, *WST*, 262–63; Kenneth E. Lewis, *The Carolina Backcountry Venture: Tradition, Capital, and Circumstance in the Development of Camden and the Wateree Valley, 1740–1810* (Columbia: University of South Carolina Press, 2017), 114, 213. James Chesnut was originally from Ireland. John Chesnut was born in Virginia on June 18, 1743.

10. Sellers, *Charleston Business*, 90; Player, *Ely Kershaw*; Kershaw, *Family*, 18. Sellers wrote that the year of the wagons was "1786"—obviously a misprint of almost two decades.

11. James Parton, *Life of Andrew Jackson*, 3 vols. (New York: Mason Bros., 1860), 1:48–50.

12. Friedrich Kapp, *The Life of John Kalb, Major-General in the Revolutionary Army* (New York: Henry Holt, 1884), 46–47.

13. Historic Camden Foundation, "Colonial Pottery at Historic Camden: Revolution and Trade," March 2021.

14. Camden Timeline; Lewis, *Carolina Backcountry*, 174; Henderson, *WST*, 262–63; Kirkland and Kennedy, *Historic Camden: Part One*, 95–96. Sarah Cantey was born on February 15, 1753.

15. Historic Camden Foundation, "Colonial Pottery"; *South Carolina Gazette*, April 11, 1774.

Chapter 2

1. Kirkland and Kennedy, *Historic Camden: Part One*, 106–07.

2. Cemetery Association of Camden marker; Camden Timeline; R.E. Beard, Jr., "Camden: Old in Years, Young in Spirit," *Sandlapper*, vol. 1, no. 1 (January 1968): 29; Kirkland and Kennedy, *Historic Camden: Part One*, 106–08.

3. *South Carolina Gazette*, July 11, 1774; Sellers, *Charleston Business*, 89.

4. Sellers, *Charleston Business*, 90. An earlier reference noted the different spellings of the Wyly name. For uniformity, I have chosen to use "Wyly" throughout this narrative.

5. "Camden: Strategic Key" historical marker; Camden Timeline.

6. *South Carolina Gazette*, January 11, 1775; Kirkland and Kennedy, *Historic Camden: Part One*, 108–09.

7. E. Alfred Jones, ed., "The Journal of Alexander Chesney: A South Carolina Loyalist in the Revolution and After," *The Ohio State University Bulletin*, vol. 26, no. 4 (October 1921), 100–01.

8. Historic Camden Foundation, "Colonial Pottery."

9. Ashe and McCrady, *Cyclopedia*, 1:118.

10. Wilmot G. DeSaussure, *The Names as Far as Can Be Ascertained of the Officers Who Served in the South Carolina Regiments* (n.p., 1886), 13–14; Kirkland and Kennedy, *Historic Camden: Part One*, 110–11; Edward McCrady, *The History of South Carolina in the Revolution: 1775–1780* (New York: Macmillan, 1901), 6. Thomson was nicknamed "Danger" or "Old Danger" for his fearlessness in battle.

11. McCrady, *1775–1780*, 10–11; Henderson, *WST*, 251.

12. Player, "Colonial Catawba"; Kirkland and Kennedy, *Historic Camden: Part One*, 117–19.

13. Robert S. Lambert, *South Carolina Loyalists in the American Revolution* (Columbia: University of South Carolina Press, 1987), 84; Kirkland and Kennedy, *Historic Camden: Part One*, 104–05, 212–13. Various accounts use either "Carey" or "Cary." The latter is used in this narrative.

14. Howe, 1:369; William M. Dabney and Marion Dargan, *William Henry Drayton & the American Revolution* (Albuquerque: University of New Mexico Press, 1962), 94, 97.

15. Kirkland and Kennedy, *Historic Camden: Part One*, 111–12, 115, 117–19.

16. Keith Krawczynski, *William Henry Drayton: South Carolina Revolutionary*

Patriot (Baton Rouge: Louisiana State University Press, 2001), 207; Marvin Cann, "Prelude to War: The First Battle of Ninety Six: November 19–21, 1775," *South Carolina Historical Quarterly* (October 1975), 212–13; R.L. Barbour, *South Carolina's Revolutionary War Battlefields: A Tour Guide* (Gretna, LA: Pelican, 2002), 14–15, 95–96; R.W. Gibbes, *Documentary History of the American Revolution Consisting of Letters and Papers Relating to the Contest for Liberty, Chiefly in South Carolina in 1776 and 1782* [hereafter referred to as Gibbes, *1776 and 1782*] (New York: D. Appleton, 1857), 247. In the early 1700s, traders enroute from Charleston estimated the village was ninety-six miles from the Cherokee town of Keowee, thus giving the community its name, which endures to this day. A much larger battle would occur at Ninety Six later in the conflict, as will be seen.

17. McCrady, *1775–1780*, 112.

18. McCrady, *1775–1780*, 112–13; Kirkland and Kennedy, *Historic Camden: Part One*, 116. I give here only a brief narrative of the political machinations of the time. It is beyond the scope of this work to do otherwise.

19. Kirkland and Kennedy, *Historic Camden: Part One*, 119—Extracts from the Minutes of the Council of Safety. For their service during this period, Boykin and his men were paid a combined total of some 1,508 pounds.

20. Nat and Sam Hilborn, *Battleground of Freedom: South Carolina in the Revolution* (Columbia: Sandlapper Press, 1970), 56, 58; Kirkland and Kennedy, *Historic Camden: Part One*, 116–17. The Battle of Sullivan's Island, as it was known, was the first British attempt to capture Charleston. The iconic moment occurred when Sgt. William Jasper raised the earliest precursor of the South Carolina flag over the palmetto fort. Days after the victory, word filtered south of the Declaration of Independence being signed, July 4, 1776, in Philadelphia. Soon after, the fort was renamed Fort Moultrie in honor of Col. William Moultrie, who commanded during the battle and had earlier designed the early South Carolina banner. The "narrow channel" mentioned is present-day Breach Inlet.

21. Kirkland and Kennedy, *Historic Camden: Part One*, 110, 120.

22. Hilborn, 63–64; Kirkland and Kennedy, *Historic Camden: Part One*, 114, 115, 120. Charlton's home was in the vicinity of Hobkirk Hill and was burned, probably by the British, at some point during the war. He survived and returned to Camden as a merchant after the conflict. Charlton died at Camden in 1795, based on records of the Camden Orphan Society, included in the latter reference above.

23. Lambert, 84; Kirkland and Kennedy, *Historic Camden: Part One*, 104–05, 212–13.

24. Historic Camden Marker; Henderson, 261; Kirkland and Kennedy, *Historic Camden: Part One*, 97. The magazine was about 150 yards east of the Great Wagon Road—present-day Broad Street/U.S. 521.

25. Lewis, *Carolina Backcountry*, 193, 195, 197; Kirkland and Kennedy, *Historic Camden: Part One*, 121.

26. Lewis, *Carolina Backcountry*, 193, 195, 197; Kirkland and Kennedy, *Historic Camden: Part One*, 121.

27. Johnson, *Traditions*, 465; Lewis, *Carolina Backcountry*, 197, 199.

28. Robert D. Bass, *Swamp Fox: The Life and Campaigns of General Francis Marion* (Orangeburg, SC: Sandlapper, 1974), 22–23; Kirkland and Kennedy, *Historic Camden: Part One*, 122–23.

29. Thiemann Scott Offutt, et al., *Patriotic Maryland and the Maryland Society Sons of the American Revolution* (Baltimore: Maryland Society Sons of the American Revolution, 1930), 27. Lewis, *Carolina Backcountry*, 206, 351.

30. McCrady, *1775–1780*, 352, 354; Kirkland and Kennedy, *Historic Camden: Part One*, 124; Lewis, *Carolina Backcountry*, 195, 199.

31. Hilborn, 94–95; McCrady, *1775–1780*, 385; Kirkland and Kennedy, *Historic Camden: Part One*, 124–25, 380; Lewis, *Carolina Backcountry*, 200. Stono Ferry was an American defeat but prompted the British to withdraw from the Charleston vicinity.

32. Henry Lumpkin, *From Savannah to Yorktown: The American Revolution in the South* (Columbia: University of South Carolina Press, 1981), 288–89; Edward McCrady, *The History of South Carolina in the Revolution: 1780–1783* (New York: Macmillan, 1902), 435.

Chapter 3

1. Lumpkin, 42–43; Lucian Agniel, *Rebels Victorious: The American Revolution in the South 1780-1781* (New York: Ballantine, 1975), 47. Agniel wrote that the fleet arrived off Georgia in 1781, an obvious error.
2. Kirkland and Kennedy, *Historic Camden: Part One*, 127–28, 132.
3. *Ibid*. It will be recalled that a portion of Kershaw's regiment was in Williamson's brigade at the battle of Stono Ferry. Williamson is a very controversial figure, apparently leaving Camden and not reinforcing Lincoln's garrison at Charleston, also serving as a double agent, for both sides, later in the war. It is unclear if some militiamen from Camden were in Williamson's ranks when his command passed through the town in 1780.
4. Lumpkin, 42–43; Frank Porterfield, *The Porterfields* (Roanoke: Southeastern Press, 1947), 73; Kirkland and Kennedy, *Historic Camden: Part One*, 127–28. It appears that the Camden magazine received supplies in irregular fashion, accounting for some munitions available at one time but not another. With Caswell was his second-in-command, Brig. Gen. Griffith Rutherford, whom we will meet again a few months later. Woodford's 750 or so troops were from Virginia and North Carolina, reaching Charleston on April 6, 1780.
5. F.B. Heitman, *Historical Register of Officers of the Continental Army during the War of the Revolution: April, 1775, to December, 1783* (Washington, D.C.: n.p., 1893), 249; Player, *Ely Kershaw*; Kershaw, *Family*, 18, 75. When the three Kershaws came to the colonies, they left behind four other brothers and a sister in England. One of those brothers was John Kershaw, whom William addressed in the March 22, 1781, letter from Charleston mentioned above.
6. Gervais to Henry Laurens, May 13, 1780—Henry Laurens Papers, University of South Carolina Digital Collections, South Caroliniana Library; Agniel, 51; Heitman, 249; Player, *Ely Kershaw*; Kershaw, *Family*, 18.
7. Banastre Tarleton, *A History of the Campaigns of 1780 and 1781, in the Southern Provinces of North America* (London: T. Cadell, printer, 1787), 26.
8. Alexander Garden, *Anecdotes of the American Revolution—Second Series* (Charleston: A.E. Miller, 1828), 135–36; Charles Ross, ed., *Correspondence of Charles, First Marquis Cornwallis*, 3 vols. (London: John Murray, 1859), 1:45.
9. Garden, *Anecdotes, Second Series*, 136; William Dobein James, *A Sketch of the Life of Brig. Gen. Francis Marion and a History of His Brigade* (Marietta, GA: Continental Book Co., 1948), 1. Brownfield's account is included in James's book.
10. Buford to Virginia Assembly, May 26, 1780—George Washington Papers, Library of Congress.
11. Brownfield in James's *Sketch*, 2.

Chapter 4

1. Charles Stedman, *The History of the Origin, Progress, and Termination of the American War*, 2 vols. (London: "Printed for the Author," 1794), 2:192–93; W.H. Wilkin, *Some British Soldiers in America* (London: Hugh Rees, 1914), 118–19; Agniel, 29–30; Tarleton, *History*, 27. The Seventeenth dragoons were attached to Tarleton's force as a training unit and were known for the skull and crossbones on their headgear.
2. Agniel, 24–25.
3. *Annual Biography and Obituary for the Year 1834*, vol. 18 (London: Longman, Rees, Orme, Brown and Green, 1834), 273; Agniel, 26–30; Wilkin, 118–19.
4. Robert D. Bass, *Gamecock: The Life and Campaigns of General Thomas Sumter* (New York: Holt, Rinehart and Winston, 1961), 51.
5. Player, *Ely Kershaw*; James Piecuch, "Massacre or Myth? Banastre Tarleton at the Waxhaws, May 29, 1780," *Southern Campaigns of the American Revolution*, vol. 1, no. 2 (October 2004), 4. At least one source claims that Joseph and Ely Kershaw were paroled on June 10, 1780, rather than shortly after Charleston's surrender, when most, if not all, of the militia were paroled to their homes.
6. Tarleton, *History*, 27; Bass, *Gamecock*, 53; Agniel, 52–53.
7. Tarleton, *History*, 28. Tarleton claimed that the intelligence gathered at Camden indicated that Buford left Rugeley's on May 26, which is erroneous.
8. Tarleton, *History*, 77–78.
9. Agniel, 52–53; Tarleton, *History*, 77–78.

10. Brownfield in James's *Sketch*, 2; Tarleton, *History*, 77–78.
11. Agniel, 52–53; Brownfield in James's *Sketch*, 2; Tarleton, *History*, 28, 79.
12. Brownfield in James's *Sketch*, 3.
13. Tarleton, *History*, 29; Brownfield in James's *Sketch*, 3.
14. Richard Cannon, *Historical Record of the Seventeenth Regiment of Light Dragoons: Lancers* (London: John W. Parker, 1841), 30–31; Tarleton, *History*, 29–30.
15. Tarleton, *History*, 28–30.
16. Ibid.
17. Brownfield in James's *Sketch*, 5.
18. Tarleton, *History*, 30–31.
19. Ibid., 30; Brownfield in James's *Sketch*, 3. In my opinion, the best investigation of this phase of the battle is to be found in James Piecuch's "Massacre or Myth? Banastre Tarleton at the Waxhaws, May 29, 1780," included in the bibliography.
20. Brownfield in James's *Sketch*, 4.
21. Cannon, *Historical Record*, 30–31.
22. Hilborn, 118; Brownfield in James's *Sketch*, 5–6.
23. Brownfield in James's *Sketch*, 5–6; Bass, *Gamecock*, 53.
24. Stedman, 2:193; Tarleton, *History*, 30–31.
25. Benson J. Lossing, ed., *Lives of Celebrated Americans: Comprising Biographies of Three Hundred and Forty Eminent Persons* (Hartford: Thomas Belknap, 1869), 244; Tarleton, *History*, 31–32; Hilborn, 118.
26. Hilborn, 118; Parton, 1:69–70; Lossing, *Lives*, 244.
27. Ross, *Correspondence*, 1:45. In the entirety of this dispatch, Tarleton mentions Buford once, incorrectly identifying him as "Burford."
28. Hilborn, 120–21; Tarleton, *History*, 31–32, 84.
29. Hilborn, 120–21; Tarleton, *History*, 31–32, 84. The Waxhaws battlefield is located in the rural community of Buford on SC Route 522 (present-day Rocky River Road) just south of its intersection with SC Route 9 in Lancaster County.

Chapter 5

1. Mason L. Weems and Peter Horry, *Life of General Francis Marion* (Philadelphia: J.B. Lippincott, 1857), 197–98.
2. Walter Scott Seton-Carr, *Rulers of India: The Marquess Cornwallis* (Oxford: Clarendon Press, 1890), 8; Agniel, 6, 9, 10, 13–16; Ross, *Correspondence*, 1:9, 13.
3. Walter Scott Seton-Carr, *Rulers of India: The Marquess Cornwallis* (Oxford: Clarendon Press, 1890), 8; Agniel, 6, 9, 10, 13–16; Ross, *Correspondence*, 1:9, 13.
4. Walter Scott Seton-Carr, *Rulers of India: The Marquess Cornwallis* (Oxford: Clarendon Press, 1890), 8; Agniel, 6, 9, 10, 13–16; Ross, *Correspondence*, 1:9, 13.
5. Ross, *Correspondence*, 1:14; Seton-Carr, 8. A plain, marble slab enclosed the vault, not even bearing her name, although it was added in 1851. The "thorn-tree" flourished until March 1855, when it was relocated due to renovations being done at the church. It was "carefully replanted in the churchyard, but did not live more than three years afterward." Seton-Carr gives Cornwallis's birthdate as December 31, 1738, while other sources say he was born on January 1, 1739. Thus, the contention appears to be about a few hours overnight more than 250 years ago!
6. Kirkland and Kennedy, *Historic Camden: Part One*, 142; Lewis, *Carolina Backcountry*, 139, 206. Charles Ogilvie is primarily known for his 1763 marriage to Mary Michie, an heiress who inherited some 3,900 acres of land in the Camden region from her late father. Lynches, also called "Lynch's," Creek is today known as Lynch's River. We will use Lynches Creek and Little Lynches Creek in this narrative.
7. Ross, *Correspondence*, 1:488–89.
8. Stedman, 194; Kirkland and Kennedy, *Historic Camden: Part One*, 143; Player, *Ely Kershaw*.
9. Tarleton, *History*, 32; Mellen Chamberlain, *Memorial of Captain Charles Cochrane, a British Officer in the Revolutionary War* (Cambridge: University Press, 1891), 6.
10. Historic Camden Marker; Player, *Ely Kershaw*; Kenneth E. Lewis, "Camden: A Frontier Town in Eighteenth Century South Carolina," *University of South Carolina Research Manuscript Series* (October 1976), 62; Kenneth E. Lewis, *A Functional Study of the Kershaw House Site in Camden, South Carolina* (Columbia: Institute of Archaeology and Anthropology, University of South Carolina, 1977), 9; Kirkland and Kennedy, *Historic Camden: Part One*, 274.

11. Lambert, 84; Tarleton, *History*, 86–87; Lewis, *Carolina Backcountry*, 212; Historic Camden Foundation, "Sickness & Survival: Kershaw House Gains New Medical Exhibit," July 2021, 104–05; Lewis, "Camden: A Frontier Town," 62.
12. Historic Camden Marker; Tarleton, *History*, 85; Kirkland and Kennedy, *Historic Camden: Part One*, 132–33.
13. "Camden: Strategic Key" historical marker; Jones, *Journal*, 79–80.
14. Ross, *Correspondence*, 1:45.
15. Tarleton, *History*, 85–86; Stedman, 195; Henry B. Carrington, *Battles of the American Revolution* (New York: A.S. Barnes, 1876), 498; Roger Lamb, *An Original and Authentic Journal of Occurrences During the Late American War* (Dublin: Wilkinson & Courtney, 1809), 302.
16. Lewis, "Camden: A Frontier Town," 61, 63; Historic Camden Foundation, "Sickness & Survival: Kershaw House Gains New Medical Exhibit," July 2021; Lambert, 84.
17. Lewis, "Camden: A Frontier Town," 61, 63; Historic Camden Foundation, "Sickness & Survival: Kershaw House Gains New Medical Exhibit," July 2021; Lambert, 84.
18. *Camden* (SC) *Journal*, quoted in Kirkland and Kennedy, *Historic Camden: Part One*, 277, no further date available; Stedman, 2:198.
19. Adelaide L. Fries, ed., *Records of the Moravians in North Carolina* (Raleigh: Edwards & Broughton, 1930), 4:1543–44.
20. Robert D. Bass, "Banastre Tarleton: Butcher or Hero?" *Sandlapper*, vol. 6, no. 3 (March 1973), 49–50.
21. Chamberlain, *Memorial*, 8.
22. Michael J. O'Brien, *A Hidden Phase of American History: Ireland's Part in America's Struggle for Liberty* (New York: Dodd, Mead, 1919), 192–93; Tarleton, *History*, 85–86; Lambert, 84.
23. Tarleton, *History*, 32, 85.
24. Agniel, 51; H.L. Landers, *The Battle of Camden, South Carolina, August 16, 1780* (Washington, D.C.: U.S. Government Printing Office, 1929), 31–32; Tarleton, *History*, 86.
25. Lewis, *Carolina Backcountry*, 206–07.
26. Bass, *Swamp Fox*, 26, 120; Stedman, 2:195–96; Landers, 31–32; Tarleton, *History*, 86–87. McArthur's command was also known as the 71st Fraser's Highlanders, the 71st Regiment of (Highland) Foot, and the "Frasers" referencing Major General Simon Fraser who had raised and organized the regiment in Scotland after the war began.
27. Stedman, 2:196; Tarleton, *History*, 87–88.
28. Landers, 31–32; Stedman, 2:196; O'Brien, 192–93; Lambert, 85.
29. Wilkin, 74–75, 89.
30. *Ibid*.
31. O'Brien, 190–91; Wilkin, 75–76.
32. Wilkin, 76–77.

Chapter 6

1. Kapp, *The Life of John Kalb*, 198; Landers, 4–5; William Seymour, *A Journal of the Southern Expedition, 1780-1781* (Wilmington: The Historical Society of Delaware, 1896), 3; Otho Williams in Johnson, *Traditions*, 485; Kirkland and Kennedy, *Historic Camden: Part One*, 146.
2. Rufus Wilmot Griswold, William Gilmore Simms, and Edward Duncan Ingraham, *Washington and the Generals of the American Revolution* (Philadelphia: J.B. Lippincott, 1856), 269.
3. Kapp, *The Life of John Kalb*, 1, 2, 4; Lumpkin, 57. Both "DeKalb" and "De Kalb" have become acceptable over time. DeKalb is used in this narrative.
4. Hilborn, 71, 73; Kapp, *The Life of John Kalb*, 47. Lafayette's full name and title was Marie Joseph Paul Yves Roch Gilbert du Motier, Marquis de Lafayette.
5. Kapp, *The Life of John Kalb*, 199–200; Landers, 5–6.
6. Lumpkin, 58; Lossing, *Lives*, 295; Agniel, 30, 55; National Park Service, "Horatio Gates," Saratoga National Historical Park, www.nps.gov.people.horatio-gates.
7. Seymour, 3–4; *Pennsylvania Gazette*, September 6, 1780, in Frank Moore, *Diary of the American Revolution from Newspapers and Original Documents*, 2 vols. (New York: Charles Scribner, 1859), 2:310.
8. Otho Williams in Johnson, *Traditions*, 486; Lumpkin, 290; revolutionarywar.us/com; Yorktown Battlefield—National Park Service nps.gov/york/learn/historyculture/armandbio.htm; Lumpkin, 290. It will be recalled that the Pulaski Legion passed through Camden on its way to the coast.

9. John Austin Stevens, "The Southern Campaign," *Magazine of American History*, vol. 5, no. 4 (October 1880), 284; Bass, *Gamecock*, 62–63.

10. John Frost, *The Book of the Army: Comprising a General Military History of the United States* (New York: D. Appleton, 1846), 177–78; John S. Jenkins, *The Lives of Patriots and Heroes Distinguished in the Battle for American Freedom* (Auburn: J.C. Derby, 1847), 74; Lumpkin, 58; Lossing, *Lives*, 295; Agniel, 30, 55; National Park Service, "Horatio Gates," Saratoga National Historical Park, www.nps.gov.people.horatio-gates.

11. *Ibid*. The Continental army was originally named the Army of the United Colonies. Of Saratoga, most histories of the Revolution refer only to the climatic combat on October 7. Burgoyne surrendered to Gates ten days later—October 17—after retreating from Saratoga.

12. Lossing, *Lives*, 295; Lumpkin, 58.

13. Otho Williams in Johnson, *Traditions*, 486; *Historical Magazine*, vol. 10, no. 8 (August 1886), 250.

14. Frost, 177–78.

15. Otho Williams in Johnson, *Traditions*, 486; revolutionarywar.us/com; Yorktown Battlefield—National Park Service, nps.gov/york/learn/historyculture/armandbio.htm. Lumpkin, 290; Benson J. Lossing, ed., *The American Historical Record, and Repertory of Notes and Queries*, 3 vols. [hereafter *AHR*] (Philadelphia: Samuel P. Town, 1873), 2:106. Williams was born in Prince George's County, Maryland, in 1748 and had a stellar war record, eventually leading to his promotion to brigadier general.

16. Lumpkin, 58–59; Lossing, *AHR*, 2:105–06.

17. Christopher L. Ward, *The Delaware Continentals: 1776–1783* (Wilmington: The Historical Society of Delaware, 1941), 337; Landers, 14–15; Frost, 179.

18. Otho Williams in Johnson, *Traditions*, 487; Seymour, 4.

19. Ross, *Correspondence*, 1:487, 490. Cornwallis to Clinton from Charleston, June 30, 1780, and Cornwallis to Germain from Camden, August 20, 1780. In the Clinton dispatch, Cornwallis mistakenly refers to Lt. Col. Charles Porterfield as a general.

20. Stedman, 2:197; Peter McCandless, "Revolutionary Fever: Disease and War in the Lower South, 1776–1783," *Transactions of the American Clinical and Climatological Association*, vol. 118 (2007), 233.

21. Barbour, 49–53. Great Falls is about thirty miles northwest of Camden. Barbour states erroneously that the Rocky Mount battle was on August 1.

22. Lumpkin, 59, 290.

23. *Southern Patriot*, July 28, 1828; Barbour 51–53.

24. Parton, 1:71–72. Italics are from the cited work.

25. Carrington, 503; Tarleton, *History*, 98–99.

26. McCrady, *1775–1780*, 618–19; Henderson, *WST*, 262–63; Kirkland and Kennedy, *Historic Camden: Part One*, 143–44.

27. Player, *Ely Kershaw*, 18; Lewis, *Carolina Backcountry*, 206–07. Some accounts state that Joseph Kershaw was captured at the battle of Camden, which is erroneous. We will soon learn more about the Kershaws' fate in the coming months.

28. Johnson, *Traditions*, 467–68; Lossing, *AHR*, 2: 110. Hampton was the grandfather of famed Confederate Lt. Gen. Wade Hampton III of South Carolina. Mathis was a Methodist minister after the Revolution. In 1819 he wrote his recollections from that time, which will be discussed later.

29. Landers, 18–19; Tarleton, *History*, 99. Kirkland and Kennedy, *Historic Camden: Part One*, 151. Tarleton refers to the stream as "the west branch of Lynche's [sp] Creek." In addition to the artillery, Rawdon's force here was the 23rd, 33rd, and 71st Highlanders, all infantry regiments, the Volunteers of Ireland, Lt. Col. John Hamilton's corps, and forty or so dragoons of Tarleton's Legion.

30. *Archives of Maryland* (Biographical Series), msa.maryland.gov; Landers, 18–19; Tarleton, *History*, 99. Some accounts list Smallwood as a major general, which is erroneous. He was promoted to that rank in September.

31. Tarleton, *History*, 101.

32. *Ibid.*, 100; Bass, *Swamp Fox*, 36.

33. Ross, *Correspondence*, 1:54–55; Tarleton, *History*, 100–02.

34. Ross, *Correspondence*, 1:54–55; Tarleton, *History*, 100–02.

35. Walter Clark, ed., *The State Records of North Carolina*, 30 vols. (Goldsboro,

NC: Nash Bros., Book and Job Printers, 1907), 14:552–53.

36. *Ibid.* Sumter to Maj. Thomas Pinckney, August 12, 1780.

Chapter 7

1. Stedman, 2:228; Wilkin, 78; Clark, *State Records*, 15:53. Martin to Lord George Germain, August 18, 1780.

2. Tarleton, *History*, 103; *Annual Register, or a View of the History, Politics, and Literature, For the Year 1780* [hereafter cited as *AR 1780*] (London: J. Dodsley, 1781), 231.

3. John Robert Shaw, *A Narrative of the Life & Travels of John Robert Shaw, the Well-Digger, Now Resident in Lexington, Kentucky* (Lexington: Daniel Bradford, 1807), 28.

4. McCrady, *1775–1780*, 666; Clark, *State Records*, 14:556.

5. Landers, 23; Senf in Stevens, "Southern Campaign," 275, 276.

6. McCrady, *1775–1780*, 667. Since both sides actively employed spies, this is very likely a fact-based episode.

7. Senf in Stevens, "Southern Campaign," 275, 276; Landers, 21; Bass, *Gamecock*, 78. Isaacs and his North Carolinians were detached from militia Brigadier General Griffith Rutherford's brigade.

8. Landers, 21–23; Tarleton, *History*, 147. Based on an August 15, 1780, letter from "Sumpter" to Gates, "Mr. Whitear's" ferry was located "five miles below Camden." In his July 17, 1780, dispatch to Baron De Kalb, Sumter, who sometimes spelled his name "Sumpter," advised securing the ferries on the Santee River. Whether this knowledge had any impact on Gates's order to seal off the Wateree ferries is unknown, but is likely, since Sumter certainly knew the South Carolina backwoods much better than Gates.

9. Stevens, "Southern Campaign," 275, 276; Tarleton, *History*, 147–48; Bass, *Gamecock*, 78, 79. Bass states the afternoon haul consisted of "fifty of the British light infantry marching from Ninety-Six [sp] ... a drove of three hundred cattle and a flock of sheep." Some accounts refer to this crossing as "Camden Ferry." The engineer Senf's account in Stevens states the detachment consisted of 70 men from the "71st & 33d Regts" who were captured as they "came from Ninety Six to join the Enemy at Camden."

10. Bass, *Swamp Fox*, 36; McCrady, *1775–1780*, 570–71. "The country from Camden to the seacoast between the Pee Dee and the Santee rivers was the theatre of his [Marion's] exertions," McCrady noted.

11. Tarleton, *History*, 103–04; *Rivington's Gazette*, January 3, 1781. Some sources state that *Rivington's* was known as the *Royal Gazette* from December 1777 to November 1783.

12. Stedman, 2:228–29; Clark, *State Records*, 15:556. Martin to Germain from Camden, August 18, 1780.

13. *AR 1780*, 232; Ross, *Correspondence*, 1:492—Cornwallis to Germain, August 21, 1780; Stedman, 2:229–30; Clark, *State Records*, 15:53.

14. *Ibid.*

15. Senf in Stevens, "Southern Campaign," 276; Wilkin, 78; Landers, 23; Ward, 347; Otho Williams in Johnson, *Traditions*, 494.

16. Landers, 27–28; Otho Williams in William Johnson, *Sketches of the Life and Correspondence of Nathaniel Greene: Major General of the Armies of the United States in the War of the Revolution*, 2 vols. (Charleston: A.E. Miller, 1822), 2:493–94.

17. Frost, 179; Landers, 25–26; Carrington, 514; Seymour, 5; Lossing, *Lives*, 316–17. Seymour claimed that "we" began the march about 8 p.m. It is unclear whether he was mistaken or if some units of the army actually started moving before 10 p.m. Major John Armstrong, Jr., 23, was born in Carlisle, Pennsylvania, and educated at Princeton. There, in 1775, he joined the American army as a volunteer in a Pennsylvania regiment and soon afterward was appointed aide-de-camp to General Hugh Mercer. When Mercer was killed at Princeton early in 1777, Armstrong was assigned the same position with General Gates, with the rank of major and was with Gates at Saratoga. Armstrong's father was General John Armstrong of Pennsylvania, who had an outstanding record in the French and Indian War. After the Revolution, young Armstrong was elected to Congress, also serving as a minister to France, among other posts. He was a brigadier general in

the War of 1812 and later served as secretary of war in the Monroe administration.

18. Seymour, 5; Otho Williams in Johnson, *Traditions*, 494; Carrington, 513–14; Landers, 25–26. Jalap is a Mexican vine whose roots were used as a laxative. Here the word is used as a synonym for laxative.

19. Wilson Gee, *The Gist Family of South Carolina and Its Maryland Antecedents* (Charlottesville: Jarman's, 1934), 13–14, 16. At the Long Island battle, Gist was a major, leading the regiment while his two superior officers were in New York on administrative duties.

20. Albert Lee, *History of the Thirty-third Foot* (Norwich, UK: Jarrold & Sons, 1922), 132.

21. Stedman, 2:229–30; Tarleton, *History*, 104.

22. Senf in Stevens, "Southern Campaign," 275, 276; Tarleton, *History*, 104; Guilford Dudley, "A Sketch of the Military Service Performed by Guilford Dudley, Then of the Town of Halifax, North Carolina, During the Revolutionary War," *The Southern Literary Messenger* [hereafter *SLM*], vol. 11 (1845), 145; Landers, 40–41.

23. Tarleton, *History*, 104; Clark, *State Records*, 14:584; Dudley, *SLM*, 146–47. Magill's letter to his father was undated, but likely written very soon after the battle.

24. Otho Williams in Johnson, *Traditions*, 494; Landers, 41; Seymour, 5.

25. Magill letter in Clark, *State Records*, 14:584; Dudley, *SLM*, 231; Lamb, 303; Tarleton, *History*, 104–05; Stedman, 208; Otho Williams in Johnson, *Traditions*, 494.

26. Magill letter in Clark, *State Records*, 14:584; Dudley, *SLM*, 231. In contrast to Dudley's account that Drew gave the retreat order, Magill claimed that Porterfield "ordered the retreat."

27. Tarleton, *History*, 145–46—Gates to Samuel Huntington, President of the Continental Congress, August 20, 1780; Ross, *Correspondence*, 1: 493—Cornwallis to Germain, August 21, 1780; Landers, 50.

28. Lamb, 303; *Pennsylvania Gazette*, September 6, 1780, in Moore, 2:311; Kirkland and Kennedy, *Historic Camden: Part One*, 157–58. Lamb was referring to Lt. Col. Porterfield.

29. Ross, *Correspondence*, 1:493—Cornwallis to Germain, August 21, 1780;

Carrington, 515; Arthur Aspinall, ed., *The Correspondence of George, Prince of Wales* (New York: Oxford University Press, 1967), 192–97; Otho Williams in Johnson, *Traditions*, 494–495; Senf in Stevens, "Southern Campaign," 276. Casualty statistics from this specific encounter were apparently never calculated, instead incorporated in various totals for the entire battle on August 16. Williams's claim about Gates' "astonishment" of Cornwallis being in front of him directly conflicts with Col. Senf's note that Gates learned of Cornwallis' presence through "Certain Intelligence" received on August 15.

30. Otho Williams in Johnson, *Traditions*, 495; Landers, 44–45. The six front-line cannon were posted in pairs, two between the North Carolina and Virginia militia; two between Gist's Continentals and the swamp; and two on the road.

31. Jesse Forbes Pugh, *Three Hundred Years along the Pasquotank: A Biographical History of Camden County* (Durham: Seeman Printery, 1957), 95; David Schenck, *North Carolina: 1780-81, Being a History of the Invasion of the Carolinas* (Raleigh: Edwards & Broughton, 1889), 94; McCrady, *1775-1780*, 668; Landers, 45; Lossing, *Lives*, 96–97. Dixon was a Continental major and lost his position during a reorganization of the army in May 1778. Coming to North Carolina, he volunteered as a militia officer under Caswell.

32. Ross, *Correspondence*, 1:507—Cornwallis to Germain, August 21, 1780; Stedman, 2:208; Landers, 42–43.

33. Tarleton, *History*, 105; Shaw, 29; Otho Williams in Johnson, *Traditions*, 495.

34. Dudley, *SLM*, 234–35.

Chapter 8

1. Otho Williams in Johnson, *Traditions*, 495; Pinckney letter to William Johnson, July 27, 1822, *Sketches of the Life and Correspondence*, 2:250–51; Landers, 46, 90. In his letter, Pinckney refers to Stevens as a colonel, which is erroneous.

2. Lamb, 303, 305; Tarleton, *History*, 105–06; Landers, 43. "Fuzileers" is correct here; the regiment's name changed to "Fusiliers" in 1881.

3. Francis Duncan, *History of the Royal Regiment of Artillery*, 2 vols. (London: John Murray, 1782), 1:366–67; Lamb, 303; Tarleton, *History*, 105–06; Landers, 43. McLeod's name is also spelled as "Macleod" in at least one British account.

4. Otho Williams in Johnson, *Traditions*, 495; italics are in the source. The Brown Bess, in at least two models, was the standard issue infantry musket of the British army for several decades. Introduced in the 1760s, this durable flintlock was also the most common firearm among the Americans, being seized from captured storehouses early in the conflict and taken in battle. In general, the Brown Bess weighed ten pounds and fired a .75-caliber round, although a later model, introduced in 1768, was a bit lighter and shorter. This musket saw service in the American Revolution, the War of 1812, and the Napoleonic Wars.

5. Ross, *Correspondence*, 1:493—Cornwallis to Germain, August 21, 1780; Otho Williams in Johnson, *Traditions*, 495–96; Ward, 346–47; Lamb, 303–04; Tarleton, *History*, 106–07; Kirkland and Kennedy, *Historic Camden: Part One*, 163. Tarleton repeats Cornwallis's misconception about the American movement, writing that Gates "not approving of the situation of Caswall's [sp] and Stevens' brigades was proceeding to alter their position." Another minor point: Cornwallis claimed that he himself saw the enemy in motion, while Tarleton related that the "circumstance being observed by the British, was reported to Earl Cornwallis." One of several variations of Stevens's exhortation is "Come on, my brave fellows, you have bayonets as well as they."

6. Otho Williams in Johnson, *Traditions*, 495–96; Tarleton, *History*, 107; McCrady, *1775–1780*, 677–78; Henry Lee, *Memoirs of the War in the Southern Department of the United States* (London: Sampson Low, Son, & Marston, 1869), 187.

7. Steven D. Smith, James B. Legg, Tamara S. Wilson, and Jonathan Leader, *The Archaeology of the Camden Battlefield: History, Private Collections, and Field Investigations* [hereafter cited as Smith, *Archaeology*] (Columbia: South Carolina Institute of Archaeology and Anthropology, 2009), 23; Gates to Samuel Huntington, August 20, 1780 in Tarleton, *History*, 145–47; Shaw, 30; Otho Williams in Johnson, *Traditions*, 495–96.

8. Dudley, *SLM*, 281–82.

9. Otho Williams in Johnson, *Traditions*, 496; Stedman, 2:209; Ross, *Correspondence*, 1:493—Cornwallis to Germain, August 21, 1780; Tarleton, *History*, 107; Shaw, 29; Agniel, 61. Next in number to the Brown Bess, the Americans also wielded thousands of the French Model 1766 Charleville infantry musket, named for the French town and armory where they were produced. Of a French shipment of 37,000 arms sent to Portsmouth, NH, during the conflict, the bulk of the weapons were .69-caliber Charlevilles. Remnants of Charlevilles have been found at the Camden battlefield.

10. Seymour, 6; Senf in Stevens, "Southern Campaign," 277; Ross, *Correspondence*, 1:493; Tarleton, *History*, 107; Shaw, 29.

11. Otho Williams in Johnson, *Traditions*, 496; *Archives of Maryland*, 10; Landers, 49; Carrington, 517; Tarleton, *History*, 107.

12. Otho Williams in Johnson, *Traditions*, 496; *Archives of Maryland*, 10; Landers, 49; Carrington, 517; Tarleton, *History*, 107. Some sources identify John C. Jones as a major, but pension records list him as a captain.

13. Ross, *Correspondence*, 1:493—Cornwallis to Germain, August 21, 1780; Shaw, 29, Johnson, *Traditions*, 496.

14. Otho Williams in Johnson, *Traditions*, 496; *Archives of Maryland*, 10; Landers, 49; Carrington, 517; Tarleton, *History*, 107. One source states that the British Legion "had pursued the militia until they were started to the rear" and then participated in the assault on Smallwood's command, which is inaccurate.

15. Gates to Samuel Huntington, August 20, 1780, in Tarleton, *History*, 145–47; Magill letter in Clark, *State Records*, 14: 585; Pinckney letter in Clark, 14:250. Pinckney refers to his fellow officer as "McGill," which is apparently misspelled.

16. Clark, *State Records*, 14:585; Seymour, 6.

17. Gates to Samuel Huntington, August 20, 1780, in Tarleton, *History*, 145–47; Magill letter in Clark, *State Records*, 14:585.

18. John H. Wheeler, *Historical Sketches of North Carolina, From 1584 to*

1851 (Philadelphia: Lippincott, Grambo and Co., 1851), 239. In later years, Brevard recalled that his "hardest fighting" was at Eutaw Springs in 1781, but he never forgot the Camden debacle.

19. Kapp, *The Life of John Kalb*, 233; Kirkland and Kennedy, *Historic Camden: Part One*, 190-91; Otho Williams in Johnson, *Traditions*, 496.

20. Kapp, *The Life of John Kalb*, 233; Kirkland and Kennedy, *Historic Camden: Part One*, 190-91; Otho Williams in Johnson, *Traditions*, 496. If Williams indeed encountered Ford, a question remains: why did the former not find DeKalb or Gist and tell either or both about the First Maryland's rout?

21. Carrington, 517; Ross, *Correspondence*, 1:493—Cornwallis to Germain, August 21, 1780.

22. Hunter in William Henry Foote, *Sketches of North Carolina, Historical and Biographical* (New York: Robert Carter, 1846), 424-25.

23. Hunter in Foote, *Sketches*, 424-25; Otho Williams in Johnson, *Traditions*, 496; Lumpkin, 66; Kirkland and Kennedy, *Historic Camden: Part One*, 187-88; *Camden Journal*, June 19, 1830; Otho Williams in Johnson, *Traditions*, 496; Tarleton, *History*, 107; Dudley, *SLM*, 281-82. Whether DeKalb was propped against a wagon, wagon wheel, or "against a pine post" is unclear, from various sources. Any or none could have been possible as the Baron was being roughly handled in the fever of combat. Grossly erroneous is at least one account stating that DeKalb "died that evening" and that his body was taken to Camden for burial. Another local DeKalb tale that appears to be way more fiction than fact claimed that when the Baron was brought into Camden after the battle, the British halted at a water pump to allow him to drink. It was there that the general died. The pump was supposedly located on what is now DeKalb Street just east of the Broad Street intersection. The biggest problem here is that Camden in 1780 was about a mile from the location of the present town. Also, DeKalb died three days after the battle, based on the account of Du Buysson, the general's aide who was at his bedside to the end.

24. Lamb, 304-05; Shaw, 30; Pugh, 95; Otho Williams in Johnson, *Traditions*, 495-96.

25. Tarleton, *History*, 107-08.

26. Heitman, 199; Williams in Johnson, *Traditions*, 497; Landers, 53; Offutt, 48; Dudley, *SLM*, 281-82; Charles J. Peterson, *The Military Heroes of the Revolution* (Philadelphia: William A. Leary, 1848), 407-08; Ward, 326. Lt. Colonel Vaughan led the Delaware regiment, composed of eight companies and about 275 officers and men in total, at Camden. Vaughan was in charge, since the Blue Hens' commander, Col. David Hall, Jr., was away on furlough. The regiment numbered some 320 of all ranks when it moved south in April, the attrition due to the long, tough march stretching into middle August. Major Anderson was killed at Guilford Court House, March 15, 1781.

Chapter 9

1. Tarleton, *History*, 107-08; Dudley, *SLM*, 282.

2. Gee, 153; David Ramsay, *Ramsay's History of South Carolina* (Charleston: Walker, Evans & Co., 1858) 207; Minnie R.H. Long. *General Griffith Rutherford and Allied Families* (Milwaukee: Wisconsin Cuneo Press, 1942), 41; Stedman, 2:210; Tarleton, *History*, 108.

3. Gee, 153; David Ramsay, *Ramsay's History of South Carolina* (Charleston: Walker, Evans & Co., 1858) 207; Minnie R.H. Long. *General Griffith Rutherford and Allied Families* (Milwaukee: Wisconsin Cuneo Press, 1942), 41; Stedman, 2:210; Tarleton, *History*, 108.

4. Otho Williams in Johnson, *Traditions*, 498; Seymour, 6. The captain's last name may actually have been "Lamar."

5. Dudley, *SLM*, 281-83; *Pennsylvania Gazette*, September 6, 1780, in Moore, 2:312.

6. Otho Williams in Johnson, *Traditions*, 498; Dudley, *SLM*, 284.

7. Otho Williams in Johnson, *Traditions*, 498; Dudley, *SLM*, 284.

8. Ward, 589; Landers, 53; Otho Williams in Johnson, *Traditions*, 497.

9. Ward, 589; Landers, 53; Otho Williams in Johnson, *Traditions*, 497.

10. Alexander Garden, *Anecdotes of the American Revolution*, 3 vols. (Brooklyn: The Union Press, 1865), 2:252. Hanger

was known for his wry sense of humor, and since DeKalb's baggage wagon was taken safely out of danger, this account should be considered with some doubt. The ageless animosity between Britain and France also may have contributed to Hanger referring to the monkey—whether the animal existed or not—as a Frenchman. Hanger's comments that his "arm was too well employed" and that he "ceased to destroy" indicates that his saber was being swung often and repeatedly at the Americans fleeing the battlefield, at least to his recollection—or imagination.

11. Wheeler, *Historical Sketches*, 1:194; Schenck, 99; Bass, *Gamecock*, 80; Otho Williams in Johnson, *Traditions*, 499; George F. Scheer and Hugh F. Rankin, *Rebels & Redcoats* (New York: World Publishing Co., 1957), 410.

12. E.W. Caruthers, *Interesting Revolutionary Incidents: Second Series* (Philadelphia: Hayes & Zeil, 1856), 147, 148; Pugh, 95; Catherine S. Albertson. *In Ancient Albemarle*, North Carolina Society, Daughters of the Revolution (Raleigh: Commercial Printing Co., 1914), 96; "The American Revolution in North Carolina—Isaac Gregory." www.carolana.com; William S. Powell, ed., *Dictionary of North Carolina Biography*, 6 vols. (Chapel Hill: University of North Carolina Press, 2000), 2:367; Tarleton, *History*, 108.

13. Otho Williams in Johnson, *Traditions*, 496; *Rivington's Gazette*, January 3, 1781.

14. Landers, 61; Lumpkin, 66; Lee, *History of the Thirty-Third Foot*, 124; Tarleton, *History*, 109; Shaw, 30. Noted military historian Henry Lumpkin listed British losses at 331 of all ranks. Lee stated that Cornwallis left Camden on "the morning of the 15th of August" to fight Gates, which is erroneous. The battle occurred on the 16th.

15. Landers, 62; Lumpkin, 291; Agniel, 62.

16. Smith, *Archaeology*, 25; Landers, 62; Garden. *Anecdotes*, 2:285—italics are from the source. The officer survived and gave this account to Garden, who served under "Light-Horse Harry" Lee and later General Nathanael Greene, who will be discussed later.

17. Lamb, 306; Tarleton, *History*, 110; Bass, *Gamecock*, 82.

Chapter 10

1. Kirkland and Kennedy, *Historic Camden: Part One*, 274–75, 380.

2. Gray, 156; Kapp, *The Life of John Kalb*, 234; Kirkland and Kennedy, *Historic Camden: Part One*, 190–91; Cornwallis to Clinton, August 29, 1780, from Camden; Lewis, *Carolina Backcountry*, 217, 378. Some accounts claim the wounded DeKalb was taken to the "Blue House" but Lewis, an esteemed historical archaeologist who spent decades on studies and projects dealing with colonial Camden and its pre-history, points out that the Blue House was not built until a few years after the Revolution. We will discuss Porterfield much more a bit later.

3. Clark, *State Records*, 15:166–67. Williamson to Thomas Benbury, speaker of the House of Commons of the North Carolina Assembly, December 1, 1780, from Edenton, NC.

4. Caruthers, 147–48; Albertson, 96.

5. Charles Cotesworth Pinckney, *Life of General Thomas Pinckney* (hereafter Pinckney, *Life*) (Boston: Houghton Mifflin, 1895), 56, 79–80; Ashe and McCrady, *Cyclopedia*, 1:118–19. Col. Charles C. Pinckney was captured when Charleston fell in May 1780, and remained a prisoner until the war ended. He would later become a major general in the U.S. army and die on August 16, 1825, the forty-fifth anniversary of his brother's wounding and capture at the battle of Camden.

6. Pinckney, *Life*, 80. Of this episode with Tarleton and the seized horses, the grandson, Reverend Pinckney, wrote: "As this is the only good thing I have ever heard of Tarleton, I am bound in justice and in gratitude to record it. A bold and reckless rider, he ever left a bloody track behind him. No British officer was more cordially hated in the South."

7. *Scots Magazine*, 1780, 42:488; Duncan, 367; Lamb, 306.

8. Clark, *State Records*, 15:166. Williamson to Benbury, December 1, 1780.

9. Historic Camden Foundation, "Sickness & Survival"; Clark, *State Records*, 14:559.

10. George Hanger, *The Life, Adventures and Opinions of Col. George Hanger*, 2 vols. (London: Johnson & Stryker, 1801), 2:413; Clark, *State Records*, 15:166–

67—Williamson to Benbury; *South Carolina and American General Gazette*, August 23, 1780.

11. *Maryland Gazette*, October 13, 1780. Allman also claimed that some Loyalist militia of unknown strength had arrived at Camden the day before his escape and were to serve for three months.

12. Henry Clinton, *Observations on Earl Cornwallis' Answer* (Philadelphia: John Campbell, 1866), 21. Extract from Cornwallis to Germain, August 21, 1780.

13. Fries, *Records*, 4: 1559–1560; Wheeler, *Historical Sketches*, 194; Schenck, 99; Bass, *Gamecock*, 80; Otho Williams in Johnson, *Traditions*, 499; Scheer and Rankin, 410. Williams's reference is to Buford's defeat at the Waxhaws.

14. Clark, *State Records*, 14:560, 575; Heitman, 88, 131, 416.

Chapter 11

1. Ross, *Correspondence*, 1:493—Cornwallis to Germain, August 21, 1780; Tarleton, *History*, 110–11. Turnbull led the New York Volunteers while Ferguson commanded a mixed force of Loyalist militia. Cornwallis dispatched the orders on the night of August 16.

2. Tarleton, *History*, 111–14; Stedman, 2:212–13; Shaw, 30.

3. Tarleton, *History*, 114–15; Ross, *Correspondence*, 1 493—Cornwallis to Germain, August 21, 1780; Stedman, 2:212–13; Bass, *Gamecock*, 83; Kirkland and Kennedy, *Historic Camden: Part One*, 200–01. As mentioned earlier in this narrative, Campbell was noted as leading the detachment that burned Sumter's summer home during the pursuit of Buford's force in May. Tarleton also lost twenty or so horses in the Fishing Creek battle.

4. Shaw, 30–31; Bass, *Swamp Fox*, 43–45; Henderson, *WST*, 251; Johnson, *Traditions*, 537–38; Clark, *State Records*, 15:166–67—Williamson to Benbury, December 1, 1780.

5. *Rivington's Gazette*, September 13, 1780.

6. *South Carolina and American General Gazette*, August 23, 1780.

7. Ross, *Correspondence*, 1:493—Cornwallis to Germain, August 21, 1780; McCrady, *1775-1780*, 709–11.

8. Kapp, *The Life of John Kalb*, 236–37; Charles Caldwell, *Memoirs of the Life and Campaigns of the Hon. Nathaniel Greene* (Philadelphia: Robert Desilver, 1819), 139–40; Kirkland and Kennedy, *Historic Camden: Part One*, 275; Griswold, Simms, and Ingraham, 271. Kapp wrote that a "solitary tree" marked the grave.

9. John Thomas Scharf, *History of Maryland from the Earliest Period to the Present Day: 1765-1812*, 3 vols. (Baltimore: John B. Piet, 1879), 366.

10. Clark, *State Records*, 14:568.

11. Tarleton, *History*, 145–47; Landers, 54–56.

12. *Ibid.*

13. Bass, *Swamp Fox*, 44–46; Lumpkin, 266; Agniel, 65; Bass, *Gamecock*, 22, 51, 88–89; Seymour, 8. It will be recalled that Cornwallis ordered "divisions" of prisoners sent from Camden to Charleston in groups of 150. Agniel states this action occurred on August 20, which is inaccurate. A lingering question—for me, at least—is why Tarleton did not burn this plantation, a short distance from Nelson's Ferry, when his force embarked on its pursuit of Buford's column on May 27, 1780. Situated about a half mile from the Camden road, it seemingly would have been hard to miss, unless Tarleton passed it on a different route, which isn't hard to imagine since he was in unfamiliar territory and the British had few maps, all bad or at most unreliable. The Great Savannah home belonged to the family of Sumter's wife, Mary. If he had approached the plantation, did Tarleton know this? Was he more focused on tracking down Buford? There are myriad questions here. What we do know is that Tarleton's men torched Sumter's summer home in the High Hills of Santee the next day in a vain attempt to capture the Gamecock.

14. Fries, *Records*, 4:1559-1560. The Moravians, a denomination of Protestantism, purchased land in North Carolina in 1753, calling it Wachovia. They were supposedly neutral during the Revolution but traded with the Americans. Salem was renamed Winston Salem in 1913. The Moravian account states that Major Armstrong was accompanied by a "Colonel Armstrong" who was the major's "brother." This appears to be erroneous. The major did have a brother named James

Armstrong, but the latter was from Pennsylvania and not an officer in the war. The colonel mentioned is apparently James Armstrong of North Carolina, who was in the Continental army—although some claim he was in the state militia at this time—wounded at Stono Ferry and unrelated to Major Armstrong.

15. Clark, *State Records*, 15:61–62; Lewis, *Carolina Backcountry*, 216.

16. Schenck, 101–02; Heitman, 354; Ramsay, *History of South Carolina*, 207; John H. Wheeler, *Reminiscences of North Carolina and Eminent North Carolinians* (Columbus, OH: Columbus Printing Works, 1884), 399. Davie wrote the dispatch from Charlotte. He was promoted to colonel a few days later.

17. McCandless, *Revolutionary Fever*, 236; Foote, *Sketches*, 425; losthistory.net/battleofcamden/index.htm. Hunter became a Presbyterian minister after the war.

18. Ross, *Correspondence*, 1:59; Schenck, 98.

19. Clinton, *Observations on Earl Cornwallis' Answer*, 19–20. Extract from Cornwallis to Clinton, August 23, 1780.

20. Seymour, 7.

21. Carrington, 505.

22. Clinton, *Observations on Earl Cornwallis' Answer*, 21–22, Extract from Cornwallis to Clinton, August 29, 1780; Earl Cornwallis, *An Answer to that part of the Narrative of Lieutenant-General Sir Henry Clinton Which relates to the Conduct of Lieutenant-General Earl Cornwallis, During the Campaign in North America, in the Year 1781* (London: J. Debrett, 1783), 58; Bass, *Swamp Fox*, 12; *South Carolina and American General Gazette*, August 23, 1780. Lt. Col. Alexander Innes led a battalion of the South Carolina Royalists, primarily operating in and around Savannah. Innes was badly wounded at Musgrove's Mill in August 1780; thus, it is unclear who commanded his battalion in the Camden garrison.

23. Clark, *State Records*, 15:62, 166–67—Extract of letter from Williamson to England, August 30, 1780; a Major Despond to Williamson, September 1, 1780; Williamson to Thomas Benbury, December 1, 1780.

24. "The Fortified Post" historical marker, Historic Camden; Lewis, *Carolina Backcountry*, 213–14.

25. Stevens, "The Southern Campaign." *Magazine of American History*, 7, 272–74. Washington to Clinton, October 18, 1780.

26. Clark, *State Records*, 14:585—Magill letter to his father; Carrington, 517.

27. New York *Royal Gazette*, September 16, 1780.

28. *Rivington's Gazette*, September 13, 1780; Scheer and Rankin, 410.

Chapter 12

1. Gates to Washington, September 3, 1780, in Clark, *State Records*, 15:65–66; Ward, 355–56; Robert K. Wright, Jr. *The Continental Army* (Washington, D.C.: U.S. Army Center of Military History, 1983), 164; Landers, 56, 62. Wright states the Fifth Maryland, commanded by Lt. Col. Benjamin Ford, was sent to reinforce Greene in February, and in many histories is mistakenly identified as the Second Maryland Regiment. Ford led the Sixth Maryland at Camden in August 1780, but the Sixth was among units disbanded during the retooling of the Maryland Continentals. Whatever the case in the Maryland reorganization, it would be weeks, even months, before the ranks were filled and the recruits somewhat ready to take the field.

2. Gates to Washington, September 3, 1780, in Clark, *State Records*, 15:65–66; Ward, 355–56; Robert K. Wright, Jr. *The Continental Army* (Washington, D.C.: U.S. Army Center of Military History, 1983), 164; Landers, 56, 62.

3. Gates to Washington, September 3, 1780, in Clark, *State Records*, 15:65–66; Ward, 355–56; Robert K. Wright, Jr. *The Continental Army* (Washington, D.C.: U.S. Army Center of Military History, 1983), 164; Landers, 56, 62.

4. Stevens, "The Southern Campaign," *Magazine of American History*, vol. 7, 279–80. Greene wrote on September 5, 1780, from his camp at Kennemark, RI, to that colony's Governor William Greene—a distant relative. The general's information at this point was that Generals Smallwood and Gist were killed in action, which was inaccurate, and DeKalb wounded, which he was, mortally.

5. Elizabeth F. Ellet, *The Women of the American Revolution*, 3 vols. (New

York: Charles Scribner, 1856), 3:2, 239–41. David McCalla, Thomas's brother, had earlier moved to South Carolina and was staying with the family of Capt. John Nixon, whom we will meet a bit later. In author Elizabeth Ellet's third volume of *The Women of the American Revolution*, published in 1856, she relies heavily on the work of Daniel Green Stinson for her information on the South Carolina women, including Sarah McCalla, who were the unsung heroines of the conflict there. Stinson was the son of a Revolutionary War soldier, William Stinson. Growing up in the Catawba River region of the state—specifically Chester District as it was known then—young Daniel was mesmerized by war stories told by people who actually lived during that turbulent period. He also "frequented places" where these folks met "to talk over their battles and adventures." As a lawyer and magistrate in later years, Stinson worked with Revolutionary pensioners, aiding them with their paperwork and also documenting their experiences. In her preface to volume 3, Ms. Ellet is quite generous in her praise of Stinson and his role in gathering reputable accounts for inclusion in her work. All of the Ellet-related footnotes in this book should be remembered for the interest and attention to detail supplied by Daniel Stinson. Without Ellet and Stinson, the heroics of these women in the Camden story and the overall saga of the Revolution, would likely have been lost forever.

6. Ellet, 3:242–44.
7. Ibid., 3:245–48.
8. Ibid., 3: 248–50, 268.
9. Pugh, 95; *Virginian-Pilot*, August 14, 2011. The general was able to return to active duty in the war, later serving as a state representative before his death in 1800.
10. Carrington, 518; Shaw, 31; Stedman, 215; Ross, *Correspondence*, 1:46; Wheeler, *Historical Sketches*, 1:58. Paterson's name is spelled "Pattison" and "Patterson" in various sources.
11. Carrington, 518; Shaw, 31; Stedman, 215; Ross, *Correspondence*, 1:46; Wheeler, *Historical Sketches*, 1:58.
12. Bass, *Gamecock*, 86; Derek Smith. "Gideon's Sword: Kings Mountain," *Army*, vol. 39, no. 8 (August 1989), 53; Shaw, 31; Stedman, 2:216. The Highlanders continued to be staggered by sickness, thus it is doubtful that the full regiment was protecting Tarleton. Major George Hanger led the British Legion during Tarleton's illness.
13. Cornwallis to Clinton, September 22, 1780, in Henry Clinton, *Observations on Earl Cornwallis' Answer*, 29; Bass, *Gamecock*, 86; Derek Smith, "Gideon's Sword," 53; Shaw, 31; Stedman, 2:216.
14. Clark, *State Records*, 15:167–68—Williamson to Benbury, December 1, 1780.
15. Pinckney, 80–81; Steven D. Smith, James B. Legg, Tamara S. Wilson, and Jonathan Leader, *"Obstinate and Strong": The History and Archaeology of the Siege of Fort Motte* (Columbia: South Carolina Institute of Archaeology and Anthropology, 2007), 16. Reverend Charles Pinckney, the major's grandson, wrote that Betsy Pinckney went to her husband's aid after "the departure of the British from Camden," which is erroneous, and makes no mention of Mrs. Brewton's role. The reverend also refers to the Motte home as "St. Joseph's," which also is inaccurate.
16. Derek Smith, "Gideon's Sword," 53, 55; Ross, *Correspondence*, 1:59.
17. Ross, *Correspondence*, 1:59; Stedman, 2:224; Tarleton, *History*, 168–69.
18. Shaw, 34; Stedman, 2:225.
19. Shaw, 34; Stedman, 2:225; Hanger, *Life, Adventures*, 2:408–09, 410–12.
20. Gray, 142
21. Ellet, 3:250–52, 267–68.
22. Ibid.
23. Tarleton, *History*, 169–70; Stedman, 216–17.
24. Ross, *Correspondence*, 1:59–60.
25. Ibid.
26. *Magazine of American History* [hereafter *MOAH*], 7:321; Duncan, *History*, 1:367; Clark, *State Records*, 15: 167–68—Williamson to Benbury, December 1, 1780.

Chapter 13

1. Lewis, *Carolina Backcountry*, 207, 257.
2. Lewis, "Camden: A Frontier Town, 61–62; *MOAH*, 7:321; Ross, *Correspondence*, 1:498; Edward McCrady, *The History of South Carolina in the Revolution: 1780-1783* (New York: Macmillan, 1902), 95; Wilkin, 81.

3. Wright, 163; Landers, 57; Kirkland and Kennedy, *Historic Camden: Part One*, 183; Bass, *Swamp Fox*, 114. Baron von Steuben, the former Prussian army officer, was sent south to assist Greene, staying in Virginia to establish a logistical structure and refurbishment of Virginia's troops when Greene went to North Carolina to relieve Gates.

4. James D. Bailey, *Some Heroes of the American Revolution* (Spartanburg, SC: Band & White, Printers, 1924), 46; Tarleton, *History*, 205; McCrady, *1775-1780*, 12; Ellet, 3:252-53. McCrady and Bailey incorrectly identify the Rugeley in command here as Rowland Rugeley, Henry's brother.

5. Barry Isaacs, "Lt.-Col. Elijah Isaacs" (n.p., 2017), 3-5; Bailey, 132; Barbour, 68-69.

6. Stedman, 2:232; Agniel, 82; Carrington, 529; Kirkland and Kennedy, *Historic Camden: Part One*, 173; Wheeler, *Historical Sketches*, 263.

7. Garden, 1:65-66.

8. *Ibid.*, 1: 65; Stedman, 2: 233.

9. George Washington Greene, *The Life of Nathanael Greene, Major-General in the Army of the Revolution*, 3 vols. (New York: Hurd and Houghton, 1871), 1:4-5, 24-26; Agniel, 16-19.

10. Greene, *Life of Nathanael Greene*, 1:73; Agniel, 19-23, 24.

11. Jenkins, 109; Carrington, 529; Agniel, 82; Kirkland and Kennedy, *Historic Camden: Part One*, 173; Wheeler, *Historical Sketches*, 263.

12. Jared Sparks, *Correspondence of the American Revolution; Being Letters of Eminent Men to George Washington*, 3 vols. (Boston: Little, Brown, 1853), 3:165-67; Wright, 165; Carrington, 531-32. Lee's Legion was a mixed force of cavalry and infantry, some 280 total troops. Lee was the father of future Confederate general Robert E. Lee.

13. Garden, 1 66-67.

14. Agniel, 83-84; *London Gazette*, February 13, 1781—letter from Leslie to Germain, December 19, 1780.

15. Agniel, 84-85; Carrington, 532. Carrington, likely meaning *two weeks*, wrote that Greene "remained in camp" at Charlotte for "two months" which is erroneous.

16. Lossing, *Lives*, 295-96; Elizabeth Bryant Johnston, *George Washington Day by Day*. (New York: Baker & Taylor, 1895), 147; Charles W. Snell, *National Register of Historic Places Inventory—Nomination Form—Gen. Gates House, Traveller's Rest* (Washington, D.C.: National Park Service, U.S. Department of the Interior, 1972), 7-8; Kirkland and Kennedy, *Historic Camden: Part One*, 183-84.

17. "The Fortified Post" historical marker, Historic Camden; Lewis, *Carolina Backcountry*, 213-14; Hilborn, 135; "The Camden District—Revolutionary War Trails"—www.historic-camden.net.

18. "The Fortified Post" historical marker, Historic Camden; Lewis, *Carolina Backcountry*, 213-14; Hilborn, 135; "The Camden District—Revolutionary War Trails"—www.historic-camden.net. My description of the Kershaw House defenses is based on a photo of a scale model of the house during the Revolution and shown in the Hilborns' book. The model was being displayed at the Midlands Exposition Center in or about 1970.

19. Hanger, *Life, Adventures*, 2:408-09, 410-12. Hanger claimed that he left North Carolina with some troops—whom he did not identify—ordered to Camden, thus bypassing Cornwallis's eventual encampment at Winnsboro, which appears unlikely.

20. Clark, *State Records*, 15:167-68—Williamson to Benbury, December 1, 1780.

21. Ellet, 3:253.

22. Pinckney, 82-83; Smith, "*Obstinate and Strong*," 16. The major gradually regained use of his leg and by September 1781 was in Virginia serving as an army recruiter. There he met Lafayette, the two enjoying a friendship lasting the rest of their lives.

23. Carrington, 527-28.

Chapter 14

1. Wilkin, 81; Lewis, "Camden: A Frontier Town," 62.

2. *South Carolina and American General Gazette*, January 27, 1781. Hamilton's notice was written from Camden on December 19, 1780, and ran over several days.

3. Ellet, 3:253-56.

4. *Ibid.*

5. Ross, *Correspondence*, 1:80–81.
6. Lumpkin, 294–95; Agniel, 87–88, 104–05.
7. Caruthers, 13–14, 395; Agniel, 104–05; Ross, *Correspondence*, 1:83.
8. Caruthers, 395–96.
9. Ellet, 3:254–56.
10. William P. Palmer, ed., *Calendar of Virginia State Papers and Other Manuscripts: 1652-1781*, Vol. 1 (Richmond: R.F. Walker, Superintendent of Public Printing, 1875), 479; Porterfield, 73–75; *Southern Campaigns American Revolution Pension Statements and Rosters*—http://revwarapps.org./s8965. Parentheses were in the Porterfield source. Some accounts state that Lt. Col. Porterfield died in October 1780, which is erroneous. Robert Porterfield served as a brigadier general in the War of 1812.
11. William P. Palmer, ed., *Calendar of Virginia State Papers and Other Manuscripts: 1652-1781*, Vol. 1 (Richmond: R.F. Walker, Superintendent of Public Printing, 1875), 479; Porterfield, 73–75; *Southern Campaigns American Revolution Pension Statements and Rosters*—http://revwarapps.org./s8965. Parentheses are in the Porter source. It is unclear if the debt was paid.
12. Ellet, 3:256–57.
13. Parton, 1:73–75, 88–89.
14. *Ibid.*, 1:90–91.
15. *Ibid.*
16. Gibbes, *1776 and 1782*, 23.
17. Johnston, *George Washington*, 24; Agniel, 109. Greene was at Guilford Court House, NC, when he granted Morgan's leave.
18. Ellet, 3:259–61, 274. Italics in original.
19. *Ibid.*, 3:262–64.
20. *Ibid.*, 3:241, 266–67; 275.
21. Kershaw, 76—William Kershaw to John Kershaw, March 22, 1781.

Chapter 15

1. Paul David Nelson, *Francis Rawdon-Hastings, Marquess of Hastings: Soldier, Peer of the Realm, Governor-General of India* (Madison, NJ: Fairleigh Dickinson University Press, 2005), 91–92; Bass, *Swamp Fox*, 186; Agniel, 118; Scheer and Rankin, 451–52; Todd Braisted, ed., *Diary of Henry Nase: King's American Regiment*, Nase Family Papers (n.d.: Archives Division, New Brunswick Museum), 16.
2. Braisted, *Diary*, 16; Agniel, 117–18; Nelson, 91–92; Scheer and Rankin, 451–52.
3. Francis V. Greene, *General Greene* (New York: D. Appleton, 1897), 230; J.C. Stockbridge, "The Surrender of Cornwallis in England," *Magazine of American History*, vol. 7, no. 5 (November 1881), 431—Pierce to St. George Tucker, July 20, 1781, from the High Hills of Santee; Scheer and Rankin, 453; Seymour, 23. Seymour added that when he and his Blue Hen comrades encamped at "one Mr. Cheek's plantation" on April 3, they had marched 2,456 miles since leaving their quarters in Morristown the previous spring.
4. Scheer and Rankin, 453–54; Balfour to Germain, May 1, 1781, in *Pennsylvania Gazette*, August 22, 1781; Wilkin, 81. Beaufort, SC, was occupied by the British but later evacuated when Savannah was besieged by American and French forces in September–October 1779.
5. Scheer and Rankin, 455; Kirkland and Kennedy, *Historic Camden: Part One*, 222; R.W. Gibbes, *Documentary History of the American Revolution Consisting of Letters and Papers Relating to the Contest for Liberty, Chiefly in South Carolina in 1781 and 1782* [hereafter cited as Gibbes, *1781 and 1782*] (Columbia: Banner Steam-Power Press, 1853), 53, 81–82—Greene to Marion, April 17, 1781; Gray, 150.
6. Bass, *Gamecock*, 151.
7. Ward, 427; Seymour, 23–24. Seymour was not in Kirkwood's company.
8. *Annual Register, or a View of the History, Politics, and Literature, for the Year 1781* (London: J. Dodsley, 1782), 24:80–81; Agniel, 118; Nelson, 91–92; Scheer and Rankin, 451–52.
9. Carrington, 571; Lumpkin, 179; McCrady, *1780-1783*, 187, 190; Nelson, 93. Some accounts list Coffin as a brevet major. Turnbull's New York Volunteers may have been led by Captain Bernard Kane, at least one source states.
10. Ward, 430; *American Historical Record*, 2: 104; Kirkland and Kennedy, *Historic Camden: Part One*, 224–25. The *American Historical Record* account here and in forthcoming references is based on Samuel Mathis's June 26, 1819, letter

to then-General William R. Davie, a copy of which was shared with Benson Lossing, editor of the *AHR*, by former North Carolina governor David L. Swain in January 1852. Mathis conversed with some American officers before and after the Hobkirk Hill battle but was not an eyewitness. He is also remembered as a relative of the Kershaw family, helping them through the ordeal of the British occupation of Camden.

11. *Annual Register, 1781*, 24:81; Seymour, 25; Carrington, 571.

12. Bass, *Gamecock*, 153; Wilkin, 82; Kirkland and Kennedy, *Historic Camden: Part One*, 224; William Gordon, *The History of the Rise, Progress, and Establishment, of the Independence of the United States of America*, 4 vols. (London: Dilly and Buckland, 1788), 4:82. Fraser's command is identified as the South Carolina Provincial Regiment in some sources.

13. Kirkland and Kennedy, *Historic Camden: Part One*, 222-23, 225. A Dr. Matthew Irvine acted as a guide for Greene, based on at least two sources. A few accounts refer to "Big Pine Tree Creek" and "Little Pine Tree Creek." For clarity, I call the main waterway simply Pine Tree Creek.

14. *Annual Register, 1781*, 24:81; Seymour, 25; Carrington, 571.

15. Parton, 1:91-92.

16. Carrington, 570; George Washington Greene, 1:244-45; Lumpkin, 178-79.

17. Gordon, 4:82; Kirkland and Kennedy, *Historic Camden: Part One*, 228-29; *Annual Register, 1781*, 24:81; Seymour, 25; Carrington, 571; *Potter's American Monthly*, 4:101-04. Otho Williams referred to the deserter as a "villain of a drummer"—Williams to his wife, Elie Williams, April 27, 1781.

18. *Royal Gazette*, May 9, 1781. Questions about the deserter drummer remain to this day.

Chapter 16

1. Scharf, *History of Maryland*, 2:418; McCrady, *1780-1783*, 191; Seymour, 24; Carrington, 570; Ward, 432; Lumpkin, 299.

2. Scharf, *History of Maryland*, 2:418; McCrady, *1780-1783*, 191; Seymour, 24; Carrington, 570; Ward, 432; Lumpkin, 299. The Virginia Continental regiments are sometimes identified as the First and Second Virginia. Ford's Maryland Continentals are sometimes identified as the Second Maryland, all of this due to reorganization. It is unclear whether two or all three of Harrison's guns were engaged in this battle. Greene had dispatched another gun to assist Marion about this time. So valuable was artillery to both sides that more than 200 North Carolina militia "just arrived" and not included in Reed's force, escorted the six-pounder. A "what-if" of the battle would be how the addition of these militia might have altered the outcome.

3. Offutt, 48,49; Scharf, *History of Maryland*, 2:418; Agniel, 123; McCrady, *1780-1783*, 191; Seymour, 24; Carrington, 570; Ward, 432; Lumpkin, 299.

4. Johnson, *Traditions*, 364; Schenck, 410-11; Historical Marker Database—"Death of Stewart," www.hmdb.org. The slain officer was Lt. Col. James Stuart of the Queen's Guards. He and Smith had apparently crossed blades at Cowpens and renewed their antagonism at Guilford. Stuart is often identified as "Stewart," but a monument erected to his memory on the Guilford battlefield in 1895 or 1896—in what is now the Guilford Court House National Military Park—has Stuart engraved on it.

5. Ward, 433; *Calendar of the General Otho Holland Williams Papers* (Baltimore: Maryland Historical Society, November 1940), 48-49; Francis V. Greene, 214—Edward Giles to Otho Williams, August 29, 1781; Archive.org—William Beatty, Jr., to William Beatty, Sr., March 3, 1781—The letter was written twelve days before the battle of Guilford Court House, Beatty's bivouac some ten miles from that location at the time he wrote.

6. *Royal Gazette*, May 9, 1781; *Annual Register*, 1781, 82; Lossing, *American Historical Record*, 2:106; George Washington Greene, 1: 245; Lumpkin, 182. Lumpkin describes the combatants as Americans versus Americans. I used "colonials" here because in my narrative I refer to "Americans" as those who fought for the United States of America, as stated in the Declaration of Independence.

7. Seymour, 25; *Annual Register*, 1781,

82; *Royal Gazette*, May 9, 1781. Some accounts state the battle opened at 10 a.m. which, based on the British timeline, including the delay in starting, is erroneous. The unidentified British officer's report in the *Royal Gazette* giving the time as 11:05 a.m. appears to be the most accurate, based on events. Otho Williams also gives the time of the attack as "about eleven o'clock"—Williams to Elie Williams, April 27, 1781, in *Potter's American Monthly*, 4:101–04. Several accounts wrongly refer to "Elie" as Williams's brother.

8. Ward, 432; McCrady, *1780-1783*, 189–90; Seymour, 25; *Royal Gazette*, May 5-9, 1781; Greene to Samuel Huntington, April 27, 1781, in *Pennsylvania Gazette*, May 30, 1781.

9. Seymour, 25; *Royal Gazette*, May 9, 1781; Greene to Huntington, April 25, 1781, in Henry Steele Commager and Richard B. Morris, editors, *The Spirit of Seventy-Six* (New York: Harper & Row, 1975), 1175–76.

10. McCrady, *1780-1783*, 191–92; Ward, 432; William Gilmore Simms, *The Life of Nathaniel Greene, Major General in the Army of the Revolution.* (New York: Derby & Jackson, 1856), 218.

11. McCrady, *1780-1783*, 191–92; Ward, 432; Simms, *Life of Greene*, 218.

12. McCrady, *1780-1783*, 192–93; Otho Williams to Elie Williams, April 27, 1781, in *Potter's American Monthly*, 4:101–04; Ward, 433; Greene to Huntington, April 25, 1781, in Commager and Morris, 1175–76. At least one account states Beatty was shot in the heart.

13. McCrady, *1780-1783*, 193–94; Greene to Huntington, April 25, 1781, in Commager and Morris, 1175–76.

14. Lossing, *American Historical Record*, 2: 109; Johnson, *Traditions*, 364; Schenck, 410–11; McCrady, *1780-1783*, 194. Italics *Cut and Thrust* in the source.

15. Greene to Huntington, April 25, 1781, in Commager and Morris, 1175–76; Bailey, 52; Lumpkin, 183.

16. Balfour to Germain, May 1, 1781, in *Pennsylvania Gazette*, August 22, 1781; Bailey, 53; Lumpkin, 183; Simms, *Life of Greene*, 222–23. The italic *undone* is mine.

17. *Annual Register, or a View of the History, Politics, and Literature, For the Year 1781* (London: J. Dodsley, 1782);

Otho Williams to Elie Williams, April 27, 1781, in *Potter's American Monthly*, 4:101–04; Lossing, *American Historical Record*, 2:109. Since the battle was spread out and fast moving—at least as far as eighteenth-century infantry tactics allowed—it is reasonable to assume that some, if not most, of the British officers paroled on the field were freed by Washington, who surprised them on his sweeping flank movement.

18. Parton, 1:92–93.

19. Ross, *Correspondence*, 1: 97.

20. Gordon, 4:85; Otho Williams to Elie Williams, April 27, 1781, in *Potter's American Monthly*, 4:101–04; Heitman, 114; *Pennsylvania Gazette*, August 22, 1781; Lumpkin, 183.

21. Nelson, 96; Otho Williams to Elie Williams, April 27, 1781, in *Potter's American Monthly*, 4:101–04; Lossing, *American Historical Record*, 2:109; Simms, *Life of Greene*, 222. Italic *Five* is mine.

22. Ross, *Correspondence*, 1:97; *Royal Gazette*, May 9, 1781; Gordon, 4:89; Horry and Weems, 71.

23. Bass, *Gamecock*, 158—The aide was Major William Pierce, Jr.; Scharf, *History of Maryland*, 2:420—Greene to President Joseph Reed of Maryland, August 6, 1781.

24. Schenck, 412; Seymour, 26; Otho Williams to Elie Williams, April 27, 1781, in *Potter's American Monthly*, 4:101–04.

25. Bailey, 52.

26. Johnson, *Traditions*, 365; Lossing, *American Historical Record*, 2:109; Schenck, 410–11; Gordon, 4:86–87.

27. Johnson, *Traditions*, 365; Lossing, *American Historical Record*, 2:109; Schenck, 410–11; Gordon, 4:86–87.

28. Parton, 1:93. Parton wrote that the exchange was negotiated between the unidentified American captain and the "British general," which is erroneous. Rawdon was a lieutenant-colonel.

29. Parton, 1:93–94; Hilborn, 187.

Chapter 17

1. Bass, *Swamp Fox*, 185–86; Carrington, 569. Cornwallis planned to rendezvous with Phillips's command at Petersburg, VA. The earl's troops arrived there on May 20, learning that Phillips had died of a "sudden illness" in the town

a week earlier. The infamous Brig. Gen. Benedict Arnold had assumed command, replacing Phillips, by the time Cornwallis reached Petersburg. Phillips's troops had marched into Petersburg on May 8.

2. Seymour, 26; Ward, 439; Lewis, *Carolina Backcountry*, 227; William Johnson, *Sketches of the Life and Correspondence*, 2:85–86.

3. Rawdon to Cornwallis, May 24, 1781, published in the *London Gazette*, July 31–August 4, 1781. The *Gazette* was not a daily paper, hence the odd date of publication. Bass, *Swamp Fox*, 190–91; *Royal Gazette*, May 9, 1781—This unidentified officer provided some accurate information in his narrative about the battle, but this part dealing with Greene's casualties seems inflated, whether by him or the "deserters" he described. Nelson, 96.

4. Bass, *Swamp Fox*, 192; Rawdon to Cornwallis, May 24, 1781, published in the *London Gazette*, July 31–August 4, 1781.

5. Rawdon to Cornwallis, May 24, 1781, published in the *London Gazette*, July 31–August 4, 1781; Greene to Washington, May 14, 1781, in Sparks, *Correspondence*, 3:310; Lewis, "Camden: A Frontier Town," 63; Braisted, *Diary*, 18.

6. *Royal Gazette*, May 9, 1781—The "Tanner" refers to Greene's early profession as a tanner of animal hides.

7. Rawdon to Cornwallis, May 24, 1781, published in the *London Gazette*, July 31–August 4, 1781; Greene to Washington, May 14, 1781, in Sparks, *Correspondence*, 3:310.

8. *Yorkville* (SC) *Enquirer*, April 26, 1877; "Colonial Pottery."

9. Hanger, *Life, Adventures*, 2:412–13.

10. "Sickness and Survival."

11. Bass, *Swamp Fox*, 196; Kirkland and Kennedy, *Historic Camden: Part One*, 277–78. Kennedy and Kirkland wrote that Kershaw family traditions claimed the destruction in the house occurred after Rawdon departed, "a party of Tories from the Waxhaws" responsible for the carnage. The pair contend that since Americans were nearby and entered the gutted village just after the evacuation that "this seems improbable."

12. Harriette Kershaw Leiding, *Historic Houses of South Carolina* (Philadelphia: J.B. Lippincott, 1921), 171; Kirkland and Kennedy, *Historic Camden: Part One*, 277.

13. Bass, *Swamp Fox*, 192; Greene to Washington, May 14, 1781, in Sparks, *Correspondence*, 3:310.

14. Wilkin, 84; Seymour, 27; Lewis, *Carolina Backcountry*, 230; Johnson, *Traditions*, 365; 469; Leiding, 172; Johnson, *Traditions*, 365; Smith, "Obstinate and Strong," 17. The British were fortifying Rebecca Motte's home and the area around it by January 1781, shortly after Major Thomas Pinckney and his family departed for Charleston.

15. Ross, *Correspondence*, 1:97–99. Cornwallis's dispatch to Rawdon apparently was in response to two letters he had received from Rawdon about Hobkirk Hill. In his report to Clinton, he enclosed copies of Rawdon's messages, stating that their arrival had "relieved me from the most cruel anxieties."

16. Wilkin, 84–85; Rawdon to Cornwallis, May 24, 1781, published in the *London Gazette*, July 31–August 4, 1781; Smith, "Obstinate and Strong," 30; Braisted, *Diary*, 18. The Loyalist soldier Henry Nase wrote that the "whole army" reached Nelson's Ferry by May 12, which appears to be erroneous.

17. Parton, 1:94–95.

18. John C. Fitzpatrick, ed. *The Diaries of George Washington: 1748-1799*, 4 vols. (Boston: Houghton Mifflin, 1925), 2:226–27; Greene to Washington, May 14, 1781, in Sparks, *Correspondence*, 3:310; Johnston, *George Washington*, 88. Washington's June 14 diary entry may have referred to both the May 14 message to which Sparks refers and to a May 16 dispatch Fitzpatrick stated was in the Washington Papers in the Library of Congress in 1925. It seems likely that Washington received these two missives from Greene, since his diary mentions "agreeable accts" sent from the latter. Due to the communications issues of the time, Washington likely would have gotten both dispatches about the same time. Greene's "other recent victories" included the collapse of most of the British outposts in South Carolina, while Ninety Six and Fort Augusta in Georgia were "invested."

Chapter 18

1. *Calendar of the General Otho Holland Williams Papers*, 106; Scheer and Rankin, 458–59.

2. "Sickness and Survival."
3. Lumpkin, 203–04; Agniel, 126; Wilkin, 86; Tarleton, *History*, 507.
4. Stevens, "Southern Campaign," 272—Greene letter from the "High Hills of Santee," August 8, 1781 also published in Gordon, 4:98.
5. Scharf, *History of Maryland*, 2:420—Greene to President Joseph Reed of Maryland, August 6, 1781.
6. Lewis, *Carolina Backcountry*, 229; Scheer and Rankin, 460; *New York Packet*, October 4, 1781, in Moore, 2:474–75; Gibbes, *1781 and 1782*, 132–34.
7. Lossing, *American Historical Record*, 2: 106; Offutt, 49; Scharf, *History of Maryland*, 2: 397, 399–400; Lumpkin, 277–78; Lewis, *Carolina Backcountry*, 230. Any reader of Scharf's work in a research or reference realm should be cautious of possibly egregious errors in this book, one being that Greene replaced Gates in command of the southern army in "the winter of *1880*..."—the italics are mine. Howard was disabled by his wounds at Eutaw Springs but went on to be a three-term Maryland governor beginning in 1788 and in 1795 declined a post as secretary of war in Washington's cabinet. He was, however, a peacetime brigadier general, a U.S. senator, and a member of the Maryland Senate before his death in October 1827 at age seventy-five. Some sources claim that the British commander Stewart had been promoted colonel in May 1780, which is erroneous. He was a lieutenant colonel at Eutaw Springs, not making "full-bird" colonel until May 1782.
8. Clark, *State Records*, 15:644–45; Kershaw, *Family*, 13; Kirkland and Kennedy, *Historic Camden: Part One*, 277; Lewis, *Carolina Backcountry*, 231–32—Joseph Kershaw erroneously wrote that the British entered Camden on May 28, 1780. The letter was written at "Fred'k Town," apparently Frederick, MD.
9. *Calendar of the General Otho Holland Williams Papers*, 57—Williams to Field, November 22, 1781; "Sickness and Survival"; Lossing, *American Historical Record*, 2:106. Williams was promoted brigadier general in May 1782. In peacetime, he was a judge and collector of customs in Baltimore before his death in July 1794.
10. Lorenzo Sabine, *The American Loyalists, or Biographical Sketches of Adherents to the British Crown in the War of the Revolution* (Boston: Charles C. Little and James Brown, 1847), 81, 176, 200, 214, 231, 257, 261, 283, 315, 325, 362, 402, 530, 580–581, 603, 660; Jenkins, 169. The Alexander Garden mentioned here was the father of the officer of the same name who served in Lee's Legion and later as an aide to Nathanael Greene. The senior Garden was a noted physician and botanist as well as a Loyalist. His deportment caused a lasting rift between father and son.
11. Lossing, *American Historical Record*, 2:295–96; Johnston, *George Washington*, 147; Charles W. Snell, *National Register of Historic Places Inventory—Nomination Form—Gen. Gates House, Traveller's Rest* (Washington, D.C.: National Park Service, U.S. Department of the Interior, 1972), 7–8; Kirkland and Kennedy, *Historic Camden: Part One*, 183–84. Verplanck's Point is located in present-day Westchester County, NY.
12. Garden, *Anecdotes*, 1:65; Jenkins, 171–72.
13. Kirkland and Kennedy, *Historic Camden: Part One*, 378–80; Lewis, *Carolina Backcountry*, 232, 254–55; Johnson, *Traditions*, 469; Kershaw, *Family*, 20.
14. Kershaw, *Family*, 18–19; Kirkland and Kennedy, *Historic Camden: Part One*, 379–80; *Charleston Evening Gazette*, November 16, 1785.
15. Kirkland and Kennedy, *Historic Camden: Part One*, 378; Lewis, *Carolina Backcountry*, 232, 254–55; Johnson, *Traditions*, 469; Kershaw, *Family*, 20.
16. Kirkland and Kennedy, *Historic Camden: Part One*, 378; Lewis, *Carolina Backcountry*, 232, 254–55; Johnson, *Traditions*, 469; Kershaw, *Family*, 20.
17. Leiding, 173; Kirkland and Kennedy, *Historic Camden: Part One*, 277.
18. Ramsay, *History of South Carolina*, 304–05.
19. Derek Smith, "Potter's Raid—'Our Errand through the State,'" *North & South*, vol. 10, no. 2 (July 2007), 72–73; *New York Herald*, March 20, 1865.
20. *Camden (SC) Chronicle*, May 30, 1947; Leiding, 173; Kirkland and Kennedy, *Historic Camden: Part One*, 277; *Edgefield (SC) Advertiser*, June 9, 1909. The 129th anniversary of the battle was about two months after the monument dedication.

21. Peterson, *The Military Heroes*, 407–08; Robert Kirkwood, Jr., Historical Marker at Robert Kirkwood Library near Wilmington, DE. Capt. Robert Kirkwood, Jr., was born in 1756, a native of New Castle County, DE. He entered the army in 1776 as a lieutenant and fought at Long Island, Trenton, and Princeton. Promoted to captain in December 1776, he fought at Brandywine, Germantown, and Monmouth. "This self-sacrificing soldier risked his life oftener, perhaps, than any other officer in the army," stated one account. He also fought at Cowpens, Guilford Court House, and Eutaw Springs. With the war winding down in 1782, Kirkwood returned to Delaware and married Sarah England. After her death five years later, Kirkwood was granted land in the Northwest Territory, settling in Ohio. Land disputes between Native American tribes and settlers moving into the region resulted in bloody clashes, including the Northwest Indian War of 1786–1795. During this conflict, Kirkwood reentered the army and was killed at St. Clair's Defeat—also called the Battle of Wabash—on November 4, 1791.

Chapter 19

1. Snell, 8; www.patriotresource.com. A variation of the Vallance name is Valens, sometimes found in the branch of her family's genealogy records. General Montgomery fell at the battle of Quebec in 1775.
2. Jenkins, 112; Lossing, *Lives*, 296; Snell, 8; Kirkland and Kennedy, *Historic Camden: Part One*, 184.
3. Jenkins, 112–13; Lossing, *Lives*, 295–96; Kirkland and Kennedy, *Historic Camden: Part One*, 183–84; Johnston, *George Washington*, 147; Snell, 7–8. Mary Vallance Gates died in 1810. Both "Traveller's" and "Traveler's" Rest are used in various accounts regarding the Gates home, which is located at Kearneysville in what is now Jefferson County, WV. The house was in Berkeley County, VA, until 1863 during the Civil War when West Virginia broke away to become a state in the Union, changing the county's name in the process.
4. Seton-Carr, 9–10, 15–17; Agniel, 151–54.
5. Hilborn, 206–08; Wilkin, 86–87. Wilkin referred to Hayne as "Haynes," which is inaccurate.
6. Wilkin, 86–88.
7. *Annual Biography and Obituary for the Year 1828*, vol. 12 (London: Longman, Rees, Orme, Brown and Green, 1828), 151, 153, 154–56, 157. The Anglo-Nepalese War—known in earlier accounts as the Ghurka War—was a conflict between Britain and the Kingdom of Nepal. The Maratha wars pitted the British against the Maratha Empire, which inhabited much of India in the early nineteenth century.
8. *Ibid*. It will be recalled that Sarah had several unpleasant encounters with Rawdon while bringing food and clothing to her POW husband at Camden as she worked to gain his freedom. On the other hand, Porterfield benefitted from Rawdon's generosity after the former was severely wounded at the battle of Camden.
9. *Ruddiman's* (London) *Weekly Register*, January 30, 1782; Bass, "Banastre Tarleton," *Sandlapper*, 6, 3 (March 1973), 51; Agniel, 158–59; Hilborn, 219–20. Some ten months after his encounter with Tarleton at Yorktown, Laurens was killed in August 1782 during a skirmish at Tar Bluff on the Combahee River in South Carolina.
10. Paget Toynbee, ed., *The Letters of Horace Walpole*, 16 vols. (Oxford: Clarendon Press, 1904), 12: 176; Bass, "Banastre Tarleton," *Sandlapper*, vol. 6, no. 3 (March 1973), 51; Agniel, 72. Italics are from Mrs. Toynbee's version. Agniel's account of these statements is somewhat different and less reliable since Mrs. Toynbee relied on actual correspondence.
11. *Annual Biography and Obituary for the Year 1834*, 18:274–75, 281; Agniel, 71, 163, 165. Tarleton married Susan P. Bertie in December 1798. They had no children, but Ban earlier had fathered a child out of wedlock at some point in his carousing, based on various accounts. In a postwar memoir, the randy Hanger wrote that as a young man, "a carpenter's wife was the first object of my early affections" and that he often "risked breaking my neck in getting over the roof" of his boarding house at night to spend time with "some favorite grisette of Windsor." While studying at Eton, he confessed to his lust for "the daughter of a vendor of cabbages."
12. Jenkins, 169; Greene, *Life of Nathanael Greene*, 3: 529–30; Charles C. Jones, Jr., *Sepulture of Major General Nathanael Greene and of Brig. Gen. Count*

Casimir Pulaski (Augusta, GA: n.p., 1885), 6.
13. Greene, *Life of Nathanael Greene*, 3:531-33; Agniel, 157.
14. Greene, *Life of Nathanael Greene*, 3:531-33; Agniel, 157.
15. Greene, *Life of Nathanael Greene*, 3:531-33; Agniel, 157.
16. Jenkins, 170; Agniel, 157; Greene, *Life of Nathanael Greene*, 3:531-34.
17. Jones, *Sepulture*, 6-7; Greene, *Life of Nathanael Greene*, 3:534-35. Jones wrote that Greene's funeral was on "the 20th of April, 1786," an obvious mistake since Greene was very much alive during that spring's planting season at Mulberry Grove.
18. Jenkins, 171; Greene, *Life of Nathanael Greene*, 3:536-37. Knox was Washington's chief of artillery in the Revolution, later serving as the nation's first secretary of war. In 1793, Eli Whitney, a tutor for the Greene children, invented the cotton gin at Mulberry Grove, monumentally improving and transforming cotton production in the South and elsewhere.
19. Jones, *Sepulture*, 7, 10; Agniel, 158. Agniel wrote that the monument was built in 1820, which is erroneous.
20. Auguste Levasseur, *Lafayette in America in 1824 and 1825*, 2 vols. (New York: Clayton & Van Norden, 1829), 2:56, 58, 59-62. Capitalization of "GREENE" is from the source.
21. Ibid.
22. Jones, *Sepulture*, 10.

Chapter 20

1. Fitzpatrick, *Diaries*, 4: 183; Kirkland and Kennedy, *Historic Camden: Part One*, 306-07; Henderson, 260. Kershaw died seven months after Washington's visit. Columbia became the state capital in 1786.
2. Johnston, *George Washington*, 77; Fitzpatrick, *Diaries*, 4:183-84. Johnston stated that Washington's remarks about DeKalb and his tours of the Camden battlegrounds were on May 25, which is erroneous. She also wrote that the battle of Camden was in 1782, also inaccurate.
3. Thomas J. Kirkland and Robert M. Kennedy, *Historic Camden: Part Two—Nineteenth Century* (Columbia: The State Company, 1926), 64-65.

These men composed the "committee of arrangements."
4. *Southern Chronicle and Camden* (SC) *Literary and Political Register*, March 5, 1825, published in Kirkland and Kennedy, *Historic Camden: Part Two*, 64-65; "Hobkirk's Hill District" brochure, published by www.ClassicallyCarolina.com.
5. Levasseur, *Lafayette in America*, 2:40-41; *Southern* (Camden, SC) *Chronicle*, March 19, 1825; Kirkland and Kennedy, *Historic Camden: Part 2*, 66-69. The Cross Creek settlement in North Carolina was renamed Fayetteville in the late 1700s in honor of Lafayette. Others in Salmond's group included Brigadier Gen. James Blair, military officer of the day, and Major John Cantey, chief marshal, assisted by William McWillie, Esquire.
6. Levasseur, *Lafayette in America*, 2:41; Kirkland and Kennedy, *Historic Camden: Part Two*, 69-70, 72. From a prominent family, James Chesnut later rose to fame as a Confederate general and husband of Mary Chesnut, whose wartime diary is a staple of Civil War literature.
7. Www.s.c.grandlodgeofafm.org, November 11, 2016; Levasseur, *Lafayette in America*, 2:41.
8. Camden (SC) *Southern Chronicle*, March 26, 1825; Kapp, *The Life of John Kalb*, 250-52; Levasseur, *Lafayette in America*, 2:41-42.
9. Kapp, *The Life of John Kalb*, 251-52; Levasseur, *Lafayette in America*, 2:42; Leiding, 173.
10. Www.s.c.grandlodgeofafm.org, November 7, 2016; Kirkland and Kennedy, *Historic Camden: Part Two*, 81-82.

Chapter 21

1. Ellet, 3:276-77.
2. *Ibid.*, 3:277-78, 280-81, 284. Archibald Gill served to the end of the conflict with South Carolina state troops.
3. *Ibid.*, 3: 284-85, 288. The couple lived at Big Spring, SC, for years after the war, before moving to Perry County, AL, in 1820.

Chapter 22

1. Gregory J.W. Urwin, "When Freedom Wore a Red Coat," *Army History*, Summer 2008, 13-14.

2. Ibid.
3. Tarleton, *History*, 91–92.
4. George H. Moore, *Historical Notes on the Employment of Negroes in the American Army of the Revolution* (New York: Charles T. Evans, 1862), 16; Agniel, 64.
5. Gibbes, *1776 and 1782*, 25, Sumter to Marion, February 20, 1781.
6. Stedman, 2:217.
7. Agniel, 157.
8. Moore, *Historical Notes*, 15.

Chapter 23

1. Scharf, 366. The proposed 1780 inscription by the legislators stated that DeKalb was "in the 48th year of his age." This is erroneous, since the general was 59 when he fell at Camden.
2. Edwin J. Scott, *Random Recollections of a Long Life: 1806 to 1876* (Columbia, SC: Charles A. Calvo, 1884), 18; Kirkland and Kennedy, *Historic Camden: Part Two*, 76.
3. Kirkland and Kennedy, *Historic Camden: Part Two*, 76–79; Camden District Revolutionary War Trails brochure; Landers, 57.
4. Kirkland and Kennedy, *Historic Camden: Part Two*, 76–79; Camden District Revolutionary War Trails brochure; Landers, 57.
5. Kirkland and Kennedy, *Historic Camden: Part Two*, 79–80; Derek Smith, *Sumter After the First Shots* (Mechanicsburg, PA: Stackpole Books, 2015), 301–02.

Chapter 24

1. *Jewish Daily Bulletin*, July 28, 1926; Bennett Muraskin, "Benjamin Nones: Profile of a Jewish Jeffersonian," *American Jewish History*, vol. 83, no. 3 (September 1885), 381; Leon Huhner, *The Jews of South Carolina from the Earliest Settlement to the End of the American Revolution* (Baltimore: Lord Baltimore Press, 1904), 56.
2. Nones to Jefferson, March 18, 1801 in Founders Online; Barnett A. Elzas, *The Jews of South Carolina* (Philadelphia: J.B. Lippincott, 1905), 96.
3. Nones to Jefferson, March 18, 1801 in Founders Online; Barnett A. Elzas, *The Jews of South Carolina* (Philadelphia: J.B. Lippincott, 1905), 96.
4. Henry S. Morais, *The Jews of Philadelphia—Their History from the Earliest Settlements to the Present Time* (Philadelphia: The Levytype Company, 1894), 457; *Jewish Daily Bulletin*, July 28, 1926.
5. *Baltimore Sun*, 1886, no further date available; Kirkland and Kennedy, *Historic Camden: Part Two*, 77–78; Elzas, 97.
6. Muraskin, 381; Morais, 457.

Appendix

1. *Camden Journal and Southern Whig*, January 24, 1835; Kirkland and Kennedy, *Historic Camden: Part Two*, 169–70.
2. Landers, 57.
3. Camilla Jess, "Where the Spirits Still Walk," *South Carolina Smiles—2008*, South Carolina Department of Parks, Recreation and Tourism, www.Discover SouthCarolina.com.
4. Edward Boltwood Hull, *Guide-Book of Camden* (Camden, SC: Author, 1918), 33–34.
5. Hull, 32–33; "Agnes of Glasgow" marker placed by the Cemetery Association of Camden.
6. *Lancaster* (SC) *Ledger*, October 12, 1853.
7. Tarleton, *History*, 109–10.
8. Hanger, *Life, Adventures*, 2:410–11.
9. John Knight, "Four Battle Flags of the Revolution: Captured by Lt.-Col. Banastre Tarleton," *Journal of the American Revolution*, August 27, 2019. www.allthings liberty.com; Antiques and the Arts Weekly—"Four Flags Recaptured For $17.4 Million at Sotheby's," June 27, 2006.

Bibliography

Agniel, Lucian. *Rebels Victorious: The American Revolution in the South 1780–1781.* New York: Ballantine, 1975.
Albertson, Catherine S. *In Ancient Albemarle.* North Carolina Society, Daughters of the Revolution. Raleigh: Commercial Printing Co., 1914.
"The American Revolution in North Carolina—Isaac Gregory." www.carolana.com.
Annual Biography and Obituary for the Year 1825, vol. 9. London: Longman, Rees, Orme, Brown and Green, 1825.
Annual Biography and Obituary for the Year 1828, vol. 12. London: Longman, Rees, Orme, Brown and Green, 1828.
Annual Biography and Obituary for the Year 1834, vol. 18. London: Longman, Rees, Orme, Brown and Green, 1834.
Annual Register, or a View of the History, Politics, and Literature, for the Year 1780. London: J. Dodsley, 1781.
Annual Register, or a View of the History, Politics, and Literature, for the Year 1781. London: J. Dodsley, 1782.
Arnold, Benedict. *The Present State of the American Rebel Army, Navy, and Finances, Transmitted to the British Government in October, 1780.* Edited by Paul L. Ford. Brooklyn, NY: Historical Printing Club, 1891.
Ashe, Samuel A., and Edward McCrady Jr. *Cyclopedia of Eminent and Representative Men of the Carolinas of the Nineteenth Century.* 2 vols. Madison, WI: Brant & Fuller, 1892.
Aspinall, Arthur, ed. *The Correspondence of George, Prince of Wales.* New York: Oxford University Press, 1967.
Bailey, James D. *Some Heroes of the American Revolution.* Spartanburg, SC: Band & White, 1924.
Balch, Thomas, ed. *Papers Relating Chiefly to the Maryland Line During the Revolution.* Philadelphia: T.K. and P.G. Collins, Printers, 1857.
Barbour, R.L. *South Carolina's Revolutionary War Battlefields: A Tour Guide.* Gretna, LA: Pelican Publishing Co., 2002.
Barnes, Timothy M. "Loyalist Newspapers of the American Revolution, 1763–1783: A Bibliography." *Proceedings of the American Antiquarian Society*, vol. 83, pt. 2 (1973): 217–40.
Bass, Robert D. "Banastre Tarleton—Butcher or Hero?" *Sandlapper*, vol. 6, no. 3 (March 1973).
———. *Gamecock: The Life and Campaigns of General Thomas Sumter.* New York: Holt, Rinehart and Winston, 1961.
———. *Swamp Fox: The Life and Campaigns of General Francis Marion.* Orangeburg, SC: Sandlapper Publishing Co., 1974.
Beard, R.E., Jr. "Camden: Old in Years, Young in Spirit." *Sandlapper*, vol. 1, no. 1 (January 1968).
Bell, Landon C. *The Old Free State: A Contribution to the History of Lunenburg County and Southside Virginia.* 2 vols. Richmond: William Byrd Press, 1927.
Blake, John L. *The American Revolution, Including also the Beauties of American History.* New York: Derby & Jackson, 1856.

Blanco, R.L. "Medicine in the Continental Army, 1775–1781." *Bulletin of the New York Academy of Medicine*, vol. 57, no. 8, October 1981.
Bostick, Doug. "The Battle of Stono Ferry." American Battlefield Trust, 2021. http://www.battlefield.org.
Boyle, Esmerelda. *Biographical Sketches of Distinguished Marylanders*. Baltimore: Kelly, Piet & Company, 1877.
Braisted, Todd, ed. *Diary of Henry Nase: King's American Regiment*. Nase Family Papers. Archives Division, New Brunswick Museum, Canada, n.d.
Briggs, Stephanie J. "The 71st Fraser's Highlanders." n.p. 2014.
Bunce, Oliver B., ed. *The Romance of the Revolution*. New York: Bunce & Brother, 1852.
Burgess, James M. *Chronicles of St. Mark's Parish, Santee Circuit and Williamsburg Township, South Carolina: 1731–1885*. Columbia, SC: Charles A. Calvo Jr., 1888.
Caldwell, Charles. *Memoirs of the Life and Campaigns of the Hon. Nathaniel Greene*. Philadelphia: Robert Desilver, 1819.
Calendar of the General Otho Holland Williams Papers. Baltimore: Maryland Historical Society, November 1940.
Calver, William L. and Reginald P. Bolton. *History Written with Pick and Shovel*. New York: New York Historical Society, 1950.
The Camden District: Revolutionary War Trails. www.historic-camden.net.
Camden Timeline. Cityofcamden.org.
Cann, Marvin. "Prelude to War: The First Battle of Ninety Six: November 19–21, 1775." *South Carolina Historical Quarterly*, October 1975.
Cannon, Richard. *Historical Record of the Seventeenth Regiment of Light Dragoons: Lancers*. London: John W. Parker, 1841.
———. *Historical Record of the Twenty-Third Regiment, or the Royal Welsh Fusiliers*. London: Parker, Furnivall & Parker, 1850.
Capt. William Beatty's Journal, Maryland Line: 1776–1781. http://archive.org/stream/capt.wm.beattysjournalmarylandline1776-1781.
Carney, Richard. *Catawba Indian Nation*. Charlottemuseum.org.
Carrington, Henry B. *Battles of the American Revolution*. New York: A.S. Barnes, 1876.
Caruthers, E.W. *Interesting Revolutionary Incidents: Second Series*. Philadelphia: Hayes & Zeil, 1856.
Chamberlain, Mellen. *Memorial of Captain Charles Cochrane, A British Officer in the Revolutionary War*. Cambridge, MA: University Press, 1891.
Clark, Walter, ed. *The State Records of North Carolina*, 30 vols., Nash Brothers, Book and Job Printers, Goldsboro, NC: 1907. [The records were published from approximately 1886 to 1907 by several North Carolina publishers. Volumes 15 and 17, cited in this book, were printed by Nash in 1898 and 1899 respectively. Volume 14, also cited, was published in then Winston, NC, by "M.I. & J.C. Stewart, Printers to the State" in 1896. Clarke edited all three volumes. Other editors of the records over the years were Stephen B. Weeks and William L. Saunders].
Clinton, Henry. *Narrative of the Campaign in 1781 in North America*. Philadelphia: John Campbell, 1865.
———. *Observations on Earl Cornwallis' Answer*. Philadelphia: John Campbell, 1866.
———. *Observations on Mr. Stedman's History of the American War*. London: J. Debrett, 1794.
Coakley, Robert W., and Stetson Conn. *The War of the American Revolution: Narrative, Chronology, and Bibliography*. Washington, D.C.: U.S. Army Center of Military History, 1975.
Coffin, Henry E. *A Memoir of General John Coffin*. Reading, UK: E. Blackwell and Son, 1860.
Commager, Henry Steele, and Richard B. Morris, eds. *The Spirit of Seventy-Six*. New York: Harper & Row, Publishers, 1975.
Cornwallis, Earl. *An Answer to that part of the Narrative of Lieutenant-General Sir Henry Clinton Which relates to the Conduct of Lieutenant-General Earl Cornwallis, During the Campaign in North America, in the Year 1781*. London: J. Debrett, 1783.

Bibliography 275

Dabney, William M., and Marion Dargan. *William Henry Drayton & the American Revolution*. Albuquerque: University of New Mexico Press, 1962.
Davie, William R. *The Revolutionary War Sketches of William R. Davie*. Raleigh: Division of Archives and History, North Carolina Department of Cultural Resources, 1976.
Dawson, Henry B. *Battles of the United States by Sea and Land*. 2 vols. New York: Johnson, Fry and Company, 1858.
DeSaussure, Wilmot G. *An Account of the Siege of Charleston, South Carolina in 1780*. Charleston, SC: The News and Courier Book Presses, 1885.
_____. *The Names as Far as Can Be Ascertained of the Officers Who Served in the South Carolina Regiments*. Published By Order of the (SC) General Assembly, 1886.
Dole, Esther Mohr. *Maryland during the American Revolution*. Baltimore: Waverly Press, 1941.
Dudley, Guilford. "A Sketch of the Military Service Performed by Guilford Dudley, Then of the Town of Halifax, North Carolina, During the Revolutionary War." *The Southern Literary Messenger*, vol. 11 (1845). New York: AMS Press, 1965.
Duncan, Francis. *History of the Royal Regiment of Artillery*. 2 vols. London: John Murray, 1782.
Ellet, Elizabeth F. *The Women of the American Revolution*, 3 vols. New York: Charles Scribner's, 1856.
Elzas, Barnett A. *The Jews of South Carolina*. Philadelphia: J.B. Lippincott, 1905.
Fanning, David. *The Narrative of Colonel David Fanning: A Tory in the Revolutionary War with Great Britain*. New York: Alvord, 1865.
Fisher, Sydney G. *The Struggle for American Independence*, 2 vols. Philadelphia: J.B. Lippincott, 1908.
_____. *The True History of the American Revolution*. Philadelphia: J.B. Lippincott 1902.
Fitzpatrick, John C., ed. *The Diaries of George Washington: 1748-1799*, 4 vols. Boston: Houghton Mifflin, 1925.
Foote, William Henry. *Sketches of North Carolina, Historical and Biographical*. New York: Robert Carter, 1846.
Fries, Adelaide L., ed. *Records of the Moravians in North Carolina*, 11 vols. Raleigh: Edwards & Broughton, 1930.
Frost, John. *The Book of the Army: Comprising a General Military History of the United States*. New York: D. Appleton, 1846.
Garden, Alexander. *Anecdotes of the American Revolution*. 3 vols. Brooklyn, NY: The Union Press, 1865.
_____. *Anecdotes of the American Revolution: Second Series*. Charleston, SC: A.E. Miller, 1828.
_____. *Anecdotes of the Revolutionary War in America*. Charleston, SC: A.E. Miller, 1822.
Gee, Wilson. *The Gist Family of South Carolina and its Maryland Antecedents*. Charlottesville, VA: Jarman's Inc., 1934.
Gervais, John Lewis. Letter to Henry Laurens, May 13, 1780., Henry Laurens Papers, USC Digital Collections, South Caroliniana Library, University of South Carolina https://digital.library.sc.edu/.
Gibbes, R.W. *Documentary History of the American Revolution Consisting of Letters and Papers Relating to the Contest for Liberty, Chiefly in South Carolina in 1781 and 1782*. Columbia, SC: Banner Steam-Power Press, 1853.
_____. *Documentary History of the American Revolution Consisting of Letters and Papers Relating to the Contest for Liberty, Chiefly in South Carolina in 1776 and 1782*. New York: D. Appleton, 1857.
Gordon, William. *The History of the Rise, Progress, and Establishment, of the Independence of the United States of America*. 4 vols. London: Dilly and Buckland, 1788.
Gray, Robert. "Col. Robert Gray's Observations of the War in Carolina." *South Carolina Historical and Genealogy Magazine*, vol. 11, no. 3 (July 1910): 139-59.
Green, Edwin L. *The Indians of South Carolina*. Columbia, SC: The University Press, 1920.
Greene, Francis V. *General Greene*. New York: D. Appleton, 1897.
Greene, George Washington. *The German Element in the War of American Independence*. Cambridge, MA: Riverside Press, 1876.

———. *The Life of Nathanael Greene, Major-General in the Army of the Revolution*, 3 vols. New York: Hurd and Houghton, 1871.
Gregg, Alexander. *History of the Old Cheraws*. New York: Richardson and Co., 1867.
Griswold, Rufus Wilmot, William Gilmore Simms and Edward Duncan Ingraham. *Washington and the Generals of the American Revolution*. Philadelphia: J.B. Lippincott, 1856.
Groves, Percy. *Historical Records of the 7th or Royal Regiment of Fusiliers: 1685–1903*. Guernsey, UK: Frederick B. Guerin, 1903.
Hanger, George. *An Address to the Army; In Reply to Strictures by Roderick McKenzie, on Tarleton's History of the Campaigns of 1780 and 1781*. London: James Ridgway, 1789.
———. *The Life, Adventures and Opinions of Col. George Hanger*. 2 vols. London: Johnson & Stryker, 1801
Hartley, Cecil B. *Heroes and Patriots of the South; Comprising Lives of General Francis Marion, General William Moultrie, General Andrew Pickens and Governor John Rutledge*. Philadelphia: G.G. Evans, 1860.
Heitman, F.B. *Historical Register of Officers of the Continental Army during the War of the Revolution: April, 1775, to December, 1783*. Washington, D.C.: n.p., 1893.
Henderson, Archibald. *Washington's Southern Tour*. Boston: Houghton Mifflin, 1923.
Hilborn, Nat and Sam. *Battleground of Freedom—South Carolina in the Revolution*. Columbia, SC: Sandlapper Press, 1970.
Historical Statements Concerning the Battle of Kings Mountain and the Battle of Cowpens. Washington, D.C.: U.S. Government Printing Office, 1828.
Historic Camden Foundation. "Colonial Pottery at Historic Camden: Revolution and Trade." March 2021. HistoricCamden.org.
Historic Camden Foundation. "Sickness & Survival: Kershaw House Gains New Medical Exhibit." July 2021. HistoricCamden.org.
Hobkirk's Hill District brochure. ClassicallyCarolina.com.
Horry, Peter, and Mason L. Weems. *The Life of General Francis Marion, a Celebrated Partisan Officer in the Revolutionary War*. Philadelphia: Joseph Allen, 1848.
Hosack, David. *A Biographical Memoir of Hugh Williamson, M.D., LL.D*. New York: C.S. Van Winkle, 1820.
Howe, George. *History of the Presbyterian Church in South Carolina*, 2 vols. Columbia, SC: Duffie & Chapman, 1870.
Huhner, Leon. *The Jews of South Carolina from the Earliest Settlement to the End of the American Revolution*. Baltimore: Lord Baltimore Press, 1904.
Hull, Edward Boltwood. *Guide-Book of Camden*. Camden, SC: Author, 1918.
Isaacs, Barry. "Lt.-Col. Elijah Isaacs." n.p., 2017.
James, William Dobein. *A Sketch of the Life of Brig. Gen. Francis Marion and a History of His Brigade*. Marietta, GA: Continental Book Co., 1948.
Jenkins, John S. *The Lives of Patriots and Heroes Distinguished in the Battle for American Freedom*. Auburn, NY: J.C. Derby & Co., 1847.
Jess, Camilla. "Where the Spirits Still Walk." *South Carolina Smiles—2008*. South Carolina Department of Parks, Recreation and Tourism. www.DiscoverSouthCarolina.com
Johnson, Joseph. *Traditions and Reminiscences Chiefly of the American Revolution in the South*. Charleston, SC: Walker & James, 1851.
Johnson, William. *Sketches of the Life and Correspondence of Nathaniel Greene: Major General of the Armies of the United States in the War of the Revolution*. 2 vols. Charleston, SC: A.E. Miller, 1822.
Johnston, Elizabeth Bryant. *George Washington Day by Day*. New York: Baker & Taylor, 1895.
Johnston, Elizabeth L. *Recollections of a Georgia Loyalist*. New York: The Bankside Press, 1901.
Jones, E. Alfred, ed. "The Journal of Alexander Chesney: A South Carolina Loyalist in the Revolution and After." *The Ohio State University Bulletin*, vol. 26, no. 4 (October 1921).
Jones, Charles C., Jr. *Sepulture of Major General Nathanael Greene and of Brig. Gen. Count Casimir Pulaski*. Augusta, GA: n.p., 1885.
Jones, Thomas. *History of New York During the Revolutionary War*. 2 vols. New York: Trow's Printing & Bookbinding Co., 1879.

Kapp, Friedrich. *The Life of John Kalb, Major-General in the Revolutionary Army.* New York: Henry Holt and Co., 1884.
Kershaw, Peter G.D. *A Kershaw Family, 1670–1970.* Port Charlotte, FL: n.p., 1974.
Kirkland, Thomas J., and Robert M. Kennedy. *Historic Camden—Part One—Colonial and Revolutionary.* Columbia, SC: The State Company, 1905
_____. *Historic Camden—Part Two—Nineteenth Century.* Columbia, SC: The State Company, 1926.
Knight, John. "Four Battle Flags of the Revolution: Captured by Lt.-Col. Banastre Tarleton." *Journal of the American Revolution*, August 27, 2019. Allthingsliberty.com.
Krawczynski, Keith. *William Henry Drayton: South Carolina Revolutionary Patriot.* Baton Rouge: Louisiana State University Press, 2001.
Lamb, Roger. *An Original and Authentic Journal of Occurrences During the Late American War.* Dublin: Wilkinson & Courtney, 1809.
Lambert, Robert S. *South Carolina Loyalists in the American Revolution.* Columbia: University of South Carolina Press, 1987.
Landers, H.L. *The Battle of Camden, South Carolina, August 16, 1780.* Washington, D.C.: U.S. Government Printing Office, 1929.
Landrum, J.B.O. *Colonial and Revolutionary History of Upper South Carolina.* Greenville, SC: Shannon & Co., Printers and Binders, 1897.
Lee, Albert. *History of the Thirty-third Foot.* Norwich, UK: Jarrold & Sons, Ltd., 1922.
Lee, Henry. *Memoirs of the War in the Southern Department of the United States.* London: Sampson Low, Son, & Marston, 1869.
Lee, Henry, Jr. *The Campaign of 1781 in the Carolinas: With Remarks Historical and Critical on Johnson's Life of Greene.* Chicago: Quadrangle Books, 1962.
Leiding, Harriette Kershaw. *Historic Houses of South Carolina.* Philadelphia: J.B. Lippincott, 1921.
Levasseur, Auguste. *Lafayette in America in 1824 and 1825.* 2 vols. New York: Clayton & Van Norden, Printers, 1829.
Lewis, Kenneth E. "Camden: A Frontier Town in Eighteenth Century South Carolina." *University of South Carolina Research Manuscript Series* (October 1976).
_____. *The Carolina Backcountry Venture: Tradition, Capital, and Circumstance in the Development of Camden and the Wateree Valley, 1740–1810.* Columbia, SC: University of South Carolina Press, 2017.
_____. *A Functional Study of the Kershaw House Site in Camden, South Carolina.* Columbia, SC: Institute of Archaeology and Anthropology, University of South Carolina, 1977.
Long, Minnie R.H. *General Griffith Rutherford and Allied Families.* Milwaukee: Wisconsin Cuneo Press, 1942.
Lossing, Benson J., ed. *The American Historical Record, and Repertory of Notes and Queries*, 3 vols., Philadelphia: Samuel P. Town, Publisher, 1873.
_____. *Lives of Celebrated Americans: Comprising Biographies of Three Hundred and Forty Eminent Persons.* Hartford, CT: Thomas Belknap, 1869.
_____. *The Pictorial Field-Book of the Revolution.* 2 vols. New York: Harper & Bros., 1852.
Lumpkin, Henry. *From Savannah to Yorktown: The American Revolution in the South.* Columbia, SC: University of South Carolina Press, 1981.
McAllister, J.T. *Virginia Militia in the Revolutionary War.* Hot Springs, VA: McAllister Publishing Co., 1913.
McCandless, Peter. "Revolutionary Fever: Disease and War in the Lower South, 1776–1783." *Transactions of the American Clinical and Climatological Association*, vol. 118 (2007): 225–49.
McCrady, Edward. *The History of South Carolina in the Revolution: 1775–1780.* New York: Macmillan, 1901.
_____. *The History of South Carolina in the Revolution: 1780–1783.* New York: Macmillan, 1902.
McKenzie, Roderick. *Strictures on Lt. Col. Tarleton's History of the Campaigns of 1780 and 1781 in the Southern Provinces of North America.* London: "Printed for the Author," 1787.

McRee, Griffith J. *Life and Correspondence of James Iredell*. 2 vols. New York: D. Appleton, 1857.
Meriwether, Robert L. *The Expansion of South Carolina: 1729–1765*. Kingsport, TN: Southern Publishers, Inc., 1940.
Monk, Will. "The Myth of 'Granny Gates.'" *Journal of the American Revolution*, October 2, 2014. Allthingsliberty.com.
Moore, Frank. *Diary of the American Revolution from Newspapers and Original Documents*, 2 vols. New York: Charles Scribner's, 1859.
Moore, George H. *Historical Notes on the Employment of Negroes in the American Army of the Revolution*. New York: Charles T. Evans, 1862.
Morais, Henry S. *The Jews of Philadelphia: Their History from the Earliest Settlements to the Present Time*. Philadelphia: The Levytype Co., 1894.
Muraskin, Bennett. "Benjamin Nones: Profile of a Jewish Jeffersonian." *American Jewish History*, vol. 83, no. 3 (September 1885): 381–85.
Neal, Jim, and Bill Segars. *Churches in South Carolina Burned During the American Revolution: A Pictorial Guide*. Columbia, SC: n.p., 2022.
Neal, John Washington. "Life and Public Services of Hugh Williamson." *Historical Papers*, Series 13, Trinity College Historical Society. Durham, NC: The Seeman Printery, 1919.
Nelson, Paul David. *Francis Rawdon-Hastings, Marquess of Hastings: Soldier, Peer of the Realm, Governor-General of India*. Madison, NJ: Fairleigh Dickinson University Press, 2005.
O'Brien, Michael J. *A Hidden Phase of American History: Ireland's Part in America's Struggle for Liberty*. New York: Dodd, Mead, 1919.
O'Neal, John B. *Biographical Sketches of the Bench and Bar of South Carolina*. 2 vols. Charleston, SC: S.G. Courtnay & Co., 1859.
Offutt, Thiemann Scott, et al. *Patriotic Maryland and the Maryland Society Sons of the American Revolution*. Baltimore: Maryland Society Sons of the American Revolution, 1930.
Oliphant, Mary C. Simms. *The New Simms History of South Carolina*. Columbia, SC: The State Co., 1940.
Palmer, William P., ed. *Calendar of Virginia State Papers and Other Manuscripts: 1652–1781*. Vol. 1. Richmond: R.F. Walker, Superintendent of Public Printing, 1875.
Paltsits, Victor H., ed. *Original Papers Relating to the Siege of Charleston, 1780*. Charleston, SC: Walker, Evans & Cogswell Co., 1898.
Parton, James. *Life of Andrew Jackson*, 3 vols. New York: Mason Bros., 1860.
Patterson, Samuel W. *Horatio Gates: Defender of American Liberties*. New York: Columbia University Press, 1941.
Peterson, Charles J. *The Military Heroes of the Revolution*. Philadelphia: William A. Leary, 1848.
Piecuch, James. *The Battle of Camden: A Documentary History*. Charleston, SC: The History Press, 2006.
———. "Massacre or Myth? Banastre Tarleton at the Waxhaws, May 29, 1780." *Southern Campaigns of the American Revolution*, vol. 1, no. 2 (October 2004): 4–10.
Pinckney, Charles Cotesworth. *Life of General Thomas Pinckney*. Boston: Houghton Mifflin, 1895.
Pinckney, Thomas. "Thomas Pinckney Letter to William Johnson." *Historical Magazine*, vol. 10, no. 8 (August 1886): 244–53.
Player, Lance. "The Colonial Catawba of the Carolinas." Historic Camden Foundation, August 2020.
———. "Ely Kershaw: A Patriot Remembered." Historic Camden Foundation, November 2021.
Porterfield, Frank B. *The Porterfields*. Roanoke: Southeastern Press, 1947.
Powell, William S., ed. *Dictionary of North Carolina Biography*. 6 vols. Chapel Hill: University of North Carolina Press, 2000.
Pugh, Jesse Forbes. *Three Hundred Years along the Pasquotank: A Biographical History of Camden County*. Durham, NC: Seeman Printery, 1957.

Ramsay, David. *History of the American Revolution*, 2 vols. London: J. Johnson and J. Stockdale, 1789.

———. *The History of the Revolution of South Carolina: From a British Province to an Independent State*. 2 vols. Trenton, NJ: Isaac Collins, 1785.

———. *Ramsay's History of South Carolina*. Charleston, SC: Walker, Evans & Co., 1858.

Rauch, Steven J. "Southern (Dis) Comfort: British Phase IV Operations in South Carolina and Georgia, May–September 1780." *The U.S. Army and Irregular Warfare, 1775–2007: Selected Papers from the 2007 Conference of Army Historians*. Ed. Richard G. Davis. Washington, D.C.: US Army Center of Military History, 2007, pp. 33–58.

Ross, Charles, ed. *Correspondence of Charles, First Marquis Cornwallis*. 3 vols. London: John Murray, 1859.

Royall, Anne. *Mrs. Royall's Southern Tour or Second Series of the Black Book*. 3 vols. Washington, D.C.: n.p., 1831.

Rubin, Ben. "The Rhetoric of Revenge: Atrocity and Identity in the Revolutionary Carolinas." *Journal of Backcountry Studies*, vol. 5, no. 2 (2010): 1–46.

Sabine, Lorenzo. *The American Loyalists, or Biographical Sketches of Adherents to the British Crown in the War of the Revolution*. Boston: Charles C. Little and James Brown, 1847.

Salley, A.S. "President Washington's Tour through South Carolina in 1791." *Bulletins of the Historical Commission of South Carolina*, no. 12 (1932).

Scharf, John Thomas. *History of Maryland from the Earliest Period to the Present Day: 1765–1812*. 3 vols. Baltimore: John B. Piet, 1879.

———. *History of Western Maryland*. 2 vols. Philadelphia: Louis H. Everts, 1882.

Scheer, George F., and Hugh F. Rankin. *Rebels & Redcoats*. New York: World Publishing Co., 1957.

Schenck, David. *North Carolina—1780–81, Being a History of the Invasion of the Carolinas*. Raleigh: Edwards & Broughton, 1889.

Scott, Edwin J. *Random Recollections of a Long Life: 1806 to 1876*. Columbia, SC: Charles A. Calvo, 1884.

Sellers, Leila. *Charleston Business on the Eve of the American Revolution*. Chapel Hill: University of North Carolina Press, 1934.

Seton-Karr, Walter Scott. *Rulers of India: The Marquess Cornwallis*. Oxford: Clarendon Press, 1890.

Seymour, William. *A Journal of the Southern Expedition, 1780–1781*. Wilmington, DE: The Historical Society of Delaware, 1896.

Shaw, John Robert. *A Narrative of the Life & Travels of John Robert Shaw, the Well-Digger, Now Resident in Lexington, Kentucky*. Lexington, KY: Daniel Bradford, 1807.

Simms, William Gilmore. *The History of South Carolina, From Its First European Discovery to Its Erection into a Republic*. Charleston, SC: S. Babcock & Co., 1840.

———. *The Life of Francis Marion*. New York: Henry G. Langley, 1844.

———. *The Life of Nathanael Greene, Major General in the Army of the Revolution*. New York: Derby & Jackson, 1856.

———. *South Carolina in the Revolutionary War: Being a Reply to Certain Misrepresentations and Mistakes of Recent Writers, in Relation to the Course and Conduct of this State*. Charleston, SC: Walker and James, 1853.

Smith, Derek. "Dawn of Hell: British Steel at Camden." 1988. Unpublished ms.

———. "Gideon's Sword: Kings Mountain." *Army*, vol. 39, no. 8 (August 1989): 52–58.

———. "Potter's Raid: 'Our Errand through the State.'" *North & South*, vol. 10, no. 2 (July 2007).

———. *Sumter after the First Shots*. Mechanicsburg, PA: Stackpole Books, 2015.

Smith, J. Spear. *Memoir of the Baron De Kalb*. Baltimore: John D. Toy, 1858.

Smith, Steven D., James B. Legg, and Tamara S. Wilson. *The Archaeology of the Camden Battlefield: History, Private Collections, and Field Investigations*. Columbia, SC: South Carolina Institute of Archaeology and Anthropology, 2009.

Smith, Steven D., James B. Legg, Tamara S. Wilson, and Jonathan Leader. *"Obstinate and Strong": The History and Archaeology of the Siege of Fort Motte*. Columbia, SC: South Carolina Institute of Archaeology and Anthropology, 2007.

Snell, Charles W. *National Register of Historic Places Inventory—Nomination Form—Gen. Gates House, Traveller's Rest.* Washington, D.C.: National Park Service, U.S. Department of the Interior, 1972.

Snowden, Yates, ed. *History of South Carolina.* 5 vols. Chicago: Lewis Publishing Co., 1920.

Sobol, Donald J. *Lock, Stock and Barrel.* Philadelphia: Westminster Press, 1965.

Southern Campaigns American Revolution Pension Statements and Rosters. http://revwarapps.org.

Sparks, Jared, *Correspondence of the American Revolution; Being Letters of Eminent Men to George Washington.* 3 vols. Boston: Little, Brown, 1853.

Stedman, Charles. *The History of the Origin, Progress, and Termination of the American War.* 2 vols. London: "Printed for the Author," 1794.

Stevens, John Austin. "The Southern Campaign." *Magazine of American History*, 5, no. 4 (October 1880): 241–80.

Stockbridge, J.C. "The Surrender of Cornwallis in England." *Magazine of American History*, vol.7, no. 5 (November 1881): 321–38.

Sweet, Ethel Wylly. "Agnes of Glasgow." *Sandlapper*, 11, no. 10 (November 1978).

Tarleton, Banastre. *A History of the Campaigns of 1780 and 1781, in the Southern Provinces of North America.* London: T. Cadell, 1787.

Tarleton, C.W. *The Tarleton Family.* Concord, NH: Ira C. Evans, 1900.

Thacher, James. *Military Journal of the American Revolution.* Hartford: Hurlbut, Williams, 1862.

Thayer, Theodore, *Nathaniel Greene: Strategist of the American Revolution.* New York: Twayne, 1960.

Thomson, William. *Military Memoirs, Relating to Campaigns, Battles, and Stratagems of War, Ancient and Modern.* London: W. Marchant, 1804.

Tipping, Henry Avray. *The Story of the Royal Welsh Fusiliers.* London: George Newnes, 1915.

Toynbee, Paget, ed. *The Letters of Horace Walpole.* 16 vols. Oxford: Clarendon Press, 1904.

Turner, Joseph Brown, ed. *The Journal and Order Book of Captain Robert Kirkwood of the Delaware Regiment of the Continental Line.* Wilmington, DE: The Historical Society of Delaware, 1910.

Urwin, Gregory J.W. "When Freedom Wore a Red Coat." *Army History* (summer 2008): 6–23.

Wallace, David Duncan. *The History of South Carolina.* New York: American Historical Society, 1934.

Ward, Christopher L. *The Delaware Continentals: 1776–1783.* Wilmington, DE: The Historical Society of Delaware, 1941.

Weems, Mason L., and Peter Horry. *Life of General Francis Marion.* Philadelphia: J.B. Lippincott, 1857.

Wheeler, John H. *Historical Sketches of North Carolina, from 1584 to 1851.* Philadelphia: Lippincott, Grambo and Co., 1851.

———. *Reminiscences of North Carolina and Eminent North Carolinians.* Columbus, OH: Columbus Printing Works, 1884.

Wilkin, W.H. *Some British Soldiers in America.* London: Hugh Rees, 1914.

Williams, Samuel C. "The Battle of King's Mountain: As Seen by the British Officers." *Tennessee Historical Magazine*, vol. 7, no. 1 (April 1921): 51–66.

Winsor, Justin. *Narrative and Critical History of America*, 8 vols. Boston: Houghton Mifflin, 1888.

———. *Reader's Handbook of the American Revolution, 1761–1783.* Boston: Houghton Mifflin, 1893.

———. *The United States of North America.* 8 vols. Boston: Houghton Mifflin, 1888.

Wright, Robert K., Jr. *The Continental Army.* Washington, D.C.: U.S. Army Center of Military History, 1983.

Zeller, Bob. "How France Helped Win the American Revolution." American Battlefield Trust, www.battlefields.org.

Newspapers and Magazines

American Historical Record
Antiques and the Arts Weekly
Army
Baltimore News
Baltimore Sun
Bamberg (SC) *Herald*
Camden (SC) *Chronicle*
Camden (SC) *Journal*
Camden (SC) *Journal and Southern Whig*
Camden (SC) *Southern Chronicle*
Camden (SC) *Weekly Journal*
Charleston (SC) *Evening Gazette*
Edgefield (SC) *Advertiser*
Gazette (Philadelphia) *of the United States*
Historical Magazine
Jewish Daily Bulletin
Lancaster (SC) *Ledger*
Lancaster (SC) *News*
London Chronicle
London Gazette
Maryland (Annapolis) *Gazette*
Magazine of American History
New Jersey Journal
New York *Herald*
New York *Packet*
New York *Royal Gazette*
New York *Royal Gazette Extraordinary*
North & South
Pennsylvania Gazette
Potter's American Monthly
Rivington's Gazette
Royal (Charleston, SC) *Gazette*
Royal Gazette Extraordinary
Royal South Carolina Gazette
Ruddiman's (London) *Weekly Register*
Scots Magazine
South Carolina and American General (Charleston) *Gazette*
South Carolina Historical and Genealogy Magazine
Southern Chronicle (Camden, SC)
Southern Chronicle and Camden (SC) *Literary and Political Register*
Southern Patriot (Charleston, SC)
The (Columbia, SC) *State*
The Union (SC) *Times*
Virginian-Pilot (Norfolk, VA)
The (Winnsboro, SC) *News and Herald*
Yorkville (SC) *Enquirer*

Websites

American Battlefield Trust—www.battlefields.org.
Archives of Maryland (Biographical Series) msa.maryland.gov.
Carolana.com.
Charlottemuseum.org.
CityofCamden.org.
ClassicallyCarolina.com
Documenting the American South, University of North Carolina—www.docsouth.unc.edu.
Founders Online, National Archives—www.founders.archives.gov/documents.
Georgian Papers Online, Royal Archives, Royal Collection Trust—http://gpp.rct.uk.
HathiTrust Digital Library—www.hathitrust.org.
Historical Marker Data Base—www.hmdb.org.
Historic Camden Foundation—www.historiccamden.org.
Internetarchive.com
Journal of the American Revolution—www.allthingsliberty.com.
Losthistory.net.—www.losthistory.net/battleofcamden/index/htm.
National Park Service, Saratoga National Historical Park—www.nps.gov.people.horatio-gates and www.nps.gov/sara.
Newspapers.com
Patriot Resource—www.patriotresource.com.
Southerncampaign.org.

Index

Abbotts Creek 55
Act of Assembly 11
Adair, John 136, 137, 164, 165
Adamson, John 22
African Americans at Camden 233
African slaves 233, 234
Agnes of Glasgow 3, 243, 244
Agniel, Lucien 110, 217
Alexander, Col. 72, 129
Alexander, Dr. Isaac 118
Allman, William 116, 117
Ancrum, William 16
Ancrum, Lance and Loocock 12, 13, 18
Anderson, Maj. Archibald 99, 104, 133
Anderson, Edward H. 226
Andrews, Samuel 122
Anglo-Nepalese War 216
Annapolis, Md. 146, 236, 237, 243
Arbuthnot, Adm. Marriot 30, 32
Archbishop of Canterbury 49
Armand, Col. Charles 88, 106, 146
Armand's Legion 2, 65, 67, 68, 84, 87, 89, 106, 134
Armstrong, Maj. John, Jr. 84, 87, 90, 125, 146, 213
Arnold, Maj. Gen. Benedict 66
Ashley River 238
Atkins, Charles 156
Augusta, Ga. 19, 29, 35, 57, 168, 179, 196, 198, 222, 224

Balfour, Lt. Col. Nisbet 55, 58, 137, 138, 170, 183, 185, 197, 198
Baltimore News 237
Baltimore Sun 237, 240
Baptists in Camden 19
Bartlam, Betty 195
Bartlam, Honour 195
Bartlam, John 15, 16, 20, 195, 200
Bartlam, Mary 195, 200
Battle of Blackstock's Ford 147

Battle of Brandywine 8, 38, 69, 100, 135, 148
Battle of Brier Creek 8
Battle of Brooklyn 60
Battle of Bunker Hill 8, 56, 60, 74
Battle of Camden 5, 121, 122, 124, 125, 127, 130, 131, 133, 134, 141, 142, 146, 150, 156, 167, 176, 177, 178, 195, 200, 203, 211, 213, 215, 225, 229, 244
Battle of Cowpens 6, 158, 159, 161, 163, 177, 192, 203, 215
Battle of Eutaw Springs 6, 185, 203
Battle of Fishing Creek 5, 120, 121, 122, 125, 127, 128, 129, 130, 135, 148, 156, 159, 217, 231, 232
Battle of Germantown 38, 100, 148, 177
Battle of Guilford Courthouse 6, 166, 167, 170, 177, 186, 187, 190, 192, 213, 215, 218
Battle of Harlem Heights 8
Battle of Hobkirk Hill 6, 185, 186, 190, 191, 192, 194, 197, 200, 200, 202, 203, 203, 225, 226, 234, 246
Battle of Kettle Creek 8
Battle of Kings Mountain 5, 85, 140, 142, 148, 158, 159, 163, 179, 192, 215
Battle of Lexington and Concord 5, 7, 20, 38, 149, 214
Battle of Long Island 85
Battle of Monmouth 8, 61, 74, 86, 100, 148, 177
Battle of Montreal 8
Battle of Moore's Creek 90
Battle of Musgrove's Mill 121, 172
Battle of Oriskany 8
Battle of Princeton 38, 49, 100
Battle of Quebec 8
Battle of Saratoga 8, 27, 64, 66, 67, 68, 75, 81, 85, 111, 112, 124, 134, 158
Battle of Stono Ferry 8, 147
Battle of Trenton 8, 27, 38, 49, 100, 148
Battle of Waxhaws 5, 115, 134, 193, 195, 217, 247

284 Index

Battle of White Plains 38, 60, 100, 177
Battle of Zama 168
"Bayonets of the Revolution" 85
Beatty, Col. William 178
Beatty, Capt. William, Jr. 178, 181, 185
Beaufort, S.C. 21, 59, 244
Belton, Jonathan 22
Benbury, Thomas 154
Benson, Capt. Perry 177, 179
Berkeley County, Va. 66
Berkeley County Military District 21
Bethabara, N.C. 125
Bethania, N.C. 125
Bethesda Presbyterian Church 226, 238
Bethune, S.C. 1
Bineham, Benjamin 226
Bishop, Drury 53
Bishop, John 164
Bishop, Nicholas 164
Bishopville, S.C. 1
Black River 74
Blair, Lt. John 118
Blanding, Abram 228, 237
Blanding, William 226, 243
Blaney Drag Strip 2
Bordeaux, France 225
Boston, Mass. 8, 17, 60, 63
Boston Tea Party 17
Bowman, Jacob 23
Bowyer, Henry 43
Boykin, Dr. E.M. 237, 238
Boykin, Francis 20, 22
Boykin, John 22
Boykin, Samuel 21, 22, 23, 25, 30
"Br. Bonn" 55
Braddock, Gen. Edward 66
Bradley, James 72
Bradley, Samuel 18
Brandenburg-Bayreuth 63
Brest, France 201
Brevard, Capt. Alexander 100
Brewton, Mrs. Robert 139
Brier Creek 8
Brisbane, James 206
British East Florida 22, 25
British Legion 37, 38, 44, 50, 59, 77, 78, 86, 94, 99, 112, 116, 117, 119, 138, 158, 247
Broad River 22, 53, 143, 158, 169
Broad Street 13, 15, 113, 136, 171, 227
Brown, James 27
Brown, John 53
Brown, Judy 123
Brown, Nancy 231
Brown, Lt. Col. Thomas 58
Browne, Daniel 23, 58
Brownfield, Robert 36, 41, 42, 49

Bryan, Col. Samuel 70, 72, 86, 94
Buckingham Palace 218
Buffalo Creek 178
Buffalo Ford 64
Buford, Col. Abraham 5, 33, 34, 35, 36, 37, 38, 39, 40, 41, 42, 43, 46, 47, 55, 56, 64, 71, 78, 117, 120, 134, 193
Burgoyne, Gen. John 60, 66, 75, 81, 112, 127
Burndale 73
Burnet, Dr. A.W. 238
Butler, Brig. Gen. John 90, 96

Calcutta, India 215, 216
Camden Archives & Museum 211
Camden County, N.C. 90, 257
Camden District 5, 14, 15, 17, 2017, 208, 243
Camden District Militia Regiment 9, 22
Camden Female Academy 227
Camden Hotel 228
Camden Journal 55
Camden Journal and Southern Whig 243
Camden Orphan Society 209
Cameron, Alexander 26
"Camp Camden" 36
Campbell, Maj. Alexander 170
Campbell, Capt. Charles 38, 77, 119, 120
Campbell, Flora Muir 216
Campbell, Lt. Col. George 171
Campbell, Lt. Col. Richard 176, 178, 180, 181, 182, 185
Campbell, Lord William 20, 21, 23
Cannon, Richard 44
Cantey, James 9, 22
Cantey, John 18
Cantey, Mary 14
Cantey, Samuel 18, 21
Cantey, Sarah 16
Cantey, Zach 9, 12, 22, 173
Cantey family 209
Capt. Starke 228
Carden, Maj. John 70, 71
"Carey's Fort ("Carey's Place") 52, 80, 153
Carlisle, Lord 50
Carlos, Wash 237
Carn, Samuel 206
Carolina Cup 211
Carter, Benjamin 226, 228
Carter, Capt. 237
Carter, John C. 226
Carter, Robert 18, 19
Cary, Col. James 22, 26, 52, 80
Cary, Nathaniel 22, 52
Casity, Thomas 18

Cassels, Henry 18
Caswell, Brig. Gen. Richard 33, 34, 36, 69, 71, 75, 85, 90, 95, 99, 100, 107, 108, 109, 111, 114, 118, 121, 124, 125, 126, 129
Catawba Indians 3, 11, 12, 13, 14, 15, 21, 23, 25, 30, 207
Catawba Path 14
Catawba River 11, 135, 151, 157, 158
Catawba Town 23
Cato, Guinea 3
Cayle, John 28
Charleston Exposition 238
Charleston, S.C. (Charles Town) 2, 5, 6, 7, 8, 11, 12, 14, 15, 18, 19, 20, 21, 22, 24, 25, 26, 28, 29, 30, 32, 33, 34, 35, 38, 40, 51, 52, 53, 56, 58, 61, 62, 62, 64, 65, 68, 69, 72, 73, 74, 75, 80, 81, 82, 83, 117, 121, 125, 126, 127, 128, 129, 130, 135, 137, 138, 142, 143, 148, 151, 154, 155, 156, 160, 163, 165, 168, 170, 185, 187, 188, 190, 192, 193, 194, 197, 198, 199, 203, 203, 206, 208, 209, 215, 221, 229, 234, 238, 239, 244
Charleston Military District 21
Charlotte, N.C. 32, 39, 41, 45, 46, 69, 84, 108, 109, 117, 118, 120, 123, 124, 128, 129, 133, 137, 138, 139, 140, 141, 143, 147, 150, 152, 157, 161, 177, 185, 200, 201, 225
Charlton, Thomas 20, 22, 23, 26, 50, 115, 193, 195, 196, 202, 203
Cheraw, S.C. 12, 14, 19, 151, 152, 204, 227
Cheraw Military District 21
Cherokee Indians 11, 23, 26
Chesnut, James, Jr. 227
Chesnut, James, Sr. 14, 226
Chesnut, John 9, 12, 14, 16, 19, 20, 22, 30, 72
Chester County, S.C. 208
Chester District, S.C. 21, 135, 159, 163, 165
Chesterfield County, S.C. 21
Church Street 123
Ciples, Lewis 226, 237, 238
Claremont County, S.C. 208
Clarendon County, S.C. 208
Clarke, Ethan 219
Clay, Mrs. 114
Clermont 39, 78, 80, 83, 85, 153
Clinton, Gov. George 130
Clinton, Maj. Gen. Sir Henry 5, 7, 8, 31, 32, 34, 35, 38, 50, 53, 54, 57, 60, 61, 75, 116, 121, 127, 129, 138, 140, 146, 157, 167, 170, 191, 197, 206, 208, 215, 218, 244, 246
Clitherell, Dr. James 206
Cochrane, Maj. Charles 42, 43, 51, 56, 74
Coffin, Capt. John 171, 182, 184
Coleman, Lt. Samuel 118

Colleton County Military District 21
Collington, Ensign John W. 110
Columbia, S.C. 12, 224, 240
Committee of Continental Association 20
Concord, Mass. 5, 7, 20, 38, 149, 214
Congaree Indians 11
Congaree River 21, 76, 114, 139, 192, 196, 197, 224
"Congratulators" 205
Congress of the Province of South Carolina 19
Conyers, James 18
Cooper River 61
Cornwall, England 48
Cornwallis, Lt. Gen. Charles, Lord 2, 3, 5, 6, 31, 35, 37, 38, 39, 40, 41, 45, 46, 48, 49, 50, 52, 53, 54, 55, 56, 57, 58, 59, 60, 61, 65, 66, 70, 74, 75, 76, 77, 78 79, 81, 82, 83, 86, 87, 89, 90, 91, 94, 97, 98, 99, 101, 102, 103, 109, 110, 111, 112, 113, 115, 116, 117, 119, 120, 121, 122, 124, 126, 127, 128, 129, 130, 131, 134, 135, 137, 138, 139, 140, 141, 145, 146, 147, 148, 149, 150, 151, 152, 154, 155, 156, 157, 158, 159, 160, 161, 167, 168, 169, 170, 174, 175, 184, 185, 190, 191, 192, 196, 197, 198, 201, 204, 205, 208, 209, 211, 214, 215, 216, 217, 218, 224, 225, 232, 233, 234, 239, 243, 344, 245, 246
Cornwallis, Charles (son) 49
Cornwallis, Jemima Tulleken Jones (Lady Cornwallis) 49, 50, 75
Cornwallis, Mary 49
Cotton, Capt. Richard 110
Council of Safety (provincial) 20, 23, 24, 25
Countess of Loudoun 216
Coventry, R.I. 206
Cowper, Basil 206
Craven County Military District 21
Crawford, Robert 28
Crawford, Lt. Thomas 161
Cross Anchor, S.C. 121, 147
Cross Creek, N.C. 19, 36, 58, 69, 167
Cruger, Lt. Col. John H. 58
Cruit, Ensign John 43, 44
Culford estate 50
Cumberland Island 219
Cummings, Hettie 73, 237
Cunningham, Patrick 23
Cunningham, Robert 23
Curacao 37

Darlington, S.C. 209
Daughters of the American Revolution 210

286   Index

Davie, Maj. William R. 70, 71, 108, 109, 122, 126, 187, 196
Deas, James S. 226
Debose family 209
"Declaration of Association" 20
Declaratory Act 49
Deep River 64, 65, 67, 167, 168
DeKalb, Maj. Gen. the Baron Johan 5, 15, 62, 63, 64, 65, 67, 68, 69, 71, 89, 90, 93, 97, 98, 100, 101, 102, 103, 105, 109, 111, 113, 122, 131, 134, 146, 147, 167, 209, 210, 211, 225, 226, 227, 228, 229, 235, 237, 238, 239, 240, 243, 245
De la Motta, Capt. Jacob 239, 240
Delaware "Blue Hens" 97, 133, 169
Delaware River 60
De Leon, Abraham 226, 227, 240, 241
De Leon, Jacob 239, 240
DeLoach, Bratton 210
DeLoach family 209
De Rochambeau, Lt. Gen., the Comte 72, 204, 217
DeSaussure family 209
De Soto, Hernando 11
Deveaux, Jacob 206
Dickey, Edward 18
Dillinger, John 211
Dinkins, Sam 48
Dixon, Lt. Col. Henry, "Hal" 90, 96, 97, 101, 109, 114, 115
Dobson, Capt. Henry 104
Doby, James C. 209
Doby, John 226
Donovan, Lt. Jeremiah 87
Dorchester, S.C. 30
Dorchester Parish 25
Douglas family 209
Dounie, John 206
Downes, Major 54, 193
Doyle, Maj. John 136, 142, 161, 167, 171
Doyle, Lt. Col. Welbore E. 167
Drayton, William Henry 5, 17, 18, 22, 25
Drayton Hall plantation 75
Drew, Capt. Thomas H. 87, 88, 90
DuBose, Isaac 9, 20, 22
DuBose, Samuel Wilds 209
Du Buysson, Charles-François, Le Chevalier 1101, 102, 122, 123, 134, 239
Dudley, Guilford 88, 91, 92, 96, 97, 104, 106, 107
Dunlap, George 28
Dunn, Sylvester 18

Earl of Moira (see Francis, Lord Rawdon)
Edenton, N.C. 154
Edisto Island, S.C. 222
Edmunds, Lt. Col. Elias 85
Egan, Michael 54
Eleuthera, Bahamas 145
Eleventh Virginia Regiment (Continental) 35
Elgin, S.C. 2
Elkins's Ford 80
Elzas, Barnett A. 239, 240, 241
England, Maj. Richard 129
English, James 209
English, Joseph 54, 193
English, Joshua 18, 22
English, Robert 22, 54, 193
Enoree River 121
Eton 48
Eutawville, S.C. 203
Evans, Josiah 28

Fairfield County, S.C. 21, 208
Fayetteville, N.C. (see Cross Creek, N.C.) 19
Fearnought 118
Fenwicke, Edward 206
Ferguson, Maj. Patrick 59, 138, 140, 148
Few, Col. 72
Field (or Fields), Capt. James 205
Fifteenth Regiment of Foot 60
Fifth Maryland Continentals 133, 176, 178, 182
Fifth Regiment of Foot 60
Fifth Virginia Continentals 176
First Continental Artillery 118
First Continental Congress 17
First Grenadier Guards 48
First Maryland Brigade 90, 93, 98, 99
First Maryland Continentals 74, 101, 133, 176, 181
First Partisan Corps (see Armand's Legion) 65
First Royal North Carolina Regiment 58, 156
Flanders 216
Flat Rock Creek 22
Fletchall, Thomas 23
"Flux" sickness 139
Ford, Lt. Col. Benjamin 101, 177, 178, 180, 181, 182, 185, 200
Forks of Saluda Military District 21
Fort Duquesne 85
Fort Granby 168, 192, 196, 198
Fort Lee 38, 49, 60
Fort Motte 168, 196, 197, 198, 202, 205
Fort Moultrie 34
Fort Sullivan 25
Fort Ticonderoga 66
Fort Washington 38, 60

Index

Fort Watson 168, 172, 174, 192
"Fortune" 156
Forty-fifth Regiment of Foot 66
Fourth Virginia Continentals 176, 185
Franklin, Benjamin 27
Fraser, Maj. Thomas 172, 179, 184
Frederick County, Md. 178
Fredericksburg, Va., 224
Fredericksburg settlement 12
French and Indian War 14, 21, 27, 66, 151
French Revolutionary Wars 216
Friday's Ferry 163
Frierson, Aaron 18
From Savannah to Yorktown 110
Furman, the Rev. Richard 19

Gales, Kit 48
Gamble, John 18
Garden, Alexander 206
Garden, Dr. Alexander 151
Gaspee affair 149
Gassaway, Capt. 127
Gates, Elizabeth Phillips 66, 213
Gates, Maj. Gen. Horatio 3, 5, 6, 64, 65, 66, 67, 68, 69, 71, 72, 73, 74, 75, 76, 77, 78, 79, 80, 81, 82, 83, 84, 85, 86, 87, 88, 89, 90, 93, 94, 95, 96, 99, 100, 103, 105, 108, 109, 110, 111, 115, 116, 117, 118, 119, 120, 122, 123, 124, 125, 127, 128, 130, 131, 132, 133, 134, 139, 146, 148, 150, 151, 152, 153, 167, 169, 194, 201, 202, 206, 209, 211, 213, 214, 215, 220, 225, 231, 239, 243, 245
Gates, Mary Vallance 213
Gates, Robert 66, 150, 213
Gayle, Josiah 122
George Ancrum, Jun., and Company 18
Georgetown, S.C. 5, 36, 37, 58, 63, 143, 168, 172, 191
Germain, Lord George 50, 70, 82, 110, 117, 120, 129, 159, 167, 183, 185
Ghazipore, India 215
Gibbons, William 220
Gibbs, Zacharias 53
Gill, Archibald 231
Gill, Ellen 231
Gill, James 231
Gill, John 231
Gill, Margaret 231
Gill, Mary 3, 231, 232
Gill, Robert (father) 231
Gill, Robert (Robert's son) 231, 232
Gill, Thomas 164, 231, 232
Gist, Christopher 85
Gist, Brig. Gen. Mordecai 85, 90, 94, 96, 97, 98, 100, 101, 103, 104, 105, 123, 146
Gist, Nathaniel 85

Gist, Col. Thomas 85
Glasgow, Samuel 9
Glen, John 206
Gordon, Moses 18
Goshen, N.C. 64
Graff, Bishop 55, 125
Grahame, Lt. Gov. John 219, 221
Granby, S.C. 12
Grand Lodge of Masons of South Carolina 230
Grannys Quarter Creek 22, 78, 106
Granville County Military District 21
Gray, Robert 142
Great Falls, S.C. (see Rocky Mount) 70
Great Savannah 125
Great Wagon Road (see Great Waxhaw Road) 13, 19, 36, 152, 153
Great Waxhaw Road (see Great Wagon Road) 108, 171, 179
Green Dragoon 46, 104, 117, 119, 120, 138, 217, 247
Greene, Catherine Littlefield "Kitty" (general's wife) 149, 219, 220
Greene, George Washington (general's grandson) 219, 220
Greene, Molly Mott (general's mother) 149
Greene, Maj. Gen. Nathanael 1, 3, 6, 49, 64, 134, 135, 146, 147, 148, 149, 150, 151, 152, 159, 163, 166, 167, 168, 169, 170, 171, 172, 173, 174, 175, 176, 177, 178, 179, 180, 181, 182, 183, 184, 185, 186, 187, 188, 190, 191, 192, 194, 195, 196, 197, 199, 200, 201, 202, 203, 204, 205, 206, 207, 209, 211, 219. 220, 221, 219, 220, 221, 222, 223, 225, 246
Greene, Nathanael (general's father) 149
Greene Street 211
Gregory, Brig. Gen. Isaac 90, 96103, 109, 114, 137
Guilford Court House 133, 167
Gum Swamp 14, 79, 86, 243
Gum Swamp Creek 14
Gunby, Col. John 99, 109, 176, 177, 178, 180, 181, 182, 191, 202

Habbersham (or Habersham), Joseph 27
Haddrell's Point 61
Haldane, Lt. Henry 52, 130
Halifax, Nova Scotia 63
Hall, Harvey 1
Hall, Mildred 1
Hamilton, Alexander 132
Hamilton, Lt. Col. John 58, 86, 110, 115, 156
Hammond, Col. LeRoy 26
Hampton, Capt. Wade 73

Index

Hampton County, S.C. 21
Hanger, Maj. George 74, 94, 99, 108, 141, 151, 154, 195, 218, 246, 247
Hanging Rock 55, 70, 71, 73, 75, 78, 79, 86, 109, 116, 126, 147
Hannibal 168
Hardman, Maj. Henry 133
Harrington, William Henry 204
Harris, Maj. James 106
Harrison, Col. Charles 176
Harrow school 60
Hart, the Rev. Oliver 22
Harvey, Lt. James Leigh 110
Hastings, Lady Elizabeth 60
Hawes, Lt. Col. Samuel 176, 178, 180, 182, 183
Hayes, Dr. John M. 116
Hayne, Col. Isaac 202, 203, 215, 216
Hays, Dr. MacNamara 126
Heard, John 18
Hebrew Legion 239, 240
Hessian troops 57, 76
Hewlett, Capt. 116
High Hills of Santee 38, 48, 200, 201, 204
Hillsborough, N.C. 35, 64, 65, 69, 116, 117, 118, 122, 124, 128, 133, 134
Hinds, Patrick 206
Historic Camden books 236
Historic Camden Foundation 195, 211
A History of the Campaigns of 1780–1781 in the Southern Provinces of North America 218, 245
Hobkirk, Thomas 171
Hobkirk Hill 76, 171, 173, 174, 177, 178, 183, 184, 211, 226
Hobkirk Inn 238
Hooper (or Hopper), Thomas 54, 193
Horry, Col. Peter 245
Howard, Lt. Col. John Eager 104, 163, 177, 181, 182, 187, 211
Howe, Brig. Gen. Robert 29
Howe, Maj. Gen. William 60
Huettendorf, Germany 63
Huger, Brig. Gen. Isaac 35, 36, 171, 176, 178, 182
Hunter, Col. 72
Hunter, Henry 18
Hunter, Lt. Humphrey 102, 126
Huntington, Samuel 124

Innes, Lt. Col. Alexander 129
Irvin, Mr. 72
Isaacs, Lt. Col. Elijah 79, 120, 147
Isle of Palms, S.C. (see Long Island, S.C.) 25

Jackson, Andrew (father) 15, 47
Jackson, Andrew (son) 3, 15, 45, 46, 71, 161, 162, 173, 184, 188, 189, 198, 199
Jackson, Elizabeth Hutchinson ("Betty") 15, 45, 46, 161, 188, 198, 199
Jackson, Hugh 15, 45, 71
Jackson, Robert 15, 45, 71, 161, 162, 184, 188, 189
Jackson County, Fla. 209
Jackson's Creek 55
Jackson's Creek Loyalist militia regiment 20, 55
James Laurens & Co. 12
Jaquett, Capt. Peter 101, 133
Jasper, Sgt. William 229
Jefferson, Thomas 124, 150, 160, 226, 239, 240, 241
Jewish Daily Bulletin 240
"Jewish Legion" 240
The Jews of Philadelphia 240
The Jews of South Carolina 239, 241
John Wylly and Company 18
John's Island 30
Johnson, Mrs. Alexander 209
Johnson, Dr. 130
Johnson, Gov. Robert 11
Johnson Square 222, 223
Johnston, Charles 206
Johnston, Robert 12
Jones, Charles C., Jr. 221
Jones, Capt. John C. 99

Kalb, John Leonard 15, 63
Kalb, Margaret Putz 63
Kapp, Friedrich 63, 240
Kelley, Abram 26
Kelso, George 232
Kelso, Isabella 231, 232
Kelso, Margaret 231
Kelso, Samuel, Jr. 232
Kelso, Samuel, Sr. 232
Kennedy, Robert M. 14, 236
Kennington, Edward 28
Keowee (Cherokee village) 23
Keowee River 26
Kershaw, Ely 5, 6, 13, 14, 19, 21, 21, 22, 26, 33, 34, , 51, 52, 57, 58, 72, 128, 145, 165, 208
Kershaw, George (Joseph and Sarah's son) 19
Kershaw, James (Joseph and Sarah's son) 19, 204, 207
Kershaw, the Rev. John 209
Kershaw, John (Joseph and Sarah's son) 19, 204, 207, 224, 226
Kershaw, John (Joseph's brother in Yorkshire) 165

Index

Kershaw, Joseph ("father" of Camden) 5, 6, 12–16, 18–22, 25, 27–30, 32–34, 39, 50–52, 57, 58, 72, 128, 145, 165, 195, 204, 207–209, 224–225, 237
Kershaw, Brig. Gen. Joseph Brevard 209, 228
Kershaw, Joseph (Joseph and Sarah's son) 19
Kershaw, Mary (Joseph and Sarah's daughter) 113, 123
Kershaw, Mary Cantey (Ely's wife) 145
Kershaw, Rebecca 30
Kershaw, Samuel G. (Joseph and Sarah's son) 207
Kershaw, Sarah (Joseph and Sarah's daughter) 19
Kershaw, Sarah (Joseph's wife) 19, 8, 72, 113, 197, 202, 204, 209
Kershaw, Dr. T.G. 209
Kershaw County, S.C. 21, 208
Kershaw, William 6, 13, 34, 72, 128, 165, 208
Kershaw and Company 18
Kershaw and Hoyle (store) 18
Kershaw and Wyly (store and company) 18, 30
Kershaw Lodge of Freemasons 228
Kershaw Volunteers 209
Kettle Creek 8, 33
King Charles II 11
King George II 11
King George III 7, 22, 0159, 218
King Hagler 13, 21, 244; *see also* Nopkehee
King Louis XVI 72
King Prow 21
King Street 15
King's American Regiment 166 171, 179, 180, 181, 193
King's Dragoon Guards (First Regiment) 38
Kingstree, S.C. 74
Kinlock, Capt. David 39, 40, 41, 42
Kirkland, Moses 23
Kirkland, Thomas J. 14, 236
Kirkwood, Capt. Robert 104, 133, 169, 177, 179, 211, 226
Kirkwood Common 211
Kirkwood Hotel 211
Kirkwood Lane 211
Kleinert, Mr. 118
Knox, Gen. Henry 204, 201
Knox, Sarah 231
Kriegenbroun 63

Lafayette, George Washington de 226, 228
Lafayette, Marquis de 5, 60, 63, 209, 221, 222, 225, 226, 227, 229, 237, 239, 243
Lafayette Hall 227
"Lafayette Jewel" 228
"Lafayette Trowel" 229
Lake Marion 203
Lamb, Sgt. Roger 89, 94, 95, 103, 112, 115
Lamprie's Point 40
Lancaster County, S.C. 208
Lancaster Ledger 244
Landers, Lt. Col. H.L. 84, 87, 110
Lang family 209
Langham, Sgt. Elias 76, 78
Laurens, Henry 20, 25
Laurens, Col. John 217
Lausanne mansion 229
Lee, Maj. Gen. Charles 38, 67
Lee, Lt. Col. Henry "Light Horse Harry" 150, 152, 168, 170, 172, 174, 184, 185, 190, 192, 198
Lee's Legion 151, 190
Leiding, Harriette Kershaw 209
Lemar, Capt. William 106
Lenud's Ferry 35, 37, 68
Leslie, Maj. Gen. Alexander 143, 151, 158
Levasseur, Auguste 222, 226, 227
Levi 243
Lexington, Mass. 60
Life of General Francis Marion, a Celebrated Partisan Officer in the Revolutionary War 245
Life of John Kalb 240
Lincoln, Maj. Gen. Benjamin 5, 8, 9, 29, 30, 32, 34, 35, 57, 62, 64, 114, 118, 239
Little Lynches Creek 73, 75, 78
Little Pine Tree Creek 173
Little River 119
Liverpool, England 37
Lockhart, Capt. Samuel 87
Logtown (or Log Town) 14, 76, 77, 169, 170, 171, 177, 183, 191
London, England 38, 60, 217
London Chronicle 56
Long Island, S.C. 25
Loocock, Aaron 16, 19
Lord Camden 13
Lumpkin, Henry 68, 110, 179, 185
Luzerne, Chevalier de la 207
Lynches Creek 21, 50, 73, 81
Lynches River *see* Lynches Creek
Lyttleton Street 52

Magill, Maj. Charles 81, 88, 100, 114, 124, 131
Magazine Hill 52, 204
Malcolm, Capt. Allan 110

Malta 216
Manhattan Island, N.Y. 213
Marion, Brig. Gen. Francis 26, 80, 81, 125, 163, 166, 167, 168, 170, 172, 174, 184, 185, 186, 190, 191, 196, 198, 203, 215, 234, 245, 246
Marquess of Hastings 216
Marquois, Lt. William 115, 144
Marshall, John 19, 28, 29, 30
Martin, Gov. Josiah 77, 82, 83
Mason, the Rev. William 218
Masons 123
Mathis, Daniel 13
Mathis, Samuel 9, 22, 73, 202
Mathis, Sarah 13
Mathis, Sophia 13
McArthur, Maj. Archibald 58, 81, 138
McCalla, David 165
McCalla, John 135
McCalla, Sarah 3, 135, 136, 137, 142, 147, 154, 156, 157, 159, 161, 163, 164, 165, 217, 232
McCalla, Thomas 135, 136, 137, 142, 154, 157, 161, 165
McClure, Mary 232
McCrady, Edward 81
McCulloch, Capt. Kenneth 116
McDonald, Middleton 28
McGirth, James 21
McGirtt, Daniel 22, 24
McKenzie, Capt. Charles Barrington 114
McLeod, Lt. John 94, 115
McLeod, the Rev. Robert 228
McPherson, Lt. Angus 244
McRae, Duncan 12, 22
McWaters, John 142
Mecan, Maj. Thomas 71
Meeting Street 113, 123, 153
Meroney, John 209
Middleton family 238
"Middleton Place" 238
Miles, John 122
Miller, Capt. James 19, 20
Millhouse, Robert 12
Mills, Elizabeth 231
Mills, John 232
Mills, Margaret 231
Mills, Mary 231
Mills, Robert 228
Moira (or Lord Moira) *see* Rawdon, Lt. Col. Francis, Lord Rawdon
Monck's Corner, S.C. 53, 68
Monterey Square 223
Montgomery, Janet L. 213
Montgomery, Maj. Gen. Richard 213
Montgomery, Robert 28

Moore, George 225
Moore, Isham 18
Morais, Henry 240
Moravians 55, 125
Morgan, Brig. Gen. Daniel 151, 152, 157, 158, 159, 163, 168, 179
Morgan, Capt. Simon 177
Morristown, N.J. 5, 62, 111
Motte, Rebecca Brewton 114, 139, 196
Moultrie, Brig. Gen. William 29, 30, 229
Mount Joseph plantation 114, 139, 140, 154
"Mount Pleasant" 13
Mt. Zion Institute 143
Mulberry (Chesnut home) 226
Mulberry Grove plantation 219

Naples, Italy 216
Nase, Henry 166, 193
Nash, Gov. Abner 65
Nassau (schooner) 145
Nassau, Bahamas 72, 128
Neilson, David 18
Nelson, Gov. Thomas, Jr. 160
Nelson's Ferry 37, 51, 52, 53, 65, 125, 143, 198
Newburgh, N.Y. 163, 206, 213
"Newburgh Conspiracy" 213
New Providence Island 72, 204
New Windsor, N.Y. 206
New York City 30, 49, 57, 59, 60, 61, 63, 127, 171, 191, 204
New York Dragoons 180
New York Herald 210
New York Volunteers 20, 58, 116, 129, 137, 142, 171, 179
Newport, R.I. 72
Ninety Six, S.C. 23, 35, 53, 57, 58, 77, 79, 80, 86, 117, 140, 143, 145, 152, 168, 172, 179, 196, 197, 198, 200, 215
Ninety Six Military District 21, 58
Nixon, Col. Henry G. 227
Nixon, Capt. John 164
Nixon, Mrs. Mary Adair 137, 164, 165, 232
Nones, Maj. Benjamin 239, 240, 241
Nones, Miriam 241
Nopkehee 13; *see also* King Hagler
North Island 63

Ogilvie, Charles 50
O'Hara, Brig. Gen. Charles 159
Old Presbyterian Meeting House (see Presbyterian Meeting House)
Old St. David's Church 14
Orangeburg, S.C. 20, 26, 117, 126, 168, 196, 198

Orangeburg Military District 21
Oxford University 37, 38, 74

Paint Hill 172
Palmetto Conservation 211
Palmetto Regiment 209
Parton, James 71, 162, 184, 189, 199
Pasquotank River 90
Paterson, Brig. Gen. James 59, 137
Patten, Maj. John 104
Patton, Robert 19
Payn, John 18
Pearson, Lt. Thomas 41
Pee Dee River 12, 58, 68, 69, 78, 85, 167, 168
Perkins, Benjamin 209
Perkins, Charles 209
Perkins, John 18
Perroneau, Robert 206
Petersburg, Va. 35, 62, 63, 134
Petty, Luke 28, 30
Philadelphia, Pa. 17, 38, 60, 61, 62, 63, 67, 86, 124, 134, 146, 155, 201, 204, 208, 224, 226, 239, 240
Phillips, Capt. James 19
Phillips, John 54, 55
Phillips, Maj. Gen. William 191
Pickens, Brig. Gen. Andrew 117, 166, 168, 203, 215, 246
Pierce, Maj. William 168
Pinckney, Betsy *see* Pinckney, Elizabeth (Betsy)
Pinckney, Col. Charles C. (Thomas's brother) 114, 155
Pinckney, the Rev. Charles C. (Thomas's grandson) 115
Pinckney, Elizabeth (Betsy) Motte 114, 139
Pinckney, Maj. Thomas 67, 93, 100, 114, 115, 118, 139, 140, 154, 155
Pine Tree Creek 13, 36, 171, 173, 178, 196
Pine Tree Hill (also Pine Tree) settlement 12, 13, 14, 125
Pitcairn, Maj. John 56
Port Royal, Bermuda 58, 72, 145
Port Royal Island, S.C. 8
Porterfield, Lt. Col. Charles 69, 84, 86, 87, 88, 89, 90, 91, 92, 96, 114, 122, 123, 124, 134, 146, 160, 217
Porterfield, Capt. Robert 160
Portsmouth, England 50
Potowomut, R.I. 149
Potter, Brig. Gen. Edward E. 210
Potter's Raid 210
Pound Ridge, N.Y. 247
Powers, Mrs. Henrietta 209

Presbyterians at Camden 15
Presbyterian Meetinghouse 123, 153
Presbyterians at Waxhaws 45
"Prescott" 225
Prevost, Maj. Gen. Augustine 29, 30
Prince of Wales 216, 218, 246
Provost Dungeon 215
Pulaski, Brig. Gen. Casimir 29, 65, 222, 223, 239
Pulaski Legion 29, 30, 65, 239, 241
Purrysburg, S.C. 28, 29

Quaker Cemetery 14, 153
Queen Charlotte 218
Queen's Rangers 58

Ramsay, David 235, 236
Ramsey's Mill 167
Ramsour's Mill 158
Random Recollections 236
Rawdon, Lt. Col. Francis, Lord 3, 6, 31, 56, 58, 59, 70, 71, 72, 73, 74, 75, 76, 77, 78, 86, 89, 94, 97, 100, 101, 102, 115, 117, 135, 136, 137, 138, 140, 142, 145, 152, 153, 154, 155, 156, 158, 159, 160, 161, 163, 164, 166, 1167, 168, 170, 171, 172, 173, 174, 175, 176, 178, 179, 180, 181, 183, 184, 185, 186, 187, 188, 190, 191, 192, 193, 194, 195, 196, 197, 198, 199, 200, 201, 202, 204, 209, 215, 216, 224, 233, 246, 247
Rawdon, John, Lord 55, 60, 61
"Rawdon Town" 200
Read (or Reade), Col. James 177
Rebels Victorious 110
Reed, Joseph 191
Rehoboth, Mass. 243
Reichel, Brother 126
Revenge 216
Revolutionary War Visitors Center 211
Reynolds, Sir Joshua 218, 247
Richardson, Col. Richard 19, 21, 22, 24, 28
Richardson, William 19
Richland County, S.C. 21, 208
Richmond, Va. 224
Rivington's Gazette 132
Robertson, Capt. 179, 180
Robinson, Joseph 23
Robinson, Mary 218
Rochambeau, Lt. Gen., the Comte *see under* De Rochambeau)
Rocky Mount 58, 70, 71, 73, 79, 120
Roebuck, Maj. Benjamin, Jr. 147
Roebuck, Col. Benjamin, Sr. 147
Romulus 57
Rose, Alexander 206
"Rose Hill Farm" 213, 214

292 Index

Ross, Charles 49, 127, 149, 158
Ross, Isaac 19
Royal Artillery 144
Royal Engineers 52
Royal Gazette 131, 194
Royal Welsh Fuzileers *see* Twenty-third Regiment of Foot
Rugeley, Henry 22, 39, 78, 84, 147, 153
Rugeley, Rowland 22
Rugeley's Mill 39, 79, 81, 83, 86, 89, 106, 108, 109, 111, 115, 119, 123, 147, 185
Rutherford, Brig. Gen. Griffith 29, 75, 84, 90, 96, 106, 113, 117, 125, 126, 147
Rutledge, Gov. John 21, 25, 26, 33, 35, 36, 39, 203, 207, 208

St. Augustine, Fla. 148
St. George Parish 25
St. James Palace 218
St. Mark's Parish 14, 16, 19, 20
St. Matthews, S.C. 114
St. Paul's Parish 25
Salem, N.C. 55, 118, 125
Salisbury, N.C. 36, 39, 69118, 128, 129, 133, 139, 184, 205
Salmond, Thomas 226, 227
Salmond family 230
Saluda River 22, 35, 53, 59, 125, 198
Sanders Creek 14, 79, 84, 86, 175, 183, 183, 245
Santee canal 210
Santee Indians 11
Santee River 35, 37, 66, 74, 81, 160, 172, 197
Saunders, Capt. John 58
Savannah (schooner) 72
Savannah, Ga. 8, 24, 27–32, 57–59, 64, 65, 83, 114, 138, 147, 168, 204, 206, 219–224, 244
Savannah River 22, 35
Sawney's Creek 192
Saxe Gotha Parish 20
Schenck, David 127, 257, 260–62, 266–67
Schuyler, Maj. Gen. Philip 66
Scipio 168
Scott, Edwin J. 236
Scott, John 206
Second Continental Congress 7
Second Continental Light Dragoons 247
Second Maryland Brigade 85, 90, 133, 177
Second Partisan Corps (see Lee's Legion) 150
Second Punic War 168
Second S.C. Continentals 36
Senf, Col. John C. 79, 80, 83, 86, 124
Seven Years' War 27, 49
Seventeenth Light Dragoons 37, 42, 59

Seventy-first Highlanders 58, 75, 81, 86, 94, 98, 114, 117, 138, 211, 244
Seymour, Sgt-Maj. William 64, 69, 84, 85, 88, 98, 106, 128, 168, 169, 180, 186, 191, 196
Shakespeare, William 218
Shannon family 209
Shaw, John Robert 78, 91, 97, 98, 103, 110, 121, 137, 141
Shawnee Indians 13
Sheridan, Richard Brinsley 218
Sherman, Maj. Gen. William T. 209
Siege of Charleston 74
Siege of Savannah 186
Simms, William Gilmore 229
Singleton, Capt. Anthony 93, 94, 176, 180
Singleton, Matthew 18, 19
Sixth Maryland Continental Regiment 101, 133, 178
Sixty-third Regiment of Foot 60, 81, 170
smallpox outbreaks 73, 116, 121, 129, 135, 162, 202
Smallwood, Brig. Gen. William 74, 85, 88, 90, 93, 98, 99, 123, 128, 146
Smith, Eleazer 122
Smith, Capt. John 177, 178, 182, 187, 188
Smith, Mark 2
Snow Campaign 24, 34
Snow's Island 167
South Carolina Gazette 12, 16, 18, 19
South Carolina General Assembly 28
South Carolina Loyalist Dragoons (see New York Dragoons) 171
South Carolina Provincial Congress 20, 21, 26, 28
South Carolina Provincial Regiment 172, 179
South Carolina Royalists military unit 172
Sowerby, Yorkshire, England 12
Spring Hill redoubt 8, 58
Stamp Act 49
Stapleton, Dr. 45
"Star" redoubt 52
Stateburg, S.C. 38
Stedman, Maj. Charles 45, 47, 48, 50, 51, 54, 55, 57, 59, 70, 77, 83, 85, 88, 91, 97, 105, 138, 140, 141, 143, 148, 234
Steel, Thomas 142
Stevens, Brig. Gen. Edward 78, 83, 84, 89, 90, 93, 95, 108, 121, 131, 133
Stevens, John Austin 201
Stewart, Lt. Col. Alexander 201, 202, 203
Stewart, Capt. Patrick 94
Stokes, Capt. John 43, 44
Stono Ferry 8, 30, 45, 71, 114
Stono Indians 11

Index

Strother, Mr. 72
Stuart, John 26
Stubblefield, Col. George 116
Suffolk, England 48, 49
Sullivan's Island 25, 26, 34
Summerville, George 28
Sumter, Brig. Gen. Thomas 5, 19, 21, 38, 65, 66, 70, 71, 73, 76, 79, 80, 82, 109, 112, 120, 121, 122, 125, 128, 129, 130, 133, 135, 147, 153, 158, 159, 163, 166, 168, 169, 170, 172, 174, 184, 185, 186, 192, 196, 198, 203, 215, 231, 234, 246
Sumter County, S.C. 21
Sutton, Jasper 14, 18, 81
Sutton, Mary Chesnut 14
Swift Creek 13

Talbot, Capt. William 42
Tarleton, Lt. Col. Banastre 3, 5, 31, 36, 37, 38, 39, 40, 41, 42, 43, 44, 45, 46, 47, 48, 51, 52, 55, 56, 57, 59, 68, 71, 72, 73, 74, 75, 76, 81, 86, 87, 88, 91, 94, 96, 98, 99, 102, 103, 104, 105, 106, 107, 108, 109, 110, 113, 115, 119, 120, 121, 125, 137, 138, 139, 140, 142, 143, 147, 153, 158, 159, 190, 193, 196, 201, 209, 217, 218, 221, 232, 234, 245, 247
Tarleton, Jane Parker 37
Tarleton, John 37
Tarleton-Fagan, Christopher 247
Tarleton's Legion (see British Legion) 44, 58, 78, 87
Taylor, Capt. James 21, 121
Taylor, John 21
Taylor, Col. Thomas 21, 80, 121
Taylor, Thomas 21
Tennent, the Rev. William 22, 23
Third Anglo-Maratha War 216
Third Regiment of Foot 201
Third Virginia Detachment 35
Thirty-third Regiment of Foot (West Riding Regiment) 58, 86, 88, 94, 97, 98, 99, 110, 111, 117, 137, 138
Thompson, Charles 131
Thomson, Lt. Col. William 20, 21, 24, 25, 26
"Traveller's Rest" 66, 152, 213
Treaty of Paris 6, 207
Trinity Church 214
Troup, Gov. George 222
Tucker, Richard 122
Turin, Italy 49
Turkey Creek 158
Turnbull, Lt. Col. George 20, 58, 70, 119, 142, 145, 171
Twelve Mile Creek 15
Twenty-third Regiment of Foot (Royal Welsh Fuzileers) 58, 71, 86, 88, 88, 89, 94, 96, 98, 103, 112, 115, 117, 138
Tybee Island, Ga. 32
Tyger River 147

Union XV Corps 210
University College Oxford 60
Upper Saluda Military District 21
Urwin, Gregory J.W. 234

Valentine, William 206
Vallance, Mary see Gates, Mary Vallance
Vaughan, Lt. Col. Joseph 104, 116
Verplanck's Point, N.Y. 206
Vickers, Dr. Samuel 205
Virginia Assembly 36
Virginia Light Dragoons 35
Viscount Loudoun 216
Volunteers of Ireland 56, 58, 59, 60, 61, 86, 94, 97, 110, 115, 117, 136, 138, 145, 171, 179, 180

Wade, Joseph 164, 165
Wallace, Lt. William 118
Walpole, Horace 218
Wando River 15
Washington, George 7, 21, 27, 38, 49, 62, 63, 64, 65, 66, 67, 85, 90, 130, 131, 134, 135, 146, 148, 150, 163, 167, 169, 186, 187, 193, 196, 199, 205, 206, 209, 213, 217, 221, 223, 224, 226, 227, 234, 236, 239, 245, 246
Washington, Col. William 52, 68, 134, 147, 158, 163, 173, 177, 180, 183, 187
Wateree Ferry 52, 77, 79, 80, 119, 121, 135, 153, 161, 192
Wateree Indians 3, 11, 12, 14
Wateree River 12, 15, 16, 18, 19, 22, 26, 50, 51, 53, 58, 59, 74, 79, 80, 82, 86, 112, 119, 133, 137, 143, 173, 202, 208, 224
Watson, Lt. Col. John W.T. 172, 184, 191, 192
Watts, Garret 96
Waxhaw, N.C. 2, 15, 41, 45, 46, 48, 51, 54, 55, 56, 59, 64, 67, 68, 71, 78, 79, 84, 108, 117, 120, 138, 161, 188, 198, 199
Waxhaw Creek 15
Waxhaw Indians 11, 15
Wayne, Maj. Gen. "Mad Anthony" 135, 219
Weatherspoon, David 9
Webster, Lt. Col. James Webster 86, 88, 94, 95, 97, 98, 99, 103, 110, 115, 138, 159, 167
Weems, "Parson" Mason L. 245
West Indies 37

West Riding Regiment (see Thirty-third Regiment of Foot)
Wheeler, John H. 138
Whitaker, John 9, 22
Whitaker, the Rev. Jonathan 227
Whitaker, Willis 9, 22
Whitaker's Ferry 80
White, Col. Anthony 68, 134
White Oak 237
White's Mill 138
Williams, Col. Otho H. 68, 69, 81, 83, 84, 85, 87, 88, 91, 93, 94, 95, 96, 99, 100, 101, 103, 104, 106, 107, 108, 110, 117, 131, 133, 172, 176, 182, 184, 185, 186, 187, 200, 201, 205
Williamsburg District 81
Williamson, Brig. Gen. Andrew 22, 23, 24, 30, 33
Williamson, Dr. Hugh 114, 115, 121, 126, 129, 130, 139, 144, 154
Wilmington, N.C. 166, 167, 190, 191, 224
Wilson, Col. 126
Wilson, David 18
Wilson, William 19
Winchester, Va. 163
Winn, Col. Richard 72

Winnsboro, S.C. 6, 143, 145, 146, 147, 150, 151, 154, 157, 159
Winston-Salem, N.C. (see Salem, N.C.)
A Winter's Tale 218
Witherspoon, John 9, 18
Woodford, Brig. Gen. William 34
Woolford, James 127
Woolford, Lt. Col. Thomas 79, 80, 120, 127
Workman, John 209
World War I 240
Wright's Bluff 33
Wright's Ferry 152
Wylie, William 164
Wyly, John 22, 27
Wyly, Samuel 9, 12, 13, 14, 22
Wynyard, Lt. George 110

"Yankee Doodle" 165
York County, S.C. 21
Yorkshire, England 12
Yorktown, Va. 6, 48, 204, 205, 214, 215, 217, 232
Young, Alexander 229
Young, Dr. James A. 238
Young, Mary 227
Young, Mrs. Mary R. 209

www.ingramcontent.com/pod-product-compliance
Lightning Source LLC
Chambersburg PA
CBHW032032300426
44117CB00009B/1035